Building the Intentional Unive

Building the Intentional University

Minerva and the Future of Higher Education

Edited by Stephen M. Kosslyn and Ben Nelson

Foreword by Senator Bob Kerrey

The MIT Press
Cambridge, Massachusetts
London, England

First MIT Press paperback edition, 2018

© 2017 Massachusetts Institute of Technology

This book was set in Stone Sans and Stone Serif by Toppan Best-set Premedia Limited. Printed and bound in the United States of America.

Library of Congress Cataloging-in-Publication Data is available.

ISBN: 978-0-262-03715-0 (hardcover: alk. paper), 978-0-262-53619-6 (pb.)

10   9   8   7   6   5

This book is dedicated to Kevin Harvey and Sheldon H. Schuster, who enabled and enable Minerva through principled daring and vision.

We owe both of you everlasting thanks for allowing us to realize our dream.

Contents

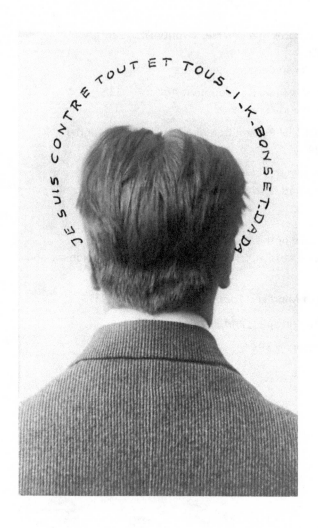

JE SUIS CONTRE TOUT ET TOUS – I – K – BONSET–DADA

Foreword: Higher Education in the Twenty-First Century

Senator Bob Kerrey

Debates in America have become distressingly binary. Something is either good or it is bad. You are either for it or against it. Anything in the middle is considered a weak alternative unworthy of consideration by principled humans. Complex solutions to complex problems get ignored. Uninformed public opinion has become the dominant force determining too many outcomes. Facts and careful analysis have been discredited, along with the experts for whom history and predictive modeling are a way of life. Either decisions are postponed or the decision makers become so demoralized they abandon the effort.

The debate over higher education is no exception. On one side are those who say that a college education is overpriced or, worse, a complete waste of money. On the other side are those who defend the status quo with modifications so slight as to barely dent the current way that universities are organized.

This book is grounded in the belief that college is not, as its harshest critics assert, a waste of money. Taken as a whole, U.S. institutions of higher education add more value to our economy, our communities, our culture, and our leaders than any other kind of institution. Higher education in the United States is radically decentralized and diverse. As an enterprise, U.S. higher education has built a comparative advantage with respect to education in the rest of the world. It generates more than $30 billion annually in foreign tuition and a balance of payments surplus on the national ledger.

Further, the research conducted by U.S. universities is the envy of the world. Past research has helped the private sector create jobs and wealth, made it possible to reduce suffering and cure previously untreatable diseases, helped us understand who we are, and much more. Without the research done at our colleges and universities, the United States would be much poorer and less impressive than it is today.

We can and should debate whether the amounts we are spending on public research are sufficient. We can and should debate our priorities. But all evidence points to the conclusion that supporting research in American universities will continue to produce great advances in our understanding of the universe and our capacity to improve the quality of life on Earth.

This book is an attempt to answer this question: How would you organize the structure of a university if you were to start with a blank sheet of paper? Answering this question helps avoid the angry, destructive accusations and counteraccusations that all too often characterize arguments over American universities. The book is a compilation of ideas—and progress reports with respect to their implementation—offered by people who share a passion for higher education, a belief that change is needed, and a deep concern that the necessary change is happening too slowly.

In the midst of the disorienting detail of any text of this kind, you should remember that moment when a great teacher enabled you to change the course of your life, that moment when you were mentored through whatever challenge you were facing outside the classroom. Recently, I had dinner with a friend who is a naturalized U.S. citizen and a highly respected surgeon. He acquired his skills at a university. He has saved and improved tens of thousands of lives. This man became a surgeon because his father was a surgeon. His father became a surgeon because a single teacher in a rural one-room school inspired him to pursue very high intellectual goals, well beyond the tending of sheep on his family's farm.

The ideas laid out in this book represent a sincere attempt to increase the number of those moments. Those who have dedicated their lives to this goal deserve our respect and thanks. My hope is that the book will help them make the serious and difficult decisions to improve their college or university.

I do understand how difficult those decisions can be. I served sixteen years in elected politics, four as governor of Nebraska and twelve as senator from that state. Thereafter, I served ten years as president of a university. I do not consider myself to be either an academic or an expert on academia. I do know a little about politics, including the politics of higher education. My comments are offered in the hope that some of what I have learned might be of value to those looking for ways to participate in constructive change.

In particular, most Americans do not understand the role played by the voluntary system of regulating colleges and universities. Most do not understand the importance of regional accreditation in determining the quality and the cost of college. Most do not understand how academic and administrative decisions get made inside U.S. colleges. As a consequence, they do not appreciate how difficult it can be to make even obviously good decisions that would improve outcomes. And most do not understand how important the boards of governors of colleges and universities are in supporting academic leaders when they do what good leaders do: make difficult choices they believe will improve their institution.

In discussing these processes and procedures, I will offer criticism that I expect will be uncomfortable for some in academia and may even provoke them to respond. I welcome that possibility. I want to be clear from the outset that this criticism does not subtract from my great admiration for the men and women who have chosen to make teaching, research, and administration their life work. Quite the contrary—I have a deep appreciation for how much easier it is to suggest change than to make it happen. Academics have a reputation for being politically liberal, but when it comes to abandoning the safety of the status quo they can be quite conservative.

I also want to make three important contextual declarations before beginning my critique. First, we are not all created equal. Not every teacher and not every student are great. The shifting of the bell curve to make it appear that we are all exceptional is a big mistake. There is no more need for us to feel inadequate in the company of intellectual superiority than there is when we watch the athletic performance of the gymnast Simone Biles.

It is in our interest to acknowledge that there are born among us men and women capable of profound intellectual insights and accomplishments. Our universities need to be the places where those intellectual talents are given support, development, and protection.

Second, it is just as important that those of us without the gift of genius are given the chance to discover, create, and collaborate our way to a better life. This does not mean that everyone should go to college. However, given the downward pressure on the wages of unskilled workers and those with only high school degrees, the burden should be on us to prove that we have done all we can to make certain that equal opportunity is more than a bitterly hollow political promise.

Those who have been the beneficiaries of an elite education need to be alert to the possibility their experience will cause them to care only about the success of one institution of higher education, namely, their alma mater. Opponents of the creation of public land grant colleges, the GI bill, and our community colleges also worried about the watering down of our elite colleges. Such worries were misplaced. These expansions helped build the American middle class and have made all of higher education better.

Acts to promote equal opportunity must begin long before a student reaches high school. It is a big mistake to wait until then to begin to prepare students for college careers or to lament the amount of remedial education needed for such preparation. It is clear to me from an examination of the facts that household income correlates with success on college entrance exams and that education must begin no later than the moment of birth. If a child is behind in reading and math in fourth grade, the odds favor that child's being behind when it comes time to apply for college.

To be clear: I do not believe it helps to coddle any student into habits that allow him or her to ignore the causal link between efforts and results. We all tend to take credit for our successes and to blame others for our failures. Adult leaders who encourage this tendency in students are not doing them a favor.

Third, no matter what is done to lower costs, college is going to be too expensive for many who would benefit from the opportunity for advanced study. Economic need is a real and compelling problem. We must constantly labor to solve it if we want our world to develop in an equitable and peaceful fashion.

My own analysis is that students need more equity, not more debt. They certainly do not need the kind of lifetime debt our current federal loans resemble, especially for those who do not complete their degree work. They need more work opportunities to help pay the bills. And they need the college they attend to be on the hook for no less than 25 percent of that debt if the student defaults. This would help ensure that colleges make certain that their curriculum prepares their graduates for the workplace of today and tomorrow.

The focus of my critique of higher education is on three interrelated problems: costs are too high, most undergraduate curricula do not prepare graduates for the challenges they face, and technology is only grudgingly deployed in the service of students. All three of these problems are actively debated today and are addressed in the following chapters. What is missing is a recognition of three barriers that make progress difficult.

The first barrier is the way higher education is regulated. Peer-reviewed regional accreditation has been a success, especially through a process known as self-study. High regional standards have contributed to the quality of American colleges and universities. Credits from a regionally accredited institution can be transferred to other regionally accredited institutions. I will note that the practice of allowing the incoming institution to decide which credits to accept adds cost without simultaneously adding demonstrable value. Regionally accredited colleges can charge more for their credits because transferability makes regional accreditation much more valuable to the student.

Unfortunately, regional accreditors also make it almost impossible for high-quality, lower-cost entrants to receive accreditation before their first class graduates. This means there is relatively little competitive pressure on incumbent institutions to change. It is much easier to get regulatory permission to do heart transplants than to get regulatory approval to teach political science.

This difficulty is the direct result of the fact that the boards of directors of the regional accreditors are composed of representatives of the incumbent institutions. It is simply not in their interest to approve any application that is a genuine competitive threat. It is not just quality that suffers. Limiting supply during a time of rising demand has contributed to annual price increases that are greater than the rate of inflation.

The solution would be for the regional accreditors to offer regulatory approval before new entrants have enrolled any students. Doing so would make it possible for a new enterprise to raise the capital or solicit the gifts that will be needed to hire faculty and build operating systems. Despite their arguments to the contrary, it would be easy to establish transparent and consistent quality standards to permit the regional institutions to bring competition, which would offer higher-quality and lower-price alternatives to the status quo.

The need is greatest for those students who are not going to a community or a four-year college. Training students in the competencies that current employers demand does not require us to know what workplace skills will be needed ten years from now. It does require us to feel a sense of urgency to prepare our students for the jobs that are available today.

It probably also requires me to discuss the relative advantages of enterprises that are tax-paying, for-profit institutions and those that are tax-subsidized, not-for-profits. Those who have an ideological preference for one or the other should be required to push beyond their opinions and prejudices to defend their position with facts.

If raising capital for a private tax-paying business can help prepare young men and women for jobs that elevate their self-worth, we and our government should support this. If soliciting contributions for a charitable tax-subsidized cause gets the job done, we should support that effort too. My own strongly held view is that an enterprise does not become morally superior as a consequence of a decision about how its corporation is organized.

There has been substantial abuse by for-profit educational enterprises that have taken advantage of federal programs that allow them to generate most of their cash from taxpayers. The public and their political leaders are right to demand higher performance and hard evidence that we are getting our money's worth. However, this demand should simply result in an even regulatory playing field. You should not be penalized simply because you are willing to pay property and income taxes.

The second barrier to change is an ingrained, poorly understood, and almost universally practiced decision-making process called "shared governance." Shared governance means that faculty must have a role in deciding the future of their institution. For the most part, this is a reasonable and good thing to do. It causes problems when it becomes a means for academia to ignore the facts at hand.

Here are some of those facts. Lectures might make it easier to teach, but they are a terrible way to learn—and yet, they continue to dominate the academic landscape. The marginal cost of knowledge dissemination is being driven to zero by technology, but colleges still charge thousands of dollars for course credits that do just that. Memorization of facts and figures produces short-term success in passing examinations but imparts very little postgraduate value.

Academic leaders constantly declare the importance of critical thinking but seldom apply critical thinking when they organize their academic work. They resist honest, open, and accountable evaluations of their teaching. They ignore the value of practice-based learning. As a consequence, the general education curriculum consists of coursework that satisfies the needs of university departments much more than it does the needs of the graduating student.

Worst of all, too many in academia ignore the inconvenient evidence that our graduates have not acquired the habits needed to continue the lifetime pursuit of knowledge or to solve the problems they will face when they graduate. This puts the students at risk, our democracy at risk, and the comparative advantage of the United States in higher education at risk.

The third barrier to change is board governance. Good corporate governance for public and not-for-profit colleges and universities is just as important as it is in the for-profit world. Too often board members are recruited to help raise money. Too often they are given little training in what is expected of them beyond fundraising. Too often boards respond to noisy critics who are more concerned about protecting students from unpleasant intellectual ideas instead of responding to the unpleasant reality of student debt. Too often boards panic when an administrator, who is trying to make constructive change happen, generates opposition.

I believe that addressing all three of these issues would help higher education improve. They do not require revolutionary changes and we don't need a revolution. We need steady and measurable improvement. Persuading the regional accreditors to grant accreditation prior to enrolling the first student if the institution agrees to high-quality standards will give us steady improvement. Making certain that shared governance leaves room for administrators to make academic decisions that are grounded in good research, even if those decisions are not in the short-term interest of some faculty members, will do the same. Paying attention to the importance of having board members who are recruited to do more than just raise money and who understand they must support administrators when narrow, status quo opposition arises will contribute to creating an environment in which shared governance improves overall performance.

In this book, you will find many detailed descriptions of what our colleges and universities could and should do. Not only would these actions enable higher education in the United States to maintain its comparative advantage, they would also help us feel better about the quality of the world's future business, government, and not-for-profit leaders.

One final statement: I am optimistic that our institutions of higher education will continue to improve. I am optimistic that a sufficient number of brave and good choices will be made by academics, administrators, board members, and regulatory authorities. Mostly, I am optimistic because so many Americans are willing to voluntarily give their money and time to this cause. Far too many wise and generous men and women are committed to our success for me to believe that we will fail.

Preface

Ben Nelson

The Minerva journey has been both long and short. For an institution born in Silicon Valley, almost everything about Minerva's timeline appears to be unfolding in slow motion. As Minerva's founder, I spent eighteen months, beginning in September 2010, working on the idea before the initial funding was secured. Nearly two years elapsed from the beginning of work until the first employee started, and another two years elapsed before a pilot group of students came on board in September 2014. In total, it was a five-year process from the day full-time work began on Minerva to the day tuition-paying students began their first year in San Francisco. In the world of academia, five years from conceiving an idea to becoming the most selective university program in American history is, for most, hard to fathom in its brevity. This book is not a history of Minerva the institution but an overview of the concepts and philosophies that underpin Minerva—and a report on what we've learned as we've implemented the first new conception of a classical liberal arts program in nearly a century.

The concepts and philosophies on which Minerva was founded would not have come to fruition were it not for two unrelated pairs of individuals. The most important pair was my parents, who brought me up in a world of far transfer without knowing either the term or the concept. This novel way of thinking was given formal structure during my first year at the University of Pennsylvania when another pair of individuals, Lee Benson and Ira Harkavy, cotaught a yearlong course on the history of universities and their interactions with their community. It was this class, and in particular the study of the founding principles of so many great institutions of higher education in the United States, that opened my eyes to the shortcomings of those very institutions in the modern era as they moved away from the ideals of Franklin, Jefferson, Dewey, and others.

I returned to the idea of a revised curriculum in the late summer of 2010. I realized that the best way to implement it would be to create a new institution from scratch—an institution that would provide a superior education based on first principles and would remain true to those principles. Such an institution could serve as a model for other universities the world over. For the next year and a half, the idea of building the world's greatest university received far more ridicule than support. But over the course of twelve short months, between December 2011 and December 2012, seven key people joined me to realize this ideal philosophy in forming the institution that Minerva is today. Minerva would not exist were it not for each one of those seven.

I met former Nebraska senator and governor and then president of the New School, Bob Kerrey, in June 2011 through my friend and mentor in the education space, Jon Bischke. Senator Kerrey was immediately enthusiastic. He said, "Not only must you be successful with Minerva, you will be successful with Minerva—it's too important for you not to." In December 2011, Senator Kerrey joined Minerva's newly formed board of advisers, and a year later he became Executive Chairman of the Minerva Institute for Research and Scholarship. Along the way, Senator Kerrey moved mountains to make Minerva a reality. He played a vital role in helping us cement our relationship with the Keck Graduate Institute, the most recent member of the Claremont University Consortium; receiving regulatory approval to operate; and gaining the legal authority to invite students from all over the world to the United States, Germany, Argentina, and beyond. It is unlikely that Minerva would be an operating entity today without Senator Kerrey's vocal support and highly visible work at an important point in the institution's history.

A couple of months after first meeting Senator Kerrey, I met Peter Thiel for the first (and only) time. Like many others, Thiel didn't think Minerva was practicable, but unlike others he explained why: it was a chicken-and-egg problem, he said. To build the best brand in undergraduate education, he argued, you needed the best students. To attract the best students, you needed the best university brand. Unless someone figured out how to jumpstart the brand, Minerva would not materialize. I dreamed of doing just that by having Larry Summers provide a public endorsement of Minerva. Summers, formerly of Harvard, was perhaps the most famous university president since Eisenhower and widely respected for his systemic thinking and brilliant insights. I arranged a meeting with Summers through my friend of more than fifteen years, Phil Bronner, and Bronner's friend Phil Deutch, who knew Summers well. By December 2011, Larry Summers had become Chair of Minerva's advisory board (he was soon joined by Kerrey, Patrick Harker, and Lee Shulman) and became the first and most prominent academic to publicly back the concept. Summers was animated by the idea of bringing a world-class education to many students who simply had no chance at traditional universities, because of capped foreign enrollment. He was quickly taken with Minerva's solution to that problem. Summers's involvement was crucial both to get Minerva off the ground and to give the program the credibility that was essential to establishing the value of the educational system we were about to develop. To have a former president of Harvard University publicly back Minerva was a transformative event and went a long way toward solving Minerva's chicken-and-egg problem.

The following month, January 2012, I was ready to formally pitch the Minerva Project, the corporation that would build the technology, publish the curriculum, and cultivate the brand behind Minerva, to Benchmark Capital, Silicon Valley's most respected venture capital firm. I contacted one of Benchmark's partners, Matt Cohler, who arranged a series of four meetings for me to discuss Minerva with Benchmark's five other partners. At the second meeting, I met Kevin Harvey, one of Benchmark's four original founding partners and a legend among venture capitalists. As the late Bill Campbell, a mentor to Harvey, told me after the event, the Minerva idea hooked Harvey, who saw its transformational potential. By February 2012, we had agreed on the terms of the largest financial commitment in the history of Silicon Valley to an institutional founder with nothing but a concept. Not only was that initial $25 million commitment a move that no other venture capital firm in Silicon Valley had the foresight, desire, and capacity to make, but, coming from the most respected investment firm of the time, this investment, along with the backing of Summers and Kerrey, put Minerva on the map as the audacious endeavor that it is. Even more important, Harvey has been and continues to be a mentor to me and a steady hand on Minerva's board (alongside SpaceX President Gwynne Shotwell, Ambassador Philip Lader, and TAL Founder Bangxin Zhang), amply providing wisdom, clarity of purpose, and unwavering support.

At the same time that the financing came together, I contacted another person introduced by Bischke, Jonathan Katzman. Katzman, whom I first met in the summer of 2011, is one of the most respected product executives in Silicon Valley and had been CEO of his own company, Xoopit, which he sold to Yahoo. Katzman was interested in making his next step in education, and he agreed to join forces with me rather than start his own venture. Katzman not only brought credibility to Minerva with the very best engineers, designers, and product experts in Silicon Valley,

he also infused the Minerva initiative with the best of Silicon Valley's sensi-
bility. Katzman's exceptional process-orientation keeps the Minerva senior
team working efficiently. He also brings a strong moral compass to the
organization, being a vocal advocate for both access and healthful living
for students. In four short years, Katzman and his small team built the
most sophisticated live interaction education platform in the world on a
technology base that didn't exist when Katzman began work—a feat that is
impossible to imagine being executed by any other team under any other
leader.

On a Monday morning in September 2012, a month after Katzman formally joined Minerva, I received a phone call from Richard Winn, who had
recently left the regional accreditor, the Western Association of Schools and
Colleges (WASC), and whom I had asked to help Minerva. Winn told me
that Teri Cannon, WASC's executive vice president, had left the organization the previous Friday and that Minerva should try to work with her. On
Tuesday, we had lunch, and thirty minutes into the lunch, Cannon became
Minerva's Chief Accreditation Officer. Cannon got to work the next day and
systematically thought through every possible partner for Minerva in the
region. After nearly a year on the job, the relationship with KGI was signed,
and a few short months later the agreement was approved by the regional
accreditor. Seven additional approvals followed, for five undergraduate
programs and two master's degree programs, at a pace that is unheard of.
Our partnership with KGI would not have been possible without Cannon's
working with KGI's visionary president, Shelly Schuster (who is a codedica-
tee of this book), nor could we have navigated the approval process without
Cannon's guiding hand. What is more, three years after Cannon joined
Minerva she took on additional far-reaching responsibilities in managing
all of student affairs and operations—a gigantic task made more difficult by
our lean staffing model and global reach.

Less than a month after I first met Cannon, I had a breakfast meeting
with Robin Goldberg. When I was the CEO of Snapfish I was used to competition, but few other companies could best Snapfish's growth. Blurb was
an exception and was a thorn in Snapfish's side for a number of years. This
was all the more irritating to me because I found their actual product to be
rather clunky but their marketing extraordinarily good. When I was rumi-
nating over who should be defining and executing for Minerva's brand, I
wanted to talk to the person who did that for Blurb. That was Goldberg.
Former Chief Marketing Officer of Blurb and before that Lonely Planet,
Goldberg was not thinking of leaving the company, but the challenge of
Minerva appealed to her, and by December she was at Minerva full time

as Chief Experience Officer. Goldberg and her team built and defined the Minerva brand, explained Minerva to the world, generated press coverage of Minerva, and attracted 50,000 applicants to the Minerva Schools for our first three classes. They were also in charge of the student immersion programs in San Francisco and around the world, while managing the professional development agency for Minerva students, faculty, and staff. Goldberg's facility in marketing and sales, branding and P&L management, public relations and direct response marketing is unlike that of any other marketing executive we have ever encountered.

A week after first meeting Goldberg, I attended a Renaissance Weekend conference in Napa Valley. In the lobby of the hotel I bumped into a friendly woman, Dr. Robin Rosenberg, and, as is customary at that event, made polite conversation. After asking me what I did, Rosenberg suggested that my wife and I join her and her husband for lunch. Rosenberg's husband was Dr. Stephen Kosslyn, former dean of social science at Harvard University, one of the youngest tenured professors in the history of that institution's Psychology Department and, at the time of the luncheon, the director of Stanford's prestigious Center for Advanced Studies in Behavioral Sciences. At the end of an engrossing lunchtime discussion, Kosslyn suggested that the group schedule a dinner. In between the two events, I called Larry Summers and asked his opinion of Stephen Kosslyn. Summers's response: "There is no better person for you to hire but you won't be able to get someone of Stephen Kosslyn's stature." At the end of that dinner, Kosslyn suggested that the group schedule a lunch, at which point I asked Kosslyn whether he would be interested in joining Minerva in some capacity, to which Kosslyn said yes. Shortly thereafter, Kosslyn became Minerva's Founding Dean and Chief Academic Officer. Summers's assessment, at least the first half, could not have been more accurate. Not only is Kosslyn's understanding of the science of learning vast, not only is he a polymath with wide-ranging knowledge of a dizzying number of fields, not only is he one of the most respected social scientists of the past few decades, he is also the hardest-working, least hierarchical academic I have ever met (and this is coming from the son of a workaholic academic who, at seventy-nine, is still working seven days a week on the bench). Although the Minerva curriculum is vast and was assembled by a broad team, Kosslyn was the one who saw how to take my skeletal ideas and turn them into reality. What is more, he oversaw and edited virtually every lesson plan of every course in both the first- and the second-year curricula. Kosslyn cowrote with Cannon every proposal for accreditation. And all of this doesn't even mention being the public face of Minerva to the academic world, which included writing a substantial part of and editing this book. Looking back at the grand sweep of the Minerva curriculum as it stands today, it is almost laughable that I thought it feasible to build.

Indeed, the enormous contributions of each of these seven individuals make my original concept seem that much more absurd. Not only did each one of them achieve what by any measure would have seemed impossible, as is evidenced in this book, each has delivered at a level higher than anyone could have reasonably expected. They embody our motto, "Achieving Extraordinary."

The senior team at Minerva is unusually accomplished and effective, but it could not have done so much so well without a lot of help. We would also like to acknowledge the entire Minerva faculty, staff, and student body, who built Minerva together and deserve incalculable credit for doing what appeared a near impossibility just a half dozen years ago. The various authors of the chapters in this book and the people acknowledged in each chapter deserve particular recognition. The families that supported each of these individuals, allowing them to devote so much time and energy to building Minerva, are also deeply appreciated.

In addition, we thank the team at the MIT Press, starting with our editor, Phil Laughlin, and the press's director, Amy Brand, who not only believed in Minerva but also believed in this project. We also thank the project manager for the volume.

I   What We Teach and Why

Minerva can do things that established universities can only dream of doing because we can push the reset button on higher education, start from scratch, and ensure that every decision is aligned with first principles. These advantages are nowhere more evident than in the curriculum. In the early days of Minerva, the entire staff could sit around one table. At one such session we hammered out what we wanted our students to be able to do after they graduated. This was a crucial first step. Every aspect of the curriculum was subsequently developed with this goal in mind: to give students the cognitive tools they would need to succeed after they graduated (where success was defined relative to our criteria).

The nine chapters in part I summarize the results of these deliberations and decisions. The first three chapters detail the conceptual foundations of the curriculum. Chapter 1, "Why We Need a New Kind of Higher Education," provides an overview of what we teach and why. This chapter establishes a broad, sweeping context for the rest of the book. Chapter 2, "Practical Knowledge," addresses one central innovation in our curriculum: the idea that students should learn skills and knowledge that will enable them to adapt to a changing world after they graduate. Our goal is to provide students with the core competencies of thinking critically, thinking creatively, communicating effectively, and interacting effectively. This chapter introduces the "habits of mind" and "foundational concepts," or HCs, that underlie each of these four core competencies. Chapter 3, "Foundations of the Curriculum," provides an overview of the design principles that undergird all of our courses: content should not be the focus; the curriculum must be structured; courses should be seminal; and students need information and guidance to make wise choices. These principles guided our decisions on what to include in the curriculum, what to exclude, and how to structure the curriculum, majors, concentrations (i.e., focused tracks within the major), and individual courses. Unlike at other institutions of higher learning, our courses not only build on one another systematically but also are highly structured at the outset and less structured in subsequent years (when the training wheels can be removed, as it were). This chapter explains the rationale for the way our courses are ordered over the four years of an undergraduate education at Minerva.

The next six chapters build on the first three, providing in-depth reviews of the key components of the curriculum. Chapter 4, "A New Look at General Education," sets out the rationale for our first-year general education program. All of our students take the same four yearlong courses during their first year. These "cornerstone" classes, like all Minerva classes, are small seminars, have no lectures, and rely entirely on fully active learning. This chapter contrasts the Minerva model with the dominant approaches to general education. Each of the next four chapters addresses a different one of our four "cornerstone" courses. Chapter 5, "Multimodal Communications and Effective Communication," explains how we teach students to communicate effectively, drawing on material from rhetoric, linguistics, philosophy, history, literature, psychology, neurobiology, and design theory. Chapter 6, "Formal Analyses and Critical Thinking," focuses on a set of critical thinking abilities, namely, those that stem from logic, statistics, algorithmic thinking, and decision science. In this seminar students learn to identify and debunk logical fallacies, to use statistics effectively, and to use formal tools (e.g., those of game theory) to make decisions. Chapter 7, "Empirical Analyses and Creative Thinking," explains how this seminar introduces the scientific method as a framework for conceiving how to make new discoveries and solve problems. The course strives to instill a deep understanding of how evidence is used creatively to generate hypotheses, test hypotheses, draw conclusions, recognize biases, and develop novel solutions and designs. Chapter 8, "Complex Systems and Effective Interaction," describes how this course leads students to understand key characteristics of complex systems and then apply those insights. Most social systems are complex systems, and students learn to apply their understanding of complex systems to social interactions, including interactions that emerge from or are associated with ethical conflicts, debate, negotiation, and leadership.

Finally, we consider the trajectory of undergraduate education at Minerva. Chapter 9, "A New Look at Majors and Concentrations," describes the way our majors are structured to give students interdisciplinary, cross-disciplinary, and transdisciplinary training that looks to the future. We treat each major and concentration as a source of detailed and focused practical knowledge. Like all Minerva courses, however, the majors and concentrations are seminal: they are starting points, not ends in and of themselves. They provide the springboard for a two-year independent capstone research project and help students design senior tutorials that allow them to pursue their own plans and interests.

In short, the chapters in part I of this book review the foundations of a Minerva education and then describe in detail the goals, structure, and substance of the curriculum. We not only outline a new way to look at how a curriculum can be constructed and organized but also describe a novel curricular arc, one that has the sole goal of giving our students the intellectual tools they need to succeed after they graduate.

1   Why We Need a New Kind of Higher Education

Stephen M. Kosslyn and Ben Nelson

Minerva was born out of the intersection of two core beliefs. The first is that we are facing a dire, cross-sector, global shortage of effective leaders. The second is that education, and specifically higher education, must play a critical role in solving this problem. It is almost a cliché that education is crucial to the future of humanity. However, public discourse, government programs, philanthropy, and entrepreneurial efforts that bear on higher education center on expanding the percentage of the population that receives a college education—preferably one that is accessible, affordable, and demonstrates high rates of completion. This is fine as far as it goes, but it doesn't go far enough. The question of what should constitute a college education is not nearly as prominent as it should be. Unless that question is answered, solving the other problems facing higher education could easily lead to a poor curriculum, flawed pedagogy, and low standards.

Minerva's journey began with an open-ended version of that simple question: If you could reinvent higher education for the twenty-first century, what would it look like? Several observers of higher education have addressed this question, but these authors typically focused on the potential of a reengineered existing institution instead of specifying the goals of higher education and then presenting a conception of the educational process that could achieve those goals (e.g., Carey, 2015; Craig, 2015; Selingo, 2013). Although such proposals typically are based on thoughtful analyses and extrapolations, they are only partial glimpses into a possible future—and it is difficult to evaluate them without having a more complete picture of how they would fit into the emergent whole. Moreover, there is no way to know whether these ideas would actually work as hoped; they often sound good on paper but have not been tested, let alone implemented.

Minerva has done something different: we have rethought the system of higher education from the ground up, using student outcomes as the lodestar in redesigning the institution. But Minerva isn't simply a rethinking exercise; we took our ideas and implemented them, too. To do so, we raised tens of millions of dollars; assembled a first-rate team; built an entirely new curriculum, pedagogy, and education delivery system; recruited an extraordinary faculty; selected some of the highest-potential students in the world; and implemented a globally immersive student experience never before seen in higher education. We have built a new university program from the ground up. Our goal is not simply to rival the best existing programs but to demonstrate that higher education can take a critical and significant step forward.

Minerva has now been in operation for three years, and we have learned a great deal about ways to reshape all facets of higher education. This book summarizes those learnings. Minerva is nothing if not ambitious; we aim not only to educate an international body of superb students who will work together to make the world a better place but also to demonstrate a host of best practices that will change higher education, writ large. The goal of this book is twofold: to present one evidence-based model for a future of higher education and to challenge all institutions of higher education either to adopt our system or to devise something better that we at Minerva should adopt.

What Problems Need to Be Solved?

Minerva is a response to problems that all institutions of higher education confront. Specifically, higher education currently is facing four overarching problems. First, higher education is not fulfilling its promise: students are leaving college woefully unprepared for life after graduation. They do not receive or develop the cognitive tools they need to succeed personally and professionally in a highly complex world (Bok, 2013; Bowen & McPherson, 2016).

Second, college is too expensive, and most students leave it with debt—which isn't ideal for their earning potential, not to mention the great costs borne by government (i.e., taxpayers) and private entities in the form of subsidies, grants, endowment allocations, and so on (Kelly & Carey, 2013). In fact, in 2015 the average American student graduated owing $30,100 (Institute for College Access and Success, 2016). In some ways this debt burden adds injury to insult: if college prepared students to succeed after they graduated, the cost might be defensible.

Third, more than half of students don't graduate (Bowen & McPherson, 2016). And even when they do, they have often been intellectually absent during much of their time in college: Many don't even bother to attend class, let alone pay attention and think about what is being discussed.

Finally, many qualified students around the world do not have access to a first-rate college education (Craig, 2017; Watkins, 2013). American universities, for example, typically have quotas on how many non-American students they will take. For instance, Harvard University typically accepts, on average, only slightly more than a dozen students from China in a class of some 1650 students (Harvard University, 2017). Does this really make sense?

We designed Minerva from the start to address these large problems. First, unlike comparable institutions' curricula, Minerva's curriculum focuses on what Benjamin Franklin, Thomas Jefferson, and other founders of the United States described as "useful knowledge." We have shaped this idea into what we call "practical knowledge." Our aim is not to teach knowledge and skills for their own sake; rather we equip our students with intellectual tools they can use to adapt to a changing world and achieve their goals. To be clear: we do not offer only a vocational or preprofessional program. We don't train students to succeed at specific jobs, and we don't offer only programs that prepare students to enter any specific profession. Rather, we provide a very broad liberal arts education, giving students intellectual tools that will help them adapt to a changing world. We want our students to be able to succeed at jobs that don't exist yet.

Second, regarding cost: Minerva's tuition and fees are less than a third of what peer institutions charge, despite being the only highly selective undergraduate program in the United States where 100 percent of classes have fewer than twenty students per class. How is this possible? Simple: attending Minerva merely requires living in a leased residence hall and buying a computer. We have no stadiums, no lawns, no gyms, not even a climbing wall. Thus we are not saddled by construction costs, maintenance costs, or the administrative overhead associated with either. Moreover, we employ no secretaries, we have no overstaffed divisions—in fact, we have no academic departments and thus no department heads, no department staffs, and so on.

Third, regarding lack of engagement, which results in either a large dropout rate or head-spinning grade inflation: the Minerva program is designed in every respect to give personalized attention to every student. Our program ensures that each student is engaged with the curriculum and the community on a daily basis. All of our classes are seminars; we have no lectures at all. Thus students not only bond with each other, they also develop personal connections with the faculty. Moreover, all of our seminars rely exclusively on active learning: all students are expected to be actively involved in every class. Thus, no student can get lost—faculty not only know every one of their students' names but are also aware of how students are doing in class and provide regular feedback. This, in combination with the strong bonding among students that comes from traveling the world together, greatly increases engagement and reduces dropout rates.

Fourth, Minerva is accessible to all qualified students—in fact, we accept *all* qualified applicants. We have no quotas and do not attempt to "balance" classes based on gender, country of origin, age, or any other demographic variable. Moreover, we are need-blind; students who cannot afford even our low costs receive a combination of work-study, modest loans, and grants.

By starting from scratch, with no legacy systems and no entrenched stakeholder interests, we were able to implement sweeping innovations. We have created a new curriculum; we have developed new pedagogies, grounded in the science of learning; we have used technology in novel ways to deliver small seminars in real time and to assess student and faculty performance; we have devised ways to use the city as a campus, relying on local resources instead of duplicating them; and we have developed an international hybrid residential model whereby students take classes on their computer but live together, rotating through different cities around the world.

Minerva has created and utilizes the first university program built for the twenty-first century. In setting up this program, we had to confront the realities of all aspects of higher education, from admissions through instruction, to career development, to building a brand.[1] In the rest of this chapter we provide a brief overview of what we have done and sketch out the reasons why we have taken this approach. The chapters that follow go deeper into each of these topics, providing details on exactly what we have done and how we intend to develop further.

What We Teach and Why

Virtually every American university curriculum has three components (Bok, 2013): general education, the major, and electives. General education courses are supposed to provide breadth, preparing students for life after college, but often they comprise merely a set of distribution requirements that are neither designed with any particular goal in mind nor are part of a coherent program. The academic major is supposed to provide depth in one area but typically is of little or no use to students after graduation. (How many literature majors become English professors? How many art history majors become art historians?) The electives are supposed to allow students to focus on topics they are interested in, but typically elective courses are just whatever happens to interest the faculty, with little thought given to what is useful for students.

Minerva has redesigned each of these three components.

• First, our general education curriculum consists of four yearlong courses, which are tightly coordinated to provide a wide range of "practical knowledge"—knowledge students can *use* to adapt to a changing world, allowing them to achieve their goals (see chapter 2). Students take these four courses during their first year, which provides them with intellectual tools that will help them develop into leaders, be innovators, be broad, adaptive learners, and adopt a global perspective. To address these aims, we focus on four core competencies: critical thinking, creative thinking, effective communication, and effective interactions. And we do not simply pay lip service to helping the students learn these competencies: the entire year revolves around introducing about one hundred specific learning objectives, each of which focuses explicitly on an aspect of one of the four core competencies. This material is at the foreground of what students concentrate on in class.

• Second, our majors do not rely on traditional organizations of disciplines, nor are they centered on today's (or yesterday's) trendy topics (e.g., anything with "studies" after an adjective). Rather, our majors center on fields that will help students in their lives after college. Each of our majors has two components. Students first take three or four (depending on the major) "major core" courses, which provide foundational knowledge and orient students to the major as a whole. After taking these courses, students then select a set of courses that are organized into distinct "concentrations." Concentrations often investigate topics at different levels of analysis (e.g., in the natural sciences such concentrations are molecules and atoms, cells and organisms, and earth's systems) or are associated with distinct research approaches (e.g., data-intensive, theoretical, or applications-oriented approaches). Students can double major and have up to three concentrations.

• Third, electives—both those within and outside the major—at Minerva are very student-centered. We offer three kinds of electives: (1) All students take a two-year capstone course in a topic they select. They design a research project under the guidance of a faculty advisor and—if necessary—a content expert. (2) In their senior year, students will identify four topics of interest that stem from their concentration(s). We then will identify three students with overlapping interests and pair them with an appropriate professor. The four of them will then design a syllabus, and the students take the course. Depending on their major(s), students may take up to four such courses. (3) Finally, students may select major core or concentration courses outside their major and take these courses as electives, which ensures that exploration outside a main area of interest will be in seminal ideas of a field as opposed to fringe pursuits (see chapter 3).

The Minerva curriculum is unique in how it is structured. As students move through the curriculum, they have increasingly more choice in what they take. In the first year, when students take the general education program, they have no choice at all. Rather, all students receive the same broad foundation, acquiring intellectual tools that will serve them for the rest of their lives. In the second year, students choose major core courses, now selecting between six and eight courses from sixteen alternatives. They then select a major. In the third year they take concentration courses within a major (or majors, if they choose more than one) and begin their capstone project. And in the fourth year, they will take the bulk of their elective courses, complete their capstone courses, and typically design at least two (and up to four) senior tutorials, which directly address student interests. Finally, in a monthlong special session after the fourth year called Manifest, we will require all students to present their capstone projects and revise them after receiving feedback.[2]

Thus, as students progress through the curriculum and gain the appropriate foundations for what they will do next, they increasingly personalize their studies to achieve their own goals. By the end of the curriculum they are poised to move on to the next chapter of their lives.

How We Teach

Two separate domains came together at Minerva to shape how we teach: the science of learning and twenty-first-century technology.

Minerva is the only school (of any sort) that systematically uses the science of learning in every session of every one of its courses. The science of learning is not new; research on this topic has been published for more than a century. The science of learning addresses ways in which humans perceive, organize, and store information and then subsequently retrieve that information from memory. A trove of useful discoveries is freely available in professional journals, and many books have been written that distill this knowledge. We have organized this literature into sixteen distinct principles (described in chapter 11), which are drawn upon in each class we offer. We have organized these principles into two broad maxims. The first encompasses principles that rely on the finding that the more people process ("think through") information, the more likely they are to remember it—whether or not they try to do so. The second maxim encompasses principles that rely on the finding that we understand, retain and later recall material best when we use associations to organize it and then associate it with what we already know.

Our efforts to apply systematically the principles of the science of learning have led us to offer only active-learning seminars. The literature is crystal clear in showing that students learn best when they have to use the material, not simply sit passively and hear it described (e.g., Freeman et al., 2014).

Because we did not need to replace legacy practices or negotiate with stakeholders to modify traditional practices, we were able to draw on what is known about the science of learning and use this information systematically in every session of every course.

But more than that, we developed a new kind of pedagogy, which allows us to use the science of learning effectively (see chapter 12). We call this pedagogy *fully active learning.* Fully active learning requires that 100 percent of the students are engaged at least 75 percent of the time and relies on using a "radically flipped classroom." That is, in a typical university course, lectures occur during class time and students do homework outside of class time. In a flipped classroom, homework is done in class (where the teacher and other students are available as resources) and lectures are provided before class. In Minerva's radically flipped classroom we moved both the homework and the knowledge dissemination to before class and reserved class time for using the information in various ways (e.g., solving problems, role playing, debating). The in-class activities rely on fully active learning and require students to use information acquired through readings and pre-class video viewings, in the service of mastering critical thinking, creative thinking, effective communication, and effective interaction. Class sessions at Minerva do not focus on information transmission but rather on learning to use information in different ways. To ensure that students are fully engaged, we have developed special engagement techniques that require students to pay attention. For example, we warn students at the outset of an activity that they will be expected at the end to compare and contrast the different positions that were discussed (see chapter 12).

To facilitate this sort of teaching and learning, all classes at Minerva are taught using a cloud-based software program we have developed, called the Active Learning Forum (ALF) (see chapter 15). We use this software for two main reasons. First, the ALF enables us to use fully active learning in ways that are very difficult or cost-prohibitive in an offline setting. The ALF incorporates tools—such as polls, voting, collaborative editing, and the ability quickly to compose breakout groups in various ways—that are difficult to duplicate in a traditional classroom. Second, because the ALF collects a massive amount of data on each student's performance, it allows us to personalize the intellectual development path for each student—which is simply impossible to do via any other education medium, online or offline. In short, the ALF allows us to teach more effectively and helps students learn more effectively.

As a beneficial side effect, the ALF allows students to take classes, and faculty to teach classes, anywhere in the world. This means the following: (1) We can be flexible about where students reside during term time. This not only allows students to travel when necessary or desirable (for personal or educational reasons) but also facilitates students' living and working together in cities around the world. (2) Students living in different cities around the world can be in the same seminar, which allows them to bring their experiences into class for compare-and-contrast exercises. (3) We can recruit first-rate faculty from all over the world without requiring them to uproot their lives to join Minerva.

The real power of our approach to pedagogy flows from the fact that we built the ALF with the science of learning and fully active learning in mind from the start. The ALF incorporates tools that are explicitly designed to facilitate our pedagogy, as well as to enable long-term educational outcomes that are simply not possible without it. Moreover, the ALF facilitates our creating and revising the curriculum, and, because each session is recorded, it helps us assess (and coach, when appropriate) the faculty. The whole has emerged to be much more than the sum of its parts.

An American International Model

Minerva's international orientation has led to one of the most distinctive but also one of the most easily replicated aspects of the Minerva model. Universities often target specific kinds of students, and this is very much an institutional choice; we do not suggest that other institutions adopt Minerva's approach to admissions (which is entirely egalitarian, with no attempt to balance students according to different criteria or even limit the number of students). Similarly, universities typically provide their education primarily in the location where they have existing infrastructure. We also recognize that Minerva's global rotation program is not well suited to all or even most entering first-year students. Nevertheless, it is useful to explain the philosophies that underlie both the composition of the Minerva student body and our global immersion program. In so doing, we outline the benefits of our approaches to the intellectual development of students.

Many citizens of a given country believe that universities should help their country compete on the world stage. Universities fulfill this part of their mission in two ways. First, they educate professionals who are needed to meet the needs of society, such as dentists, social workers, accountants, and architects. Second, universities educate decision makers who are expected to lead the country to a better future, such as politicians, business people, journalists, scientists, and inventors. Clearly, the emphasis on education for these two groups, those working toward meeting the needs of society and those working toward roles as future leaders, should be different. One can imagine a highly effective dentist who may not have great facility with thinking through generalizable second-order effects (although that skill would probably be useful). However, most of us would not be excited by the prospect of a nation's president or a company's CEO who lacked these analytical skills. In an increasingly globalized world, such decision makers not only shape local society but also have a broader societal impact, despite their often considering only the small sliver of society that they believe their actions will affect.

Clearly, a purely local orientation to education does not serve the country or these particular students well, especially during the undergraduate years, when students can develop along many trajectories and hence need a broad background of knowledge and skills. Even the most international education systems, however, are remarkably provincial. For example, in Australian universities—which probably have the most internationally oriented student body of any major university system in the world—only 21 percent of entering bachelor's degree students in 2015 came from outside Australia (Australian Government, 2016). American universities have far fewer slots reserved for international students. In 2015, U.S. colleges and universities hosted 1.13 million foreign students (U.S. Immigration and Customs Enforcement, 2015) out of a total of 20.5 million students (National Center for Education Statistics, 2015). Moreover, only about 10 percent of American undergraduates study abroad (NAFSA, 2016). But even this figure is misleading because many study abroad programs do not provide cultural immersion; instead, American students live with and spend most of their days with other native English speakers, often from their home country. Neither statistic supports claims by elite institutions that they train globally minded leaders.

Minerva's approach is markedly different. We have designed our curriculum, student experience, pedagogical model, and institutional structure specifically to help our students have a broad societal impact (as opposed to focusing on more narrow professions). But more than this, we have designed Minerva to help our students create, run, or influence major institutions—especially institutions with a broad global reach.

This focus also shapes our admissions philosophy. If we find an applicant who has the clear potential to become a transformational leader or innovator, how could we justify rejecting that person because of a lack of space? Similarly, even if applicants are intelligent or have impressive backgrounds, if they do not have the level of potential of those for whom we designed the program, how could we justify admitting them? Unlike all of our peer institutions, we accept *all and only* students who are qualified, regardless of country of origin, age, gender, wealth, family prominence, or other demographic characteristics.

Minerva is deeply international, both because we do not have quotas for regions or other characteristics and because we know that talent is broadly distributed around the world, and hence we spread our outreach efforts accordingly. Fewer than one quarter of Minerva students are American, and no single group constitutes a majority. We take seriously our responsibility to provide these exceptional students with the international experience they will need to be successful; thus we ensure that they benefit from being in the most diverse undergraduate student body in the world and that they get the most out of living and studying in cities located in seven different countries during their four-year tenure—San Francisco, Seoul, Hyderabad, Berlin, Buenos Aires, Taipei and London. Minerva leases at least one residence hall in each city, where students live together; students use the residence as a base, from which they take advantage of programs that immerse them in the culture of each location.

Why do we encourage our students to travel the world? Three main reasons: first, we believe that the future is increasingly international (Friedman, 2005), and that leaders and innovators in the twenty-first century should be comfortable interacting with people from many different cultures. And there's no better way to foster such an orientation than by actually living and interacting with people on their home turf. Second, we treat the city as a campus and use its resources both in our required curriculum and in optional cocurricular activities. As part of our focus on practical knowledge, every course includes at least one location-based activity that requires students to apply what they have learned in class to a situation in their city of residence. In addition, we offer a wide range of optional cocurricular activities that also draw on what the students have learned in class. Lastly, deep learning of conceptual frameworks can only occur when those frameworks are applied in multiple, varied contexts. And what better way for our students to master the learning objectives we teach them than to apply them to day to day living in cultures as radically different as India and Argentina?

However, we must underscore that Minerva is a deeply American institution. Not only do we adhere to the structure of an American education, offering a four-year, liberal arts education leading to a bachelor's degree, we also bring a distinctly American attitude to education: We believe that education is the great equalizer, that it can open up opportunities for everyone. In fact, our emphasis on practical knowledge is deeply rooted in American traditions that reach back to our founders and were strengthened by John Dewey and other members of the late nineteenth-century functionalist movement (e.g., Dewey, 1913/1969; Hook, 1939).

A Lifelong Experience

We have taken to heart the idea that college should be a springboard for a successful, productive and meaningful life. We not only have designed the curriculum to help students thrive after graduation but also have built mechanisms and institutions to help students develop their careers. At most universities, graduating students can expect help in preparing their résumés, but little else. We have taken a different approach.

First, we assign students a career coach during their first year. Rather than waiting to call on a professional coach when careers hit roadblocks, we provide expert guidance during the first year to avoid many potential roadblocks. Having started such support early, we continue to provide it throughout our students' four years at Minerva and even after graduation—we provide such support throughout a Minervan's career.

Second, we have instituted a "talent agency" that actively helps students find appropriate summer internships during their school years and then will help them find positions after graduation. This talent agency helps students according to their individualized goals, not simply by curating a short list of employers that come to the university. This service will not stop when the student has his or her first job: we allow students to access the service for the rest of their lives. We take seriously our commitment to student

PUBLICITY SERVICES

success. We pair this with lifelong publicity services to help our students amplify their work in the popular press.

Finally, we provide the social and emotional infrastructure to help students succeed. Minerva provides a higher ratio of mental health providers to students than any university, with a strong emphasis on proactive resiliency education. Moreover, we explicitly teach students life skills, ranging from basic cooking techniques to time management. Our goal is to provide students with fishing rods, not fish.

At Minerva, we recognize that we need to educate the whole person, and we have set up processes and procedures to help the students help themselves. We don't take this commonly stated goal as something that is "nice to have" but rather as something that is critical for the sake of the world.

Conclusion

Because Minerva was created from scratch, we were able to take a step back and consider our long-term goals. We had the extraordinarily rare opportunity to be principled in all respects—to have good reasons for doing what we do. But more than that, we were able to design all aspects of the university experience not only to address our goals but also to ensure that the various aspects of the program work together when doing so. We designed the curriculum, the pedagogy, the technology, the global orientation, and the student services systems to promote students' intellectual, social, and emotional well-being, with only a single overarching goal in mind: the success of our students. Ultimately, this is the only metric that matters.

Notes

1. Academics sometimes cringe at the word "brand," but that's what it is: To succeed, a university must develop a reputation for having specific qualities and characteristics—and its name and any identifying logos and marks must become associated with these qualities and characteristics. In other words, it must develop a brand.

2. We also offer an optional master's degree in applied arts and sciences, which students can take concurrently with their undergraduate studies. Students in this program take additional, graduate-level courses and conduct a team master's project, with their report of one component of this project serving as a master's thesis.

References

Australian Government. (2016). Higher education statistics. https://www.education.gov.au/higher-education-statistics

Bok, D. (2013). *Higher education in America*. Princeton, NJ: Princeton University Press.

Bowen, W. G., & McPherson, M. S. (2016). *Lesson plan: An agenda for change in American higher education*. Princeton, NJ: Princeton University Press.

Carey, K. (2015). *The end of college*. New York, NY: Riverhead Books.

Craig, R. (2015). *College disrupted: The great unbundling of higher education*. New York, NY: Macmillan.

Craig, R. (2017, January 27). Make America first in higher ed: Open the door. *Inside Higher Ed*. https://www.insidehighered.com/views/2017/01/27/us-should-ease-not-restrict-access-its-colleges-international-students-essay

Dewey, J. (1913/1969). *Interest and effort in education*. Boston, MA: Houghton Mifflin.

Freeman, S., Eddy, S. L., McDonough, M., Smith, M. K., Okoroafor, N., Jordt, H., et al. (2014). Active learning increases student performance in science, engineering, and mathematics. *Proceedings of the National Academy of Sciences of the United States of America*, *111*(23), 8410–8415.

Friedman, T. L. (2005). *The world is flat*. New York, NY: Farrar, Straus and Giroux.

Harvard University (2017). Harvard International Office Statistics. http://www.hio.harvard.edu/statistics

Hook, S. (1939). *John Dewey: An intellectual portrait*. New York, NY: John Day Co.

Institute for College Access and Success. (2016). Student debt and the class of 2015. http://ticas.org/sites/default/files/pub_files/classof2015.pdf

Kelly, A. P., & Carey, K. (2013). *Stretching the higher education dollar: How innovation can improve access, equity, and affordability*. Cambridge, MA: Harvard Education Press.

NAFSA: Association of International Educators. (2016). Trends in U.S. study abroad. http://www.nafsa.org/Policy_and_Advocacy/Policy_Resources/Policy_Trends_and_Data/Trends_in_U_S__Study_Abroad

National Center for Education Statistics. (2015). Fast facts: Back to school statistics. http://nces.ed.gov/fastfacts/display.asp?id=372

Selingo, J. J. (2013). *College unbound: The future of higher education and what it means for students*. Seattle, WA: Amazon Publishing.

U.S. Immigration and Customs Enforcement. (2015, August). SEVP (Student and Exchange Visitor Program): Student and exchange visitor information system. SEVIS by the numbers: General summary quarterly review, August 2015. https://www.ice.gov/sites/default/files/documents/Report/2015/sevis_bythenumbers_aug15.pdf

Watkins, K. (2013, January 16). Too little access, not enough learning: Africa's twin deficit in education. *Brookings*, https://www.brookings.edu/opinions/too-little-access-not-enough-learning-africas-twin-deficit-in-education

2   Practical Knowledge

Stephen M. Kosslyn

Many believe that the primary goal of universities is to produce educated citizens. What does it mean to be an educated person in the twenty-first century?

Minerva's response to this question is unusual. We have designed our curriculum to focus on what we call *practical knowledge*. Practical knowledge is knowledge one can use to adapt to a changing world, which allows one to achieve one's goals. It is not preprofessional (it is not "pre" anything; it is useful in its own right) and it is not vocational (it is not narrowly focused on a single application). Moreover, practical knowledge is not just a collection of facts. Rather, practical knowledge is broad and generative; it includes both skills and knowledge (including theories). Practical knowledge provides the foundations of a solid liberal arts education, of a broad understanding of the world around us. Practical knowledge is often deep: As the great social scientist Kurt Lewin (1945) once said, "Nothing is so practical as a good theory" (p. 129). Good theories allow one to explain novel phenomena and anticipate how events will unfold even in unfamiliar contexts. Good theories are useful.

In this chapter I provide an overview of how we have fleshed out the concept of practical knowledge and why we have fleshed it out the way we have.

Practical Knowledge in the Curriculum

Our approach to developing a curriculum is very different from that typically used in American universities. Most modern American universities build their academic programs around a specific set of discipline-based topics; in fact, course catalogs from different universities are remarkably similar. The underlying assumption is that any educated person should know a certain core set of facts (e.g., how different political systems operate) and be able to use a core set of specific skills (e.g., how to read and write at a relatively high level).

In American universities, this material is taught in all three parts of the standard university curriculum noted in chapter 1: general education, the major, and electives. General education is supposed to give students broad foundations, the major is supposed to give students depth and focus in one domain, and electives are supposed to allow students to explore subjects that they personally want to study.

Chapter 4 discusses four models of general education, which differ primarily in terms of what sort of material is taught. However, we can also consider the structure of the general education curriculum itself. Several ways of organizing this part of the curriculum are popular, but two are most common. The simplest program to design and run is a distribution requirement system. Students are told they need two courses from category A (e.g., arts and humanities), two from category B (e.g., the natural sciences), and so on. Typically, this list is largely populated by introductory courses in different areas. In no case that I am aware of is any effort made to relate material from courses in one category to material in courses from another category.

A second approach is to provide special survey courses that integrate much material, such as courses with titles like Western Civilization or Science and Religion. Key criticisms here are that such courses can't cover everything (and hence some crucial areas are overlooked) and that the treatment of what is covered is necessarily superficial. Moreover, this approach requires additional effort for the faculty who prepare and teach these specialized courses and draws additional resources from the university. Again, material in one of these courses is rarely, if ever, explicitly related to material in the other courses.

In my view, both approaches fall short. In neither case are breadth requirements part of a coherent program. But more important, both approaches typically rely on lectures that are designed to disseminate sets of knowledge and skills. This approach is problematic because many studies have shown that students forget such lectures at an alarming rate. For example, in his classic work, *Audiovisual Methods in Teaching*, Dale (1969) reported that students recalled less than 20 percent of a lecture even three days later(!). Bligh (2000) reported even worse recall, less than 10 percent after three days. Even with cued recall (in which hints are given), college students recalled only slightly more than 20 percent of names and about 37 percent of concepts they had learned twenty-seven months earlier in a course on cognitive psychology (I estimated these numbers from figure

2, on p. 401, of Conway, Cohen, & Stanhope, 1991; in addition, it is worth noting that these students may have revisited at least some of this material in subsequent classes, during the time after it was originally introduced). In an important study, Semb, Ellis, & Araujo (1992) concluded that "passing scores for recall tests [in class] should be set at over 90 percent to ensure that performance will be above 60 percent following a 4-month or 11-month interval" (p. 10). How often is 90 percent considered the lowest "passing score"?[1]

The emphasis on memorizing content is pervasive in the standard curriculum: it is present not only in general education but also in the major and in electives. Moreover, the major is supposed to provide depth, but the material typically is of little or no use to students after graduation. Often faculty treat students in their majors as budding professors-in-the-making, but very few actually go on to teach that subject. In fact, only about 2 percent of Americans complete a Ph.D. (U.S. Census Bureau, 2016).

We at Minerva have rejected the idea that higher education is primarily about information transmission, about leading students to memorize knowledge and skills. In the twenty-first century, the Internet serves as a kind of external memory, allowing users to access a vast array of information easily and quickly. Yes, people must have some idea of the range of what is known, and must know enough to be able to think about topics clearly, but it is difficult to justify emphasizing information transmission as the primary goal of our classes. Instead at Minerva we focus on practical knowledge; we intentionally selected material that should be broadly useful to the students, that should help them adapt to a changing world. And rather than simply ask them to memorize this material, we help them to learn to use it in various ways. But what does it mean to be broadly useful to a student? And how do we decide?

Minerva's Educational Goals

Let's begin by taking a step back and considering why anyone might want his or her child to attend college. I raise this question from the point of view of the parents, who have ample real-world experience and perspective. (From the point of view of the student, the answers might be very different, often heavily weighting short-term goals such as social life or athletic programs.) Here I want to consider what college might do to equip a student to succeed in life after college, both professionally and personally. What should college do to help the student succeed in the long term? Let's consider four possible goals of higher education.

Goal 1: Understanding leadership and working with others

Many colleges' mission statements say that they want to train leaders. What does this mean? Not everybody can be a leader at any given time; a group usually has only one leader. And in any event, students typically are not going to be hired to serve as leaders immediately after they graduate.

In my view, training students to be leaders is the wrong way to frame this goal. At Minerva, we want students to understand leadership. Yes, they need to develop key characteristics of successful leaders and need to have the foundations that will allow them to grow into being effective leaders. But at least as important, they need to know when it is appropriate for them to be a leader and when it is appropriate to defer to someone else's leadership. Moreover, when they are not functioning as a leader, they need to know how to work with the leader so that everyone is pulling the oars in the same direction.

More generally, whether or not they are functioning as the leader, students need to know how to work effectively with others. Most of the world's current problems are so difficult that no one individual working alone will be able to solve them. Rather, groups of people will have to work together, leveraging each other's strengths.

Thus, higher education not only should teach the skills that enable one to become a leader, but also should teach students how to work effectively with leaders and more generally how to work effectively with others who have different strengths and weaknesses.

Goal 2: Understanding innovation

Another commonly stated goal is to train innovators. But do we really want to train students to try to innovate all of the time? Probably not. Students need to learn when it is likely to be useful to innovate. The first step is simply to find out whether a good solution to a problem already exists, and how to evaluate whether that solution would work in a specific case. Why reinvent a well-oiled, fully functional wheel? Students need to have a high degree of information literacy, and must know how to search for sought information efficiently and effectively. Moreover, they must be inoculated against the "not invented here" syndrome. It does not matter where a good solution comes from; if it exists, using it is better than inventing another solution just to have something new. Only if an existing solution falls short should one work to devise a new solution. We don't want (or need) everything always to be new.

In addition, is it really possible to train someone to be creative? The empirical literature suggests that there are in fact heuristics and techniques that can help people be more creative (e.g., McGuire, 1997), but not everyone will formulate useful innovations (Finke, Ward, & Smith, 1996). Thus, part of what students need to learn is how and when they can best contribute to useful innovations.

I doubt that many would argue with the two goals just discussed. But if the overarching aim is to help students learn to contribute to society, these cannot be the only goals of higher education. Let's consider two more goals:

Goal 3: Thinking broadly and adaptably

The Greek philosopher Heraclitus of Ephesus (c 535–475 BC) reportedly said, "The only thing constant is change." This truism has become abundantly clear in the digital age, when sweeping changes seem to occur every couple of years. Thus, students must be given broadly useful intellectual tools that will help them adapt to a changing world. They should have the intellectual tools to grow, to adjust to the times and master jobs that don't exist yet. It's clearly a mistake to train students to succeed only in current jobs, in light of how quickly the world is changing.

Moreover, most of the changes students will experience in their lifetimes are not easily predicted (e.g., Tetlock & Gardner, 2015). Thus the ability to adapt requires a broad education. One needs skills and abilities that will apply to a wide range of effects wrought by change.

Goal 4: Attaining a global perspective

Increasing numbers of people from different backgrounds and cultures are interacting and working together. Hence, a fourth goal is that students should be comfortable working with people from very different backgrounds and cultures who have different values and worldviews. And they should be comfortable functioning in different cultures. Minerva tries to achieve this goal in two ways. One way is to have a truly diverse student body, with students from all over the world who interact on a daily basis. The other way is to have students live and function in very different cultures, moving from city to city (see chapters 22 and 23).

Few if any universities would disagree with any of the four goals I just summarized. But these goals—or ones very much like them—usually end their lives stuck in mission statements and are never translated into any specific aspect of education. Why? In part because faculty members prefer to teach in their own disciplines, and achieving these goals requires a broader scope and reach. In addition, many faculty do not prioritize teaching, and hence are not motivated to expend the effort to reach these goals. Rather, they prefer to pursue their own research—which makes sense in light of the incentive structures in many universities: in virtually all top-tier universities, hiring, promotion, salary decisions, and various perks follow from research accomplishments, not teaching.

But these are not the only reasons why most universities do not focus on achieving the four goals described above. For the most part, it is not immediately clear how one would go about teaching material that would achieve these goals. Moreover, it often isn't clear how one would assess whether such goals have been achieved; if you cannot measure the outcomes, many would argue, there's no point in trying to teach the material.

Four Core Competencies

To achieve these four goals, we must teach practical knowledge. The first step is to consider what knowledge and skills would help students achieve each goal. The empirical literature can be of use here. In particular, solid research has identified the personal qualities, practices, and approaches that underlie successful innovation and leadership. For overviews of characteristics of creative people, see Csikszentmihalyi (1996), Feist (1998), Feist and Barron (2003), Grosul and Feist (2014), and Simonton (2000, 2008); for overviews of characteristics of effective leaders, see Derue et al. (2011), House and Aditya (1997), Judge, Colbert, and Ilies (2004), Lord, De Vader, and Alliger (1986), and Zaccaro (2001, 2007). We reviewed this material, and also considered the characteristics that employers seek when hiring new staff, noting that they value employees who can think broadly and adaptively. We not only interviewed employers ourselves to ascertain such characteristics but also relied on published surveys (e.g., Hart Research Associates, 2013; see also National Association of Colleges and Employers, 2016).

We organized the most robust personal qualities, practices, and approaches identified in the literatures, interviews and surveys into four core competencies, which were:

- Thinking critically
- Thinking creatively
- Communicating effectively
- Interacting effectively[2]

It is clear that one needs all four of these competencies to be an effective leader or a valuable member of a team. Similarly, it is clear that one needs all four to be an effective innovator: to be successful, one needs not only to be creative but also to be able to filter one's own ideas critically, to communicate them to others, and to work with others to implement these ideas.

And a broad, adaptive thinker must master all four competencies, as should someone who intends to function effectively in a global context.

None of these four competencies is surprising or controversial. In fact, virtually every university claims to train students to be critical thinkers and creative thinkers (see, e.g., Bok, 2013; Rosovsky, 1991). However, the evidence suggests that universities often do not achieve these stated goals (e.g., Arum & Roksa, 2011).

Analyzing the four core competencies

At Minerva we aim to teach students the practical knowledge that undergirds each of these four core competencies. But how do we make these relatively abstract competencies sufficiently specific and concrete that they can be taught?

To formulate specific learning objectives, we conceived of practical knowledge in terms of *production systems* (e.g., Newell & Simon, 1972). A production consists of a condition/action pair. When the condition is satisfied, the action is performed. For example, a production might specify, "If it's raining, get an umbrella." The condition is "If it's raining" and the action is "get an umbrella." When the action is produced, it in turn can serve as the condition for another production, such as "If you want an umbrella, look in your closet," and that action in turn can serve as the condition for yet another production, and so on. In a production system, a large number of productions constantly lie in wait for the appropriate conditions to be satisfied, ready and able to perform their actions.

This framework is ideal for characterizing practical knowledge, for by its very nature, practical knowledge focuses on *doing* something. We have used this framework to define two kinds of practical knowledge, "habits of mind" and "foundational concepts." Each of the four core competencies draws on both types of practical knowledge.

Habits of mind

Habits of mind are *cognitive skills that with practice come to be triggered automatically*. By virtue of being "of mind," they are cognitive; because they specify practical knowledge, you can do something with this knowledge (which follows from their being "skills"); and because they are "habits," they come to be applied automatically, without requiring conscious deliberation.[3]

For habits of mind, the condition part of the production is very well defined and applies to a narrow range of circumstances that are easy to identify. For example, one habit of mind we teach is "Tailor oral and written work for the context and the audience." The condition is that one is producing work for an audience. This condition is easy to recognize, and recognizing it can easily become automatic—with sufficient practice it can become a habit that does not require conscious thought and deliberation.

In contrast, the action component of a habit of mind may be difficult: Exactly how you should tailor your work to a particular context and audience depends on a variety of factors, such as your goal, what the audience already knows, what the audience is interested in, and how much time you have to present. Knowing when to apply a habit of mind is the easy part; if there is a hard part, it is knowing exactly what to do in relevant circumstances.

For some habits of mind, both the condition and the action may be very well defined, and hence both may become automatic with practice. For example, another habit of mind we teach is "Distinguish between categories and types of information to determine source quality." The condition is that one is confronted with different types of information and needs to determine which ones are most trustworthy; the action is to favor the most trustworthy sources when using the information. In this case, both the condition and action can become so well learned that they rarely require conscious thought and deliberation.

Foundational concepts

Foundational concepts are *fundamental knowledge that is broadly applicable*. By virtue of being concepts, they are knowledge; they are fundamental and applicable in the sense that they provide a springboard for action—you can do something with this knowledge. In this case, the condition part of the production is not narrowly defined but rather applies to a wide range of circumstances. And the relevant commonalities across the relevant circumstances typically are not easy to recognize; in contrast to habits of mind, the various situations in which a foundational concept applies typically do not readily display their common characteristics.

For example, one foundational concept we teach requires students to distinguish between correlation and causation. The condition is a situation in which it is important to distinguish between correlation and causation, which is not easy to identify: both sorts of relationships range far and wide, and few common threads (if any) exist across instances. (The action is implied: "and act accordingly," which we note when explaining the foundational concept.) We may take as an example epidemiological observations, such as the fact that people who take a baby aspirin every day have fewer heart attacks and strokes than people who do not. On first hearing this association, one's impulse is probably to interpret it as a causal relation, with the implication that we all should take a baby aspirin every day. But as described, it is not a causal relation; it is only a correlation. Many other factors could produce both effects. For example, more compulsive people may both take aspirin as requested and be more careful about their diet and exercise, and it may be the latter factors that produce the effect. Another example is the observation that people who support Donald Trump score more highly on measures of Authoritarian Personality than those who don't support him. Again, this is not necessarily a causal relationship. And the two correlations in our examples, that between taking an aspirin every day and heart attacks or strokes and that between Trump support and Authoritarian Personality, have nothing in common. Noting the regularities across the conditions of foundational concepts typically is difficult.

In contrast, once the condition of a foundational concept has been met, the action usually is straightforward; the concept is easily applied. For instance, it is not always obvious when a test of statistical significance, such as a t-test, should be used to assess whether two means reflect differences in the underlying populations, but once you have decided to use such a test, actually applying it is easy. The knowledge used is typically basic and straightforward to apply; the hard part is knowing when to apply it.

However, for some foundational concepts both the condition and the action are difficult. For example, another foundational concept we teach is "Apply algorithmic strategies to solve real-world problems." Not only is it difficult to identify situations in which such an approach is appropriate, but acting on it—by creating the relevant algorithm—can also be difficult.

In short, the key to the distinction is that the *conditions* for habits of mind are always well defined and can come to be recognized automatically, whereas the broader, more varied conditions for foundational concepts cannot be recognized automatically. In contrast, the *actions* of foundational concepts are well-defined nuggets of knowledge that typically are straightforward to apply, whereas this is rarely the case for habits of mind.

Using the distinction between habits of mind and foundational concepts

Why is the distinction between habits of mind and foundational concepts important? Conceiving of practical knowledge in terms of condition/action pairs helps us to focus our efforts in teaching. This perspective illuminates major sources of difficulty in mastering the material.

Specifically, for habits of mind, it is relatively easy to determine the condition; any difficult aspect will be knowing exactly what to do in a relevant situation. Thus we know that we need to have students use the habit of mind repeatedly, so that the condition component becomes very familiar and eventually can be applied automatically. We also know that when we do invoke a habit of mind, we should focus our efforts on helping students learn how to respond appropriately. The students need practice in using the habit of mind in a variety of situations so that they learn relevant strategies.

In contrast, for foundational concepts, the situation usually is reversed: it is relatively difficult to determine when they are applicable but it typically is relatively easy to know what to do in a given situation. Thus we know that we need to have students use the foundational concept repeatedly in situations that on the surface appear very different so that they learn to identify the crucial aspects of the condition component. The action typically is straightforward, and thus we do not need to focus as much effort on learning how to act on the foundational concept.

By conceiving of practical knowledge this way, we are led to consider exactly where to concentrate our teaching efforts—on the condition, the action, or (relatively rarely) both. This is a systematic approach to pedagogy that would not be possible at most institutions. At Minerva we have the great advantage of starting from scratch, and thus have no legacy practices to overcome. Instead we can start from first principles—as illustrated here— and try to do what will be most effective.

Teaching Habits of Mind and Foundational Concepts

One easily could formulate a very large number of habits of mind and foundational concepts (which we call "HCs," short for "habits" and "concepts"). How do we decide which HCs to introduce in our general education program? At Minerva, to be included in the curriculum, a specific habit or concept must:

1. be derived from an aspect of one of the four core competencies (thinking critically, thinking creatively, communicating effectively, interacting effectively);
2. lead students to be able to *do* something useful in ordinary life after graduation;
3. be broadly applicable, as indicated by the fact that it is used in courses offered in at least two of Minerva's majors;
4. be justified either by empirical findings, proofs, or well-established best practices (particularly those that support functioning ethically in a global context); and

5.   lead to specific behaviors that can be evaluated with rubrics. The habit
     or concept cannot be so general or so vague that it cannot be systemati-
     cally and reliably evaluated.

At Minerva, all HCs are introduced during the first year, when students
take our general education program. This program consists of four yearlong
"cornerstone" seminars: Formal Analyses (which focuses on core aspects
of thinking critically), Empirical Analyses (which focuses on core aspects
of thinking creatively), Multimodal Communications (which focuses on
core aspects of communicating effectively), and Complex Systems (which
focuses on core aspects of interacting effectively). This material is then used
(and assessed) during the ensuing three years while students major in specific subjects.

When we began to implement this approach, we were surprised to discover that we could not easily derive HCs directly from the four core competencies. Let me underline this: we discovered that we could not directly
teach critical thinking and the other three core competencies.

In retrospect, the problem should have been obvious: Each of these competencies is not one thing. For example, there is no such thing as critical
thinking in general; this is the name for a loose collection of very different
skills and abilities. For instance, let's think about how we would evaluate
a claim such as "It's impossible to teach critical thinking per se." To think
critically about this claim, we might try to remember a counterexample
(an instance in which critical thinking was taught). We might consider the
background assumptions that underlie the claim, such as what is meant by
"teaching." We also might examine the logic of the claim: what the underlying premises are, and whether the conclusion follows. We might even
consider the credibility of the source.

Now let's contrast this kind of critical thinking with what is required to
make a decision, such as whether to go to college or spend a year working.
Now we need to weigh trade-offs. This sort of critical thinking is best accomplished by setting up a payoff matrix in which we systematically compare
and contrast the costs and benefits of each course of action. Moreover, we
need to remember that humans disproportionately weight the prospect of
loss over the prospect of gain (Kahneman, 2011).

In short, the abilities needed to accomplish these two different forms
of critical thinking have almost nothing in common. They are alike in the
same way that swinging the bat, hitting a foul ball that is not caught, or
pitching a ball that goes directly over the plate are alike: all three are called
a strike, but they have nothing in common.

And in fact none of the four big core competencies—thinking critically, thinking creatively, communicating effectively, and interacting effectively—is a single thing. Rather, each is a collection of very different skills and abilities, and these different skills and abilities each require teaching different material.

At Minerva, we organize practical knowledge into a set of distinct *aspects* of each of the core competencies. In the following section, I provide one example of a habit or concept for each aspect of each of the four competencies, along with a brief summary of that HC and then an example of how that habit or concept could be used in the real world.

Competence in critical thinking

We divide critical thinking into four types, each of which draws on different habits of mind ("H" below) or foundational concepts ("C" below).

Evaluating claims (type of critical thinking)   One type of critical thinking requires evaluating claims. To do this, one must evaluate the background assumptions as well as the logic that underlies the claim (in part by looking for counterexamples). In addition, one often must be able to evaluate the quality of the evidence for the claims, which may require understanding probability, statistics, and the nature of biases. Here is an example of one of the habits of mind we teach that is employed in this form of critical thinking:[4]

Example (H): "Identify and analyze premises and conclusions." Evaluating claims, writing cogently, speaking persuasively, and debating effectively are related: all demand an understanding of how arguments work, along with the ability to dissect and analyze the arguments of others while using valid reasoning in one's own arguments. To analyze arguments, one must identify and analyze the premises and how they are related to the conclusions.

Application example: You are arguing with friends over what to do tonight. They say that they are short on money, so they want to go to a movie instead of a concert. By recognizing their main premise, concerts costs more than movies, you discover a new approach to convincing them. Their conclusion, that they can't go to a concert, is unsound if you can find a free concert.

Analyzing inferences (type of critical thinking)   Inference is the rational creation of new knowledge from old. Even if a claim is correct, the inferences one is invited to make from it may not be. Formal logic provides a method for determining which inferences are valid and which are not.

Example (C): "Describe interactions among events or characteristics at different levels of analysis to interpret phenomena." Depending on the question one is asking, a different level of analysis may be appropriate for the answer. For instance, the insurance adjuster seeking the cause of a house fire will not be interested in principles of combustion but rather may focus on a resident's habit of leaving burning candles unwatched. Any event or system can be understood at multiple levels of analysis, and it is appropriate to focus on different levels for different purposes.

Application example: Your team has been building a robot hand, and you are getting frustrated because it keeps dropping things. At first you think that the shape of the fingers is wrong, so it is not getting a good grip—but then you realize that you might be focusing on the wrong level of analysis. When you consider the nature of the materials you used to make the hand, you discover that they are too slippery—and there isn't enough friction after the hand has closed around an object. There was nothing wrong with the design of the hand, there was just a problem with the materials that you used to produce it.

Weighing decisions (type of critical thinking)   Evaluating claims and analyzing inferences are important in part because they help us decide how to act. But these types of critical thinking are not all that is required to make decisions. To make decisions rationally, one must analyze the various choices and identify their respective trade-offs.

Example (H): "Consider different types of future costs and benefits for all stakeholders." When making decisions, one must always consider trade-offs between future costs and benefits from the different perspectives of all stakeholders.

Application example: You are about to hold an annual meeting and are hosting it at the hotel you've used for the past six years. You have already printed the invitations and coordinated with the guests, speakers, and nearby restaurants. A week before the date, you receive a letter from the hotel manager informing you that he will be charging you three times what he charged the previous year. You consider the costs and benefits for each stakeholder of staying the course and holding the meeting at this hotel. For yourself, the costs are severe: you won't be able to cover your expenses. The benefits are that you are familiar with the venue and would not have to redo all of the invitations and arrangements. For the attendees, the costs are a larger registration fee and the benefits are clarity in the arrangements and meeting in a familiar venue. For the hotel manager, the costs include losing you as a client and the benefits are increased revenue—which would be limited to this one upcoming meeting (you definitely won't meet there again). Presenting all of this to the hotel manager results in a useful negotiation, whereby he increases the amount by only 50 percent (this example is based on a chapter in Carnegie, 1937.)

Analyzing problems (type of critical thinking)   Although actually solving problems requires creative thinking, the analysis that precedes this process is a form of critical thinking. This analysis focuses on understanding and organizing the problem.

Example (H): "Characterize the nature of the problem." The first step to solving a problem is to characterize exactly what the problem is. This may sound obvious, but is often ignored—people jump right into trying to solve a problem before they fully understand what it is. Characterizing the nature of the problem requires specifying the goals, the obstacles that stand between the starting situation and the goals, the constraints on possible solutions (such as limited funds), and the size of the problem. Different types of solutions are appropriate for problems that arise at different scales.

Application example: Your doctor tells you to lose weight. Why? Consider the different ways to characterize the nature of the problem (and the different implications for solutions): For you, it may be personal appearance (which may be solved with liposuction, cosmetic surgery, or a sleeve gastrectomy), but for your doctor it's a need for you to change some aspects of your blood chemistry (which can be done with pills, a change of diet regardless of weight, or perhaps no change at all if you don't mind the risk), or maybe it's about the cost of insurance (which is less expensive for people who are not obese because they have fewer operations and subsidized treatments—which could be solved by increasing your payments or reducing your coverage). By defining the problem differently, you are led to different courses of action.

Competence in creative thinking

Creative thinking leads to the production of something new. Whereas critical thinking focuses on analysis, creative thinking often focuses on synthesis. Creative thinking is at the heart of scientific discovery, the innovative solution of practical problems, and the creation of new products, processes, and services. Like critical thinking, creative thinking is not a single activity. We have organized its different facets into three types of activities, described below.

Facilitating discovery (type of creative thinking)   There are no recipes or rules for how to make new discoveries. However, certain practices and heuristics ("rules of thumb") can set the stage, facilitating discovery. Among such practices are the ability to create well-formed hypotheses, predictions, and interpretations of data. In addition, research methods can be used effectively to increase the likelihood of making a new discovery. Furthermore, one can facilitate discovery by considering systems at multiple levels of analysis.

Example (C): "Evaluate the link between initial data collection and subsequent hypothesis-driven research." Scientific research begins with observations, which then must be organized to suggest underlying patterns of regularity. Such patterns in turn suggest theories and accompanying hypotheses about the nature of the factors that may give rise to these patterns in the data. These hypotheses can then be tested. This cycle of observing, theorizing, formulating hypotheses, collecting data to test hypotheses, revising the theory and then generating and testing new hypotheses characterizes science and is often referred to as the scientific method.

Application example: You are a writer. You start working on an article about street crime in San Francisco. You notice that neighborhoods with low crime rates also have less diverse residents and have volunteer neighborhood watches. You first theorize that people simply get along better in homogeneous neighborhoods, and hence will have lower crime rates. To test this idea, you check other such neighborhoods, but find no connection. You then revise your theory to focus on the presence of a neighborhood watch, and hypothesize that this is why crime rates are low—and now turn to testing this hypothesis.

Solving problems (type of creative thinking)   A "problem" occurs when an obstacle prevents one from immediately reaching a goal. When first encountering a problem (when no known solution is available), one must use creative thinking to solve it. Often such creative thinking relies on using specific heuristics and techniques.

Example (C): "Identify and apply constraint satisfaction as a way to solve problems." Obstacles often cannot be overcome easily, in large part because there are constraints on what sorts of actions are possible or realistic. Constraints are requirements imposed on the solution; they do not determine the solution, but they do place boundaries on what is possible. Thus, part of solving a problem is to identify the constraints on what can be done. If the constraints are well defined, problems often can be solved by devising ways to satisfy all of the constraints at the same time.

Application example: You are moving into a new house and must decide where to put the furniture in your bedroom. You have an old sofa, which is missing a rear leg and sits on a telephone book—and so you don't want to put it in a location where it can be seen from behind (this is a constraint). You also have an old bed, with a headboard that must lean against the wall (another constraint). And you have two end tables, which must be placed to either side of the headboard (another constraint). A large chair and a reading lamp must be placed near each other (yet another constraint). Once you pick a wall for the sofa, in one fell swoop you may have solved the problem of how to arrange furniture in the room. The positions of the other pieces of furniture may be determined: There is only one other place where the wall can accommodate the headboard and have room for the end tables, and once it and the end tables are set up, there is only one other place large enough for the chair and the lamp. The mere act of satisfying all of the constraints simultaneously can dictate the solution to the problem!

Creating products, processes, and services (type of creative thinking)   Various methods and techniques can help one to create new products, processes, and services. Such methods and techniques include iterative design thinking, reverse engineering, and application of the principles of perception and cognition.

Example (C): "Identify gaps (in knowledge, in market offerings, in a range of ideas) that reveal where a creative solution is required." A creative solution is required only when a previous effective solution does not exist. Thus the first step in producing a new product, process, or service is recognizing that one is required. This ability requires recognizing when existing plausible solutions are inadequate.

Application example: You work for a bakery and discover that the amount of flour you order is not being adjusted according to how many bakery goods were sold in the last few days and the upcoming need for seasonal specialties (such as hot cross buns at Easter). You look, and can't find any suitable software to estimate the needed amount and order it automatically. So you hire your neighbor's son to write the code. It works so well that you are now starting a company with him to market the software to other bakeries.

Competence in effective communication

The ability to communicate effectively is crucial for leaders and innovators, who must function as broadly educated members of a community. This ability relies in large part on verbal expression; the message must be both clear and appropriate for a given audience. However, effective communication also relies on conveying appropriate information nonverbally, including through facial expressions and body language.

Using language effectively (type of communicating effectively) Most human communication occurs through language, both spoken and written; thus it is crucial to know how to use language effectively to communicate.

Example (H): "Tailor oral and written work for the context and the audience." Different audiences have different background knowledge, interests, goals, worldviews, and perspectives. To communicate effectively, one must recognize such characteristics of an audience and other factors (such as your goals and the amount of time you have), and tailor one's writing and speaking accordingly. The same message can be delivered in many ways, and these different ways will be more or less effective for different audiences.

Application example: You present a new product to the board of directors of the company. The directors are not interested in the technical details of the product but want a quick summary of its functionality, potential revenue, and how long it will take to become profitable. You present it to the engineers, and they want the technical details of the product and any potential problems that might arise in manufacturing. You present it to the sales staff, and they want to hear about the most novel and noteworthy features of the product. In presenting the product to different audiences you will need to adjust both the content and the way you present, including the length of your presentation, to communicate effectively what each audience wants and needs to know.

Using nonverbal communication effectively (type of communicating effectively) Nonverbal communication is a potent form of expression in its own right and often plays a crucial role in how well a verbal communication is received. These elements of communication color the entire message.

Example (H): "Apply principles of perception and cognition in oral and multimedia presentations and in design." A large body of research has documented many aspects of human perception and cognition, resulting in a set of principles that captures how humans organize and interpret what they see and hear. Illustrations—in published works as well as presentations and video—will communicate effectively only if they respect these principles. Similarly, objects that invite specific uses must be designed to communicate those uses clearly.

Application example: You watch people leave a building. More than half of them try to pull open the doors, but the doors are designed to be pushed outward as you exit. You look carefully at the door handles and see that they are identical to the ones on the outside of the doors—which clearly invite being pulled. You realize that the shape of the handles, with their round contour and open space that a hand could easily slide behind, implies that they should be pulled. This is the wrong message to be conveyed when the door should be pushed open.

Competence in effective interaction

We communicate not only to convey information but also as a key part of our interactions with others. However, personal interactions involve much more than simply communicating. Interactions may be intended to have a specific effect on others (such as when negotiating or trying to persuade); they may also facilitate or impede team functioning.

Negotiating, mediating, and persuading (type of interacting effectively)

Effective interactions with people require anticipating the impact of a particular message, registering the actual responses, and adjusting communications accordingly. Such dynamic interactions lie at the heart of negotiating, mediating, and persuading.

Example (H): "Prepare multidimensional best alternatives to a negotiated agreement (BATNAs)." Negotiating is partly an art, but it is also informed by empirical findings and best practices. One best practice is to have well-defined BATNAs when going into a negotiation. Each BATNA specifies what a person or party will do if negotiations fail. The key is to develop attractive alternatives in advance and to know when they outweigh specific possible outcomes from a negotiation. This practice entails preparing more than one BATNA and ordering them according to different dimensions—which will be more or less relevant, depending on how a situation evolves.

Application example: You have an old car that you've decided to sell. An acquaintance says he wants it—for the right price. You decide in advance what a fair price is. You develop two BATNAs. If the deal doesn't go through because he simply doesn't have the money, you will put an ad in the paper for 10 percent above your walk-away price and see whether you can negotiate with someone else. If the deal doesn't go through because he discovers too many things wrong with the car, you will sell it to a mechanic for parts.

Working effectively with others (type of interacting effectively)   Each of us plays many roles when interacting with others. For example, we sometimes act as a leader and sometimes act as a follower or a team member. Specific behaviors and practices can facilitate such interactions.

Example (H): "Learn to assign team roles appropriately, which requires being sensitive to the nature of the task and to the nature of specific types of roles." Leaders must recognize that each of us has different cognitive, metacognitive, and social strengths and weaknesses. These differences have implications for which sorts of roles on a team a given person can perform effectively. To assign roles, one first must analyze what sorts of skills and characteristics are needed to accomplish the task. Some of these necessary skills and characteristics depend on specific expertise; others concern interpersonal skills and temperament more generally, and are relevant to cooperative or social endeavors. By considering such factors, one is in a position to determine which people have the requisite skills and characteristics to perform specific roles effectively.

Application example: You are the leader of a team charged with developing a new product. The first step is to think about what tasks the team must perform (ranging from identifying a promising niche in the market, to designing the product, to building a prototype, to devising a marketing plan). You know the team members well. You assign them tasks based partly on their background knowledge and partly on their temperaments. For instance, you need to have a quick idea of the niche you want to fill before anything else can happen, so you first need to assign people to the group charged with identifying the niche. You assign colleagues who are especially informed, perceptive and can work quickly—you don't worry so much about whether they can think ahead to designing or marketing the product.

Resolving ethical dilemmas and having social consciousness (type of interacting effectively)   The way one resolves ethical dilemmas has a direct effect on how one interacts with others. One factor that should contribute to such thinking hinges on having social consciousness, which is a concern for others and for the common good.

Example (H): "Evaluate ethical dilemmas, framing the dilemma in a way that will help resolve it." Ethical dilemmas often hinge on discovering what course of action will be the most fair for the most stakeholders (which typically are people, but may also be corporations, animals, plants, and the environment more generally) while at the same time not undermining accepted social rules or mores (including the rule of law). To resolve such dilemmas, it is useful to consider different ways of framing the situation, looking for a way that clearly maximizes the benefits to the most stakeholders while minimizing any harm and not undermining accepted social rules or mores.

Application example: Your organization needs to hire more people, and you aren't getting enough applicants. You decide to give a bonus to all employees who bring in someone for an interview. An employee complains that this is a setup, inducing people to behave unethically: People will be biased to bring in their friends, even if they don't think the job is right for them. You acknowledge that this is an issue, and revise the policy: Employees will get a bonus only if the people they bring in are hired and stay more than three months. You also explain that you trust your employees to uphold their own ethics, as well as the company's.

Applying Practical Knowledge Widely

Minerva has devoted an enormous amount of time and energy to devising ways to teach practical knowledge. We explicitly teach the HCs that underlie each aspect of thinking critically, thinking creatively, communicating effectively, and interacting effectively; we do not simply hope that such key skills and knowledge will be incidentally acquired as students learn other material. Was this really necessary? As far as we have been able to tell, no traditional university systematically teaches practical knowledge. (In some cases, universities offer individual courses in some aspects of this material, but the courses are not part of a systematic program and usually there is no follow-up; for example, some universities offer a single course in critical thinking, but that's it.) However, in most cases, faculty members—if they think about it at all—assume that critical thinking and the other core competencies will automatically emerge as students study English, philosophy, biology, and other subjects. For example, the faculty may assume that students will learn critical thinking through learning techniques of close reading in literature classes, analytical approaches in philosophy classes, and so on. This is unlikely because of fundamental facts about how humans learn:

First, humans often do not automatically abstract general principles from examples (see, e.g., Gick & Holyoak, 1983). Thus we cannot assume that students will identify and formulate the common strategies and methods that underlie reasoning in different fields.

Second, even if people do identify the key principles that underlie a certain kind of reasoning or behavior, they are unlikely to apply those principles outside the domain in which they learned them. This problem lies at the heart of what we know from the science of learning. An anecdote is instructive here. A distinguished physicist was teaching introductory physics for nonmajors at Harvard. He decided that the students would learn better if he used everyday examples, ones they might care about. He decided to use examples from baseball (baseball involves a lot of physics). However, as it turned out, he used every baseball example he could think of in the lectures. When it came time to write the final exam, he couldn't think of any more baseball examples, so he used football examples instead. How do you think the students reacted? They accused the professor of tricking them on the final exam—they said that the whole course had been about baseball, so how could he suddenly switch and ask them about football? It wasn't fair![5]

The students were exhibiting what is called a "failure of transfer." When we humans learn skills or knowledge in one context, we often have difficulty applying them, or "transferring" them, to another context. When the contexts are similar, as occurred here, such transfer is called "near transfer." Near transfer is difficult, but nowhere near as difficult as when the contexts appear very different on the surface and may occur at very different points in time; in this case, applying the skills and knowledge appropriately is called "far transfer" (Barnett & Ceci, 2002).

To help students transfer what they learn in one context to other contexts, we at Minerva strive to ensure that students understand the underlying principles *and* that they have practice applying them in numerous different situations, with different sorts of examples. The students in the physics class would have been much better off with examples not just from sports but also from driving cars, watching apples fall from trees, and considering why water runs downhill.

To encourage both near and far transfer, we grade students on how effectively they use HCs in new contexts, well after the HCs are introduced. In fact, students are graded on how well they use and transfer HCs in every course they take during their last three years in the program.

Conclusion

We have shown that not only is it possible to characterize practical knowledge in detail, which we do with the HCs, it is also possible to teach practical knowledge systematically. We considered four uncontroversial goals for our college graduates, namely, understanding leadership and working with others, learning how to innovate, being a broadly adaptive thinker, and having a global perspective. We then considered the characteristic qualities, practices, and approaches of people who have achieved the first three goals; we organized these characteristics into four core competencies: thinking critically, thinking creatively, communicating effectively, and interacting effectively. We analyzed each of these competences into specific aspects, which positioned us for the final step: For each aspect of each of the four core competencies we defined two sets of learning goals, habits of mind and foundational concepts. This analysis in turn led us to focus on specific facets of practical knowledge when we teach. By considering in detail the nature of practical knowledge and key facts from the science of learning, we were able to shape a pedagogy that helps students learn practical knowledge—with the aim of helping them to succeed after graduation.

I have noted only a small sampling of the HCs that currently constitute the core of the Minerva curriculum (for a list of the full set, see appendix A). Undoubtedly, objections could be raised about why we've included or neglected certain HCs; in particular, one may strongly believe that we've overlooked a critical habit of mind or foundational concept—even respecting the inclusion criteria we used. In some cases, such objections may be justified, and we should modify our list accordingly. We in fact regularly update the list, adding, consolidating and sometimes deleting HCs on the basis of feedback from students, faculty, employers, internship supervisors and others. Thus, the list in appendix A must be treated as a "living document," which will evolve over time. Moreover, this process will never end: because the world is constantly changing, the practical knowledge we teach should change along with it. However, our goal will never change: we want to equip our students with the intellectual tools to adapt to a changing world, which should help them succeed after they graduate—and we will continually refine what we do in the service of this goal.

Acknowledgments

Many people helped to conceive and author the HCs. In particular, I owe a lot to conversations with Minerva deans and associate deans, present and past: Eric Bonabeau, Judith Brown, Vicki Chandler, Josh Fost, Kara Gardner, James Genone, Diane Halpern, Rich Holman, Daniel Levitin, and Brian Ross. Rena Levitt also helped me clarify the key concepts summarized here. In addition, many people contributed to the examples cited in this chapter, in particular Josh Fost, James Genone, Vicki Chandler, Megan Gahl,

Daniel Levitin, Rena Levitt, John Levitt, Kara Gardner, Judith Brown, Beth Callaghan, and Rich Holman. Minerva students Royi Noiman, and Ian van Buskirk drafted some of the application examples. I also thank Guy Davidson for comments on an earlier draft of this chapter.

Notes

1. Although similar findings are often found in this literature, results from such studies vary; the precise amount recalled depends on a host of factors, from the type of material to the recall interval. For example, at least some of the material taught in courses that are part of a cumulative sequence, particularly in STEM fields (science, technology, engineering, and math), is much more likely to be retained (e.g., see Group 3 of Pawl, Barrantes, & Pritchard, 2012).

2. Initially we had only the first three core competencies. But during a visit to Minerva, Professor Eric Mazur commented that we had missed a category, which he felt should deal with "professional behavior" (e.g., being a good team member, showing up on time, following through on commitments). We realized that he was right, and that we had conflated "interacting effectively" and "communicating effectively." Yes, communication is one key to how we interact with others, but it is not the only one. Moreover, interactions involve more than interacting with other individuals; they also involve interacting with systems and institutions. Thus it made sense to break our original third category into the third and fourth categories listed here.

3. To be more precise, with practice, information and abilities are shifted from what Kahneman (2011) calls "System 2"—the slow, serial, conscious system—to "System 1"—the fast, parallel, unconscious system.

4. This and the following examples of HCs and applications are quoted (with minor edits in some cases) from the Minerva HC Master List. As noted in the acknowledgments to this chapter, many people contributed to this material.

5. This anecdote was recounted by Eric Mazur.

References

Arum, R., & Roksa, J. (2011). *Academically adrift: Limited learning on college campuses.* Chicago, IL: University of Chicago Press.

Barnett, S. M., & Ceci, S. J. (2002). When and where do we apply what we learn? A taxonomy for far transfer. *Psychological Bulletin, 128*(4), 612–637.

Bligh, D. (2000). *What's the use of lectures?* New York, NY: Jossey-Bass.

Bok, D. (2013). *Higher education in America.* Princeton, NJ: Princeton University Press.

Carnegie, D. (1937). *How to win friends & influence people*. New York, NY: Pocket Books.

Conway, M. A., Cohen, G., & Stanhope, N. (1991). On the very long-term retention of knowledge acquired through formal education: Twelve years of cognitive psychology. *Journal of Experimental Psychology: General, 120*(4), 395–409.

Csikszentmihalyi, M. (1996). *Creativity: The work and lives of 91 eminent people*. New York, NY: HarperCollins.

Dale, E. (1969). *Audiovisual methods in teaching*. New York, NY: Dryden Press.

Derue, D. S., Nahrgang, J. D., Wellman, N., & Humphrey, S. E. (2011). Trait and behavioral theories of leadership: An integration and meta-analytic test of their relative validity. *Personnel Psychology, 4*(1), 7–52.

Feist, G. J. (1998). A meta-analysis of personality in scientific and artistic creativity. *Personality and Social Psychology Review, 2*(4), 290–309.

Feist, G. J., & Barron, F. X. (2003). Predicting creativity from early to late adulthood: Intellect, potential, and personality. *Journal of Research in Personality, 37*, 62–88.

Finke, R. A., Ward, T. B., & Smith, S. M. (1996). *Creative cognition: Theory, research, and applications*. Cambridge, MA: MIT Press.

Gick, M. L., & Holyoak, K. J. (1983). Schema induction and analogical transfer. *Cognitive Psychology, 15*(1), 1–38.

Grosul, M., & Feist, G. J. (2014). The creative person in science. *Psychology of Aesthetics, Creativity, and the Arts, 8*(1), 30–43.

Hart Research Associates. (2013, April 10). *It takes more than a major: Employer priorities for college learning and student success*. Washington, DC: Hart Research Associates for the Association of American Colleges and Universities. https://www.aacu.org/sites/default/files/files/LEAP/2013_EmployerSurvey.pdf

House, R. J., & Aditya, R. N. (1997). The social scientific study of leadership: Quo vadis? *Journal of Management, 23*(3), 409–473.

Judge, T. A., Colbert, A. E., & Ilies, R. (2004). Intelligence and leadership: A quantitative review and test of theoretical propositions. *Journal of Applied Psychology, 89*(3), 542–552.

Kahneman, D. (2011). *Thinking fast and slow*. New York, NY: Farrar, Straus and Giroux.

Lewin, K. (1945). Reserve program of group dynamics: The Research Center for Group Dynamics at MIT. *Sociometry, 8*(2), 126–136.

Lord, R. G., De Vader, C. L., & Alliger, G. M. (1986). A meta-analysis of the relation between personality traits and leadership perceptions: An application of validity generalization procedures. *Journal of Applied Psychology, 71*(3), 402–410.

McGuire, W. J. (1997). Creative hypothesis generating in psychology: Some useful heuristics. *Annual Review of Psychology, 48*, 1–30.

National Association of Colleges and Employers. (2016): Job outlook 2016: Attributes employers want to see on new college graduates' resumes. http://www .naceweb.org/s11182015/employers-look-for-in-new-hires.aspx

Newell, A., & Simon, H. A. (1972). *Human problem solving.* New York, NY: Prentice Hall.

Pawl, A., Barrantes, A., & Pritchard, D. E. (2012, December 10). What do seniors remember from freshman physics? *Physical Review Special Topics—Physics Education Research, 8*(2), 1–12.

Rosovsky, H. (1991). *The university: An owner's manual.* New York, NY: W. W. Norton.

Semb, G. B., Ellis, J. A., & Araujo, J. (1992, August). *Long term memory for different types of classroom knowledge.* Report NPRDC-TR-92-18. San Diego, CA: Navy Personnel Research and Development Center. http://www.dtic.mil/dtic/tr/fulltext/u2/ a255235.pdf

Simonton, D. K. (2000). Creativity: Cognitive, developmental, personal, and social aspects. *American Psychologist, 55*(1), 151–158.

Simonton, D. K. (2008). Scientific talent, training, and performance: Intellect, personality, and genetic endowment. *Review of General Psychology, 12*(1), 28–46.

Tetlock, E., & Gardner, D. (2015). *Superforecasting: The art and science of prediction.* New York, NY: Crown.

U.S. Census Bureau. (2016). Educational attainment: Five key data releases from the U.S. Census Bureau. https://www.census.gov/newsroom/cspan/educ/educ_attain_ slides.pdf

Zaccaro, S. J. (2001). *The nature of executive leadership: A conceptual and empirical analysis of success.* Washington, DC: American Psychological Association.

Zaccaro, S. J. (2007). Trait-based perspectives on leadership. *American Psychologist, 62*(1), 6–16.

3   Foundations of the Curriculum

Ben Nelson and Stephen M. Kosslyn

Minerva was conceived more than twenty years ago as a curricular reform plan for the University of Pennsylvania, with the goal of bringing Benjamin Franklin's ideals to the twenty-first century. True to its roots, Minerva is a systematic rethinking of every aspect of the liberal arts curriculum. A healthy debate exists over what a liberal arts curriculum really is (e.g., Nelson, 2011). One view holds that education at its core should be vocational, focusing on educating for a particular career. This leads to very narrow and specialized curricula, and different students may have very different educations. Another view is that the essence of a liberal arts curriculum is the pursuit of knowledge for its own sake—which proponents take to imply that one should not consider the potential utility of knowledge. This in turn often leads to a completely unstructured curriculum in which nothing builds on anything else. We subscribe to a third path, championed by Benjamin Franklin and Thomas Jefferson more than two centuries ago. At the time, many of the interpreters of Franklin and Jefferson's vision adopted a great books model focused on the writings of dead white men on which Western civilization was arguably built. But this leads to a curriculum that focuses on great works, which inevitably are embedded in another time and place, and is not fully aligned with Franklin and Jefferson's ultimate goals. We have taken the founders' core insights in a different direction.

The founders of the United States formed a system of government based on the concept of a representative republic—an idealized version of the governmental structure of ancient Rome. In this republic, any citizen might be called on to govern as a representative of his (and at that time, it was "his"—not "his or her") fellow citizens. Therefore, all citizens needed training in the liberal arts, those fields of knowledge that the leaders of society must draw on to make decisions. Franklin and Jefferson advocated the teaching of practical, or "useful," knowledge as the basis of an American higher education. We have adopted this perspective.

However, committing to the first principles that animated American higher education does not imply that American universities should return to the curricula of old. Educational researchers have learned an enormous amount not just about educational systems but also about how learning works, how individuals come to structure generalizable knowledge, how to provide training that allows individuals to interrogate subject matter in different ways, and so on. We believe that the basic task of a liberal arts education is to provide citizens with a set of intellectual tools that is applicable across a wide range of situations—and that therefore serves as practical knowledge. Practical knowledge, as we use the term, is knowledge that one can use to adapt to a changing world, helping one to achieve one's goals (see chapter 2). Following ideas of Jefferson and Franklin, practical knowledge is at the core of a liberal arts education, as opposed to knowledge for the sake of knowledge or vocational training.

How should we devise a curriculum to transmit practical knowledge effectively today, given all that we know? A set of design principles can lead universities to structure their curricula in ways that will help students learn both what to do and what not to do. We consider these principles in the next section.

Foundational Principles

We formulated four principles that we used to structure our curriculum. These principles can be used generally to structure curricula to promote a leading-edge liberal arts education.

Principle 1: Content should not be the focus

The first principle is that content should not be the core focus of higher education. Today we are bathed in a sea of content and can tap into vast amounts of it effortlessly with a few clicks on a keyboard. Although content is important, universities should not focus on making students memorize it. Rather, universities should assume that students (with appropriate support) can acquire most content on their own, typically before class (using the "flipped classroom" model; see chapter 12). The question is not whether to memorize content, especially in light of today's information explosion, but how to know where to find it, how to evaluate it, and what to do with it. The central task is to help students learn how to find, evaluate, analyze, and synthesize information in the service of achieving their goals.

Furthermore, the amount of content available free or nearly free online raises the question of the ethics of institutions that charge their students fees to certify that they have been able to memorize enough of that content to pass a test. To put this in perspective, the average private nonprofit four-year institution of higher education in the United States charges $33,480 for tuition and fees per year (this figure does not include room and board; College Board, 2016). If we assume that students take eight courses per year, a student will pay $4,185 to certify that he or she has been able to pass an introduction to microeconomics course or a basic calculus class. With the overwhelming majority of credits issued by universities being for work in large lecture-based classes, this translates to about $100,000 spent by each student on what is otherwise a free, publicly available service.

Moreover, universities do not even transmit information effectively—they rely heavily on lectures, which have been shown repeatedly not to be an effective way for students to learn (see chapter 12). Conscious of this fact, many universities publish statistics that make it appear as if the bulk of their education is delivered in smaller format, non-lecture-based classes—statistics that upon further examination often prove to be misleading. Columbia University serves as an example. According to *U.S. News & World Report* (2017), Columbia has the highest proportion of classes with fewer than twenty students among any of America's top one hundred ranked universities. *U.S. News & World Report* reports that Columbia has fewer than twenty students in 82.7 percent of its classes, between twenty and forty-nine students in 8.9 percent of its classes, and fifty or more students in 8.2 percent of its classes. To be kind in our analysis, let's assume that on average these three categories have twelve, thirty, and one hundred students, respectively. This means that only 47 percent of credits issued by Columbia are for classes of twenty or fewer students (although we are sure that many of those classes are lectures as well). If we assume that classes are smaller overall, say ten, twenty-five, and seventy-five students on average, the result is practically the same. If we assume that they are larger, say fifteen, thirty-five, and one hundred twenty students, again the distribution shows that a majority of credits are issued for larger classes—which are certain to be lectures.

What is worse is that Columbia's tuition and fees in 2017 are not the national average but cost $55,056 (again, excluding room and board)—which is paid by the more than half of Columbia students who are not eligible for financial aid. That means that a Columbia University student who pays the full amount, a student at an elite university with the best ratio of small to large classes, will also be paying well over $100,000 to sit in lectures and not learn effectively. Clearly, something is amiss, and surely higher education in America can do better.

Principle 2: The curriculum must be structured

The second principle follows from our belief that in order to develop the mind, universities must have a structured approach. One could think of education as a form of brain surgery: education effectively changes the structure and function of the brain. And, as with other forms of surgery, there must be a clear plan of action before the education operation actually begins. It is not acceptable to start an operation and only then start thinking about what the next step should be. When universities perform this "brain surgery" and try to grow the capability and capacity of the mind, they should not do so in a haphazard way. They should have a plan of action. And therefore the structure of the educational path, commonly known as the curriculum, is important.

The idea that the curriculum is important should not be controversial. Most institutions of higher education, however, have not carefully crafted their curricula with specific goals in mind. At first glance, a traditional American university seems to have a coherent curriculum; that is, most courses of study specify a core sequence that students must take. However, this structure pertains almost exclusively to course requirements for a major, not to general education or electives—which may consume the bulk of student time at American universities. Students often can choose from scores (or more) of different classes, and therefore can forge a large number of paths through the course offerings. But there is little rhyme or reason for the sequence they follow; the student skips around, as opposed to progressing toward a goal. Insofar as there is structure, it is imposed primarily by prerequisites: some courses require that students already have taken specific other courses. But such prerequisite course sequences are often isolated instances, not part of a larger overall structure.

In short, at most traditional institutions the structure of the curriculum is superficial, serving to organize tightly only a sequence of foundational courses within a major. For everything outside the major, a coherent structure is close to impossible or is made completely impossible by the fact that each of the classes is treated as entirely independent. There is no coordination, no overall cohesion, and no overall quality control.

Principle 3: Courses should be seminal

The first two principles imply that universities should not offer courses to disseminate information that can easily be acquired elsewhere (or at the very least should not be charging for the privilege); instead, they should provide well-structured sequences of courses that convey underlying skills and knowledge that allow students to function effectively in appropriate real-world contexts.

These requirements imply that course offerings should be judiciously selected and tightly organized. But, more than that, they imply a third principle: courses should be *seminal*, in the sense of specifying key material from which much else can grow. Seminal courses convey crucial skills and fundamental knowledge: they are generative, prompting and promoting intellectual growth. If a course is offered, students should have to take it in order to achieve a level of mastery in the relevant track of study. If a course plays such a role, then students who do not take it should not be able to call themselves proficient in that particular area of education or that particular field.

The implications of the idea that course offerings should be seminal in this sense are substantial, particularly when this principle is joined to the first two principles. This requirement implies that the course catalog will dramatically shrink: if a university offers a course that fits into a particular course of study, it should be seminal and it must fit into a tightly structured sequence. Students need not be required to take the entire sequence, but if they do choose to focus on the particular area, they will need to take a set of courses—and these courses will need to be explicitly designed to convey seminal skills and knowledge. Universities should think very carefully and thoroughly about what it is that students should be learning.

Principle 4: Students need informed choice

The fourth principle focuses on the need to help students navigate the curriculum through informed choice. When they first enter college, most students have at best only a vague idea of what they want to do after they graduate, and they need easy access to information so that they can make informed choices. In fact, most college students change their major at least once (Chen & Soldner, 2013), and perhaps 80 percent of students may do so (Garton, 2015). Systematic and informed advising is part of the solution, but so is simply providing more information about the consequences of choosing certain paths. Even more important, the curriculum must be structured to offer real choice as opposed to the illusion of choice. For example, although the course catalog may suggest otherwise, few students at traditional universities can decide as sophomores to major in biology, given that they must have already taken certain courses in their first year for that major. At Minerva, the freshman courses provide the foundations for all majors and concentrations, and the sophomore courses lead students to explore a variety of relevant subject matter before they are set on a specific path; students choose majors in the middle of the sophomore year and concentrations in the junior year, and do so knowing a lot about the choices they are making.

Broad Context and Far Transfer

The Minerva curriculum grows out of the four principles just reviewed, but more than that, it grows out of an analysis of how specifically the curriculum should prepare students for life after college. In chapter 2 we reviewed the goals of our curriculum: To help students understand leadership and know how to work with others, to know how and when to innovate, to become broad adaptive thinkers, and to attain a global perspective. These goals emerged from our reviewing relevant literatures, from interviews with employers, and from careful analyses of surveys that specifically asked employers what characteristics they sought in applicants. In addition, the Minerva curriculum is structured as it is in response to two large problems with traditional higher education curricula. In this section we consider those problems and our responses to them.

The importance of broad context

In universities abroad, almost all systems of higher education have extremely narrow curricula. They often offer any given student only what U.S. universities offer in one major. They might go into a bit more depth, but they do so in three years—and there is no broader exploration outside the chosen major. In our view such a broader exploration must be at the heart of the kind of education that citizens everywhere in the world need.

Why do we argue that students should learn information that is situated in a broad context? Let's consider what we expect of people who are in positions of great importance in the world—CEOs of large corporations, senators and members of parliament, presidents and prime ministers, the journalists and reporters who influence the influencers. One could argue that we want a CEO to understand the mechanics of business, we want senators and other elected representatives to understand the law, and we want journalists to have excellent writing skills. That is correct as far as it goes, but it doesn't go far enough. The key figures in history did not distinguish themselves solely through their expertise in a particular subject matter in a narrow field—quite the opposite: The key figures in history understood what broader frameworks they could bring to their field. If you are the CEO of a company, you need to understand how to act in a competitive environment; how to make decisions that affect people's lives; the psychology of your competitors, your customers, and your suppliers. A person in charge of government (national, state, or city) or responsible for any kind of collaboration among individuals should of course understand the law, but to have a truly large and lasting impact, that person also needs to understand the principles of economics and how to make good, well-reasoned decisions.

In short, to have a substantial and lasting impact in the real world, one needs more than expertise in a specific subject; one needs to contextualize such expertise, to understand it as part of broader systems. Helping students learn to think through broader issues is a far more important part of a university's mission than the dissemination of information within a specific field. Not many people look at their prime minister or president (or any other individual who aspires to those positions) and are upset by the fact that he or she hasn't mastered all of legal history. These are not the issues that matter to people. What matters is whether the leader or leader candidate has thought through the consequences of his or her actions and how they will affect all stakeholders.

At the same time, these individuals are surrounded by people who need to be able to work with them. The skills we want our leaders to have often are even more important for those who surround and influence them.

The importance of far transfer

Intuitively and practically, we understand the idea of a liberal arts education, but universities rarely, if ever, structure their curricula to help students learn to make wise and well-reasoned decisions. Virtually all universities profess to want to help students learn how to think critically and creatively. But how do they actually do that? Typically, they let students look through a mass of courses in different departments and pick two or three (usually based on the student's superficial impression of what will be offered in the courses, with minimal guidance at best). Worst yet, the goal of those courses is not to teach critical or creative thinking. Rather, the faculty teach particular subject matter and hope that students will pick up broader thinking skills as a side result of that process. This simply does not work. Students do not automatically distill the common threads across different kinds of thinking, and they do not automatically apply what they learn to new contexts (see chapter 2).

As reviewed in the previous chapter, the relevant underlying principle is known as *far transfer* (e.g., Barnett & Ceci, 2002). Far transfer occurs when students apply what they have learned in one context to a situation in a different time and place, one that, on the surface, does not resemble the original context. Far transfer is at the epicenter of what makes education effective. Far transfer will not be achieved if students are left on their own to identify underlying principles and then to apply them widely. Far transfer requires not only explicitly teaching relevant underlying principles but also helping students see how they apply in a wide range of different circumstances. It can be achieved only if we do not treat the educational outcome as a by-product but rather as the goal of education, and structure a university's curriculum around it.

Let's consider as an example the concept of *sunk cost*. Understanding sunk cost is critical when one wants to determine whether or not a further investment in a project makes sense. For instance, say that you have already spent $1 million building a hotel, and you know it will take an additional $1 million to complete. You then receive a new assessment that says that once constructed, the hotel will have a total value of $0.5 million. Given this assessment, you should not spend another $1 million. The fact that you have already spent $1 million on the project does not matter; this is referred to as the sunk cost. It is already spent; you cannot recover it, and therefore you should only consider your future investment versus your future return.

The concept of sunk cost is taught to everyone who studies business or economics. But the concept of sunk cost is usually taught solely in the sort of narrow context just described. However, this concept is broadly applicable. For example, say that that a friend has spent five years trying to learn to play the violin, but still sounds awful. It's time for him to renew the contract for his lessons; should he sign up for another year's worth of lessons? He might think, "I've gone this far and put so much into it, I shouldn't abandon the effort now!" But in fact perhaps he should reflect on the limits of his talent and ability, and decide whether another year of arduous practice would make any real difference. People who have studied sunk cost solely in the context of economics may not realize that the concept is applicable in this situation. Why? Because we humans have difficulty with far transfer.

Teaching with an eye toward far transfer is nearly impossible without a structured curriculum. If a professor would like to apply a concept in one class, how does she know whether or not the concept has already been introduced in another class that all of her students have taken, or whether or not it will be introduced to them in a different context in another course? A structured curriculum in and of itself, however, is not sufficient. This curriculum must be accompanied by an assessment system that allows faculty members to follow each individual student's progress in applying these concepts in different contexts. Feedback based on objective assessment is critical if students are to learn how to apply skills and knowledge in a wide range of disparate situations.

Scaffolding and Systematicity: The Minerva Approach

Perhaps Minerva's most important innovation in curricular design is the melding of choice and structure. Battles that raged before core curricula were abandoned were fought between two camps: one camp championed a rigidly planned curriculum that could ensure structured intellectual development whereas the other camp claimed that universities cannot possibly pick a set of required readings in a world with vast amounts of extraordinary intellectual achievements. Many felt that it was worth sacrificing structure in order to allow freedom of intellectual pursuits. Minerva has devised the first educational system that does not require making that trade-off—ensuring both tremendous flexibility of choice in intellectual exploration while maintaining a structure throughout our four year course of study.

We earlier noted the illusion of choice that is present in most university course catalogs, where many apparent choices are not actually available. The situation is exacerbated because the remaining choices are not what they should be. Yes, the university may have a grand course catalog, but the bulk of it consists of electives—and these electives are not selected based on any principles other than that they should be in the relevant field. This approach is problematic for three reasons:

First, it is difficult to defend why a university offers one subject versus another. For the most part, electives are offered simply because a professor has a background in the chosen field. This is the case even if the particular field is not nearly as important as one that students would be more interested in studying.

Second, because faculty members offer electives based largely on their own areas of expertise, the core goal of those courses will be imparting information in that area of expertise as opposed to exploring analytical frameworks applicable to the field. This is a subtle difference but a substantial one. The origin of the course comes from the faculty's perspective rather than from a curricular perspective.

And third, some prerequisites are difficult to require of students because the professor cannot ensure that the relevant courses will be offered. For instance, for a course on Wittgenstein, potential prerequisites might include not just a broad introductory course in philosophy and courses on logic and language but also courses on the historical context of his work. But if these courses really are prerequisites, a university must actually offer them. This is not within the control of any individual professor. Hence the likelihood that the courses are offered can be very low.

Minerva's response to these problems relies on systematizing the curriculum. We began by scaffolding the curriculum, which not only ensures that prerequisite material must be taught but also that they are continuously reinforced and built upon in future courses. This approach led us to consider carefully how to sequence the courses. Clearly, the key foundational material—our version of a general education program—had to come first (see chapters 4 through 9). As noted in chapter 1, in their first year all students take the same four yearlong courses, which introduce the core competencies of thinking critically, thinking creatively, communicating effectively, and interacting effectively.

The second year consists of a set of courses that build on these competencies, but now apply them to specific majors (see chapter 9). Even though the broad fields that constitute our majors (such as arts and humanities and social sciences) appear to be very traditional, we continue to focus on practical knowledge. Each of these courses provides the entry point to a specific aspect of a major (e.g., in social sciences, one course provides an overview of economics as applied to booms, busts, and bubbles, and another provides an overview of the cognitive sciences). These courses cover the seminal ideas that are found in most subfields of these broad areas. For us, connections among the narrow fields within a broad area are extremely important.

The third year provides specific courses that build on the second-year courses. These courses consist of a "concentration" within the major (e.g., in social sciences, the concentrations are cognition, brain, and behavior; economics and society; and politics, government, and society). Because we continue to focus on practical knowledge, our concentrations typically are interdisciplinary, even as they address traditional topics (see chapter 9). Moreover, our concentrations situate the material in a broad context. For example, if a student wants to learn the foundations necessary to grow into a position of authority after graduation, he or she might major in social sciences and select the politics, government and society concentration. Unlike at any other institution, this major and the concentration within it will require the student to acquire a background in such fields as human psychology, economics, and politics—and the student must also think through what would be required to form a better society.

At the same time, in their third year, students choose the topics for their capstone project. This two-year project requires them to contribute something new to their chosen field. The project requires them to synthesize what they have learned in the first two years and to integrate what they continue to learn into that material. The project provides a point of focus, allowing students to understand fully how the skills and knowledge they have learned can be wielded to address real-world issues.

Finally, in the fourth year students will take courses as electives, design their own seminars with faculty guidance, and finish their capstone project. For the seminars, students will first list four topics of interest, and we will assign three students who have closely overlapping interests to an appropriate professor (i.e., who has expertise relevant to those interests). The four will then devise a syllabus, and the students then will work through that syllabus, with the professor providing guidance and resources. Implementing such seminars allows us to solve the problem that electives are driven by professor versus student interest. If a course is not required to complete an educational sequence, then the subject matter is best left to students to choose.

The curriculum therefore progresses from being completely structured in the first year to being almost completely driven by the students themselves in the fourth year. The curriculum expands in a measured way when the student is prepared by the institution to assume greater and greater responsibility for the direction of his or her personal intellectual development. Throughout, each course reinforces the habits of mind, foundational concepts, and other learning objectives of those courses on which it is built. Although the entire course catalog at Minerva has seventy-one undergraduate courses, students can choose from an almost infinite number of courses because they will design their own during their final year. The foundations are sufficiently systematic and scaffolded that students are in a position to do this by their fourth year. Finally, during this year they will finish their capstone project; this project offers a way for all that comes before it to be drawn on and synthesized.

Crucially, during the second, third, and fourth years, students also take electives that are outside their majors. They acquire broader contexts not just in the courses within their major but also in at least five courses outside their major. Students choose their electives from among the same courses that other students take for their majors and concentrations during their second and third years. At Minerva we have no courses that serve solely as electives; what serves as a requirement for one student serves as an elective for another.

This design guarantees not only that the electives will be taught but also that the relevant prerequisites will be available. Moreover, because the courses are scaffolded, students learn to think deeply about the material. They learn to make decisions of consequence by interrogating the material to an unusual depth, even in fields outside their major.

Conclusion

Perhaps most important, the structure of the Minerva curriculum allows students to progress in their academic exploration and personal development when they become ready. The first-year curriculum not only introduces the foundational elements of the four core competencies, it also provides samples of content from the courses of study available at Minerva. The second year allows students to sample major requirements for up to four of the five majors offered at Minerva in the first semester and to complete the requirements for up to two majors or switch to the fifth major in the second semester. In the third year, every course offered can be used for two of the six concentrations within a major, and students can once again make informed choices about their area of focus.

It is only after three years of intensive preparation that we effectively provide our students with primary agency in the fourth year, allowing them to chart their own course of study with direct consultation and mentorship of the faculty. This serves as a transition to the real world, where choice is indeed nearly infinite for those equipped to make the most of it. At Minerva, students participate in a curriculum that is systematically and holistically designed with a single overarching purpose: to help the students succeed in their chosen career after they graduate. This goal is at the heart of Minerva's mission, which is to nurture critical wisdom for the sake of the world.

References

Barnett, S. M., & Ceci, S. J. (2002). When and where do we apply what we learn? A taxonomy for far transfer. *Psychological Bulletin, 128*(4), 612–637.

Chen, X., & Soldner, M. (2013). *STEM attrition: College students' paths into and out of STEM fields.* Washington, DC: National Center for Education Statistics.

College Board. (2016). *Trends in higher education.* https://trends.collegeboard.org/home

Garton, C. (2015, January 7). Avoid these 3 pitfalls when considering switching majors. *USA Today College.* http://college.usatoday.com/2015/01/07/avoid-these-3-pitfalls-when-considering-switching-majors

Nelson, C. B. (2011). Learning for learning's sake: The foundation for a liberal education. Washington, DC: American Council on Education. http://www.acenet.edu/the-presidency/columns-and-features/Pages/Learning-for-Learning%E2%80%99s-Sake-The-Foundation-for-a-Liberal-Education.aspx

U.S. News & World Report (2017). Columbia University. http://colleges.usnews.rankingsandreviews.com/best-colleges/columbia-university-2707

4 A New Look at General Education

Joshua Fost

The organization of this book reflects our conception of curriculum and pedagogy as existing in a two-dimensional space: *what* to teach and *how* to teach. As described in chapter 2, what we teach in our general education program is a set of habits of mind and foundational concepts—the HCs—that span four core competencies: thinking critically, thinking creatively, communicating effectively, and interacting effectively. This material is structured in a particular way, which constitutes our general education program. In this chapter I summarize this program and then contrast it with other approaches.

The Minerva Model

We think of the HCs as constituting not so much a set of things that everyone ought to know but rather a set of tools that everyone ought to use—something akin to a basic cognitive operating system. Our aim is to anchor these tools so robustly in the minds of our students that they reach for them and apply them in all relevant contexts, quickly and naturally. As with the acquisition of any kind of expertise, this requires a process that begins with conscious deliberation and continues with spaced practice in a variety of contexts, so that is how we teach: we introduce the HCs explicitly (each habit or concept has a hashtag name, e.g., #rightproblem, and accompanying explanatory text; see appendix A); we assign relevant readings and other materials accompanied by study guides; we meet in small, live seminars to practice applying the habit or concept in real-world contexts, to explore its subtleties and address confusions; and we ask students to exercise their nascent skills in independent or team-based assignments. The principles from the science of learning (see chapter 11) clearly point away from lecture and toward practice using the material, so that is how we organize our sessions; moreover, we ensure that all students are engaged at

Table 4.1

Key Features of Our General Education Program

Key features
• All first-year students take the same four courses, called the "cornerstones" (these are described in detail in chapters 5–8). Each course lasts the whole freshman year.   • Across the cornerstones, there are approximately 115 learning objectives (HCs) spanning the four core competencies (see appendix A).   • Each HC has its own 5-point mastery rubric. Rubric scores are the primary determinants of overall course grade.   • The HCs are illustrated with content from multiple domains, driven by Big Questions (see below).   • HC assessment continues in every course throughout the college career; freshman grades are continuously updated on this basis.

least 75 percent of the time—and that is what we mean by *fully active learning* (see chapter 12). Minerva seminars always center on thinking things through, making connections, and practicing skills. Only rarely—probably less than 5 percent of the total time spent in class—do they include explicit instructions for information transfer.

Learning objectives and assessment

The core implementation details for this overarching plan are summarized in table 4.1. In their first year, all students take the same four "cornerstone" courses, each one introducing approximately thirty HCs. The academic calendar is such that this means that a new habit of mind or foundational concept is introduced in approximately half the class sessions. The remainder of the sessions are either *continuation* days—needed for particularly rich HCs—or *synthesis* days, on which bundles of HCs are applied in combination. It is rare for more than one habit or concept to be introduced on a single day, but this does occur occasionally, especially when two HCs are in some sense different sides of the same coin.

We focus on formative rather than summative assessment (i.e., we prioritize low-stakes feedback provided in the early and middle stages of learning over high-stakes exam scores arriving at the end) and are intensely concerned with transparency and reliability in this process. For this reason, every one of the HCs has its own five-point mastery rubric, each derived from a common template (see table 4.2). Students receive HC rubric scores on in-class contributions and formal assignments, the latter of which are assigned weights according to their difficulty or importance.

Table 4.2

Master Rubric Template*

Rubric score	Description
1	Does not recall or use the skill or concept when prompted or does so mostly or entirely inaccurately.
2	Recalls or uses the skill or concept only somewhat accurately, by partially quoting, paraphrasing, summarizing, outlining, or applying it, or recalls or uses the skill or concept in ways that fail to address the relevant problems or goals.
3	Accurately recalls, uses, paraphrases, summarizes, outlines, or reproduces standard or straightforward examples of the skill or concept and does so in a way that addresses the relevant problems or goals.
4	Demonstrates a deeper grasp of the skill or concept by explaining it, using it to produce a sophisticated, nonstandard example, differentiating component parts, or applying critical distinctions, or analyzing relationships between component parts.
5	Uses the skill or concept in a creative and effective way, relying on a novel perspective (i.e., not one that was in course materials or is easily located in the relevant literature) to: improve an existing problem-solving technique or create a more effective one; devise a more elegant or beautiful solution than the standard; or produce an unusually clever and effective application.

Note: *All HC rubrics are customized from this template.

To ensure that students' commitment to general education goals remains firm throughout their time at Minerva, we have implemented what might be most naturally thought of as "time-traveling" grades. In sophomore and later years, students receive grades for the learning outcomes related to course content *and* grades related to their use of relevant HCs. HC grades from later years are more heavily weighted than those from the first year, so students are incentivized to demonstrate and improve their mastery continually. At graduation, the letter grade for each cornerstone course—a function of the accumulated grades for all the HCs it introduced—is finally locked in, representing each student's ability in each of the four core competencies as evinced over his or her entire college career.

Throughout this process, students are frequently reminded of their mastery of the general education goals. The Active Learning Forum's dashboard (see chapters 15 and 16) displays each student's changing scores across the entire set of HCs. These can easily be sorted according to either course of introduction or core competence. A summary report at the core-competence level also appears on term reports, and we have plans to include it as an option on per-student customizable employer-facing CVs.

Using Big Questions to organize content

We realized early that even if one wishes to focus on transferable skills and knowledge rather than overt knowledge of specific content, one still must establish some kind of organizational scheme for the content. There are several good ways of doing this, but earlier work (Fost, 2013) suggested a natural solution: use so-called Big Questions. The idea came from a recommendation by the Association of American Colleges and Universities (2007) that curricula should "engage the big questions" by "[teaching] through the curriculum to far-reaching issues, contemporary and enduring, in science and society, cultures and values, global interdependence, the changing economy, and human dignity and freedom."

The advantages of this approach are clear. First, by associating questions with instructional units—that is, natural groupings of HCs—that last two to three weeks, we ensure that the subject matter for a certain course will remain relatively stable. This strategy decreases the time and effort required to learn content related to a narrow domain and keep it in mind long enough to participate in classwork, only to discard it and repeat the process with another subject. Minerva students spend correspondingly more effort focusing on the HCs rather than on frequently changing content incidental to the learning objectives. Second, the questions provide real-world domains of application. The first of these is the Big Question associated with the unit in which the habit of mind or foundational concept is introduced. Later in the course, however, synthesis lessons bundle several HCs and apply them anew to a different question. This can occur multiple times within a course, or even between courses. For example, the Big Questions "How can we feed the world?" and "Can war be avoided?," among others, appear in several cornerstone courses. This approach harmonizes with several principles from the science of learning (see chapter 11), including spaced practice, interleaving, and building on prior associations.

Command central: The curriculum map

To see the cornerstone courses under even greater magnification, let's examine a small piece of what we call the curriculum map. This map shows, for all four freshman yearlong courses, which learning objectives will be addressed and when, using content from a particular Big Question. The excerpt shown (see table 4.3) is from the first two weeks, fall semester, of

Table 4.3

Excerpt from the Curriculum Map Showing the First Two Weeks of Empirical Analyses Course

Unit	HC(s) introduced	Big Question
Problem Solving	#selflearning	How can we feed the world?
	#rightproblem; #breakitdown	
	#gapanalysis; #constraints	
	Synthesis: #rightproblem, #breakitdown, #gapanalysis, #constraints	

the Empirical Analyses course (see appendix A for the specific HCs referenced in table 4.3).

Each row in the "HC(s) introduced" column in table 4.3 represents a single class session. Thus the first session of the Problem Solving unit introduces the habit of mind #selflearning, which is about techniques to facilitate self-study and unsupervised learning. In the next two sessions, four more HCs are introduced. Readings for all five relate either to the HCs themselves or to some aspect of the Big Question that will permit illustrations of its application. For example, in session 3 of this unit, students might read an article about how a nonprofit group approached providing agricultural assistance to an underdeveloped country. The study guide for that reading might ask students to focus on how the group used gap analysis (the focus of the #gapanalysis foundational concept) to determine which elements of the problem could be addressed with existing tools and which elements required new solutions. In class, students might share their understanding of this process, then work in groups to apply gap analysis to a slightly new problem, still related to the same Big Question, "How can we feed the world?"

Comparison with Other Approaches

Considerably more detail on the cornerstone courses is provided in chapters 5 through 8, so I will proceed now to compare our first-year curriculum with other approaches to general education. My anchor is a study by Brint and co-workers (2009), who identified four dominant models, listed here from the most popular (i.e., embraced by the greatest number of schools) to the least popular: (1) core distribution areas, (2) traditional liberal arts, (3) cultures and ethics, and (4) civic/utilitarian. Brint and colleagues' analysis, which used factor analysis to find latent structures in course catalog and other institutional data, was somewhat complex, but in essence it reduced to finding recurring patterns in the types of classes required of all students. Their sample included 292 institutions of various sizes and types and spanned the period 1975–2000. Despite the broad scope of their study, however, none of these four models captures particularly well the approach we have taken at Minerva.

The core distribution areas model

The core distribution areas model, which arose in response to the untamed chaos of free electives systems, requires that students distribute their electives across domains such as the natural sciences, social sciences, and humanities. At first glance, this approach seems to align reasonably well with our cornerstone courses, but on closer inspection the resemblance results largely from the Big Questions those courses use. It is true, for example, that our Complex Systems course draws content mostly from the social sciences, but many of the HCs it introduces are not drawn from or especially prevalent in the social sciences. In particular, the foundational unit in the fall semester introduces six complexity-related HCs, subsets of which reappear in every lesson plan throughout the year. These six HCs cover concepts such as system dynamics and emergent properties that would more typically be found in an applied mathematics course. A later unit in ethics would typically be offered by a philosophy department, and a still later unit on negotiation and mediation would be more expected of a business curriculum.

The other cornerstone courses are similarly diverse, to a greater or lesser degree. For instance, Empirical Analyses includes learning objectives concerned with problem solving (not often found … anywhere, actually), Formal Analyses includes units on symbolic logic (philosophy) and risk analysis (business, economics), and Multimodal Communications includes units on design thinking (engineering), artistic interpretation, and multimedia (fine arts).

More fundamentally, though, the core distribution areas model implicitly endorses a division of intellectual inquiry into the domains it spans. We do not endorse such a view. In our view—one represented explicitly in the criteria for new HCs (see appendix A)—each worthwhile general education learning objective ought to find application in at least several domains. Furthermore, the idea of a distribution model is that taking any one (or two or three) from among a set of sometimes hundreds of courses will provide an equivalent level of breadth for the student—a notion we summarily reject.

The traditional liberal arts model

The traditional liberal arts model is another kind of distribution model, with the difference that the mandated distribution areas eschew practical applications (as is, presumably, at least part of the intention of the core distribution model) in favor of material intended to enrich the inner lives of students. Literature, philosophy, and foreign languages constitute the canonical set of subjects, from the legacy of what Brint and colleagues call "status education." Again, this model is not particularly well aligned with ours. It is eminently possible for a Minerva student to pursue studies that have this cast, but that work would appear mostly in courses taken in the sophomore year and later and would stem from work they did within their major and through their choice of electives. Outside those electives and in the general education program per se, our curriculum focuses much more heavily on "practical knowledge"—cognitive tools that can be applied to solve real-world problems—than on pursuits intended for personal enrichment (see chapter 2).

The cultures and ethics model

The cultures and ethics model emerged in the 1960s on a tide of rising sensitivity among secular liberals that higher education was too Eurocentric. This led to curricula that required students to take courses on almost any subject as long as the scope was non-Eurocentric: Indian philosophy, South American religion, Chinese medicine, Japanese education, and so on. This approach is plainly not evident in our model. One of the reasons for this parallels our divergence from the Great Books programs: amid the cornucopia of books and cultures, we cannot discern any principled way of adjudicating which ones to select. It is not, in other words, that we deny the value in reading this or that great book or the transformative power of expanding one's perspectives to include those of an unfamiliar culture. Rather, we do not see what reasons there might be for choosing one culture over another, or one great book over another—and, in the absence of such reasons, the choice seems to invite the favoritism and bias of the curriculum designers. Great Books programs have faced exactly this challenge. Is there some evidential justification for teaching Hawthorne but not Melville? African culture but not New Guinean? We could not see any.

Nevertheless, we have tried to capture in other ways some of this model's advantages. Most plainly, we do believe that direct, lived experiences of cultural diversity will serve our students well, so we have arranged for all our undergraduates to live in seven global cities—in the Americas, Europe, India, and Asia—throughout their college careers. This geographic diversity is complemented by the diversity of the student body itself, which, although we do not set geographic quotas, shows only a minority (about 25 percent) hailing from the United States and Canada and a long, fat tail from a wide range of other countries. The impact of this diversity is reinforced by the logistics of the seven cities model: students live and travel together, remaining for four years in cohorts of just 150 students—the Dunbar number (Dunbar, 1992). These circumstances are highly conducive to a thoroughgoing, sincere understanding of other people and their values and views. We believe that this extracurricular model is well positioned to yield many of the advantages hoped for by those who endorse a cultures and ethics academic program.

The civic/utilitarian model

The civic/utilitarian model is in some ways the opposite of a distribution model in that its domain is narrow: it requires students to learn material related to American federal or state government, contemporary business, and technology. Presumably this model was informed by the view that education should prepare students for pro-social activity after graduation. It was the least stable of the four models characterized by Brint and colleagues. (By "stable," Brint and colleagues mean *exhibiting a loading on courses that was stable over time*.) This was also the youngest and most provincial model, first appearing in 1980 in midwestern and southern state colleges. Judging by the courses typically included in such programs, it is clear that they are (and were) considerably narrower than the scope of our cornerstone courses. Critical thinking and creative thinking—two of our core competencies—do not appear to be well represented in the civic/utilitarian model, nor do foundational concepts of the scientific method, complex systems, or formal analysis. The only substantive overlap appears to be this model's inclusion of effective communication skills in speaking and writing and some contact with computer science (computer programming appears prominently, though somewhat incidentally, in our Formal Analyses course).

Overall, then, our approach to general education is in many respects unique. In summarizing their findings, Brint and colleagues note that "The most notable gains during the period [1975–2000] came in basic academic skills courses (mathematics, English composition, speech/communications, and foundations) and in diversity-related and non-Western cultures courses." To be sure, those basic academic skills and other reasonably common general education requirements—such as critical thinking, ethics, and computer literacy—appear prominently in our courses, but much that appears in our courses does not appear on Brint's list at all, and our conception of these skills is much more granular than is typical.

How We Met Common Challenges

In the scholarly fora of general education—places like the pages of *The Journal of General Education*—discussions of curriculum structure are often accompanied by others equally important: those concerning implementation. In this section I review some of the ways that we either avoided or overcame structural and sociopolitical challenges faced elsewhere. As maps of the terrain, I will use Zai (2015) and Newton (2000). As Zai sees it, the core challenges include the following:

• Lack of rigor; watered-down courses
• Curricula uncoupled from assessment of student outcomes
• Internal tensions, including beleaguered or poor leadership
• External tensions, such as those from accrediting bodies and governing boards
• Attacks from social constructivists regarding the epistemic justification for enthroning a single body of knowledge

Newton (2000) sees the core issues as follows:

• A debate about whether the focus should be on the acquisition of knowledge within multiple fields or knowledge that transcends any particular field
• Questions about whether students are best served by achieving breadth or depth (and debates about whether achieving both is a live possibility)
• Concerns about who should, or can, teach general education courses, generalists or specialists
• Concerns about the dominance of the Western intellectual inheritance

Some of these challenges do not apply at Minerva and I will not address them further. For example, Zai's second bullet point, about the uncoupling of curriculum and assessment, does not apply because we are building the curriculum, learning outcomes, and assessment procedures at the same time and in a completely integrated manner. Also Zai's fourth bullet point, about external tensions, does not really apply: our approach to general education was fully explicated in our initial program application with our accreditor, and our governance is such that we do not experience almost any of the other external pressures known elsewhere, particularly at state-funded schools. Other challenges listed above can be combined: Zai's social constructivist challenge is closely related to Newton's Western centrism critique. In the remainder of this section, therefore, I address just those concerns that plausibly could have affected us but did not because of the way we organized the institution and managed its development.

Lack of rigor/watered-down courses

One set of challenges concerns academic standards and rigor. Sometimes these challenges have to do with the coherence and conceptual unity of the curriculum itself, or the degree to which curricular rigor is enforced by an intellectual community that shares a "language of ideas" and a commitment to policing the integrity of those ideas. Other concerns center on delivery: general education classes are commonly taught in large classrooms and by the least expensive (and often least experienced) faculty.

Regarding coherence, we focus on two specific issues. The first is interpersonal, namely, the extent to which one can say something definite about the recipient of a degree. One of the historical purposes of general education programs was to establish a standard level of competence and knowledge that every graduate would achieve. Prospective employers are interested in that, but so are current and prospective students. In this sense, the Minerva program coheres because everyone takes the same courses in the first year and continues to be assessed on the HCs throughout his or her undergraduate career. The cornerstone course grades that appear on a student's transcript guarantee that external audiences, and the students themselves, can compare student ability in the four high-level core competencies.

Another key issue regarding coherence is cross-course synthesis, or the degree to which the curriculum itself hangs together. This concern has a history dating back to about 1820 (Boning, 2007), which was when classical liberal arts programs began to meet competition from programs (such as those at Bowdoin, Brown, or Michigan) that offered more individualized pathways to help students prepare for specific vocations. The Minerva approach to this issue is multifaceted. As mentioned above, some Big Questions appear in multiple courses. "Can war be avoided?" is one example. These questions function as cross-course bonds, explicit demonstrations that a single real-world problem typically requires the synthesis of ideas from different core competencies. Another way we achieve the same end is through our use of final project assignments. Final projects consume the last week of each cornerstone course and require students to invoke at least two HCs from each cornerstone (eight total), combining them into a coherent approach to their chosen topic. Students complete two of these projects, one in fall semester and another in spring semester, and this work is the most heavily weighted when we calculate the students' HC grades. Last, as students progress through the year, they employ HCs introduced in one cornerstone course across the other cornerstone courses on a regular basis. In fact, there are sections in some cornerstone courses that cannot be taught—at least not optimally—without students having taken segments of other cornerstone courses.

The remainder of the academic standards concerns have already been addressed elsewhere in this chapter, if implicitly. Conceptual unity arises from how we have organized the HCs into core competencies (see chapter 2 and appendix A). There is certainly an intellectual community for the HCs, in the sense of a group of people who share a language of ideas and attend assiduously to one another's use of them. One of the requirements for a habit or concept is that there be a scholarly literature about it, but in many ways we are creating a new community for whom this structure will become a touchstone. The appellation process, that is, the granting of a hashtag name for a habit or a concept, provides that community with a common language. Indeed, even after our first year of teaching, and more so now after three years of student enrollment, it is common to hear HCs dropped by name into casual conversation.

The integrity of the proper application of these concepts and habits is facilitated by scoring rubrics, which detail exactly what we say it means to apply a concept poorly or well, and our explicit definitions, which are displayed prominently on the Active Learning Forum. There is very little room for hand waving about any habit or concept; indeed, our sharpest students have helped draw attention to vagaries in some of our early definitions, prompting revision or correction. The final concern about academic rigor—that of class size and professorial status—does not apply to us: all our "classrooms" are small (limited to nineteen students), and all professors, regardless of their collegiate appointment, participate in cornerstone course instruction. (This is true at present; time will tell whether the practice can be maintained as we grow.)

Troubled leadership and reform

Zai reports, with concern, that when programmatic reform is led by tenured faculty, these individuals tend to be more committed to their disciplines, or even to communities outside the university (such as professional societies), than to general education. They also tend to be unfamiliar with the relevant literature. At Minerva, we have intentionally avoided the incentive structures that at many institutions push faculty toward research and away from teaching. In the first place, we don't use publication quotas or impact factors to determine professorial retention or advancement. Faculty research is encouraged and supported, especially to the degree that it can include students as authentic contributors, but it is not the centerpiece of professorial success. Research is also so heavily incentivized within the broader profession that additional pressure imposed by the institution seems counterproductive. Second, and related, faculty performance is measured first and foremost by professors' successful discharge of instructional duties—this is why we say that we are *student-outcome-centric*. The general education courses are treated no differently in this regard from the disciplinary courses within the colleges. Finally, all our faculty currently teach a cornerstone course at least once and receive more than a month of training, which includes extensive sections on the science of learning, pedagogical best practices, and our general education curriculum.

Zai also reports that lack of academic rigor in some programs may have an organizational cause, namely, the low esteem general education holds in the eyes of the university's power elite. This is not a concern at Minerva. The primary architects of our program are the founder and the chief academic officer, who developed these plans in full view of the board of directors and the funding bodies. It was not merely that these entities approved of the program incidentally, it was that the program was a central reason for their endorsing the overall academic mission.

Another advantage we have with respect to reform is that we are developing our curriculum sequentially, from the freshman year forward. Because the freshman year is entirely focused on general education, to prove we were delivering on our promises we had to do our best work on those courses. There simply was no other university activity to showcase.

At some other institutions, mostly those following the core distribution areas model, there are perverse incentives for departments to persist in teaching arcane domain-specific knowledge in their general education service courses: so that the revenue associated with them cannot be captured by other departments. This leads to a kind of turfism that inhibits reform in various ways. It also breeds interdepartmental conflict, which inhibits broader interdisciplinary collaborations. At Minerva, we have avoided these problems in ways that should by now be clear: using a principled set of learning objectives unconcerned with or even hostile to disciplinary boundaries and a set of dedicated general education courses that do not produce revenue for specific colleges or departments. And because the HCs are so broadly applicable, we are confident that they will appear frequently in courses from all colleges. We do not, in other words, anticipate needing to codify special-purpose incentives to force per-college contact with the HCs.

Who can or should teach

Each of the cornerstones is interdisciplinary, so it is rare for any individual instructor to be thoroughly familiar with all the material in it—either the HCs or the Big Questions. To support them, we hold weekly hour-long meetings with all instructors who are teaching a given course at that time. Prior to the meeting the instructors review the lesson plans to be used two weeks hence, and in the hour allotted they work through any unfamiliar material or pedagogical concerns. Although the lesson plans are already complete and highly polished by the time the instructional faculty receive them, they are flexible enough to accommodate new suggestions and approaches. Also attending the meeting is a specialist—the same person for all four courses—whose role is to help each teaching team understand how its class relates to the other three. That person also passes along institutional memories as needed, including common confusions, best practices for certain topics, and the like. In some cases the dean of the college also attends these meetings.

The team-based approach is also used to develop the lesson plans in the first place. That development was managed by experienced interdisciplinary educators and the lesson plans were heavily edited. Altogether, approximately 3,400 pages of curriculum were written and reviewed by a team of eight to fifteen people over the course of two years. By using such a cross-disciplinary team to develop standardized lesson plans, we further mitigated the impact of any given professor's particular training. Nevertheless, the lesson plans are written in a way that allows us to capitalize on that training: a portion of every lesson plan is left completely free so that the class can explore particularly fruitful student questions or issues that many of them found confusing. In these moments, some professors' expertise will come to the fore. Critically, we use the weekly meetings to capture their handling of the situation and add it as an annotation to the lesson plan so that future students and instructors can benefit from it.

Multidisciplinary or transdisciplinary knowledge

On the matter of whether general education ought to include knowledge within multiple subjects or knowledge that transcends subjects, our choice has by now become clear: we deemphasize, in our general education curriculum, knowledge acquisition—that is, knowledge in the sense of a codified set of justified, true beliefs—and instead favor teaching habits of mind and foundational concepts (see chapter 2) that either help produce knowledge or help students deploy knowledge in the service of a goal. Consider, for example, the nine-week-long Scientific Method unit in Empirical Analyses or the Leadership and Teamwork unit (also nine weeks long) in Complex Systems. The learning objectives in these units include, respectively, HCs such as #plausibility, which is about the process of determining the internal and external consistency of a hypothesis, and #powerdynamics, which is about types of power and different ways and consequences of wielding it. We assign readings from the scholarly literature on these topics, but our goal is not to ensure that students remember the content of these readings. Even if that were our purpose, the brutal fact is that they would not remember much of it, as the evidence of multiple studies on higher education show. Instead, our purpose is to instill a habit of mind—that is, a regular practice that becomes automatic in the relevant contexts—or to teach a foundational concept that helps make sense of a problem. This aim is supported by the rubrics, which move quickly past mere demonstration of knowledge and toward competent praxis. A student cannot achieve mastery or receive an A grade by regurgitating information in an exam booklet: we have no exams in these courses. Rather, the student must deploy the skill or concept in the contexts it is needed, which are likely to be classes that have nothing whatever to do with their original context. Those classes, and those contexts, may occur years after the #plausibility habit was introduced. Thanks to our time-traveling grades and Active Learning Forum dashboard, the enduring importance of these general education goals remains in focus throughout students' college careers.

Conclusion

I conclude with a view expressed by Clifford (1877), written at a time—perhaps not coincidentally—when the diversity of views about general education was in its first flush.

The student who begins to learn about electricity is not asked to believe in Ohm's law: he is made to understand the question, he is placed before the apparatus, and he is taught to verify it. He learns to do things, not to think he knows things; to use instruments and to ask questions, not to accept a traditional statement ... . If Ohm's law were suddenly lost and forgotten by all men, while the question and the method of solution remained, the result could be rediscovered in an hour. But the result by itself, if known to a people who could not comprehend the value of the question or the means of solving it, would be like a watch in the hands of a savage who could not wind it up ... . In regard, then, to the sacred tradition of humanity, we learn that it consists, not in propositions or statements which are to be accepted and believed on the authority of the tradition, but in questions rightly asked, in conceptions which enable us to ask further questions, and in methods of answering questions.

References

Association of American Colleges and Universities. (2007). *College learning for the new global century*. Washington, DC: Association of American Colleges and Universities.

Boning, K. (2007). Coherence in general education: A historical look. *Journal of General Education, 56*(1), 1–16.

Brint, S., Proctor, K., Murphy, S. P., Turk-Bicakci, L., & Hanneman, R. A. (2009). General education models: Continuity and change in the U.S. undergraduate curriculum, 1975–2000. *Journal of Higher Education, 80*(6), 605–642.

Clifford, W. (1877). The ethics of belief. *Contemporary Review (London, England), 29*, 289–309.

Dunbar, R. I. M. (1992). Neocortex size as a constraint on group size in primates. *Journal of Human Evolution, 22*(6), 469–493. doi:10.1016/0047-2484(92)90081-J

Fost, J. (2013). Semantic technology and the question-centric curriculum. *Innovative Higher Education, 38*(1), 31–44. doi:10.1007/s10755-012-9219-y

Newton, R. R. (2000). Tensions and models in general education planning. *Journal of General Education, 49*(3), 165–181.

Zai, R. (2015). Reframing general education. *Journal of General Education, 64*(3), 196–217. doi:10.1353/jge.2015.0022

5 Multimodal Communications and Effective Communication

Judith C. Brown, Kara Gardner, and Daniel J. Levitin

One of the four core competencies at the heart of Minerva's curriculum is the ability to communicate effectively. It is not enough to think critically and creatively. One also must be able to communicate the result of that thinking to others and be able to persuade them of its merit, using any and all modes of communication that best fit the situation. In contrast to similar courses elsewhere, Minerva's multimodal communications course pursues these goals by drawing on a wide range of empirical discoveries from cognitive science and neuroscience, and encompasses an unusually wide range of types of communication. Moreover, the course focuses on the persistent, synchronous, and systematic application of the habits of mind and foundational concepts (HCs) to the analysis and expression of multimodal communications.

The first step in developing the ability to communicate effectively is to realize that human communications are more than just speech. They have always been multimodal. Even communication that appears to be entirely verbal almost always also involves paralinguistic cues—gestures, pointing, describing, and depicting (Clark, 2016). Our prehistoric ancestors used multimodal communications when communicating through speech, facial expressions, and hand gestures, as we still do today. In one study, storytellers were found to gesture twenty times per minute (Bavelas, Gerwing, & Healing, 2014). We also use multimodal communications when we talk to others in person or by videoconferencing (e.g., Skype or Zoom), and when we make videos that integrate written scripts, speech, music, and visual cues. Yet only in recent years has the field of multimodal communications become a formal field of academic study, with its own journals, conferences, research programs, and courses in which students can learn about this new field and use the associated knowledge and skills in their own projects.

What is the reason for this late bloom? It's not that people were oblivious to the importance of effective communication. Even in antiquity some of the great philosophers, Aristotle and Cicero among them, appreciated the central role of effective communication for the survival of civic life in their societies. Prompted by that concern, they wrote lengthy treatises on rhetoric, as the field was then called. And it required more than the simple use of sophisticated words. These scholars realized that effective communication requires a keen understanding of the performance aspects of speech and their effective use in different settings.

Like Rip van Winkle, however, the discipline of rhetoric entered, and then remained in, a long slumber. For roughly two thousand years most of the additions to it could be contained within the framework created in antiquity. Two independent yet interlinked developments woke the study of communications from its torpor and set it in a new direction. One was the digital communications revolution of the past half century. The other was the growth of cognitive science and neuroscience, which in turn was facilitated by new technologies that afforded insight into how the mind functions and the brain reacts to the signals it receives from different modes of communication and different media.

These two strands in the development of communication studies—the digital communications revolution and advances in cognitive science and neuroscience—have shaped much of the organization and content of Minerva's two-semester course, Multimodal Communications, one of four required cornerstone courses for all our first-year students. The course teaches students how to communicate effectively through writing, speaking, and the use of other media. It also teaches how the interaction of psychology, culture, and society influences how audiences interpret the messages they receive. This body of knowledge, and practice using it, strengthens our students' abilities to communicate effectively and contributes to their ability to work well with others.

Also influential in the structure and content of the course is Marshall McLuhan's astute observation that "in a culture like ours, long accustomed to splitting and dividing all things ... it is sometimes a bit of a shock to be reminded that, in operational and practical fact, the medium is the message" (McLuhan, 1964/1994). For this reason, after our students analyze certain genres and media singly, they learn to analyze them in combination. Some lessons focus on the interaction of literature and film, others on lyrics and music, yet others on multimodal and multimedia design. We want our students to understand that in the course as in life, various modes of communication generally occur simultaneously and are imbricated with the media that carry them, which are themselves part of the message they communicate. Once the students have acquired this knowledge they are given opportunities to use it and put it into effect in their own projects.

As in the other three cornerstone courses, Multimodal Communications ultimately focuses on practical knowledge—skills and knowledge students can use to adapt to a changing world, allowing them to succeed in jobs and professions that may not yet exist.

An Open Mind and Close Reading

Before our students reach the stage at which they can use effective communication strategies in their own work, they must acquire the ability to analyze what others communicate. This necessitates seeing the world as others see it, even if on further reflection and analysis disagreements remain. It also requires critical self-assessment and ethical framing—the willingness to ask questions such as "Why do I disagree with what I'm encountering? Do I have good reasons for my own stance? What are my biases? Are they rooted in ethically defensible values?" In sum, it requires developing a dialogue with previously unexamined layers of the self and one's relationship to the world. This interior dialogue and self-examination are the first step to good communication.

Our students engage in this inner dialogue and apply it to specific works of art and literature in a set of lessons on close reading that test two important HCs, open-mindedness and the ability to critique. When used in relation to each other, these HCs both provide the intellectual space for and set the limits of fruitful analysis and discussion. We do not choose materials for our students to view, listen to, or read because we believe that an educated person must engage with those particular items or because we think that they are superior to any number of other great works. Rather, we select the materials because they are effective vehicles to illustrate the foundational concepts of open-mindedness and critique, and the complex relationship between them.

New Ways to Teach Communication through Writing

Having broadened their outlook and acquired skills as critical readers, our students are then ready to tackle the craft of writing. In this domain also we take a different approach.

Using new ways to teach writing

Few images in our society are as pervasive, and arguably as pernicious, as that of the solitary writer, a genius, whose self-exile and seclusion from the world is essential for great writing and the creation of important literature. Minerva's innovative pedagogical approach to writing, by contrast, is synchronous and recurrent. The use of digital technologies, specifically the cloud-based Active Learning Forum (ALF), allows students, no matter where they are located, to work together in small groups of four or five and to see each other's work and each other's edits, as well as who is making them, displayed on the screen in real time as they are being made. It also allows the professor to observe or participate, as best suits the occasion. This synchronous process, in which the identity of the writer or editor can remain anonymous or be disclosed, combines the immediacy and intense focus of one-on-one interactions with the power of peer instruction.

Typically, these small groups then share and discuss the edited work—along with their newfound insights—with other groups in class, then reiterate the process with the entire class, thereby gaining even wider perspectives. These interactions are especially rich at Minerva because of the diverse international background of our students and the selective admissions criteria, which target creative and independent thinkers.

This writing process is very effective in both identifying and correcting common problems in one's own work and that of peers. It also helps build students' abilities to create works of greater complexity and sophistication. By providing our students with the opportunity to edit their own work and that of others on a regular and ongoing basis, our cloud-based HC-focused ALF enables our students to learn the importance of iterative editing. The process also shows the students that a great many hours of close attention are required to produce high-quality writing. We recognize that it is often easier to see flaws in other people's writing than in one's own work and that the more practice young writers have in identifying flaws in others' work, the more facile and independent they will eventually become in correcting their own writing.

Students do learn to correct infelicities in word choice, grammar, style, logic, facts, organization, and so on. But more than that, our students learn how to write convincing, evidence-based essays in which they formulate thesis statements, ascertain what information they need to support them, logically organize the exposition of their arguments, and use a variety of literary and rhetorical tools to add layers of meaning that will make their work compelling to different audiences. These lessons, all focused on HCs—ranging from #thesis, to #sourcequality, #organization, #composition,

#connotation, and #audience (see appendix A)—prepare students to inter-
pret and write on any topic for which they have acquired the necessary
knowledge, whether it be a literary, scientific, political, or personal topic.

Choice of subject matter
Because the choice of material is vast and one of the goals of a Minerva education is to help students make a positive difference in the world, the unit
on writing as a craft uses the unifying theme of utopias and the "Big Question" of whether they can or should be achieved through cloning. These
topics enable students to engage in ethical framing, critique, and finding
support for their written arguments in highly intentional and active sessions that combine different genres and modes of communication.

The Role of Body Language and Facial Expression

We also want students to understand the limits of language, how language
interacts with facial expressions and body language in different settings
and different cultures, and to use that knowledge in their own communications. This unit of the course requires students to learn about research on
body language (e.g., de Gelder, 2006) and facial expressions to determine
which gestures may be universal (California Academy of Sciences, 2009)
and which may vary cross-culturally or within cultures (Maloney, 2014).
What may seem to be an appropriately confident posture in one society
may appear arrogant in another. Similarly, a gesture or linguistic style combined with certain facial expressions or bodily gestures may have different
connotations depending on a person's social class, gender, the situation in
which it occurs, and the composition or function of the audience.

Knowledge of these interactions enables students not only to interpret
the body language of people with whom they interact but also to modify
their own body language so that it is consistent with how they want other
people to perceive them. Such self-awareness, linked to the development of
the frontal lobes as people mature (Luu, Collins, & Tucker, 2000), may not
be fully developed in college-age students. This unit aims to provide students with the tools to interpret the body language and facial expressions
of others and to become more self-aware so that they can understand what
they are communicating through their own posture and gestures.

Once students have engaged in a critical reading of scholarly works on
these subjects, they deepen their understanding by comparing their readings to real-life applications. They analyze videos from legal testimonies by
expert witnesses, closely examine the body movements of public figures

who find themselves in tense situations, and analyze scenes from fictional films (Cramer, Brodsky, & DeCoster, 2009).

We conclude this unit with videos of speeches by masterful orators who illustrate how verbal communication, body language, and facial expression can work in combination and reinforce each other. Prime examples can be found in the speeches of Martin Luther King, Jr. (1968), whose combination of body language, facial expressions, vocal tones, and rich use of connotative language bring together all these modes of communication in memorable ways. As one student remarked on hearing Dr. King's (1968) "I've been to the mountaintop" speech and observing the facial expressions and the body language that reinforced his points: "It's not just what he's saying, but the way that he's saying it. When I read the speech on the page before ever hearing it, I was already moved by the words and the poetic aspects of the speech. But his delivery turned it into something else entirely."

Teaching the Arts as a Tool of Communication

Our Multimodal Communications course also addresses the visual arts and music as forms of communication. Understanding these topics is clearly within the realm of practical knowledge, in light of their pervasive presence in the media, on websites, and increasingly in technology-mediated personal communications. These media surround us in so many contexts—advertising, street art, background music—that often we are hardly aware of them. And even when we are, as in museums and concert halls, we rarely frame them as tools for communication. Yet we should. When we watch a political ad, we would do well to consider how much the underlying music or camera angles and background might influence our views about the candidate, or how much a logo shapes our behavior when we shop for clothing. Tuning in to the ways in which we receive visual art and music in all of their forms is an important aspect of understanding effective communication. In our course on multimodal communications, we treat the visual arts and music as expressive tools, and we teach students to examine how we can use those tools to interpret and produce meaning in nonverbal forms.

The visual art and music sessions in the Multimodal Communications course are unified by two of our Big Questions: "What is the relation between a work of art and its contexts?" and "How do we make and find meaning in art?" We use a diverse range of genres—opera, symphony, song, painting, and propaganda posters—and apply our HCs to understand them. Students learn the historical context for a work and consider how that might help them interpret it. In so doing, we ask them to bring unconscious bias to the surface and consider how their preconceived notions shape their responses to music and visual art. And we require them to articulate arguments about the meaning of artworks based on observations of small details in color, shape, line, pitch, rhythm, timbre, and other features.

Communicating through the visual arts

To appreciate how visual art communicates differently from linguistic expression, students conduct close readings of two paintings from the Spanish Civil War era, Pablo Picasso's *Guernica* (1937) and Salvador Dalí's *Soft Construction with Boiled Beans (Premonition of Civil War)* (1936). With a vast number of available paintings produced by artists in different eras and different parts the world, we could have chosen many works as subjects for close analysis. These two offer several advantages: they both comment on a conflict that had global impact, the Spanish Civil War (1936–1939), and though they are from the same era and are concerned with similar socio-political issues, they exhibit contrasting styles. This enables us to analyze the variety of approaches that artists can take, even when dealing with the same or similar subjects. The techniques these artists used in their paintings were experimental and novel at the time. Picasso and Dalí both commented on and went beyond existing approaches to painting, and they called attention to color, line, the use of space, and other tools in their work.

To understand what the paintings communicate, students must carefully consider all the elements that make up the two paintings and must learn about the historical context in which they were created. Both works require active engagement from the viewer on a number of levels. As Picasso wrote, "The public who look at the picture must interpret the symbols as they understand them. [...] A painting is not thought out and settled in advance. While it is being done, it changes as one's thoughts change. And when it's finished, it goes on changing, according to the state of mind of whoever is looking at it" (PBS Learning Media, n.d.).

Communicating through music

We take a similar approach to teaching musical communication. Students study a piece by the Mexican composer Silvestre Revueltas, *Homenaje a García Lorca* (Revueltas, 1936), which is dedicated to the noted writer, who was executed by Nationalist forces during the Spanish Civil War. The piece is contemporaneous with the paintings by Picasso and Dalí, so students can use prior historical (and cultural) knowledge to inform their interpretations. During class, they meet in small breakout groups and engage in a focused analysis of the musical elements of the piece. Revueltas employs unusual timbres in his small chamber orchestra, emphasizing brass instruments and unusual percussion, such as the tam-tam. Even if students do not have a background in formal symphonic conventions, they can describe the often surprising, dissonant sounds the orchestra is producing and consider the impact these sounds have on the listener.

When students begin their analyses, they focus on details such as instrumentation, volume, the balance of dissonance and consonance, tempo, and so on. Then they consider the life and political views of Revueltas, who was a socialist and went to Spain to support the Republican side during the Spanish Civil War. Critics often emphasize Revueltas's political views when evaluating his work, rather than its musical elements. During class, students must first consider whether context, musical elements, or perhaps a combination of the two, is most critical in determining what the music communicates, and then—most importantly—they must interpret the piece.

Combining visual art and music

In addition to examining visual art and musical works individually, students consider how the modalities interact. For example, in opera, the libretto, music, costumes, and staging combine to create meanings that change over time. Students study specific operas, and their interpretations consider both the context and their own biases. By means of polls, debates, focused analysis, and other pedagogical techniques, we create opportunities for students to extend in class the work they have done beforehand using HCs to deepen their understanding of the opera. Our purpose is not to furnish our students with a broad understanding of music or art history but rather to give them a set of interpretive tools they can apply to any of the musical and visual forms of communication they encounter for the rest of their lives.

Beyond Interpretation: The Art of Persuasion

As we move from critical interpretation and questions about how to find and make meaning in art, we turn to the realm of persuasion and to complex issues surrounding the difference between persuasion and manipulation. If our students are to make a positive contribution in the world, they need to learn the tools of psychology and of multimodal communications that will help them become successful persuaders. Yet they must not be tempted to become manipulators, and they must be aware of efforts by others to manipulate them. This is why the ethical framing HC is yoked to the unit on persuasion, which we organize around the Big Question, "How is free choice manipulated?"

When we teach about persuasion we draw attention to two approaches: cognitive (or rational) and emotional. These approaches are distinguishable and sometimes work for one person or group in one context but not in another. Yet we are also mindful that in practice, these approaches often overlap and are used together.

Cognitive persuasion techniques address content. They attempt to appeal to an individual's or group's rational sense and use of systematic thinking. They are intended to appeal to an audience's reasoning as well as to its preexisting revealed positions, likely motivations, and known flexibility on certain issues.

Emotional persuasion techniques appeal instead to an audience's feelings. They aim to shape recipients' attitudes by appealing to cultural rules about what emotions are expected as well as which ones are socially appropriate and morally revealing. They may also fulfill common human desires for acceptance—to fit into or be perceived as part of social groups that enhance one' social standing and diminish one's sense of vulnerability. Because emotional experiences, whether positive or negative, are often powerful and more memorable than experiences not linked to them, using emotions and appealing to them—especially using humor, surprise, and poignancy—can be particularly effective, with longlasting effects (Wang et al., 2015).

It has long been known that persuasive communication requires knowing one's audience and adapting to the audience's needs, often in real time (Aristotle, 1994). For this reason, when we teach the HC on emotional persuasion, we frame our discussion of rhetorical devices such as storytelling, repetition, humor, and understatement in the context of social psychology theories and research in affective neuroscience. These include cognitive dissonance, attribution theory, conditioning theory, and controlled observations about human responses to authority or to situations that call for consistency, reciprocity, or consensus (Dawes et al., 2012; Harris, 2013).

Using emotion to persuade

To address these issues, students examine the persuasive power of emotions in particularly charged settings of real-life public speeches and in particularly persuasive debates in fictional film. We ask students to identify the relevance of social judgment theory, the elaboration likelihood model, cognitive dissonance theory, the narrative paradigm, ethos, pathos, and logos, among other factors they have learned about in their readings.

We introduce this material not so that our students may learn to manipulate others for nefarious purposes but so they will be aware and prepared when others employ propaganda techniques and broadcast fake news to try to influence them. We want our students to immunize themselves against adopting beliefs that contradict the evidence or their own carefully considered views.

In addition, we incorporate our students' own real-world experiences into our instruction. For example, we ask them to propose a persuasive approach to change the behavior of a fictional student who believes in helping San Francisco's homeless but who never gives them money when asked. This activity—which combines Festinger's (1957) cognitive dissonance theory and Lewin's (1947) channel factors—requires students to move beyond the task of naming and organizing the different approaches they have read about. Instead, they have to apply what they have learned to new situations they encounter in the city they call home during their first year of college.

Using location-based assignments

Because Minerva treats the city as a campus, we view San Francisco, where all first-year students live, as a rich source for additional learning through location-based assignments. For this course the location-based assignment consists of studying, visiting, and speaking with members of a local organization that holds the opposite or very different views from those of the students. The aim of this exercise is to understand how an organization tailors its messages to its intended audiences, to assess the extent to which it succeeds, and to consider what communicative approach might successfully engage the organization.

How Is Technology Changing Communications?

The last set of issues that our Multimodal Communications course addresses focuses on the effect of new technologies on communication. These are the issues that gave rise to the field in recent decades. In a wide variety of endeavors and occupations, we are now asked to present, view, and hear materials in graphic or multimedia formats such as videos or podcasts, on websites, or in PowerPoint or Keynote presentations. These communications can be enhanced with new technologies for special effects that were not available as recently as a decade ago.

Integrating cognitive and emotional responses

We approach the effect of new technologies on communication from both a cognitive perspective and an emotional-affective one, first in separate class sessions and then together. Integrating the two perspectives has the most force. A good example of how cognitive and emotional responses can be integrated occurs in the lessons on film as multimedia. Before class, students read scholarly articles on the narrative power of special effects and music in film (McClean, 2007). They also view, for example, the full-length feature film, *Inception* (Nolan, 2010); this film is particularly useful for examining the interactive aspects of media because the multiple levels of its labyrinthine plot are demarcated by means of sophisticated digital special effects, music, and sound. Students must pay close attention to all of these, both to explain how the director makes them coalesce and to re-score a short clip with new music designed to change how the audience interprets a given scene.

New kinds of communication

Interactive multimedia platforms, the product of new twenty-first-century technologies, offer another opportunity to consider how multimodal and multimedia materials can combine to communicate in new ways. To draw inferences about how they affect communications, students must understand how different modalities may be used singly or in combination to complement, undermine, or intensify each other. This is increasingly important because the number of people worldwide who use interactive media, primarily to play video games (Duggan, 2015), is growing by the millions annually. Many of these games create virtual worlds with narrative story lines that gamers find immersive and compelling (Bogost, 2007; Ciccoricco, 2013; Ryan, 2013).

Because of their immersive narratives, video games have the potential to play an important role in communication and persuasion for socially beneficial purposes. For example, some medical institutions have used them to modify diet, physical activity, or other health-related behaviors (Baranowski, T., Buday, Thompson, & Baranowski, J., 2008). Other institutions have used such games to inform and persuade the public about programs that address important social issues. Our students read about and participate in one such multimedia platform, which aims to enlist public support for solving the problem of chronic homelessness in Canada (Sweeney, 2012). As they use this platform, the students apply what they know about human-centered and multimodal design to analyze how the platform communicates its information and messages, to determine whether it does so effectively, and to suggest what could be done to improve it.

Applying design principles

Effective communication also depends on using good design principles. For example, Norman (1988) presents principles that affect the design of everyday things—and also affect communications. We teach our students to use these principles to evaluate communications or products they encounter. This knowledge also enables them to create their own successful multimodal communications in the form of interactive platforms, graphs, films, videos, or everyday objects. Our aim is to promote an appreciation for good design and intentionality so that student works are not mere assemblages of words, images, technological tools, and other resources casually appropriated through hastily chosen online search terms and a few mouse clicks. We want them to create purposeful, coherent, and integrated works such that the total impact is greater than the sum of the parts.

Conclusion

At the end of our Multimodal Communications course we bring together the HCs that students have learned throughout the year. We pay particular attention to the writing, organizing, speaking, and technical skills the students have learned, as well as the importance of having an open mind, using ethical framing, employing cognitive and emotional persuasion, and incorporating effective design in communications. We want our students to use these skills and knowledge to move people to action, to help make the world a better place. This is one of the major goals of a Minerva education. And it is also our students' goal: they want to be effective and positive leaders in the world they inhabit. Given this goal, the skills and knowledge our students learn in our course on multimodal communications will be immensely useful to them in their lifelong journey.

References

Aristotle. (1994). *Rhetoric* (W. Rhys Roberts, Trans.). http://classics.mit.edu/Aristotle/rhetoric.html

Baranówski, T., Buday, R., Thompson, D., & Baranowski, J. (2008). Video games and stories for health-related behavior change. *American Journal of Preventive Medicine, 34*(1), 74–82.

Bavelas, J., Gerwing, J., & Healing, S. (2014). Hand and facial gestures in conversational interaction. In T. Holgraves (Ed.), *Handbook of language and social psychology* (pp. 111–130). Oxford, UK: Oxford University Press.

Bogost, I. (2007). *Persuasive games: The expressive power of videogames.* Cambridge, MA: MIT Press.

California Academy of Sciences. (2009, April 6). *Science today: Facial expressions* [Video file]. YouTube. https://youtu.be/5G6ZR5lJgTI

Ciccoricco, D. (2013). Games as stories. In B. J. Robertson, L. Emerson, & M.-L. Ryan (Eds.), *The Johns Hopkins guide to digital media* (pp. 224–228). Baltimore, MD: Johns Hopkins University Press.

Clark, H. H. (2016). Depicting as a method of communication. *Psychological Review, 123*(3), 324–347.

Cramer, R. J., Brodsky, S. L., & DeCoster, J. (2009). Expert witness confidence and juror personality: Their impact on credibility and persuasion in the courtroom. *Journal of the American Academy of Psychiatry and the Law, 37*(1), 63–74.

Dawes, C. T., Loewen, P. J., Schreiber, D., Simmons, A. N., Flagan, T., McElreath, R., Bokemper, S. E., Fowler, J. H., & Paulus, M. P. (2012). Neural basis of egalitarian behavior. *Proceedings of the National Academy of Sciences of the United States of America, 109*(17), 6479–6483.

de Gelder, B. (2006). Towards the neurobiology of emotional body language. *Nature Reviews. Neuroscience, 7*(3), 242–249.

Duggan, M. (2015, December 15). Gaming and gamers. Washington, DC: Pew Research Center. http://www.pewinternet.org/2015/12/15/gaming-and-gamers/

Festinger, L. (1957). *A theory of cognitive dissonance.* Stanford, CA: Stanford University Press.

Harris, R. A. (2013). A handbook of rhetorical devices. http://www.virtualsalt.com/rhetoric.htm

King, M. L., Jr. (1968). *Martin Luther King's last speech: "I've been to the mountaintop"* [Video file]. https://www.youtube.com/watch?v=Oehry1JC9Rk

Lewin, K. (1947 November 1). Frontiers in group dynamics: II. Channels of group life; social planning and action research. *Human Relations, 1*(2), 143–153.

Luu, P., Collins, P., & Tucker, D. M. (2000). Mood, personality, and self-monitoring: Negative affect and emotionality in relation to frontal lobe mechanisms of error monitoring. *Journal of Experimental Psychology. General, 129*(1), 43–60.

Maloney, D. (2014, April 11). Facial expressions aren't as universal as scientists have thought. *Popular Science.* http://www.popsci.com/article/science/facial-expressions-arent-universal-we-thought

McClean, S. T. (2007). Trick or treat: A framework for the narrative uses of digital visual effects in film. In *Digital storytelling: The narrative power of visual effects in film* (pp. 69–102). Cambridge, MA: MIT Press.

McLuhan, M. (1964/1994). *Understanding media: The extensions of man.* Cambridge, MA: MIT Press.

Nolan, C. (Producer & Director). (2010) *Inception* [Motion picture]. USA, UK: Warner Bros.

Norman, D. (1988). *The design of everyday things.* New York, NY: Basic Books.

PBS Learning Media. (n.d.). *Guernica: Testimony of War.* [Video file]. PBS.com. http://www.pbs.org/treasuresoftheworld/a_nav/guernica_nav/main_guerfrm.html

Revueltas, S. (1936). *Homenaje a García Lorca.* Cond. Jan Latham-Koenig. Orquesta Filarmónica de la UNAM. Performance. https://www.youtube.com/watch?v=BlV54hhB4hc.

Ryan, M.-L. (2013). Interactive narrative. In B. J. Robertson, L. Emerson, & M.-L. Ryan (Eds.), *The Johns Hopkins guide to digital media* (pp. 292–298). Baltimore, MD: Johns Hopkins University Press.

Sweeney, H. (2012). *Here at home: In search of a cure for a 21st century crisis* [Interactive video] National Film Board of Canada (Executive Producer).

Wang, Y., Lucas, G., Khooshabeh, P., de Melo, C., & Gratch, J. (2015) *Effects of emotional expression on persuasion.* US Army Research Paper 340. http://digitalcommons.unl.edu/usarmyresearch/340

6 Formal Analyses and Critical Thinking

John Levitt, Richard Holman, Rena Levitt, and Eric Bonabeau

As citizens of a highly technological society, we are constantly bombarded with claims, data, and facts that we should analyze and integrate into our decision-making process. There are myriad examples of the need for this process. An illustrative example is climate change, arguably the most important issue currently facing humanity. Understanding the scope of this problem, to what extent it is caused by human activity, and what we might do to mitigate its consequences requires a number of skills, all of which are part and parcel of Formal Analyses. We must be able to understand what the data are telling us. In particular, we need to be able to identify trends in global temperature, to discern correlations and test for causation, to quantify the risks consequent on doing something or doing nothing, and then to distill this information into a cogent, logically consistent argument.

Another example comes from medicine. At one point the standard recommendation for testing for prostate cancer was to have prostate-specific antigen (PSA) assays done at regular intervals and make decisions based on changes in PSA numbers. More recently this recommendation was changed because the PSA test gave rise to a significant number of false positives, leading to unnecessary operations, with the consequence that insurance companies enacted new policies regarding when they would pay for PSA testing. The question is whether or not it would be prudent for any given man to pay out of pocket for the test (if he has the means) to try to catch a cancer as early as possible. This question is exacerbated by the fact that prostate cancer can grow very slowly; as is often pointed out, most men with prostate cancer die with it, not of it. Addressing this question requires an understanding of how data are processed, how statistical inference works, and how to quantify risks.

A final example comes from elections in the U.K. and United States, as well as the Brexit vote. In all of these instances, statements were made by both sides that incorporated logical fallacies or were based on false premises.

The tools we teach in our Formal Analyses course, including the ability to use logic to analyze statements and the ability to use concepts from statistics and the science of decision making, are essential for the electorate to make informed decisions.

The material in Formal Analyses can be found in a variety of courses at other universities, but our approach differs in crucial ways. We combine topics differently, emphasize aspects of the topics that constitute practical knowledge (in Minerva's sense), and frame the application of skills and knowledge in novel ways. At the end of the course, we expect the students to be equipped to interweave applications of game theory to a particular decision problem with statistical arguments, and then couch their analysis in a tightly reasoned logical framework. Because our goal is to improve students' ability to think critically, students not only learn how to use tools from logic, statistics, and decision theory, they also learn how to critique the use of those tools by others. For instance, a key concept emphasized throughout the course is that human biases have an impact on objectivity in analysis and decision making. Furthermore, through both the activities embedded in the Formal Analyses lessons and out-of-classroom interactions, we encourage students to question the course content itself and to recognize the limits of the applicability of the skills and knowledge they learn.

In this chapter we describe three of the central units of the Formal Analyses curriculum: analyzing arguments, evaluating evidence in the form of data, and making effective decisions in the face of risk or uncertainty. We give a brief overview of the content we emphasize and comment on some of the activities students perform to explore and practice these ideas.

Analyzing Arguments

The first major topic Minerva students encounter in Formal Analyses is the analysis of arguments—their structure, strength, uses, and abuses. This foundation supports critical thinking about all of the remaining topics not only in this course but also in the three other cornerstone courses. We focus on deductive and inductive logic. At the end of this unit, students should be able to evaluate the conclusions drawn both by themselves and by others.

Deductive logic

The goal of our study of deductive logic is to provide students with the tools to determine the validity of arguments and to recognize their soundness. Thus, students will develop a notion of "correctness" as it pertains to this type of argument—the truth of the premises guarantees the truth of the conclusion. They learn to use various formal tools to evaluate validity. Soundness can be a more difficult issue because one must know that the premises are actually true, which may require further investigation.

To understand how to use deductive logic, students learn to translate English sentences into both first- and second-order symbolic languages. Interpreting the precise meaning of complicated logical statements in natural language is one of the biggest challenges for students; careful translation into a symbolic form helps them determine the meaning or uncover inherent ambiguity in the wording of the argument (such as that caused by the colloquial use of disjunctions). Symbolic forms can also help students understand the negation of complex sentences, which may require using logically equivalent forms.

Students complete several types of exercises in the deductive logic section to practice their skills. These exercises include such typical tasks as constructing truth tables, finding logical equivalences, negating given sentences—both with and without quantifiers—and identifying the use of deductive rules.

Unlike other courses in logic, however, students are also asked to articulate implied deductive arguments in nonwritten communications. For example, if a student encounters a pictorial advertisement, he or she should be able to identify the argument that leads to the conclusion that the product or service should be bought. Furthermore, students complete tasks both inside and outside the classroom that demonstrate how deductions and validity are key components of programming languages, not just natural languages. These tasks include identifying logical inconsistencies in a given code and writing code to aid in parsing first-order symbolic statements.

In the culminating exercise of this topic, students examine arguments made by a world leader, such as those made in a speech. The goal is for students to identify where deductions are being made and then to critique them. The tools we teach students thus allow them to identify fallacious arguments—those that result from faulty reasoning (though this topic is not restricted to deduction, many fallacies occur when a valid argument is not sound).

We not only teach fallacies in formal deductive logic but also consider various informal fallacies. We find that being aware of the various informal fallacies is an aid to identifying them—and then to ameliorating them. Anecdotally, students are often amazed by the prevalence of such fallacies in political rhetoric, such as in the speeches they examine.

Inductive logic

Fallacies serve as a bridge to the next major topic, inductive logic, which has a different mechanism for evaluating how strongly premises support a conclusion. In Formal Analyses, we define inductive arguments, distinguish them from deductive arguments, and then evaluate the strength of inductive arguments from a broad perspective. This includes examining the logical entailments of inductions and studying human biases that color our conclusions.

In these lessons, students are exposed to the concepts of generalization and analogy. Although not a complete taxonomy of inductions, these two types of arguments expose students to the idea of drawing a conclusion from a sample. In the case of generalization, properties of a population are inferred from a subset of its members, whereas in the case of an analogy, properties of a sample are inferred from shared properties with another sample. For example, if we observe a small group of penguins all of which have brown feathers, we might generalize that all penguins have brown feathers. On the other hand, if we observe two species of whales that have baleens, and the first species has an average life span of fifty years, we might argue by analogy that the second species has a similar life span.

A key point that we stress to our students is that inductive conclusions are not unique in the way that deductive conclusions are. In the penguin example, we could also speculate that only penguins from a certain region have brown feathers, or draw the broader conclusion that all birds have brown feathers. This idea of multiple conclusions gives students an additional tool for discriminating between deductions and inductions.

The fact that more than one conclusion can always be drawn from an induction leads naturally to considering how one should assess the strength of such conclusions. Whereas sound deductions have necessarily true conclusions, the strength of inductive conclusions is relative to the strength of other conclusions that may be drawn from the same premises. In the penguin example, it is far more reasonable to conclude that the penguins of a certain region have brown feathers than to say with much more generality that all birds have brown feathers. Our students also often report that this conclusion is also consistent with common sense.

A related issue, which reoccurs later in the course, is the effect of human biases on coming to a conclusion. In the penguin example, why did we come to the conclusions we did, and why is it "common sense" to evaluate one conclusion as weak and one as strong? Students are exposed to the confirmation and availability biases, along with heuristics such as representativeness. They analyze inductions with these in mind in order to consider their strength. Furthermore, students are led to distinguish the conclusions drawn using Kahneman's (2011) "System 1" thinking from those drawn using his "System 2" thinking—in other words, those made with quick, automatic, "intuitive" thought (System 1) from those made after careful, deliberate, more objective analysis (System 2). We strongly advise students to prefer the latter.

Though it may be extremely difficult, if not impossible, to determine whether a strong inductive conclusion represents a truth about the world, one can determine whether a conclusion is wrong. Minerva students are shown how to examine the logical entailments of inductive arguments and to try to use such entailments to falsify conclusions. Continuing with the penguin example, we can say that if all birds have brown feathers, then any bird we encounter will have brown feathers. Thus, if we actually observe a bird without brown feathers, we have shown our conclusion to be false by *modus tollens*. This process of using evidence to make an induction and then testing results forms the backbone of the scientific method, which is further studied in the Empirical Analyses course.

Students in the Formal Analyses course practice these concepts in varied ways. In several class activities they are presented with either fictional premises or real-world observations and are then asked to draw several conclusions; then they critique the strength of these conclusions using the tools they have learned. At this point in the course we want students to develop an eye for what seems reasonable and to be alert for biases. Students are also given nonobvious but complete arguments and asked to identify whether the arguments are deductive or inductive. The point of this exercise is to determine what the burden of proof is in coming to the given conclusion.

The final activity in this topic is a student favorite. Because inductive arguments are evaluated by their strength but do not guarantee the truth of their conclusions, we ask students to debate whether or not we can ever rely on inductions. As part of this exercise, we nudge them to consider what knowledge we as humans would have without making inductions. Moreover, we emphasize that inductive conclusions always should be tentative, and often should be checked by using deductive methods. We stress that the two kinds of reasoning are frequently complementary and should be used together.

Descriptive and Inferential Statistics

The deductive and inductive approaches to inference are remarkably general. Additional formal tools may be needed, however, to analyze the strength of conclusions. In the next unit of the course, students learn and practice using tools to understand data. Minerva's Formal Analyses course covers topics in both descriptive and inferential statistics. At the end of this unit a Minerva student is able to take a real-world data set, such as a set of climate observations or business intelligence, and provide a qualitative description of its variables and their relationships based on both data visualization and quantitative tools. Furthermore, when the data are a sample representing a population, the student will be able to make accurate inferences based on sound statistical principles. Last, he or she will be able to analyze inferential conclusions reached by others, such as in a research article, and judge their strength while also understanding any limitations inherent in the methods used.

Rather than giving an exhaustive list of the statistical concepts and tools we teach, we present here a few of the key points we emphasize to help students think critically about data and statements made about them.

Descriptive statistics

For descriptive statistics, we emphasize four important tasks: detecting the appropriate measure of centrality, avoiding the post hoc ergo propter hoc fallacy, recognizing the limitations of quantitative measures of correlation, and using regression to compare the relative contributions of variables to explaining an effect. The thrust of at least the first three tasks is to avoid making unwarranted conclusions. In the case of centrality, we stress that students must consider both data type and the effects of outliers. Moreover, when trying to determine relationships between variables, we must take care not to blindly conclude causality, or to take quantities such as Pearson's r and R^2 at face value without examining other properties of the data.

To practice these concepts, students engage in a range of activities that involve both fictional and real-world data, using tools such as spreadsheets and Python. In particular, students experiment with the effects of changing variable values on various quantitative measures to learn to interpret them. Instead of performing calculations by hand, students build their own Python scripts to perform the calculations. The descriptive statistics section concludes with an open-ended project in which students find their own data and then describe the data set with the tools they have studied, taking care to avoid the pitfalls they have learned about.

Inferential statistics

For inferential statistics, students study common probability distributions and then learn to draw inferences about the parameter values of population distributions from sample statistics. We place special emphasis on both calculating and distinguishing between practical and statistical significance, along with careful interpretation of any calculated quantities and understanding the assumptions on which these calculations are based.

Evaluating statistical significance is essentially determining how likely it is that an observed difference has occurred simply by chance—an effect is statistically significant if it is unlikely to have occurred by chance. This evaluation is highly influenced by factors such as sample size, whether the sampling is done with or without replacement, whether some population parameters are known, and subjective factors such as significance levels. Minerva students learn how to set up and evaluate both one- and two-sample hypothesis tests, interpret Type I and Type II errors, and take into account the problems associated with multiple comparisons. Furthermore, students explore the use of confidence intervals as a more informative description of inferred parameter values.

The activities we use to teach this material are primarily based on problem solving. Some of these activities involve both setting up and performing significance tests for various real-world scenarios; others involve evaluating the quality of conclusions made by others when presented with an analysis of data from an experiment. Many of the specific problems have missing assumptions—to be filled in by the students—or have instructions to try different assumptions and compare the results. The goal is for students to appreciate how these changes alter the conclusions. Another effective technique is to have students design exercises for each other. This allows students not only to see analyses from a different perspective but also to explore the possible applications of statistical inference.

We consider not only statistical significance but also practical significance. Evaluating practical significance requires determining whether an effect is large enough to warrant notice or action. The point is that an effect may be statistically significant—that is, unlikely to occur as the result of chance alone—but the size of the effect could be too small to yield any practical application, or it may not be big enough to be worth the cost of application. The actual evaluation of whether an effect is considered to be practically significant is either subjective or based on complex and application-specific criteria. However, measuring effect size can be done using a formula, such as that for Cohen's d. We emphasize that a variety of formulas can be used, and a variety of substantially different measures are commonly called by the same name. We stress that students should know what they are calculating and why they are using a particular formula. Students are often asked to form and justify their own criteria for when an effect is large enough in practical scenarios with experiments, such as when a new pesticide is judged to increase crop yields, and hence farm revenues, but has costs associated with using it.

Effective Decision Making

The final major topic of the course focuses on effective decision making. Students first learn to assess risk and uncertainty. To distinguish the two, we define risk as quantifiable and uncertainty as not quantifiable. We typically quantify risk by computing or estimating the expected values of outcomes. When the risks associated with the outcomes of a decision can be identified and quantified, one can use various rational decision-making tools to find the optimal choice(s). In Formal Analyses, we focus on using decision trees and noncooperative game theory.

Furthermore, students study common biases that may affect one's ability to come to the best decision and to realize which decisions should be avoided. At the end of this unit, students are able to objectively assess the risks or uncertainties associated with the different possible outcomes of a decision—or recognize when they cannot—and apply a tool to aid in deciding on the most favorable outcome. Additionally, the students can critique the decisions of others, and when they assess these to be nonoptimal, they are able to identify factors that may have led to these decisions.

Students gain experience with these tools by applying them to both fictional and real-world scenarios. An example of such an activity is students' constructing trees to evaluate the decisions made by both sides during the Cuban missile crisis. This exercise is interesting in part because both sides may face similar sets of decisions but evaluate risks differently. Students then discuss how they might use game-theoretic techniques to model the situation, and weigh the relative merits of each tool.

Last, students learn about several cognitive biases that can undermine an objective evaluation of outcomes. These biases include narrow framing, hyperbolic discounting, the use of sunk costs, and various kinds of risk aversion, such as preferring to take the riskier choice when choosing between two alternatives that lead to net losses and preferring to take the more conservative choice when choosing between two options that have net positive expected values.

To deepen their understanding of this material, students are given scenarios and asked to evaluate decisions made by others and to identify what biases may have led to nonoptimal choices. We also ask students to make decisions under time pressure to force them to rely on Kahneman's System

1 thinking, then have them reevaluate their decisions with their peers in a longer session. Students often rely on heuristics when they have only a brief amount of time, and with this exercise they are able to see that they are more prone to the effects of the cognitive biases than when they have more time to consider the alternatives.

Conclusion

To conclude this chapter, we offer an anecdotal observation that we have made repeatedly as this course has been taught. The way of thinking developed in Formal Analyses has permeated the language of the student body. When meeting with students, it is very common to hear them remark on the existence of biases and fallacies in statements they hear and they themselves have uttered. They are able to distinguish between the different types of biases and fallacies. These ideas appear to have been absorbed and may be well on their way to becoming part of students' System 1 thinking.

Reference

Kahneman, D. (2011). *Thinking, fast and slow*. New York: Farrar, Straus and Giroux.

7 Empirical Analyses and Creative Thinking

Megan Gahl and Vicki Chandler

Minerva's Empirical Analyses cornerstone course focuses on how to apply empirical thinking and analysis creatively by taking methodology that is often implicit in science and making it explicit and broadly applicable across all fields. Class sessions address skills and knowledge that underlie problem solving, the scientific method, bias, research design, and problematic applications of the scientific method (each of which we discuss in more detail in this chapter). Because we use content to generate a context within which to practice using the skills and knowledge we teach, groups of habits of mind and foundational concepts (HCs) are strategically paired with content areas. These content areas typically are drawn from the natural sciences, illustrate the utility of the HCs, and elicit nuances of these applications.

Creativity in Empirical Analyses

Some may be surprised that the core competency associated with Empirical Analyses is thinking creatively because creativity is typically associated with artistic disciplines and scientists are often categorized as methodical and linear in their thinking. But scientists are without question creative. Devising new ways to collect data, organizing data, developing research questions to pursue, generating hypotheses, designing studies, solving problems, conducting data analyses, and interpreting the results all require creativity. Creativity is manifested in facilitating discovery, generating solutions to problems, and creating something new. Scientists regularly do all three (Dunbar, 2000; Ossola, 2014).

In Empirical Analyses we emphasize the iterative and creative aspects of empirical research and problem solving. We explicitly cultivate creativity and provide students with systematic skills and knowledge to enhance their creativity, recognize and overcome existing biases, derive novel and creative solutions to problems, and identify novel and creative problems to address. We equip students with a set of heuristics they can use to enhance their creativity, such as constructing analogies, reverse engineering, performing means-ends analysis, and developing contrarian positions. These heuristics help students grapple with any type of problem. Moreover, we teach students how to benefit from the diverse experiences represented on a research team, which often elicit creativity in approaches and solutions (Dunbar, 2000).

Self-Directed Learning

We begin Empirical Analyses by exploring the science of learning (#self-learning; see appendix A for a complete listing of HCs): we offer students a foundation of empirically tested learning techniques they can use in all their classes. Students consider the underlying principles that make specific learning techniques more or less effective for different types of material. Students then reflect on how to make their own self-directed learning more effective. We also emphasize how pedagogy at Minerva is built on effective learning principles, giving students insight into exactly why we use the active learning techniques we do and how they can best learn from engaging in class.

Problem Solving

What so often counts most in schools is the important but incomplete cognitive resource of knowledge. Fixed knowledge and algorithms are easier to teach, learn, and test than is the tangled web of processes that make up problem solving.
—Michael E. Martinez, 1998

Problem solving requires a broad set of skills and knowledge, and teaching students how to solve problems is not simple or straightforward. The central challenge is to teach students how to adapt these skills and knowledge to address specific problems. These problems can range from simple and methodical (e.g., figuring out how best to pack products into a refrigerator) to extremely complex and lacking any single best solution (e.g., solving world hunger). Our overarching approach in Empirical Analyses is to introduce skills and knowledge that facilitate a methodical and systematic approach to problem solving, which first requires identifying when a problem exists and eventually may require a novel solution. For example, figuring out how to schedule a meeting with eight busy people should not require a novel solution, but determining how best to assess students' learning might require a novel solution or a combination of existing successful solutions.

We approach the unit on problem solving in two parts: (1) characterizing a problem and (2) identifying and evaluating solutions. Individual lessons focus on acquiring specific tools for problem solving with typically two examples, one example of straightforward problem solving, to clarify the nuances of the skill or concept, and a second example in which students apply the skill or concept to a complex problem based on the Big Question for the unit.

Characterizing the problem

What is a problem? On the surface, this is a simple question, but it is often overlooked, or the problem is misidentified. Unless one has a deep grasp of the nature of the problem, the derived solution may or may not be relevant or effective. The importance of laying this groundwork before attempting to solve a problem is exemplified in a quotation often misattributed to Albert Einstein: "If I had an hour to solve a problem I'd spend 55 minutes thinking about the problem and 5 minutes thinking about solutions."

We begin with the HCs #rightproblem and #breakitdown, first focusing on ensuring that we are solving the appropriate root problem and then breaking down the problem to a tractable scale using tools such as fishbone diagrams, drill-down techniques, and the "5 Whys" (e.g., Spradlin, 2012). Characterizing the problem also depends on identifying constraints that will limit and potentially identify possible solutions and using gap analysis to ascertain the scale of the problem and whether existing solutions are sufficient (#constraints, #gapanalysis). If no existing solution exists, students then work on devising a novel solution. Students practice characterizing the problem by working with the Big Question, "How can we feed the world?," which leads to many and varied subquestions that allow students to practice identifying tractable scales and breaking down a problem.

Identifying and evaluating solutions

In some cases, the process of characterizing the problem, particularly by identifying the constraints on the solution and considering potential existing solutions (using gap analysis), leads to identification of an existing solution. In other instances a novel solution is needed, and creative approaches to solving the problem will be required. We guide students to cultivate creativity by drawing on effective methods and heuristics from across disciplines (relying on the HCs #analogies, #abstraction, #problemheuristics, and #creativeheuristics). The goal is to use these tools for creative brainstorming to identify potential solutions that may be unusual or imported from other disciplines; following this, students systematically evaluate the potential efficacy of these solutions. Students play with identifying and developing creative solutions for aspects of the Big Question, "How do we allocate water?" For example, they explore ways to reduce household water consumption in drought-prone cities in California by identifying and reverse engineering analogous solutions from the International Space Station.

Students complete this unit by developing a systematic method for solving complex problems and applying it in class and in written work. In class, students work in breakout groups role-playing consultants who have been hired to help the Mars One team solve problems related to food and water. The goal is for students to outline a systematic, step-by-step problem-solving approach to guide the Mars One team toward identifying existing and novel solutions. The discussion then broadens the scope to evaluate how one might vary the systematic approach in order to address different types of problems, leaving students with skills and knowledge that they can apply very generally.

Scientific Method

We begin our exploration of the scientific method with the vocabulary of empiricism, #epistemology, exploring the nature of knowledge and how we distinguish types of scientific knowledge. This exercise ensures that students understand the need for precise language in science. The scientific meanings of the terms *fact, theory, law*, and *hypothesis* do not always align well with the colloquial usage of these terms, which can lead to confusion. Being able to distinguish the scientific from the colloquial meanings of these terms allows students to gauge how confident scientists are in an assertion and to understand the implications of evidence.

Inductive reasoning in science

Science is an iterative process that typically begins with observations, the root of empiricism. Reliable and useful observations are made by paying attention to detail and identifying patterns, which in turn spurs curiosity and can lead to hypothesis development. Our students learn to make such observations (#observation), display patterns in data by using visualization tools (#dataviz), and consider how these patterns lead to hypotheses (#hypothesisdriven) and eventually to research studies to test those hypotheses. Students practice inductive reasoning by developing hypotheses from observational data about global warming and then fine-tuning these hypotheses as additional evidence is presented. This activity is designed to simulate the iterative process of science.

Deductive reasoning in science

Science can also be driven by deductive reasoning: overarching theories give rise to hypotheses and predictions that can be tested. Students have already studied deductive reasoning in Formal Analyses, and we draw on these skills and knowledge in the context of Big Bang theory, leading students to develop predictions from theories (#theorytesting) and to evaluate whether hypotheses are testable (#testability). We distinguish two types of testability: whether hypotheses are testable in principle (i.e., whether there are specific predictions, appropriate lines of evidence, and methods that could produce such evidence) and whether hypotheses are testable in practice (i.e., whether they are testable under the currently existing set of political, social, and technological conditions). We also teach students to assess plausibility (i.e., whether the assumptions and premises that underlie the hypothesis are coherent).

Models

We build on the scientific method by considering the uses of models in empirical analyses (#modeltypes). Students work with physical, conceptual, and computational models and identify their roles at different points in the scientific process. For example, models are often used to develop predictions, test predictions, and explore relationships among variables. We use the content area of global pandemics to address different ways that models can facilitate decision making. For example, students work with a simulation model to test predictions about whether disease containment (e.g., quarantine, minimizing potential disease transmission on public transit) or prevention (e.g., vaccination) would more effectively stem a global pandemic.

Biases

The first principle is that you must not fool yourself—and you are the easiest person to fool.
—Richard Feynman, 1997

Creative solutions are only useful if they in fact solve the relevant problem. Many studies have now documented that conclusions drawn from unaided, unsystematic human observation are often unreliable. In this unit we review the failings and biases to which humans are subject, with a focus on both identifying and potentially mitigating the effects of bias in our observations and decision making. We use the failings and successes of forensic science as a vehicle to explore the ways that emotion, vision, and cognitive function can bias our memories, perception, and ultimately our decisions. For each bias that we discuss, we provide a class demonstration so that students can experience the bias directly for themselves, and we then explore the effects of that particular bias in a forensic case study.

Our exploration of biases is rooted in cognitive science. We begin by considering the effects of memory fallibility and the advantages and trade-offs of human short-term and long-term memory, using current understanding of memory encoding and retrieval to address the problems inherent in eyewitness testimony (#memorybias). We then consider how emotions may influence decision making and affect memory (#emotionalbias), and how both top-down and bottom-up processes can focus and influence our attention and perception (#attentionperceptionbias), which in turn can bias our observations.

Decision making can also be influenced by *how* we make decisions. Thus we examine how the use of heuristics can give rise to biases (#heuristicbias) and how we may intentionally or unintentionally interpret evidence to confirm preexisting beliefs, resulting in confirmation bias (#confirmationbias). Students apply these concepts in class by considering case studies to analyze how heuristics and biases can influence a wrongful conviction. Students also debate whether the risk of confirmation bias that can result from giving forensic analysts contextual evidence outweighs the potential benefits of their having such information.

Identifying biases is only a first step. To obtain reliable knowledge and make informed decisions, we need to mitigate the biases and the potential for bias. Thus, students evaluate which forensic tools are most susceptible to bias and determine the best approaches for mitigating those biases, including both technological innovations and method modifications. In addition, students revisit the scientific method to explore at what points in the scientific process biases are most likely to occur and how such biases may be mitigated by good research study design. This discussion serves as a bridge to the next unit, on research design.

Research Design

In this unit students consider the major types of research study designs. Our overarching goals are for students to acquire the skills and knowledge they can use to evaluate studies and understand the limitations on inferences drawn from them. We emphasize the motivation for different research designs, the level of generality they confer on inferences drawn from them, and the inherent trade-offs of each approach. To explore different types of research designs, we use two content areas: how humans influence evolution and the science of aging.

Before delving deeply into specific types of research designs, we focus on the key tenets of good research design, including elements of both standard experimental and observational study design (#experimentaldesign, #observation), the types of inferences that can be drawn from each, and systematic replication and sampling (originally introduced in Formal Analyses, and specifically addressed in this course as sampling is applied in research designs). A key exercise for students is to develop criteria by which to evaluate research studies, which they subsequently iterate for each new research design that is introduced. This unit integrates aspects of the scientific method unit, the biases unit, and concepts from other cornerstone courses (e.g., the HCs #sampling and #correlation from Formal Analyses, and #levelsofanalysis and #multiplecauses from Complex Systems).

We lead students to consider the uses and potential drawbacks of a wide variety of approaches, from designs in which one cannot directly manipulate the phenomena being studied (i.e., observational studies, some types of case studies, some surveys, and most interviews) to designs with fully or partially controlled experimental conditions (i.e., true experiments, randomized controlled medical trials, and quasi-experimental designs). To gain experience with, and deep knowledge about, the advantages and limitations of each type of research design, students: (1) develop criteria with which to evaluate each type of design, (2) practice designing studies themselves, which they then critique, and (3) critique published studies and identify flaws.

To integrate their understanding of different research designs, we give students the results of one type of study and ask them to design a different type of study to test the same hypothesis, or we give students a specific problem and ask them to identify the best study design. For example, students determine which would be the most effective research method to investigate whether the Zika virus causes birth defects; they defend their choice by outlining the advantages of their chosen approach over other research methods. Students synthesize their understanding of research design by developing, administering, and analyzing the results from a survey, using peer critique and feedback at specific stages of development (e.g., hypotheses, survey design, data analysis).

Problematic Applications of the Scientific Method

At its best, empirical analyses minimize subjectivity and bias in order to help one to obtain reliable knowledge. But science is not an "inexorable march toward truth" (Gould, 1996). Beyond biases and problems in research design, sociological factors can sometimes guide science even when scientists are responsible and have the best of intentions. For example, public perception can influence what is funded, what gets published, and what research findings get attention (e.g., in the media), thereby driving scientific progress in specific directions.

Building on what has come before, we explore a range of problematic applications of the scientific method, including the underlying reasons for scientific retractions, various pseudosciences, the role of the media, and an exploration of contrarian perspectives (including evaluation of when contrarian perspectives are effective). We use scientific revolutions (i.e., when new results require a major revision or replacement of established ideas) as content throughout this unit, to lead students to practice evaluating surprising and "revolutionary" results, and we emphasize the role of skepticism in empirical analyses.

To apply and practice these skills and knowledge in class, we draw on a number of examples. For example, students learn to distinguish between scientific and pseudoscientific claims by applying their knowledge of the scientific method and data analysis to consider Blondlot's N-rays. N-rays were discovered by Blondlot shortly after the discovery of x-rays and were debunked shortly thereafter, but not before a fair number of researchers had published work on N-rays (Tretkoff, 2007). N-rays now serve as a cautionary tale to scientists to remain skeptical, even of one's own conclusions. Students evaluate whether this reported finding was an example of pseudoscience or a poor application of the scientific method (it was the latter). Students identify flaws in applications of the scientific method and learn to identify the types of flaws that would lead a study to be retracted. In addition, students compare the conclusions drawn from scientific studies in the primary literature to those reported in a popular media article that summarizes those results.

In addition, students learn that in some situations a contrarian approach might be effective, but that it is important to distinguish these from situations in which such an approach is not likely to be effective. To explore the utility of a contrarian approach specifically in science, students identify the checks that are inherent in the scientific method to ensure that a possible paradigm shift is valid.

Finally, we conclude this unit by exploring ways that our analysis of evidence can be tainted by prior beliefs. We do so by analyzing an empirical test of the efficacy of superstitions, which draws on elements of the biases, research design, and scientific method units.

Synthesis

To bring the Empirical Analyses course to completion, we lead students to synthesize what they have learned throughout the course by analyzing a case study. This case study focuses on a high-profile science paper that reported strong evidence (the authors claimed) that arsenic could be incorporated into biological molecules by microbes (Wolfe-Simon et al., 2011). Had the results of this study been valid, they would have represented a scientific revolution in theories about life and its origin on Earth, which would have strong implications for the potential for life on other planets.

This case study (modeled from a case study by Prud'homme-Généreux, n.d., from the National Center for Case Study Teaching in Science) is ripe for applying many of the Empirical Analyses HCs, as well as some HCs from other cornerstone courses. As students analyze the study's methods, potential biases, and research design and evaluate a replication of the study (Reaves et al., 2012), they recognize flaws that led the original study to be largely unsupported by the scientific community (though not yet retracted). The specific case is insightful because of the media attention and the amount of informal peer review in social media, which enable students to gain insights into how complex sociological factors can influence the progression of science or what are considered to be facts in general.

Conclusion

This long history of learning how to not fool ourselves—of having utter scientific integrity—is, I'm sorry to say, something that we haven't specifically included in any particular course that I know of. We just hope you've caught on by osmosis.
—Richard Feynman, 1997

The overarching goal of our Empirical Analyses course is to instill an appreciation for how to identify problems where creative solutions are required and how to approach producing such solutions. We use creative applications in science to illustrate this more general goal and at the same time to stress the need to maintain the highest level of integrity when addressing problems creatively. We do not hope that students have just "caught on" but instead bring the tools of scientific integrity to the forefront of the curriculum. The empirical skills and knowledge we introduce are relevant for all students, regardless of their chosen career path, because the need for creative solutions (especially in, but not limited to, science) influences so many aspects of daily life. Deciding which medical treatment will be most effective (if any), making decisions about which heuristics to use when solving problems, or identifying problems with proposed solutions to a problem—all are skills and knowledge covered in this course, and ones students are likely to employ in many facets of their lives and careers. Understanding and being able to evaluate (and know the limits of one's ability to evaluate) problems and conceive of new solutions are crucial skills for the world's next generation of problem solvers and leaders.

References

Dunbar, K. (2000). How scientists think in the real world: Implications for science education. *Journal of Applied Developmental Psychology, 21*(1), 49–58.

Feynman, R. (1997). *"Surely you're joking, Mr. Feynman!" Adventures of a curious character* (as told to R. Leighton). New York, NY: W. W. Norton.

Gould, S. J. (1996). *The mismeasure of man.* New York, NY: W. W. Norton.

Martinez, M. E. (1998). What is problem solving? *Phi Delta Kappan, 79*(8), 605–609.

Ossola, A. (2014, November 12). Scientists are more creative than you might imagine. *The Atlantic.* http://www.theatlantic.com/education/archive/2014/11/the-creative-scientist/382633

Prud'homme-Généreux, A. (n.d.). Aliens on earth? The #arseniclife affair. Buffalo, NY: National Center for Case Study Teaching in Science, University at Buffalo. http://sciencecases.lib.buffalo.edu/cs/collection/detail.asp?case_id=708&id=708

Reaves, M. L., Sinha, S., Rabinowitz, J. D., Kruglyak, L., & Redfield, R. J. (2012). Absence of detectable arsenate in DNA from arsenate-grown GFAJ-1 cells. *Science, 337*(6093), 470–473.

Spradlin, D. (2012, September). Are you solving the right problem? *Harvard Business Review*. https://hbr.org/2012/09/are-you-solving-the-right-problem

Tretkoff, E. (2007). This Month in Physics History, September 1904: Robert Wood debunks N-rays. *APS News*. https://www.aps.org/publications/apsnews/200708/history.cfm

Wolfe-Simon, F., Blum, J. S., Kulp, T. R., Gordon, G. W., Hoeft, S. E., Pett-Ridge, J., et al. (2011). A bacterium that can grow by using arsenic instead of phosphorus. *Science, 332*(6034), 1163–1166.

8 Complex Systems and Effective Interaction

James Genone and Ian Van Buskirk

It is a platitude to say that in an increasingly complex world, leaders and innovators must interact effectively with others to accomplish their goals. But what does the complexity of the contemporary world really amount to? And how exactly is this complexity relevant to effective social interaction? At Minerva, we consider a working knowledge of the answers to these questions to be an essential prerequisite to personal and professional success. That is why we devote a quarter of each student's first-year education to the study of the complex social systems in which they are embedded and to understanding the challenges and opportunities that their interactions with these systems, and with other individuals within them, provide.

The nature of complex systems has been the subject of scientific study for decades, but recent years have seen insights from biology, physics, and computer science systematically applied to analyzing human social interactions. Other universities now offer courses on this topic, but Minerva's approach is unique: Unlike other courses on complex systems, our cornerstone course Complex Systems does not focus primarily on characterizing such systems in great detail, using sophisticated mathematics to describe the ways that interactions among independent units give rise to emergent properties. We introduce the main ideas, but then quickly move on to applying this framework to human interactions. In our course we illuminate the nature of human social systems by drawing on complex systems science, along with philosophy, psychology, economics, political science, and management theory. We consider how skill in debate, negotiation, and ethical reasoning can be reframed in terms of complex systems, and how these and other skills and knowledge contribute to effective teamwork and leadership.

To begin to appreciate the utility of studying complex systems for learning how to interact effectively, we must examine the characteristics of such systems across a range of social domains. We provide an overview, and then explain how students apply their knowledge of complex systems to understanding effective social interaction.

What Are Complex Systems?

Complex systems are present almost everywhere. Classic examples include ant colonies, fish schools, bird flocks, the human brain, cities, and economies. Despite scientific consensus on salient examples, researchers and theorists have not agreed on a general description of complex systems. Often, complex systems are defined as systems composed of autonomous agents that interact with each other to produce emergent phenomena, independent of centralized coordination or control. Emergent phenomena are collective properties of systems that cannot be understood simply by examining the behavior of individual units or subgroups in the system (Mitchell, 2011). For example, ant colonies are composed of thousands of ants that communicate with each other in such a way that the colony can divide tasks, build structures, and coordinate reactions to predators. An individual ant can do none of these things, but through the interactions of many ants, the colony can.

Complex systems are often contrasted with simple and "merely complicated" systems, but the distinction is not always obvious. A car is complicated, not complex. It might seem at first that vehicular motion could be considered an emergent phenomenon, the result of the interactions among the many mechanical parts that make up a car, but this is not the case. As long as environmental effects are negligible, knowing how each individual part is operating, from the pistons to the carburetor, reveals the overall functioning of the vehicle and explains its motion. In complex systems, by contrast, the behavior of components cannot be isolated and aggregated to realize the collective behavior. Knowing the states of all the neurons in someone's brain does not tell us—at least not with present-day understanding—what that person is experiencing (O'Connor, 1994). Knowing the position and velocity of each bird in a flock does not allow us to know where the flock will move next (Ballerini et al., 2008). Predicting emergent phenomena in a complex system based solely on individual behavior may be possible in some cases, but in most cases we cannot at present make such predictions with precision and confidence.

Complex social systems

Social systems present a wide range of cases in which predicting collective behavior, as well as understanding the connection between individuals and the collective, has far-reaching implications. For example, decisions made in social systems are often intended to bring about change in the system as a whole, but rarely can system-level properties be manipulated directly. Instead, decisions affect individual agents in the system, which then affect the entire system. For instance, policy makers may decide to increase the size of a highway in the hope of reducing traffic congestion. But complexity makes it difficult to gauge exactly how interventions at one level of analysis will affect properties at another level. It may turn out that increasing the number of lanes actually worsens congestion (perhaps because it results in a disproportionate increase in the number of drivers selecting that route) and that a different intervention, such as decreasing the speed limit, would alleviate the issue more effectively (Chen, 1998).

Moreover, although it can be useful to study complex social systems in isolation, ultimately they must be understood in relation to other systems. For example, transportation systems affect and are affected by economic systems, and both in turn interact with systems of government and law. Cities are particularly salient systems of systems that, to be fully appreciated, must be examined with complexity in mind. At their core, cities are systems of people. Despite the presence of some highly influential people (e.g., the mayor, business executives, celebrities), the overall behavior of cities is ultimately leaderless and largely shaped by layers of localized interactions. For example, the mayor and the city council may attempt to use zoning laws and tax incentives to attract businesses to a neighborhood. Ultimately, however, it is the decisions of individual business owners and consumers—along with the effects of those decisions—that determine whether a particular shopping district is successful. The identity of a city is not prescribed but rather results from how individuals share ideas, make new connections, move around, buy goods, exchange services, and learn from each other.

Networks and emergent properties

Networks are the means by which people interact in cities, and in groups more generally, and the structure of these networks constrains what interactions are possible. For example, city size has a significant influence on how connected people are with others; higher population density in a city leads to more social interaction per person, which can lead to more innovation and wealth but also to increased rates of disease and crime (Bettencourt et al., 2007).

Such network effects cause feedback loops by which a system's outputs influence the functioning of the system itself. For instance, technological innovation allows more people to live in a city, and this increased population density results in more innovation and faster technological advance. To improve cities, and social interaction more generally, we need to understand how networks can be manipulated to preserve positive interactions (e.g., idea and wealth generation) and curb negative interactions (e.g., disease transmission and violence).

Viewing the identity of a city as a collection of overlapping complex systems can bring clarity to seemingly intractable issues. The clustering of people in a city to form diverse neighborhoods is often seen as unique to that particular city's geography, legislation, and history. However, an alternative approach, one based on an understanding of complex systems, involves focusing on only a few simple rules for how people decide where to live. These rules of interaction alone allow us to predict patterns of settlement and segregation that mirror what we see in the real world (Schelling, 1971). This process exemplifies the power of cities to self-organize: unorchestrated, often simple interactions among individuals lead to the appearance of coordination and order in the system. More generally, this property of distributed decision making is what can make cities, and many other complex systems, highly adaptive and resilient to changes.

Cities are particularly relevant examples of complex social systems because of the central role they play in defining and addressing the world's most pressing challenges. Cities are in turn parts of even larger systems of states and nations that interact on a global scale. A complex systems framework can be usefully applied to analyzing international relations and military conflicts (Green, 2011). For example, this framework has been used to show that asymmetric information, overconfidence, and loss aversion can be amplified by network effects and feedback and as a result make conflict between nations more likely, even when both sides agree that this outcome is best avoided (Jackson & Morelli, 2011).

Levels of analysis

Viewing interactions through the lens of complex systems is also useful on a personal level. Our daily interactions with friends, co-workers, and strangers are greatly shaped by the systems in which we interact. To improve these interactions, we must recognize that these are complex systems, and begin to untangle the web of individual and system behavior. A commonly discussed example is the interaction among members of collaborative teams. Intuitively, the most effective teams are those with the most effective members, but this is often not the case. Teams with members who possess diverse perspectives and skill sets often outperform teams with members of higher average ability but a narrower range of approaches to their work (Page, 2007).

By studying a range of complex social systems at different scales, we can recognize patterns of repeated behavior and the conditions under which the dynamics of social systems undergo significant qualitative shifts. Rioting behavior provides an illuminating example of this phenomenon: in a group of peaceful protestors, each individual can be understood as having a specific threshold for joining a riot based on the proportion of other protesters who are rioting (Granovetter, 1978). To manage such situations, political leaders and law enforcement personnel must understand where these thresholds tend to lie based on the composition of a crowd.

These examples illustrate how each of us is embedded in multiple layers of overlapping complex social systems and how the characteristics of these systems affect our behavior and the decisions we make. With this background in mind, we now turn to describing how we teach students to use their knowledge of complex systems to understand the systems they belong to and improve their interactions within them.

How We Teach Complex Systems

The overarching aim of our course on complex systems is to lead our students to learn how to interact with individuals within particular systems and to interact with systems themselves. With this goal in mind, we organize the Complex Systems course so that after learning about how complex systems function, students learn to identify the relevant characteristics of complex systems in a diverse range of social situations. The characteristics of complex systems serve as foundational concepts for the course, and we devote considerable time to them. Through this study, students develop an approach to analyzing complex systems that they can apply to understanding and determining how to interact within a variety of social systems.

By learning to view everyday social systems as complex systems, students can better formulate research questions about them and pursue these questions through scientific study and modeling. This illustrates one of the many examples of interleaving throughout the cornerstone courses: in this case, students draw on skills in problem solving, experimental research, statistical reasoning, and programming that they learn in the Empirical Analyses and Formal Analyses cornerstone courses.

Decomposing systems

Students begin by learning to identify the primary components and sub-components of a system and to frame such decompositions of systems in ways that are relevant to the behaviors they wish to understand or predict (#multipleagents). These decompositions must be made at multiple levels of analysis (#levelsofanalysis), accounting both for the most relevant groups within the system and for the individuals who make up those groups.

Students often compare different ways of breaking down the same group of individuals to evaluate which way is best suited to their purposes. For example, if a student is trying to understand the dynamics of a large corporation, he or she might analyze it along the lines of different departments or teams (product, sales, marketing, human resources) or by considering groups that cut across these teams (e.g., all employees, regardless of department or team, who are responsible for a particular product). Depending on the student's interests and aims, one of the approaches may prove more useful than others. As students repeatedly apply this technique as a first step toward understanding a system, it becomes second nature for them to approach a new system by identifying alternative ways to break it down.

Identifying emergent properties

The next major task is to identify the emergent properties that are of interest in a system, and to determine the interactions among components of the system that give rise to these properties (#emergentproperties). In the example of the corporation, a student may wish to understand why the business is consistently able to innovate at a more rapid pace than its competitors. To do so, the student must determine which individual and group interactions within the corporation give rise to innovation. This effort leads students to distinguish between *explanatory* analyses of a system (Hedström, 2006), in which one analyzes a system to discover the interactions that produce emergent properties, and *predictive* analyses, in which this understanding is used to identify possible future behaviors of the system under different conditions (Epstein, 1999).

We introduce a variety of skills and knowledge intended to help students understand emergent properties. Students may examine the network connections among individuals and groups in the system to understand better how they provide opportunities and constraints on how information travels within that system (#networks). They may also perform causal analyses to determine the primary causes of specific behaviors in the system and the secondary and tertiary effects of these causes (#multiplecauses). As noted earlier, feedback loops are often a primary driver of emergent phenomena in a system. For example, if a corporation is set up so that teams that repeatedly produce innovations are given additional resources, this may lead to increased innovation—or the opposite, depending on the structure and mechanisms of the relevant feedback loops.

System dynamics

Students also consider how behavior in a system changes over time (#systemdynamics). For example, although a company may innovate during certain market cycles, a student may wish to understand how particular political or economic events can lead the system to behave differently. Here students begin to notice patterns of behavior—in dynamical systems theory, these are known as "attractors"—that may prevail when certain sets of conditions are satisfied. Identifying both these conditions and the events that may result in a shift from one pattern of behavior to another is a key component of understanding how complex systems can adapt—or fail to do so—as conditions change.

Addressing aspects of interactions

Once students have become familiar with the process of analyzing social systems, we continue our examination of the characteristics of complex systems by introducing additional skills and knowledge that are relevant to understanding and engaging in social interactions. Our aim is to build on the framework of complex systems to give students additional ways to use this framework to understand and predict the behavior of individuals and groups. But more than that, we want to give students skills and knowledge they can use to determine what kinds of interventions in the system might help realize particular goals. These skills and knowledge include recognizing factors such as utility and motivation, which govern people's behavior and decision making; identifying ethical issues that arise in social interactions; learning how to debate and negotiate; and studying the practices of effective teams and leaders.

Individual and group psychology are central to applying the complex systems approach to social systems. Thus, we study traditional economic theories of decision making, as well as theories from behavioral economics that explore the impact of biases on decision making (#utility). Students discuss the difference between what a "fully rational" agent would be expected to do in a particular situation and how behavior can be affected by framing a situation differently (e.g., as a potential loss as opposed to a potential gain).

We also consider how stated goals may not fully reflect what drives the behavior of certain stakeholders (#motivation). Skill in detecting motivations requires emotional intelligence, and we teach our students the importance of recognizing the emotions that influence behavior in a system, both for individuals and for groups (#emotionaliq).

Understanding the causes and outcomes of behavior, however, is not sufficient for determining appropriate responses to the challenges that arise in systems. In social systems these challenges typically also have an ethical dimension (#fairness). Students must analyze whether unfair practices or distributions of resources exist in a system and determine what kinds of interventions might correct these imbalances. To this end, we introduce ethical theories for comparing different possible resolutions and teach students to balance and prioritize competing ethical principles according to relevant contextual factors in a given situation (#ethicalframeworks and #ethicalconflicts).

Students apply these tools for analyzing complex social systems by addressing some of the major challenges facing societies today. Their assignments are organized around a set of "Big Questions," including "Why do people commit crimes?," "How can we feed the world?," and "Can war be avoided?" By applying the complex systems framework to specific problems in these domains, students become familiar with how this approach can be used to deepen their understanding of a diverse range of social problems.

Students then turn to studying how to use this knowledge to make their own interactions in complex social systems more effective. We begin by studying how to change the behavior of groups and individuals through the use of incentives and disincentives (#carrotandstick), and then provide students with opportunities to develop skills in debate and negotiation (e.g., #strategize, #negotiate). Students practice these skills by examining some of the most pressing social and political challenges facing the world today, including religious freedom, education reform, immigration, environmental regulation, and health care. In addition to structured debates and simulated negotiations, students also write strategic plans and policy proposals; they specify in detail how to approach a debate or negotiation related to one of the social or political issues they examine. Students practice formulating arguments and counterarguments, and also work to identify common ground among stakeholders in a disagreement, determine points of leverage in negotiations, identify alternatives to negotiated agreements, and develop tactics for influencing the way parties perceive the terms of a dispute.

In all these cases, students attempt to anticipate the consequences of interventions using tools from the study of complex systems. For example, they consider how feedback loops in a debate can lead to the emergent property of both sides taking new perspectives that were not previously anticipated. The relationship between individual behavior and collective behavior remains a focus, informing investigations such as how the effectiveness of various incentives change as a result of interpersonal and group interactions.

Leadership and teamwork

The course then turns to an extended examination of leadership and teamwork. As they do throughout the course, students use the skills and concepts they have acquired for analyzing complex systems to understand how successful leaders and teams reach their goals and confront the problems they face. This understanding includes both analyzing the practices that effective leaders use to motivate and inspire those they lead (#leadprinciples) and identifying the characteristics of teams that work well together (e.g., #powerdynamics, #differences, #teamroles). Students learn to understand the importance of diversity of knowledge and skills in group endeavors and how teams can be organized in ways that distribute authority and decision making so that they can adapt to evolving conditions and challenges (#orgstructure). We examine the role of complexity by analyzing these factors through the lens of individual and group interactions and the properties that emerge from these interactions.

The course concludes with an exercise in self-examination, during which students are asked how they can learn to monitor their own knowledge and understand better what information they are missing (#metaknowledge) regarding both the tasks they have undertaken and their own abilities (#selfappraisal). They consider how to avoid blindly conforming to external expectations (#conformity) and how to be proactive and take responsibility for the results of their actions (#responsibility). Students come to see themselves not as mere cogs in the complex systems in which they exist but rather as agents whose behavior and initiative have the power to change these systems, potentially in far-reaching and beneficial ways.

Conclusion

When we consider the skills and knowledge that students can attain during their undergraduate education, it is easy to underestimate the importance of learning how to interact effectively with others. Some may assume that students will learn to do so in the course of their future careers, or that it is an innate ability that need not be taught explicitly. We disagree: interaction in social systems can be improved by understanding these systems and by learning and practicing the skills that allow one to influence them. The extent to which students can improve their social interactions will have a considerable impact on their future lives and careers.

The habits of skilled leaders and change agents are often straightforward to describe, as evidenced by countless management books, but can be very difficult to learn. Minerva's Complex Systems course combines two unique approaches to this challenge: a sophisticated analytical framework for understanding social interaction, provided by the study of complex systems, and the practice of active learning, in which students apply skills and knowledge to practical problems rather than simply engaging in theoretical study.

Framing social systems as complex systems represents a new way of looking at the world, one that fundamentally changes the way we analyze and interpret the behavior we observe. This perspective leads to new insights into how different systems interact with each other and teaches students that examining the interactions among systems is an essential step in analyzing their functioning. Armed with an understanding of the characteristics of complex systems, students can begin to explain and predict their behavior and determine how to respond appropriately in order to accomplish their aims. By the end of the course, students should be able to produce realistic analyses of social systems that avoid oversimplification and to formulate possible interventions that would make these systems function better. Ultimately, we aspire to help our students make informed and well-reasoned decisions about how to engage with individuals and with social systems, both by teaching them humility in the face of the challenges involved in predicting the behavior of others and by providing them with the tools to recognize how their own behavior can influence systems for the good.

Acknowledgments

Many thanks to Josh Fost for his guidance through the literature on complex systems, numerous illuminating conversations on the nature of complexity, and feedback on a draft of this chapter.

References

Ballerini, M., Cabibbo, N., Candelier, R., Cavagna, A., Cisbani, E., Giardina, I., et al. (2008). Empirical investigation of starling flocks: A benchmark study in collective animal behaviour. *Animal Behaviour, 76*(1), 201–215.

Bettencourt, L. M., Lobo, J., Helbing, D., Kühnert, C., & West, G. B. (2007). Growth, innovation, scaling, and the pace of life in cities. *Proceedings of the National Academy of Sciences of the United States of America, 104*(17), 7301–7306.

Chen, D. D. (1998). If you build it, they will come ... Why we can't build ourselves out of congestion. *Surface Transportation Public Policy (STPP). Progress, 7*(2), 4–6.

Epstein, J. M. (1999). Agent-based computational models and generative social science. *Complexity, 4*(5), 41–60.

Granovetter, M. (1978). Threshold models of collective behavior. *American Journal of Sociology, 83*(6), 1420–1443.

Green, K. L. (2011, May). *Complex adaptive systems in military analysis.* IDA Document D-4313. Alexandria, VA: Institute for Defense Analyses. https://www.ida.org/idamedia/Corporate/Files/Publications/IDA_Documents/JAWD/ida-document-d-4313.pdf

Hedström, P. (2006). Explaining social change: An analytical approach. *Papers. Revista de Sociologia, 80*, 73–95.

Jackson, M., & Morelli, M. (2011). The reasons for wars: An updated survey. In C. Coyne & R. Mathers (Eds.), *The handbook on the political economy of war* (pp. 34–57). Northampton, MA: Elgar Publishing.

Mitchell, M. (2011). *Complexity: A guided tour.* Oxford, UK: Oxford University Press.

O'Connor, T. (1994). Emergent properties. *American Philosophical Quarterly, 31*(2), 91–104.

Page, S. (2007). Making the difference: Applying a logic of diversity. *Academy of Management Perspectives, 21*(4), 6–20.

Schelling, T. (1971). Dynamic models of segregation. *Journal of Mathematical Sociology, 1*(2), 143–186.

9 A New Look at Majors and Concentrations

Vicki Chandler, Stephen M. Kosslyn, and James Genone

In formulating Minerva's majors and concentrations, we were faced with both a unique opportunity and an enormous challenge: starting with a blank page, we had to design a curriculum from scratch. This required us to step back and ask a simple question: What will students need to succeed in their chosen fields? We have spent years working on the answer, and probably will do so for years to come. This chapter represents a progress report and an outline of where we are going in the near future.

Specifically, we have rethought the course of study for a bachelor's degree, using the core principles outlined in chapter 3: content should not be the focus,[1] the curriculum must be structured, courses should be seminal, and students need information and guidance to make wise choices. Starting with a clean slate and free of traditional departmental structures, we have addressed the question of how to design highly structured but flexible interdisciplinary courses of study in the liberal arts and sciences.

This chapter describes the philosophy, structure, and content of the curriculum for a bachelor's degree in one or more of Minerva's five colleges: Arts and Humanities, Business, Computational Sciences, Natural Sciences, and Social Sciences.

Rationale for Design

We began by asking what sorts of practical knowledge (in Minerva's sense of the term—see chapter 2) are needed to succeed in a globalized, ever-changing world. The answer to this question became the primary motivation for what we teach our students in their first year. However, although we believe that the habits of mind and foundational concepts (HCs) we introduce during the first year are essential, we also recognize that what students study in the first year is not sufficient. The curriculum needs to lead students to apply their nascent understanding of such practical knowledge to their chosen fields of study. In addition, students need to expand their foundational concepts and skills within their fields of interest. We strive to achieve these goals in our upper-level curriculum—in particular, our major core and concentration courses.

We also spent an enormous amount of time addressing another question: How should we balance breadth versus depth? Our students need breadth—which is a hallmark of a liberal arts education—and this breadth needs to be interdisciplinary, crossing traditional departmental and college boundaries. They also need enough depth to be effective in their chosen disciplines.

We recognized that our students would need certain knowledge and skills in order to be competitive with students from other institutions that offer more traditional degrees. Although it is true that we live in an information age, and it is straightforward to look up a staggering amount of information, one still must know enough to determine what is useful in a particular domain and to be able to discriminate valid, relevant information from extraneous and sometimes false information in a specific field. Moreover, certain skills and knowledge are needed in particular fields, and students must demonstrate proficiency in those areas on a transcript (and in practice). Some examples of such necessary skills and knowledge include math proficiency for graduate training in physics, chemistry, engineering, and biology; knowing how data are obtained and analyzed to generate testable hypotheses in the social sciences and natural sciences; and understanding the analytic conventions and research methods in the arts and literature, philosophy, and history.

When designing our upper-level curriculum, we soon realized that the crucial question came down to what constituted an appropriate balance between breadth and depth: We define an appropriate balance as requiring us to expand the students' knowledge and skills within specific fields and to cover the usual bases that are necessary to make students competitive. In what follows, we describe how we defined breadth and depth.

Providing Breadth

Minerva begins to provide breadth from the start of the student's undergraduate career. As noted previously (chapters 4–8), in our four first-year cornerstone courses we use content from numerous fields to introduce the HCs that underlie the four core competencies: critical thinking, creative thinking, effective interaction, and effective communication. We build on this breadth in several ways in our upper-division courses: First, the major core courses within each college expose students to a range of subfields within that general field. Second, we encourage students to pursue double majors or to take minors. Third, breadth requirements ensure that all students take courses outside their primary college.

Major core courses

The major core courses within each college are designed to orient students to a general field. However, the major core courses are not introductory; they are foundational. As such, they are inherently interdisciplinary and teach fundamental knowledge and skills in the context of specific issues and problems. The major core courses are prerequisites for taking the more advanced concentration courses.

For example, all students majoring in the natural sciences are required to take all three of the natural sciences major core courses so that they are exposed to the scope of the natural sciences and the diversity of approaches used across disciplines. These three major core courses address topics that range from the infinitesimally small (particles, atoms, molecules), to larger entities (cells and organisms), to very large entities (namely, Earth's systems). Summaries of these three major core courses follow (these summaries are taken directly from our course catalog):

NS110 Theory and Applications of Physical Interactions. Explore real-world applications of physical principles using mathematical concepts and techniques, and address qualitative and quantitative problem solving.

NS111 Implications of Earth's Cycles. Explore the origin, chemistry and role of carbon, water, silicates, and metals on Earth. Discover in depth the interplay of living systems (including humans) and Earth's systems and how expanding sensor technologies are changing the way we investigate our earth.

NS112 Evolution across Multiple Scales. Evolution is the unifying principle of all biological processes. Explore in detail how the fundamental processes within cells, individuals, and ecological communities are explained by the basic mechanisms of evolutionary change, including mutation, natural selection, and genetic drift. Discover how the latest technologies are revealing the interconnectedness of all living systems.

Similarly, in computational sciences the three major core courses are designed to address events at different levels of scale, as follows (these summaries also are taken directly from our course catalog):

CS110 Computation: Solving Problems with Algorithms. Apply core concepts in design and analysis of algorithms, data structures, and computational problem-solving techniques to address complex problems. Hashing, searching, sorting, graph algorithms, dynamic programming, greedy algorithms, divide and conquer, backtracking, random number generation, and randomized algorithms are examples of algorithms you will learn to exploit to solve problems ranging from logistics to route optimization to robotic arm control.

CS111 Structure: Mathematical and Computational Models. Use a range of mathematical and computational models to address complex problems. This course covers at a high level the core concepts central to modern mathematical and computational research: set theory, combinatorics, probability, graph theory, and differential equations, as well as modeling methods such as Monte Carlo techniques, and agent-based modeling. Topics are chosen from diverse fields, including food webs, industrial optimization, and voting—which shows the versatility and usefulness of concepts that may at first appear entirely theoretical.

CS112 Knowledge: Information-Based Decisions. Learn how to extract meaning from data using modern approaches such as Bayesian inference. Armed with this information, apply the tools of decision science to solve a wide range of problems. The course focuses primarily on applying statistical inference and formal models of decision making to design practical solutions. Students frame and quantify a range of scenarios to address real problems in the life sciences, energy, and technology industries. Discover how to make big strategic decisions with math, statistics, and simulation.

As should be clear from these course descriptions, the major core courses are broad, and serve to orient students to large swaths of a field.

Majors

Each of our five colleges has a single major, and the courses in the major are organized to ensure breadth. Typically, the upper-division advanced (i.e., concentration) courses address phenomena at different levels of scale, just as the major core courses do. In fact, in most majors each major core course provides the foundations for three more specific, advanced courses. In addition, these advanced courses are cross-organized by emphasis. Typically, courses are organized as focusing primarily on theory, on empirical findings, or on applications. Our majors require students to have breadth.

We have ensured breadth not only by including a wide range of topics within each major but also by enabling students easily to pursue a double major, a major in one college and a minor in another, or to take more than one concentration (three related courses) within a college. All of these combinations expand the interdisciplinarity of their studies.

Breadth requirement

We also ensure breadth by requiring students to take courses outside their major. For example, students who take a single major have ten electives, at least half of which must be taken from a college different from their major. At Minerva we have a novel model for electives: a requirement for one student is an elective for another. That is, no courses exist that function solely as electives, and therefore every course a student takes at Minerva is seminal (see chapter 3). Thus students who take a single major can achieve their breadth requirement by taking courses designated as major core courses in other majors or advanced courses in other majors. Students who wish to take an advanced course outside their major college must take the required major core course as a prerequisite, ensuring further breadth.

If students choose to pursue a double major in two colleges or a major in one college and a minor in another, this will reduce the number of electives they can take; they will instead take the specified major core and advanced courses for their additional major or minor. Students who pursue either a double major or a minor automatically receive breadth because they take multiple courses from at least two, if not more, colleges.

Providing Depth

Our approach to providing depth is unique. In part, depth is ensured by requiring students to focus on concentrations within the major. But more than that, the curriculum requires them to devise a capstone project and take senior tutorials—both of which lead our students to dig deeper into their areas of interest.

Concentrations

Each major has nine advanced courses, which can be taken only after taking the respective major core prerequisite course (or set of courses, in the business major). These courses are arranged in a three-by-three matrix. A concentration within a major consists of a row or a column in the matrix. We had to make strategic decisions about what concentration themes would be offered and the nature of the courses within each concentration. Using the principles outlined in chapter 3 (reviewed below), each college generated a rationale for the rows and the columns to meet the needs of students majoring in that college. For example, table 9.1 shows the matrix for social sciences. The rows correspond to different levels of scale and the columns focus on theory, data, and applications.

The subjects covered in the three rows increase in scale. The first row, Cognition, Brain and Behavior, focuses on the scale of individual

Table 9.1
Social Science Concentrations (rows and columns)

	Theory and Analysis in the Social Sciences	Empirical Approaches to the Social Sciences	Designing Societies
Cognition, Brain and Behavior	SS142 / Theories of Cognition and Emotion	SS152 / Cognitive Neuroscience	SS162 / Personal and Social Motivation
Economics and Society	SS144 / Economic Theory and Tools	SS154 / Econometrics and Economic Systems	SS164 / Global Development and Applied Economics
Politics, Government and Society	SS146 / Constructing Theories of Good Government	SS156 / World Political Systems in Practice	SS166 / Designing Constitutions

neurobiological and mental functions as the basis of behavior, with much of the emphasis on the brain and psychology. The middle row, Economics and Society, focuses on a more macro level at which patterns of group behavior are considered, with the emphasis on economics. The bottom row, Politics, Government and Society, focuses on an even more macro level, addressing the institutions and laws that shape societies, with the emphasis on political science. The columns range from more fundamental approaches (Theory and Analysis) to the most applied approaches (Designing Societies). Depending on a student's interest, he or she would pursue one or two concentrations (rows or columns), or pursue one concentration and take other courses as electives.

All of the concentration matrices have four characteristics in common. First, the courses provide additional depth to subjects that were put in a broader context in a major core (or the set of major cores, in the business major). Second, the three courses in each row and in each column form a coherent set, allowing students to focus on a specific area. Third, we selected the courses to ensure that students learn appropriate disciplinary knowledge, which will allow them to compete with traditionally trained students in the next stages of their careers, whether it is further study in graduate school or working in government or in private industry. Finally, the courses in each concentration complement each other but can be taken in any order. Thus a student who has taken the major core prerequisite(s) can take a concentration course from any column or row, in any order. This ensures that students can fulfill their concentration requirements or electives even if not every course is offered both semesters of each year, provided that each course is offered every year.

Capstone

The bulk of the major core and concentration courses are typically taken during the student's second and third years, respectively. During their third year our students also begin working on their capstone project, which is a research or creative project based on their own ideas. Capstone projects can range from devising a business plan for a startup, to a laboratory research study, to writing a play or creating an art installation. All projects, however, must be described and analyzed in a substantial written document. We set very high standards for this project: we want our students to contribute something new to their chosen field, and the methods must meet professional standards.

To begin this project, students will take a two-unit capstone class each semester of their third year. During the first semester we want the students to cast their nets widely, to take a step back and consider big, important questions they might want to address. To lead them to do this, we pair each student with another student who has a different major and ask them to identify "open questions" that are worthy of being addressed. Following this, they will develop hypotheses about answers to these questions, and then devise ways to test those hypotheses. This process involves multiple iterations and critiques from their professor and other students.

During the second semester of this capstone course we want the students to focus and ultimately produce a proposal for their independent research project. Students will begin by drafting a preliminary proposal, which may or may not be related to the open questions they considered during the first semester. Students circulate that proposal before the first day of class and then briefly present it in class. These proposals are critiqued by their professor and other students. This process involves multiple iterations of revising the proposal and then considering critiques, and culminates in a clear and compelling proposal.

The student must then find an advisor on the Minerva faculty. If the Minerva advisor is not a content expert in the student's chosen field, the student must also find and recruit an expert in that subject to serve as a mentor. In such cases, students will complete their capstone project under the guidance of both their Minerva advisor and their mentor during their senior year.

We plan to require all students to present their final capstone project to their peers, faculty, and other experts during a month-long session we call Manifest at the end of their senior year. The capstone project provides a means for students to deepen their knowledge and skills within their chosen field.

Senior tutorials and practica

Senior tutorials are designed to provide Minerva students with depth in specific subjects chosen by the students themselves. We intend these seminars to allow students to focus narrowly on topics of interest. At the end of their third year, students will submit four topics of interest that are related to their majors and concentration(s), and we will group three students with overlapping interests with an appropriate professor. The four of them then will take two weeks to design the syllabus together, and then the students take the class. The structure of these classes is modeled on the Oxford tutorial (or, at Cambridge, supervision); in our case, up to three students supplement their weekly readings and assignments with guidance, defense, and synthesis directly with an expert faculty member. Because we require these topics to build on the student's major(s), these tutorials provide greater depth in specific areas and ensure that our students are at least as well prepared in their chosen area of study as are students from traditional universities; this will serve them in good stead if they apply for postgraduate studies.

For students who have a single major, their senior year will consist of the capstone project, finishing their electives (chosen from major core and concentration courses), and two senior tutorials. Two tutorials are required per major, so that students who are pursuing a double major will have fewer electives and two additional senior tutorials. The minor does not require senior tutorials.

In the Business College, instead of tutorials the students participate in a practicum. This practicum requires students to apply the material they learned in their major core and concentration courses to a work environment. The students analyze their applications of the HCs and learning outcomes from upper-division courses to a real-world work setting and produce a substantial paper that is graded by a Minerva faculty member.

Working within Constraints

We have structured the curriculum to establish an appropriate balance between breadth and depth. To ensure that we were on the right track, we returned to the design criteria that guided us and checked to determine whether we had respected them. Using the natural sciences major as an example, we briefly illustrate how all of the design criteria outlined in chapter 3 were met as we balanced breadth versus depth.

Content should not be the sole focus

Practical knowledge lies at the heart of every one of our majors. One of our core goals is to give students the skills and knowledge they need to adapt to a changing world. We do this both by reinforcing the HCs that are introduced during the first-year cornerstone courses and by introducing new, field-specific practical knowledge in all of our courses. In addition, every one of the majors has an applied concentration (a column in the matrix), and three of the other concentrations (rows in the matrix) include one applied course.

Moreover, students receive two grades in every one of our upper-division courses, one on the content of the course and one on their ability to apply the HCs to the material. This second grade is used to adjust the grade they received at the end of the first year, up or down, as appropriate (see chapter 17). To ensure that the content introduced in the course is also practicable, we formulate course-specific learning outcomes (on which students are assessed) for upper-division courses; these learning outcomes describe transferable skills and specify knowledge that should be acquired in the course.

The curriculum must be structured

As is evident, we have structured the curriculum at multiple levels of scale, from the overall majors to the prerequisite material in the major core courses to the six different concentrations that characterize every three-by-three matrix of courses within the major. Moreover, the capstone project and senior tutorials add another layer of structure, now mixed with free choice.

Courses should be seminal

Our courses are intended to be springboards to further inquiry and study. Consider, for example our courses in science. A quick look at colleges of science and other associated colleges, such as environmental and agricultural sciences, at institutions around the world reveals numerous majors and specialties that students can pursue, ranging from fundamental discovery science to many applied fields. With twelve courses and no laboratories, how can we train the scientific leaders of the future? We do so in large part by ensuring that our courses are seminal: that they are in fact springboards and invitations, steps to many other fields and discoveries. We achieve this goal by ensuring that our major core and concentration courses rely on broad interdisciplinary approaches, the type of approaches required to address the challenging questions facing our world. The goal is to help students master the fundamental physics, chemistry, biology, and Earth systems knowledge and skills so that they can go in any direction of interest.

Moreover, every course is designed by continuously asking how fundamental the skill or knowledge is, and whether students could learn the topic in the future by applying the skills and knowledge they are learning at Minerva. As one example, we don't offer a course that solely addresses neurobiology. Yet because the courses we do offer are seminal, our students can pursue this field in a number of ways. They can take the cells and organisms concentration to learn fundamental genetics, biochemistry, and bioengineering, which they can then apply to neurobiology. If they are interested in molecular neurobiology, they can also take more molecularly oriented courses from the molecules and atoms concentration. If instead they are interested in neuroscience more broadly, they can pursue a double major, a minor, or take electives from the cognition, brain and behavior concentration in social sciences. If they are interested in computational neurobiology, they can pursue a double major, a minor, or take electives from computational sciences. In all cases they would pursue their neurobiology interests in their capstone and senior tutorials. As noted below, they would also be encouraged to do at least one summer research experience at another institution in neuroscience.

Students need information and guidance to make wise choices
We have structured the curriculum in part to ensure that students know what they would be getting into by taking specific courses. As noted earlier, the cornerstone courses use a wide range of content to illustrate the HCs. We treat such courses as "samplers" that allow students to learn something about various fields that may or may not be inviting to them. We then build on that content in the major core courses, which in turn lead down specific paths within the major.

We provide students with insight into the content of each upper-division course by organizing the learning outcomes we assess under several course objectives, which serve as high-level descriptions of what students will learn by taking the course. Table 9.2 shows course objectives and learning outcomes (each of which has a hashtag label) for NS111: Implications of Earth's Cycles.

Table 9.2

Implications of Earth's Cycles: Course Objectives and Learning Outcomes

Learn the science of systems operating at distinct scales in time and space, and how feedback and energy sources produce system states that are stable but far from equilibrium.

- #feedback: Analyze examples of positive and negative feedback in the Earth system, perturbations to such feedback, and their implications.
- #scale: Be able to determine scale, considering both time and space, and the placement of human civilization appropriately within that scale.
- #systemsthinking: Distinguish between a reductionist approach to the world and a "systems thinking" approach.

Explain the scientific narrative that includes the formation of Earth and its place in the Universe.

- #Earthdifferentiation: Explain how the Earth progressed from a homogenous mixture of rock and metal to a layered planet, including concepts of immiscibility and partial melting.
- #ageandcomposition: Analyze appropriate methods to determine age and/or composition of components in the Universe, including stars, Earth, and other planetary bodies.
- #elementstominerals: Explain the different modes of element formation, how elements combine to form molecules and minerals, and how their properties affect planetary construction and/or functioning.
- #solarsystemformation: Explain the general model for solar system formation and the supporting evidence.

Learn the major cycles on Earth and how they support Earth's systems.

- #climateregulation: Explain both the natural controls that act to stabilize Earth's climate and the natural causes of climate variability.
- #humanimpacts: Analyze the multitude of impacts that humans have on the planet, including Earth's climate and ocean, biosphere, and even human-directed evolution.
- #naturalresourcecycles: Recognize that the natural resources utilized by or affected by humans have different time scales of formation and cycling (e.g., groundwater, fossil fuels), and that certain natural resources were created at particular points in Earth's history under very different conditions.
- #platetectonics: Evaluate the multiple lines of evidence for plate tectonics, and recognize the fundamental importance of plate tectonics to virtually all other Earth cycles.

Learn how Earth has changed through time to become an environment conducive to life.

- #originoflife: Examine the evidence for when life began on Earth, and organize the "origin of life" problem into a series of discrete steps.
- #redox: Analyze the "co-evolution of life and Earth's exterior," namely, the critical role of oxidation-reduction reactions, which make life possible but which also fundamentally alter Earth's surface environment.

By our structuring the goals of every course in this way, students can understand how each lesson and assignment feeds into the overall purpose of the course and how the course in turn fits into the concentration and major.

Moreover, students receive feedback on their performance at unusually frequent intervals and thus are in a good position to know whether a specific academic path is a good fit for them (see chapter 17). Each student discusses such feedback with his or her advisor, who plays a central role in guiding the student to make wise choices about his or her studies.

In addition, we publish every syllabus in advance, so students can get a good idea of what is included in each course. As discussed in chapter 16, a Minerva syllabus is unusually detailed, indicating, among other things, the topic of each week's sessions, the course objective and learning outcomes, as well as the specific readings and assignments. Finally, students have a content expert to help them with their capstone projects, and they have a particularly close intellectual relationship with the professors in their senior tutorials.

Ensuring That Students Are Competitive

In addition to the four design criteria just addressed, we take care to ensure that our students are competitive with those from traditional universities. We expose students to multiple related fields, asking them to focus on such matters as "how we know what we know," "what are the key open questions," "what are current tools and methods to address those questions," and "what are major unknowns." For example, our aim is not only to train students to think like a scientist but also to increase their mastery of the key knowledge and skills they would need when pursuing a science-related field. This material ensures that our students are competitive in the next stage of their career, whether that is graduate training in a particular discipline, developing science policy, or holding positions in government, nongovernmental organizations, or private industry.

Our goals are similar for students pursuing a minor in natural sciences. The main difference is that they will not have as much breadth, but they will be able to go deeper into their chosen major in another college. Students who minor in natural sciences will be able to "think like a scientist" and bring these skills and approaches to a broad array of careers.

We are often asked how our students can compete in natural sciences when none of our courses have laboratory sections. Although we make ample use of computer simulations and our students work with real data in class, we firmly believe that all science majors should have authentic hands-on research experiences in which they address real research questions in a mentored environment. This is achieved by encouraging our students to pursue summer research experiences at universities and research institutions around the world. The dean of natural sciences, our faculty, and the professional development team help our students successfully compete for these opportunities. These research experiences may serve as the basis from which to develop a strong capstone project and may also stimulate students' interests in specific senior tutorials in which they dig deeper into their topic of interest.

Conclusion

We at Minerva have developed a unique curriculum, guided by first principles. This curriculum allows us to balance breadth against depth in new ways. We have achieved this balance while respecting guiding principles designed to ensure that our curriculum serves our students well.

As part of this design, we have encouraged and facilitated interdisciplinary and transdisciplinary studies, both within each major and by making it easy for students to complete a double major. At the same time, we have included requirements and structures that lead to a broad education by putting what students learn in context. Above all, a Minerva education is forward-looking: our overarching goal is to give our students the knowledge and skills to continue to learn and to adapt to a changing world.

Note

1. For upper-division courses, we reframe this as "content should not be the sole focus"—we do focus in part on content, but we use the content to illustrate a field's key concepts and principles, with the goal of helping the students to become lifelong contributors to, or consumers of, their chosen fields.

II How We Teach

One of the advantages of starting from scratch in designing Minerva's curriculum is that we were able to create and use pedagogical techniques that promote learning, without facing resistance from entrenched interests, traditions, or legacy practices. A vast empirical literature indicates that lectures, the most traditional of pedagogical techniques, are not an effective way for students to *learn,* though they are a highly effective way to *teach*: one can lecture to a very large group as easily as to a very small one. This fact has obvious economic implications, which may be one reason why lectures endure as the dominant mode of teaching.

Many of the empirical studies that document the deficiencies of lectures do more than simply challenge the efficacy of this technique—they also provide support for another approach that is demonstrably more effective: active learning. Active learning requires students to engage with the material, relying on such activities as debate, role-playing, and group problem solving. Active learning leads students to comprehend and retain much more information than do lectures.

Minerva has taken this literature to heart and designed its entire pedagogy around active learning. The eight chapters in this part of the book systematically explain how our pedagogy was developed, implemented, and employed.

Chapter 10, "Unlearning to Learn," describes how we set the stage for the effective use of active learning. We quickly discovered that both faculty and students had to be willing to unlearn some previous assumptions and habits. We knew that abandoning lectures would be difficult, but we were still surprised by some of the challenges. For example, students and faculty had to adjust to the purposes of class sessions; rather than focusing on information transmission and memorization, we stress using information to achieve specific learning goals.

The next two chapters provide the rationale for our use of active learning in all of our courses. Chapter 11, "The Science of Learning: Mechanisms and Principles," distills sixteen principles from the empirical literature on the science of learning. These principles bear on how information is acquired, stored, and later retrieved from memory when appropriate. These principles can be drawn on in different combinations, and such combinations underpin the specific active learning techniques we use in class. Chapter 12, "Fully Active Learning," reviews these active learning techniques. Active learning is contrasted with other methods (such as collaborative learning), and the idea of what we call "fully active learning" is developed. This sort of learning requires all students to be engaged at least 75 percent of the time. It is not enough to have one or two students involved in a debate; everybody else also needs to be doing something that requires them to engage with the material.

The next two chapters describe how we organize each class session and how our faculty teach and facilitate our courses. Chapter 13, "A New Team-Teaching Approach to Structured Learning," explains how we ensure that all sections of the same course, many of which are taught by different faculty, provide the same high-quality learning environment for students and a productive and stimulating working environment for faculty. This chapter also describes the monthlong training and orientation course that all of our faculty take; during this course, faculty learn a wide range of knowledge and skills, from the science of learning and active learning techniques to use of the software platform and classroom management. This course is taught using the same techniques used in the classes students take. Chapter 14, "Teaching from Lesson Plans," examines the role of the professors in our courses, all of which are taught from detailed lesson plans. The lesson plans structure and guide the sequence of events in class, ensuring that different sections of the same course provide the same material (and hence professors teaching subsequent courses can assume with assurance that all students have acquired the same background knowledge). However, the professor does not simply read the lesson plan or follow rigid instructions; rather, the professor plays a crucial role in directing the discussions and ensuring that students do in fact achieve the learning goals. This chapter shows how we design lesson plans to take advantage of the instructor's knowledge, creativity, and skills.

The final three chapters in this part of the book all focus on how the pedagogy is embedded in the Active Learning Forum (ALF), the cloud-based software program that we use to host all of our classes. Chapter 15, "The Active Learning Forum," describes how the ALF not only allows faculty to teach better (because of the various tools built into it) but also, and more important, allows students to learn more effectively, in part because of the sorts of feedback it allows us to provide. Chapter 16, "Building Lesson Plans for Twenty-First-Century Active Learning," describes a computer program that works to augment and supplement the ALF. This program facilitates the development of new syllabi and new lesson plans by automating much of the processing and providing highly structured guidelines for the remainder. This authoring tool, called Course Builder, allows us to scale easily as we grow and develop more courses—and also allows us to leapfrog the need for a learning management system entirely. Finally, in chapter 17, "Assessing Student Learning," we review how the ALF allows us to measure student academic performance. We consider how our rubrics are embedded in the ALF, how they are constructed, how they are applied, the role of different types of assignments, and how we assess transfer of skills and knowledge to new contexts. We focus on the technology that has been developed in the service of such assessments.

The overarching theme of part II of this book is the close relationship between pedagogy and technology. All of the technology we have developed has not simply been informed by the pedagogy but rather has been designed to promote the pedagogy. As the technology progressed, new opportunities for pedagogical techniques emerged (such as ways to present and discuss poll results). The pedagogy and technology have coevolved, with each one building on progress in the other.

10 Unlearning to Learn

Stephen M. Kosslyn, Robin B. Goldberg, and Teri Cannon

We at Minerva are pressing the reset button on higher education. We are in the unique situation of having no prior stakeholders, no legacy expectations, and no strong established history to bind us. Instead we can take a step back and ask, Given what we know about the science of learning, what students need to know to succeed in the twenty-first century, and the capabilities of modern technology, what should we teach and how should we teach it?

For many who have felt constrained in traditional academic environments, just hearing about this freedom is liberating and empowering. And they are right: at Minerva, we can make principled decisions based on our stated learning goals for students and our core values without being constrained by past practices and without experiencing high levels of resistance from current stakeholders.

Nevertheless, although we do not have to take into account many competing influences and interests that could lead to suboptimal compromises, we do have to work with students and faculty who have grown up in traditional institutions, and who sometimes fall back on old ways of teaching and learning out of habit. Students come from high schools that typically teach in traditional ways; faculty members have completed advanced degrees in universities that also use familiar methods. In particular, both high schools and universities typically focus on transmitting information and rely primarily on lectures to do so.

The fact that both students and faculty have been immersed for years in traditional educational methods and institutions has posed some challenges. In this chapter we summarize what we've learned about how to address these challenges. Bringing both students and faculty along on the journey we have envisioned takes time and patience. But this journey has proven very rewarding to all involved, when we have selected applicants properly and both students and faculty are willing to discard preconceived notions about what should be taught and how it should be taught.

A key ingredient to being comfortable with the Minerva pedagogy is being open to new experiences. Part of this openness involves being willing to examine assumptions and habits and being willing to unlearn old ways on encountering something new and better. The force of this observation has become evident as we've developed a new kind of curriculum, guided by empirical findings and first principles. Our curriculum is distinctive in three respects: in what we teach, how we teach it, and the means of delivery. Each of these features has required our students and faculty to face new challenges.

Adjusting to What We Teach

Higher education is often faulted for not preparing students to succeed after they graduate. Hart Research Associates has conducted several online surveys of employers. The most recent surveys, of more than three hundred employers, were conducted in January 2013 and November 2014 on behalf of the Association of American Colleges and Universities (Hart Research Associates, 2013, 2015). These reports provide a detailed analysis of employers' priorities with respect to the kinds of knowledge and intellectual skills that college students must have if they are to succeed in today's world.

Employers recognize capacities that cut across majors as critical to a candidate's potential for career success, and they view these skills as more important than a student's choice of undergraduate major. Nearly all the employers surveyed in the 2013 study, 93 percent, agreed that "a candidate's demonstrated capacity to think critically, communicate clearly, and solve complex problems is more important than their undergraduate major." In 2014 the learning outcomes that employers cited as most important were written and oral communication, teamwork, ethical decision making, critical thinking, and the ability to apply knowledge in real-world settings. Moreover, these same skills are critical for students to develop into effective citizens and fully functional human beings, in light of the increasing complexity of the world and the ready availability of vast amounts of information.

Despite these clear findings, colleges and universities rarely guide students toward mastering the skills and knowledge needed to succeed after they graduate. To address this problem, and as explained more fully in chapters 1 and 2, Minerva focuses on teaching what we call "practical knowledge," which is the knowledge and set of intellectual skills that students can use to adapt to a changing world—allowing them to succeed at a wide range of jobs and in life more generally.

Recognizing and changing old habits

Because faculty and students are accustomed to focusing on information transmission in specific topic areas rather than on developing this sort of knowledge and intellectual skills, some have difficulty prioritizing practical knowledge. Many faculty members and students, consciously or unconsciously, believe that students aren't really learning unless they are memorizing facts, figures, and concepts. This is challenging because our first year consists of four yearlong integrated general education courses intended to teach fundamental practical knowledge. And subsequent years not only return to the learning goals introduced in the first year but also provide more advanced and specialized forms of practical knowledge. A problem sometimes arises because to introduce, illustrate, and apply practical knowledge, one must put it in a concrete context (e.g., when learning how to organize an argument, the argument must be about a specific topic). Both faculty and students sometimes can't help but attend primarily to the content, the concrete context we provide to develop practical knowledge. Faculty do appreciate that the content is primarily a vehicle for teaching practical knowledge per se but often must consciously resist the siren song of content, of slipping into familiar habits and dwelling on information transmission. We have found faculty members very receptive to this change of perspective, but it does sometimes require effort.

Part of the challenge we have observed is that initially students and faculty alike may leave a class feeling that the discussion was "superficial" or that nothing was learned—but that is only because they overlook the fact that students are beginning to develop specific intellectual skills, and the content was the vehicle to achieve that end. We are clear about the role of content from the outset of our engagement with both faculty and students. We explain that the content should open doors for the students, allowing them to explore new areas on their own. We stress this role of content during our monthlong faculty training course, and our faculty do subscribe to our goals and methods. But old habits can die hard, and sometimes faculty members need feedback on their teaching to stay on course.

Mastering practical knowledge

Another interesting challenge concerning what we teach is that students sometimes believe they have already mastered specific sorts of practical knowledge. For example, students often think that they know how to craft a clear and coherent argument, but we find that they are not familiar with the organizational principles that would enable them to do so at a sophisticated and deep level. Similarly, some of our learning objectives may seem obvious at first.

We have found that often it is only with the passage of time that students realize just how much they have to learn. Sometimes the difference is most evident when they reengage with their friends from high school who attended traditional universities—and the Minerva students realize how much more developed their thinking has become after just a few months at Minerva. Sometimes the difference emerges most strongly when they are doing a summer internship, and they discover that nobody else pauses to characterize a problem before trying to solve it (this is one of the learning objectives addressed in our Empirical Analysis cornerstone course). Sometimes the lightbulb goes off when they notice that they are not in fact exercising one of the pieces of practical knowledge (e.g., adjusting what they say to be appropriate for the audience) and realize that they are falling flat.

As one way to address this problem, we sometimes administer a short multiple-choice exam at the beginning and end of every unit. We do not grade the students on their performance but do show them the results: students can use the practical knowledge introduced in a unit significantly better after the end of the unit, even though they might not have been aware how much they were learning at the time.

Adjusting to How We Teach

Ample research indicates that remarkably little learning occurs on most college campuses (e.g., Arum & Roksa, 2011). This need not be the case. Through well-documented research on the science of learning, we know an enormous amount about how humans learn (for an overview, see chapter 11). Minerva is the first institution to use the science of learning systematically not just in all our classes but also in the curricular and institutional design. This approach led us to use active learning in all classes, such as through problem solving, role-playing, engaging in debates, and the like (see chapter 12). The specific activities are all designed to take advantage of facts about how humans learn best, which led us to design activities that require students to pay close attention and to think through problems and situations.

Adjusting to active learning

Faculty sometimes question how active learning can be better than a lecture on materials they have researched extensively and thought about for many years. In addition, faculty often have a difficult time abandoning deeply ingrained methods of teaching that they've experienced throughout their educational careers. They may not feel that they are doing a good job unless they are telling and explaining things to the students. Faculty (and students) sometimes fall prey to what we call the "illusion of learning" whereby the more notes students take, the more they are assumed to have learned. But a massive amount of research has documented that this is ineffective pedagogy: students learn best when they are actively engaged, not when they are passive recipients of a lecture. Lectures do not facilitate deep learning; students rarely can apply or synthesize what they learn this way and do not retain much of it over time. Active learning has been shown to be vastly superior to traditional lectures (e.g., Freeman et al., 2014).

A common way to address this problem is to have discussion sections along with the lectures. In many courses faculty deliver two lectures and teaching assistants run a one-hour discussion section each week. But discussion is not necessarily active learning for most of the students in the class most of the time. For active learning to take place, students must actively reflect on and try to use the information (see chapter 12). Because most discussion leaders are not trained in implementing active learning, they may allow a few students to dominate or they may allow students to sit through the discussion passively. And when students do participate, the instructors may not appropriately challenge them, inducing them to engage with the material in new ways. Traditional discussion sections are often almost afterthoughts; they often are not structured or designed to facilitate learning but instead are merely opportunities for already engaged students to ask questions and express their opinions.

Team teaching

At Minerva, it's not just that faculty don't lecture and rely on active learning, they also work as a member of a team: All instructors teaching sections of the same course rely on the same detailed lesson plan notes; these notes specify learning objectives, preparatory materials, assessments, assignments, and the in-class active learning exercises (see chapters 13 and 14). We adopted this technique (drawing on one used for many years at the Harvard Business School) to provide comparable learning outcomes for students in different sections of the same course and to ensure that the science of learning is being systematically operationalized in all sections. This is also one of the ways in which we keep the quality uniformly high as we grow. Using the same lesson plans helps us reduce variability across different sections of the same course, helping all students to have comparable experiences.

Faculty who come from traditional institutions, where they were in complete control of their classrooms and pedagogical methods, can find all of this structure challenging. This is especially true of faculty who studied or taught at institutions where there were no core curricula requiring this kind of intersectional coordination. However, our faculty members typically come to thrive in this structure. Every week all the faculty who teach sections of the same course meet and review the upcoming week's lesson plans, revising and updating them as needed. During the discussion they review how well the previous week's lessons went and note ways that the lesson plans should be revised for the following year. Faculty soon learn that working as members of a team helps them teach better and helps their colleagues teach better. Faculty report that this experience is gratifying.

In addition, faculty come to appreciate the flexibility built into the lesson plans; the lesson plans leave plenty of room for the faculty to contribute creatively during each individual session. Class discussions hinge on the faculty member's ability to answer questions well and to nudge the students in fruitful directions. Despite a uniform lesson plan, all actual lessons unfold differently from one another because of differences in student responses and faculty reactions. There is also flex time built into every lesson plan, and faculty report "best practices" to their team every week— which in turn helps improve the lesson plans that will be used in the future.

Faculty effort and stimulation

The lack of complete control over the class content can also require faculty to put in more effort than they would in a traditional setting. One reason why faculty members like to lecture is because they know in advance what will unfold during the class period. Not only do they know what they are going to say, but after giving the lecture a few times, they often have a good sense of what questions the students will ask. Unlike in a Minerva seminar, faculty giving traditional lectures do not need to worry about handling challenging questions, students who are lost and vocal about their confusion, or class discussions that may veer from the learning objectives, nor do they need to worry about ensuring that all students are drawn into the activities.

Facilitating active learning requires a different set of skills than is required to lecture, especially at Minerva. Minerva faculty need to learn how to use the technology and manage the classroom activities within the allotted time. Almost anything can happen—and that initially makes some professors nervous. But we have also noticed that faculty soon find these seminars unusually stimulating. They are never bored, and they find that they learn more than they did when teaching using traditional methods. Faculty are often excited and enthused after class.

Teaching at Minerva is a different way to teach. When faculty embrace this new approach, the active, engaging classroom enables all students to help make the classes relevant and meaningful—which helps students learn. Because our faculty are dedicated to helping the students learn, they come to appreciate the strengths of our approach—but this does require an open mind and a willingness to learn and try new methods.

Student engagement

Active learning also requires work on the part of the students. Taking notes during lectures is easy; having to interact with other students and think through a difficult problem or situation is not. Students must be prepared when they enter class and must remain engaged throughout every class. They cannot be passive, back-row observers. The key to active learning is that the more students pay attention and work through material, the deeper their learning becomes (discussed in chapters 11 and 12).

Students sometimes don't initially feel at ease with the level of engagement required in a Minerva class. Nevertheless, we commonly observe that after a few weeks, they find classes more fun and stimulating than anything they had experienced previously.

Adjusting to the Means of Delivery

We aim to provide a first-rate education to all qualified students, no matter where they live, how much they can afford to pay, or what their background is. To deliver on this goal, we had to create a new classroom model that provides an educational experience that is as effective as it is cost-efficient. To that end, we developed a novel, cloud-based technology platform, the Active Learning Forum (the ALF, described in chapter 15). This platform and its associated software allow all classes to be small seminars, where students and faculty meet and interact together in real time. Every student is in the front row; all students and faculty can see each other at all times—which is not the case in a traditional classroom, not even in most small classes, where students sit in arrangements that do not allow them to see all their peers at the same time.

The ALF allows us to teach better because it has tools built in that facilitate active learning, such as the ability to conduct rapid polls, compare before-and-after poll results, and assign students to breakout groups according to different criteria. These tools not only allow us to teach better, they also help the students to learn better. Moreover, every class is recorded, and faculty members review the recordings, assess students' performance on class-specific learning objectives, and provide formative feedback. This feedback mechanism is a major benefit of the platform and a powerful tool to enhance student learning. Thus, although our students can take classes in the same room, we record a video of each student individually, which allows faculty later to use the recording to provide extensive feedback that goes far beyond grades on midterms and finals.

Of course, evaluating students after class requires considerable faculty time. Every class is ninety minutes long, and it takes at least an hour to review a class (sometimes at double speed) and identify which student contributions to annotate with specific comments. And faculty don't grade using vaguely defined categories but rather rely on standardized five-point rubrics that all faculty have learned to use in the same way. This approach helps us to have crisp, transparent criteria for assigning grades and to ensure that different faculty members grade in the same way.

We have found that because we have hired well, and our faculty are truly devoted to teaching and facilitating student learning, they adopt these methods easily and well. Our faculty care about what the students learn, and soon appreciate what we are trying to achieve with our methods. Moreover, the faculty are active collaborators—they have input on every method and procedure we use. For example, one professor noticed a peculiarity in the way our rubric scores mapped onto a standard letter-grade scale. The deans and development faculty met to discuss this observation, and immediately reworked this mapping to solve the problem. We don't always do what any individual faculty member might prefer, but they all know that their observations and ideas are taken seriously.

In addition, because we focus on active learning, it is crucial that students attend class. In a traditional model, they can skip lectures (or text through them) and simply obtain the notes. With active learning, however, they must be present and participate. Initially this puts off a few students, who are used to succeeding academically without preparing for or attending class and who see their nonacademic activities at college as equally or more important than learning. But nearly all students soon see the benefits of this approach and are socialized into participating by the vast majority of their peers, who are deeply engaged in their classes.

Conclusion

At Minerva we have learned how important it is to have an open mind, to be willing to unlearn old approaches and learn new ones—on the part of both faculty and students. The effort this requires is not for everyone; both faculty and students must be open to new experiences and convinced that it's worth giving the new approaches a try. The preliminary results indicate that this openness is well worth the effort: we have found that over the course of the freshman year, not only do students make substantial and measurable learning gains, but also most students come to realize the usefulness of practical knowledge in their internship work and daily lives.

References

Arum, R., & Roksa, J. (2011). *Academically adrift: Limited learning on college campuses.* Chicago, IL: University of Chicago Press.

Freeman, S., Eddy, S. L., McDonough, M., Smith, M. K., Okoroafor, N., Jordt, H., et al. (2014). Active learning increases student performance in science, engineering, and mathematics. *Proceedings of the National Academy of Sciences of the United States of America, 111*(23), 8410–8415.

Hart Research Associates (2013, April 10). *It takes more than a major: Employer priorities for college learning and success.* Washington, DC: Hart Research Associates for the Association of American Colleges and Universities. https://www.aacu.org/sites/default/files/files/LEAP/2013_EmployerSurvey.pdf

Hart Research Associates (2015, January 20). *Falling short? College learning and career success.* Washington, DC: Hart Research Associates for the Association of American Colleges and Universities. https://www.aacu.org/sites/default/files/files/LEAP/2015employerstudentsurvey.pdf

11   The Science of Learning: Mechanisms and Principles

Stephen M. Kosslyn

The science of learning encompasses findings in a wide range of areas, including discoveries about how humans perceive, organize, and store information and then subsequently retrieve that information from memory. We've learned a tremendous amount about how humans process and store information, and that knowledge can be used systematically in education to help students master the material they are taught.

Oddly, although the science of learning matured decades ago, it is rarely used to facilitate teaching. Instead, most classes are taught using methods that were developed over a thousand years ago. Walk into any university and you are more likely than not to see a "sage on the stage": a faculty member at the front of the class and rows of students dutifully putting in their time by sitting in class (some listening, some taking notes, but many doing e-mail, monitoring Twitter, or surfing the web). To my knowledge, Minerva is the only institution to use the science of learning systematically in all aspects of the curriculum.

Lectures are a common way to teach, but we need to distinguish between teaching and learning. Teaching focuses on information *transmission*; learning is about knowledge *acquisition*. On the face of things, the two activities should be completely aligned, but typically they are not. Teaching is often done in a way that is convenient and efficient for the professor, with little thought given to how best to facilitate student learning. Lectures are a superb way to teach: a single instructor can lecture to ten thousand people as easily as to ten. But study after study has documented that lectures are a terrible way for students to acquire information (let alone to acquire deep knowledge, which requires not just learning information but also gaining an understanding of its broader context and utility).

For example, consider a meta-analysis of 225 studies of how well students learn from lectures versus active-learning seminars (Freeman et al., 2014). This review was restricted to STEM (science, technology, engineering, and mathematics) courses, which presumably are among the most challenging offered to undergraduates. The results were dramatic. The authors reported the following:

The studies analyzed here document that active learning leads to increases in examination performance that would raise average grades by a half a letter, and that failure rates under traditional lecturing increase by 55% over the rates observed under active learning. The analysis supports theory claiming that calls to increase the number of students receiving STEM degrees could be answered, at least in part, by abandoning traditional lecturing in favor of active learning … . (p. 1)

Finally, the data suggest that STEM instructors may begin to question the continued use of traditional lecturing in everyday practice, especially in light of recent work indicating that active learning confers disproportionate benefits for STEM students from disadvantaged backgrounds and for female students in male-dominated fields. (p. 4)

Although these statements are from just one meta-analysis, the same conclusions have been reached repeatedly, and for non-STEM courses as well as STEM courses. Without question, active learning is better than passive listening to lectures.

Why, then, are lectures still the dominant mode of teaching in most universities? Part of the problem may be that those doing the teaching do not understand enough about the science of learning to take advantage of it. This is not to suggest that other problems are not also prevalent, such as the economics of universities, incentive structures, and institutional rigidity, but certainly most faculty who care about being effective instructors would benefit from a more thorough understanding of the science of learning.

In this chapter, I provide a very brief overview of the key principles of the science of learning I have gleaned from the empirical literature. I summarize two overarching principles (which I call "maxims") and then consider sixteen specific principles that fall under them. At the outset, I should note that different reviewers have organized the literature differently, producing different numbers of principles. For example, Graesser, Halpern, and Hakel (2008) identify twenty-five principles, whereas Willingham (2009) identifies only nine. The differences appear to arise primarily from what principles are considered special cases or variants of other principles. In what follows, I've chosen a level of granularity that easily maps into active learning exercises that can be used in the classroom (see chapter 12).

Distinctions and Purposes

Before we start, I need to make several distinctions and background assumptions clear.

Important distinctions

First, "learning" is the process of acquiring information, of picking it up and storing it mentally. In contrast, "memory" refers to previously acquired information that has been stored, and the term typically includes the processes of retaining the information and then subsequently digging it out of storage for use. Learning and memory are different sides of the same coin: If you don't acquire and store information, there's nothing later to retrieve; and if you can't retain and later retrieve it, it may as well not exist.

Second, it is useful to distinguish between two different sorts of memories: *Dynamic* memories exist only as long as they are actively maintained. In contrast, *structural* memories persist even when they aren't being actively considered. Here's a metaphor: imagine that someone is trying to remember the shape of a four-sided geometric form. To do so, she walks along a path she creates on a lawn, in the shape of the form. She walks this path over and over. While she is walking, the representation of the shape is dynamic; it depends on her continued movement. If she stops walking, the representation is lost. But after a while she wears a dirt path through the lawn. Once this happens, it no longer matters whether she keeps walking. She can stop slogging along the path and the shape will persist. At this point the representation has transitioned from being dynamic to being structural. A comparable distinction exists in the brain; for learning to be useful, it must engender structural changes that will endure over time.

Third, it is useful to distinguish between two different types of learning. On the one hand, we learn *declarative* information—such as vocabulary words, addresses, concepts, and theories. On the other hand, we learn *procedural* information—such as how to drive a car, how to negotiate, how to debate, and how to use the rules of grammar in speaking a second language. The following principles typically should be applied in different orders when learning the different types of information. For example, mastery of underlying rules may be more important when acquiring procedural knowledge than when acquiring declarative knowledge, and hence underlying rules should be introduced early in the process to help students form a mental model of what they should do. But in all cases, I claim, the underlying principles of learning are the same.

Fourth, the individual principles can be invoked in different combinations by what I call "application techniques." For example, explaining something to yourself will help you learn. But this activity itself is not a separate principle. Rather, it is a way to draw on a set of cognitive processes that underlie the principles, bringing them to bear on learning. I return to this point after reviewing the principles.

Purposes of the principles

The principles I describe below are intended to accomplish three aims:

First, we can draw on many of them to lead students to learn even if they do not intend to do so. This is a remarkable discovery: people often learn not (or not only) through intention but simply as a consequence of using information. An example is recalling at the end of the day what you did from the time you woke up in the morning—what conversations you had, the details of a newspaper article you read, and so on. How much of that material did you consciously *try* to remember? Very little, I would wager.

Second, by repeatedly relying on the principles I summarize below, you can transition from doing something consciously to doing it automatically. When you learned to drive a car, for example, at first it was extremely laborious. Your driving instructor told you what to do, and you did your best to follow instructions. But with practice, you soon could do those things without consciously thinking about them.

Third, these principles can help learners apply what they learned to all relevant contexts. This is a challenge because people transfer what they have learned in one context to a novel context only with effort (see chapters 2 and 3). And the more dissimilar the new context is to the one in which the material was originally learned, the harder it is to make the shift. "Far transfer" occurs when one uses learned material in very novel contexts (contexts that on the surface do not resemble the circumstances in which the material was learned) and uses it well after the material was learned (Barnett & Ceci, 2002).

Maxims

We can organize the principles of learning under two umbrella "maxims," as summarized in the following.

Maxim I: "Think it through"

The first maxim is "Think it through." The key idea is very simple: the more you think something through, paying attention to what you are doing, the more likely you are later to remember it.

This maxim is at the core of your ability to recall facts and figures from a newspaper article you read, even though you didn't try to memorize them. You stored the material in memory simply because you paid attention and thought it through. *Incidental learning* is learning that occurs without consciously trying to acquire the knowledge; it occurs as a by-product of the cognitive processing that is used to understand, analyze, or synthesize.

As you read through the list of specific principles below, you may notice something that is conspicuously absent—any mention of motivation as a principle. I've often encountered admonitions to "find out what the students are interested in, and play to those interests." But the evidence suggests that the key is to get the students engaged. They might get engaged because they are motivated to do so or simply because the situation requires it. As far as I can tell, the reasons why they are engaged will make little difference; the key is to lead them to perform the relevant cognitive processing and to pay attention while they are doing so.

This is the essence of the first maxim, "Think it through."

Maxim II: "Make and use associations"

The second maxim is "Make and use associations." Associations not only help us organize material so that it is easy to store in memory, they also give us the hooks that will allow us later to dig the material out of memory, to recall it.

A dramatic demonstration of the power of using associations to organize material was reported by Ericsson, Chase, and Faloon (1980). They asked an undergraduate student to commit to coming into the lab at least three times per week, and he did so for about a year and a half. At each session, the researchers simply read him a sequence of random digits, one digit per second, and asked him to repeat them back. They started with a single digit, which he correctly recalled. They then gave him two other randomly selected digits, which he recalled, and then three, and so on, increasing the length of each new list until he failed to recall the entire sequence (eight digits, on that first day). Each session began where the previous one had left off, with a new list of that length (with a new combination of random digits). Every set consisted of a new set of digits; he wasn't given practice learning the same set over and over. When the study finally ended, this participant could recall a list of seventy-nine random digits!

How did he do this? As it happened, the participant in the study was a long-distance runner who had run numerous marathons. He associated the random digits with times for particular segments of races. For example, if he heard "3, 4, 9, 2," he might associate these digits with the time, "3 minutes,

49.2 seconds." Thus, four digits were converted to a single "chunk" (i.e., an organized unit) using associations. This chunk is as easy to store as a single digit taken alone! He eventually devised other strategies for making such associations, such as relating digits to specific people's ages or specific notable dates.

Associations are important not only for helping us enter new information into memory so that it is stored effectively but also for helping us later to retrieve this information. Associations can serve as cues and reminders. The game of charades illustrates this process in slow motion. For example, say that the presenter gets down on all fours and moves around like an animal. The players might shout "a cat," "a dog," "a donkey." The position is a cue, which activates these concepts. The presenter then sticks her fingers up from her forehead, mimicking horns. Someone says "a deer," someone else says "a goat." The presenter then stands up and mimics having a cape with an animal running by—leading the viewers to shout out "a bull!" Each cue evokes specific associations, which in turn retrieve certain information from memory. This process of being cued to recall specific information happens all of the time, every day, virtually every time we recall something.

Sixteen Specific Principles

Now to the specific principles that underlie these two overarching maxims. I used three criteria to select and formulate these principles: First, the principle could not be explained by appeal to other principles; it had to describe how a distinct type (or types) of cognitive processing contribute to learning. Second, the principle must have been derived from highly replicable studies that demonstrated large effects on learning. Third, the principle must have straightforward implications for instruction; how to implement it in practical situations must be clear. In what follows, I provide very brief descriptions of each principle.

Principles that underlie "Think it through"

First, seven principles fall under the maxim "Think it through."

Evoking deep processing. The more cognitive operations one performs while paying attention to such operations, the more likely it is that one will later recall that information (Craig et al., 2006; Craik & Lockhart, 1972). This is the most obvious implication of the maxim "Think it through." For example, if you formulate an example of how every one of these principles can be used in a specific situation, you will remember them much better than if you simply read and understand them.

Using desirable difficulty. We can think of this as the Goldilocks rule (not too hot, not too cold—just right!). Learning is best when the task is not so easy as to be boring but not so hard as to be over the learner's head (Bjork, 1988, 1999; VanLehn et al., 2007). To get the most out of thinking it through, the person needs to be as engaged as possible—no more, no less. For example, if you are good at math, you will need more challenging examples of new mathematical concepts to stay engaged than would someone who has less knowledge.

Eliciting the generation effect. Simply recalling information—especially when effort is required—strengthens memory for that piece of information; the mere act of digging information out of memory reconstructs and strengthens the mental representation of the information. For example, a consequence of this principle is that frequent testing can enhance learning if it leads learners to recall relevant information (Butler & Roediger, 2007; Roediger & Karpicke, 2006).

Engaging in deliberate practice. In some cases, to learn effectively you need to pay attention to and think through specific aspects of what you are learning. In particular, feedback helps you to correct aspects of a mental representation when it isn't optimal (Brown, Roediger, & McDaniel, 2014; Ericsson, Krampe, & Tesch-Romer, 1993). For example, when learning French, it's good to have a native speaker listen to you and carefully correct your pronunciation. Such feedback is most effective when learners use "deliberate practice." Deliberate practice occurs when you pay careful attention to mistakes and use the ways that an error differs from the correct performance to correct subsequent performance. (This principle alone, however, is not enough to make you into an expert; Hambrick et al., 2014.)

These first four principles all focus strongly on the fact that more processing of the relevant information will produce better memory. The next three principles focus on ways to induce people to engage in additional processing. (My interrupting here and pointing this out should allow you to create two large groups for this set of principles, the first four and the second three, which respects the fact that we can store easily no more than four units in a "chunk," as discussed below.)

Using interleaving. Instead of just focusing on one type of problem (e.g., when doing math), it's best to intermix different types of problems. The same principle implies (but to my knowledge has not yet been investigated) that when learning French, it's best to do a bit of studying French, then some history, then some math, and then back to French.

This makes sense because it's easier to pay attention to something new than to sustain paying attention to the same material, extended over time. For example, all else being equal, you would probably learn the material in this chapter more effectively if you did something else after you finish this section, and returned to the second set of principles later.

Inducing dual coding. If I give you a short paragraph to remember, you will recall it better if I also include some relevant illustrations. In general, presenting both verbal and visual material enhances memory. In this case, the brain stores multiple representations in memory (some verbal, some visual—which are stored in different parts of the brain), which gives you multiple shots at later digging the information out of storage (Kosslyn, 1994; Mayer, 2001; Moreno & Valdez, 2005). Furthermore, if you are given only a name or a verbal description to remember, your memory will be vastly improved if you can visualize (i.e., form a mental image of) the named object or scene: not only will you create a second type of representation (in addition to the verbal material itself) but the mere effort of visualizing the described object or scene will enhance subsequent memory.

Evoking emotion. Leading someone to feel emotion when experiencing an event generally will enable him or her to recall that event more effectively. Emotion focuses attention and also causes the brain to devote extra resources to storing the information. Negative emotions in particular narrow attention and focus one on details. For such negative emotions, beta-blockers will remove this extra boost, which hints at the underlying pharmacological events that produce this extra processing (Erk et al., 2003; Levine & Pizarro, 2004; McGaugh, 2003, 2004). For example, if you are anxious about how an interview will go (and do not take beta-blockers), you probably will remember more details about the interview than if you are not anxious.

To summarize, I've just reviewed seven principles, all of which are special cases of the maxim "Think it through."

Principles that underlie "Make and use associations"

The second overarching maxim is "Make and use associations." It is useful to distinguish two general classes of these principles.

Structure information by using associations

The first class is "Structure information by using associations." Five principles fall in this category:

Promoting chunking. As we saw in the case of the marathon runner who could memorize staggering numbers of randomly selected digits (Ericsson et al., 1980), you can use associations you already have in your memory to organize material into relatively few chunks (organized units). People can easily store in memory three or four chunks—and remarkably, each of these units itself can contain three or four chunks. For example, if you want to learn a list of sixteen principles, figuring out ways to organize them into roughly four (or fewer) groups of four (or fewer) principles each should help. Organizing material into manageable units clearly facilitates learning (e.g., Brown, Roediger, & McDaniel, 2014; Mayer & Moreno, 2003).

Building on prior associations. When learning something new, the more associations you can find with information already stored in memory, the better (e.g., Bransford, Brown, & Cocking, 2000; Glenberg & Robertson, 1999; Mayer, 2001). For example, when meeting a new person, you might better remember his name by associating his face with that of someone with the same name whom you already know. One way to do this is to visualize the face of the person you know and then morph that mental image into the face of the new person (Kosslyn, 1994). If you do this a few times, you will associate the new person's face with that of the familiar person. And the familiar person's face is already associated with the appropriate name.

The fact that prior associations can be used to learn new information resolves an old conundrum: At one time researchers worried about a "paradox of the expert," which hinged on the fact that the more you know, the easier it is to learn even more (Reder & Anderson, 1980; Smith, Adams, & Schorr, 1978). The intuition was that the more you know, the "fuller" memory should be—and hence it should be harder, not easier, to store new information. However, researchers have learned that the more information you already know, the more existing associations you can use to store new information. The more branches you have, the more leaves and fruit can be hung on this structure. Hence there's no actual paradox.

Presenting foundational material first. When complex information is to be acquired, learning is enhanced when a teacher takes advantage of existing associations to provide the most basic material first, and then integrates new material a bit at a time (Bransford, Brown, & Cocking, 2000; Wandersee, Mintzes, & Novak, 1994). Presenting foundational material first provides a backbone to which one can attach additional information, allowing an organized mental structure to be built up over time. For example, my presenting the two general maxims first should have given you a structure for understanding the specific principles.

The following two principles build on the previous ones but focus specifically on the relationship between examples and underlying principles. (By interrupting here and pointing this out, I hope to help you create two large chunks, which should help you get your mental arms around this material.)

Exploiting appropriate examples. Abstract ideas cannot be fully understood without examples. But examples must be memorable, in part by being associated with prior information. Multiple examples of the same material must be associated with each other so that they form a cluster that is associated with the to-be-learned material. For example, when teaching the concept of far transfer, it's not enough for me to provide the example that debate techniques learned in class should then be used months later when arguing politics with friends. You would need a few different examples of far transfer, and I would need to make sure that you have associated them with each other, even though on the surface they may appear very different (Hakel & Halpern, 2005).

Relying on principles, not rote. Learning typically requires not just becoming familiar with examples but also understanding the underlying principles that organize and integrate examples (Kozma & Russell, 1997; Bransford, Brown, & Cocking, 2000). For example, the key to far transfer is to distinguish between surface characteristics (the particular example) and underlying deep characteristics (which tell you which knowledge should be transferred to the present case). For instance, the principles of debate can also be used in teaching, but that doesn't require becoming confrontational (a surface characteristic of debate) but rather being sensitive to the other person's goals and perspectives (a deep characteristic). The principles must be associated with the examples. In general, making explicit the ways that information relates abstractly (at what is called a "deep structural level" in the literature) to other information enhances memory (Chi & VanLehn, 2012).

Create rich retrieval cues   The other class of principles that falls under the maxim "Make and use associations" is "Create rich retrieval cues." The key idea here is that you need to associate distinctive information with what you learn so that you later can be effectively reminded of it when you want to recall it.

Dynamic mental representations arise from recent experiences or thoughts, and often are conscious; thus they are easy to recall. Structural representations, in contrast, are like the crates and boxes in that giant warehouse in the last scene of *Raiders of the Lost Ark*. We can retain uncounted numbers of such mental representations, and they often aren't well organized. We access these representations by using cues and reminders. For example, you might associate one of those crates with a coffin, and hence seeing that shape would remind you of it (and you then could search for other such shapes, if the initial one turned out to be incorrect). Thus, to be easily recalled, it's crucial that structural representations include characteristics that makes them easily cued later, which can include being associated with a distinctive time and place. The following principles can produce such cues.

Creating associative chaining (a.k.a using story telling). Stories are built on a series of interlocking causes and effects—this is the essence of a plot. Creating an interlocking sequence of associations that has a narrative arc—that is, a story—to integrate material will not only help you create larger chunks (stories are one way to build associations to create chunks) but, more than that, you also can use each part of the story to cue the next part when you later recall the material. Such cueing can greatly facilitate later recall of the information incorporated into the story (Bower & Clark, 1969; Graesser, Olde, & Klettke, 2002). For example, to learn the principles underlying the "Think it through" maxim, you could create a story about a friend who uses each of these principles, one at a time, in an effort to learn the computer programming language Python, adopting a new principle when the previous one proves inadequate.

Using spaced practice. Cramming may be an efficient way to study, but it's a bad way to learn. Here's an analogy: when I was young, I had a black wooden desk. I thought it would look much better if I painted it white. Being in a hurry, I ignored the advice to use several thin coats of paint rather than one thick coat. I poured on a single thick coat. At first, it seemed just fine; the black paint was covered up. But in practically no time, the paint began to chip—and soon the desk was a blotchy mess, much uglier than it was in the first place. Something similar happens with memory: Trying to store information in one fell swoop leaves it vulnerable to being lost. One reason for this is that if you cram, you will have only one set of retrieval cues, the associations set up the one time you stored the information. If you instead spread out studying over time, you will associate the material with lots of different cues (such as cues in the room or rooms where you study, your feelings at the time, and thoughts you have while considering the information).

It is much better to use information repeatedly over a relatively long span of time than to try to cram it in all at once in the course of learning it (Brown, Roediger, & McDaniel, 2014; Cepeda et al., 2006, 2008; Cull, 2000). For example, when learning this material you might want to read it once, and then reread it a few times to review.

Establishing different contexts. Far transfer is the holy grail of learning. As noted earlier, far transfer occurs when information learned in one context (e.g., a classroom) is retrieved and applied in a very different context (e.g., to a seemingly unrelated problem in a work environment years later). Far transfer appears to be possible in large part because one has learned a group of varied examples and has a firm grasp of the principles that underlie the relevant material (Hakel & Halpern, 2005; Van Merrienboer et al., 2006). But it also depends critically on knowing when learned information is relevant. To facilitate this, one should associate the material with numerous different contexts. For example, studying in different places will enhance your ability later to use the information in different contexts.

Avoiding interference. Distinctive retrieval cues are crucial in part because they can help the learner avoid interference from other information (Adams, 1967; Anderson & Neely, 1996). Psychologists have documented two types of interference. *Proactive interference* occurs when material you have learned previously interferes with learning new information. For example, if you learned Spanish, you might have a problem learning that "de" is pronounced "duh" in French, not "day" as it is in Spanish. *Retroactive interference* occurs when learning new material impairs your ability to recall previously learned material. In the language example, once you learn the French pronunciation, you might have difficulty recalling the Spanish one. Creating distinctive retrieval cues can help you avoid both types of interference (e.g., you could associate the French pronunciation with an image of a French person having difficulty understanding why a learner is having this problem, perhaps dismissively saying "duh," and a Spanish person taking a siesta in the middle of the "day").

Using the Principles

The principles just summarized encompass a set of processes that underlie all learning. The principles are like letters of the alphabet; different combinations of the same principles can be used in different types of learning.

Many "application techniques" have been developed to evoke different combinations of processes to produce effective learning. For example, researchers have shown that people learn effectively by explaining things to themselves (e.g., Chi et al., 1994). Creating an explanation is a special case of the generation effect, and checking to ensure that it is correct is part of deliberate practice. Thus the method is effective not because it introduces a new kind of cognitive processing but because it effectively recruits combinations of processes that underlie specific principles. Similarly, mnemonics can be a very effective way to learn. In fact, I relied on two of them in the above (the descriptions of learning new names and of avoiding interference both involved mnemonics). But there's nothing special here: mnemonic techniques involve combinations of specific processes, such as deep processing and drawing on previous associations to form new ones.

Conclusion

The sixteen principles reviewed here underlie all forms of learning, ranging from learning a golf swing to learning copyright law to learning about the principles of learning. In many cases, you initially learn a set of rules or instructions that must be consciously mediated (through Kahneman's [2011] "System 2"), and only after practice does the material become automatic (through Kahneman's "System 1").

We at Minerva designed our curriculum from scratch and could be systematic and principled in doing so. We decided to take advantage of the science of learning, and so designed (and are continuing to design) every one of our classes to rely on application techniques: Every class is built around active learning, and every one of our active learning exercises draws on combinations of the principles just described. If these principles are respected in how material is presented and used, students will learn effectively—sometimes without even trying to learn.

Acknowledgments

Brianna Smrke helped me clarify earlier versions of many of the ideas presented here, Behnam Arzaghi did a great job catching errors, and Laurence Holt provided astute feedback that shaped the presentation. I also wish to thank Diane Halpern and Daniel Levitin for useful conversations on this and related topics.

References

Adams, J. A. (1967). *Human memory*. New York, NY: McGraw-Hill.

Anderson, M. C., & Neely, J. H. (1996). Interference and inhibition in memory retrieval. In E. L. Bjork & R. A. Bjork (Eds.), *Memory: Handbook of perception and cognition* (2nd ed., pp. 237–313). San Diego, CA: Academic Press.

Barnett, S. M., & Ceci, S. J. (2002). When and where do we apply what we learn? A taxonomy for far transfer. *Psychological Bulletin, 128*(4), 612–637.

Bjork, R. A. (1988). Retrieval practice and maintenance of knowledge. In M. M. Gruneberg, P. E. Morris, & R. N. Sykes (Eds.), *Practical aspects of memory: Current research and issues* (Vol. 1, pp. 396–401). New York, NY: Wiley.

Bjork, R. A. (1999). Assessing our own competence: Heuristics and illusions. In D. Gopher & A. Koriat (Eds.), *Attention and performance XVII: Cognitive regulation of performance: Interaction of theory and application* (pp. 435–459). Cambridge, MA: MIT Press.

Bower, G. H., & Clark, M. C. (1969). Narrative stories as mediators for serial learning. *Psychonomic Science, 14*(4), 181–182.

Bransford, J. D., Brown, A. L., & Cocking, R. R. (Eds.). (2000). *How people learn* (expanded ed.). Washington, DC: National Academy Press.

Brown, P. C., Roediger, H. L., III, & McDaniel, M. A. (2014). *Make it stick: The science of successful learning*. New York, NY: Belknap Press.

Butler, A. C., & Roediger, H. L., III (2007). Testing improves long-term retention in a simulated classroom setting. *European Journal of Cognitive Psychology, 19*(4/5), 514–527.

Cepeda, N. J., Pashler, H., Vul, E., Wixted, J. T., & Rohrer, D. (2006). Distributed practice in verbal recall tasks: A review and quantitative synthesis. *Psychological Bulletin, 132*(3), 354–380.

Cepeda, N. J., Vul, E., Rohrer, D., Wixted, J. T., & Pashler, H. (2008). Spacing effects in learning: A temporal ridgeline of optimal retention. *Psychological Science, 19*(11), 1095–1102.

Chi, M. T. H., de Leeuw, N., Chiu, M.-H., & LaVancher, C. (1994). Eliciting self-explanations improves understanding. *Cognitive Science, 18*, 439–477.

Chi, M. T. H., & VanLehn, K. A. (2012). Seeing deep structure from the interactions of surface features. *Educational Psychologist, 47*(3), 177–188.

Craig, S. D., Sullins, J., Witherspoon, A., & Gholson, B. (2006). The deep-level reasoning effect: The role of dialogue and deep-level-reasoning questions during vicarious learning. *Cognition and Instruction, 24*(4), 565–591.

Craik, F. I. M., & Lockhart, R. S. (1972). Levels of processing: A framework for memory research. *Journal of Verbal Learning and Verbal Behavior, 11*(6), 671–684.

Cull, W. L. (2000). Untangling the benefits of multiple study opportunities and repeated testing for cued recall. *Applied Cognitive Psychology, 14,* 215–235.

Ericsson, K. A., Chase, W. G., & Faloon, S. (1980). Acquisition of a memory skill. *Science, 208*(4448), 1181–1182.

Ericsson, K. A., Krampe, R. T., & Tesch-Romer, C. (1993). The role of deliberate practice in the acquisition of expert performance. *Psychological Review, 100*(3), 363–406.

Erk, S., Kiefer, M., Grothe, J., Wunderlich, A. P., Spitzer, M., & Walter, H. (2003). Emotional context modulates subsequent memory effect. *NeuroImage, 18*(2), 439–447.

Freeman, S., Eddy, S. L., McDonough, M., Smith, M. K., Okoroafor, N., Jordt, H., et al. (2014). Active learning increases student performance in science, engineering, and mathematics. *Proceedings of the National Academy of Sciences of the United States of America, 111*(23), 8410–8415.

Glenberg, A. M., & Robertson, D. A. (1999). Indexical understanding of instructions. *Discourse Processes, 28*(1), 1–26.

Graesser, A. C., Halpern, D. F., & Hakel, M. (2008). 25 principles of learning. Washington, DC: Task Force on Lifelong Learning at Work and at Home. (For a summary, see Graesser, A. C. (2009). *Journal of Educational Psychology, 101*(2), 259–261.)

Graesser, A. C., Olde, B., & Klettke, B. (2002). How does the mind construct and represent stories? In M. C. Green, J. J. Strange, & T. C. Brock (Eds.), *Narrative impact: Social and cognitive foundations* (pp. 231–263). Mahwah, NJ: Lawrence Erlbaum Associates.

Hakel, M., & Halpern, D. F. (2005). How far can transfer go? Making transfer happen across physical, temporal, and conceptual space. In J. Mestre (Ed.), *Transfer of learning: From a modern multidisciplinary perspective* (pp. 357–370). Greenwich, CT: Information Age Publishing.

Hambrick, D. Z., Oswald, F. L., Altmann, E. M., Meinz, E. J., Gobet, F., & Campitelli, G. (2014). Deliberate practice: Is that all it takes to become an expert? *Intelligence, 45*(1), 34–45.

Kahneman, D. (2011). *Thinking fast and slow.* New York, NY: Farrar, Straus and Giroux.

Kosslyn, S. M. (1994). *Image and brain.* Cambridge, MA: MIT Press.

Kozma, R., & Russell, J. (1997). Multimedia and understanding: Expert and novice responses to different representations of chemical phenomena. *Journal of Research in Science Teaching, 43*(9), 949–968.

Levine, L. J., & Pizarro, D. A. (2004). Emotion and memory research: A grumpy overview. *Social Cognition, 22*(5), 530–554.

Mayer, R. E. (2001). *Multimedia learning*. New York, NY: Cambridge University Press.

Mayer, R. E., & Moreno, R. (2003). Nine ways to reduce cognitive load in multimedia learning. *Educational Psychologist, 38*(1), 43–52.

McGaugh, J. L. (2003). *Memory and emotion: The making of lasting memories*. New York, NY: Columbia University Press.

McGaugh, J. L. (2004). The amygdala modulates the consolidation of memories of emotionally arousing experiences. *Annual Review of Neuroscience, 27*, 1–28.

Moreno, R., & Valdez, A. (2005). Cognitive load and learning effects of having students organize pictures and words in multimedia environments: The role of student interactivity and feedback. *Educational Technology Research and Development, 53*(3), 35–45.

Reder, L. M., & Anderson, J. R. (1980). A partial resolution of the paradox of interference: The role of integrating knowledge. *Cognitive Psychology, 12*(4), 447–472.

Roediger, H. L., III, & Karpicke, J. D. (2006). The power of testing memory: Basic research and implications for educational practice. *Psychological Science, 1*(3), 181–210.

Smith, E. E., Adams, N., & Schorr, D. (1978). Fact retrieval and the paradox of interference. *Cognitive Psychology, 10*(4), 438–464.

Van Merrienboer, J., Jeroen, J. G., Kester, L., & Pass, F. (2006). Teaching complex rather than simple tasks: Balancing intrinsic and germane load to enhance transfer of learning. *Applied Cognitive Psychology, 20*, 343–352.

VanLehn, K., Graesser, A. C., Jackson, G. T., Jordan, P., Olney, A., & Rose, C. P. (2007). When are tutorial dialogues more effective than reading? *Cognitive Science, 31*(1), 3–62.

Wandersee, J. H., Mintzes, J. J., & Novak, J. D. (1994). Research on alternative conceptions in science. In D. L. Gabel (Ed.), *Handbook of research on science teaching and learning* (pp. 177–210). New York, NY: Macmillan.

Willingham, D. T. (2009). *Why don't students like school? A cognitive scientist answers questions about how the mind works and what it means for the classroom*. New York, NY: Jossey-Bass.

12 Fully Active Learning

Joshua Fost, Rena Levitt, and Stephen M. Kosslyn

Minerva is faced with a unique challenge because all classes are taught in real time, as synchronous seminars delivered on the computer. We are competing against all the distractions the Internet has to offer: Twitter, Facebook, texting, e-mail, and their electronic cousins. No one is looking over the shoulders of our students, and many temptations tug at them to drift off to other pursuits during class. Thus we needed to develop new teaching methods that would induce students to stay engaged.

In this chapter we summarize a host of new methods we have developed and adapted to keep students engaged during class—not just interested and stimulated but involved in the sorts of cognitive processing that promote learning and facilitate far transfer. Many of these engagement methods draw on features of the Active Learning Forum (ALF), and we have learned a lot about which techniques are more or less effective.

Key Terms and Associated Concepts

At the outset, we need to clarify a few key terms and associated concepts and to put our approach in a broader context. Let's begin with the concept of *active learning*. Freeman and co-workers' (2014) consensus definition is that active learning "engages students in the process of learning through activities and/or discussion in class, as opposed to passively listening to an expert. It emphasizes higher-order thinking and often involves group work" (pp. 8413–8414). They also cite Bonwell and Eison (1991), whose definition of active learning is "instructional activities involving students in doing things and thinking about what they are doing" (p. iii). We have no quarrel with either of these definitions but believe they can be sharper. We propose the following:

Definition: Learning is *active* to the extent that it engages the cognitive processes associated with comprehension, reasoning, memory, and pattern perception.

These cognitive processes are discussed in chapter 11, which summarizes a set of principles that describe how these processes function in learning. As stated there, these principles can be subsumed under the two overarching maxims "Think it through" and "Make and use associations."

Fully active learning

As we use the term, *fully active learning* requires all students to be engaged at least 75 percent of the time while in class. That is, rather than just professors inviting students to be involved in discussions, fully active learning hinges on activities and exercises that require students to engage in the sorts of cognitive processing that engender learning—namely, those processes mentioned above.

Freeman and co-workers mention that for many educators, active learning often involves group work. Other authors agree, and sometimes combine active learning and collaborative learning—which requires students to work in small groups toward a common goal—into a single category, at least for the purposes of assessing high-impact pedagogical practices. For example, Kuh (2003), reporting on findings from the 2006 National Survey on Student Engagement (NSSE), refers to the "active and collaborative learning movement." Part of the motivation for combining the two practices may be the observation that collaborative learning is likely to be active because members of a group cannot passively receive information. At least there is no "continuous exposition" from an authoritative teacher, to borrow another of Freeman and co-workers' (2014) terms.

Contrasting pedagogies

Kilgo, Sheets, and Pascarella (2015) also combine the active and collaborative learning categories and strongly endorse their efficacy above and beyond most other high-impact practices, writing that "active and collaborative learning and undergraduate research were consistently significant, positive predictors for nearly all of the liberal arts educational outcomes" (p. 521). The combination of active and collaborative learning proved more effective than service learning, first-year seminars, and learning communities, among other methods.

At Minerva, we distinguish between active learning and collaborative learning. More specifically, we see collaborative learning as a special type of active learning. All of our classes are active in the sense that students "do meaningful learning activities and think about what they are doing," rather than passively receive information from the instructor (Prince, 2004).

However, only some of our activities are collaborative in the way that most authors use the term.

Our most frequent use of collaborative learning occurs in "breakout group" activities. In these, our small seminar (maximum of nineteen students) subdivides into groups that typically range in size from two to five students. The breakout groups typically work together privately for ten to fifteen minutes, and then the whole class reconvenes for a debrief, such as a collective sharing of a solution, a critique, and so forth. Collaborative learning at Minerva also occurs when group assignments are completed out of class. This kind of work constitutes approximately 10 to 15 percent of the assignments in our first-year curriculum. Overall, collaborative learning is a common feature of our in-class and out-of-class pedagogy, but it is by no means the only form of active learning that we use.

Another sense of the term active learning extant in the literature concerns student-centered learning (SCL). Lee and Hannafin (2016), citing Jonassen (1991), position SCL as one of the paradigmatic forms of active learning. A comparison of its characteristics with Minerva's pedagogical techniques, however, reveals that the two are not the same—and in some ways are actually opposed. For Lee and Hannafin, when students engage in SCL they analyze ill-defined content that they themselves select, to achieve learning goals that they themselves negotiate. Some implementations of problem-based learning take this approach. For most Minerva classes (the exception being senior tutorials, described in chapter 9), the *base* content for a class session—that is, the material that forms the core of the activities—is selected by the course designers (often not the instructors, and certainly not the students), as are the learning objectives and the lines of inquiry meant to help students master them. Students are encouraged to supplement the required preparation with self-directed research. Indeed, we regard this as so vital to student success that we introduce it as an HC, #selflearning, in the first week of our general education courses. (HCs are habits of mind and foundational concepts, described in chapter 2 and appendix A.)

But such self-selected *and* self-directed inquiry only occasionally forms the basis for a class. It does appear from time to time in assignments done out of class, such as the heavily weighted final projects in our first-year curriculum and the capstone projects in the third and fourth years of study. Overall, however, SCL embraces a much greater level of student autonomy over what is to be learned than does our pedagogy, and SCL has a much smaller level of precision of the predefined learning objectives than is found in Minerva's curriculum.

However, some elements of SCL do parallel our methods. For example, SCL and Minerva's fully active learning both see the instructor primarily as a facilitator rather than as the source of knowledge, and both typically see students as active builders of knowledge rather than receivers. We are all constructivists in this sense; we agree that knowledge cannot merely be received. Instead, it must be examined, critiqued, contextualized, applied, and synthesized with other knowledge—and students are the ones who must do this work (Deslauriers, Schelew, & Wieman, 2011). As noted earlier, the most important reasons for adopting this view are the principles from the science of learning.

In short, we distinguish active learning from collaborative learning and also from student-centered learning. We always use active learning, sometimes use collaborative learning, and sometimes use elements of SCL.

Most of the rest of this chapter is dedicated to explaining in more detail the specific techniques we use to craft active learning activities in the sense defined above.

Pedagogical Tools

Fully active learning relies on specific pedagogical techniques we have developed and tools built into the ALF. The heart of each lesson plan is its set of activities, which build on preclass assignments (described in chapter 14). We established a set of design practices that maximize the amount of active learning in each activity. Our guiding question is, "What is everybody else doing?" That is, for each activity, we focus not just on what the current speaker or actor (e.g., someone solving an equation) is doing but also on what the rest of the class is doing: we don't want students ever to sit passively and listen to what others are saying or doing. Rather, we want all students to be as engaged as possible for as much of the time as possible.

In the service of reaching this goal, we designed two practices: The first is to be deliberate and explicit about our pedagogical technique, and the second is to include as often as possible an explicit "engagement prompt" that tells all students what they should be doing when they are not actively producing a work product (e.g., speaking, writing, or otherwise acting). Both practices are described in detail below.

Varied activity types

People habituate after they do the same thing over and over—and either stop doing it or stop paying attention to what they are doing. Thus, if we require students to do the same sort of activity repeatedly, engagement will flag and they will tune out. Effective active learning therefore must include a wide variety of types of activities. The prototype activities in our initial lesson plans drew from various approaches in active learning (Barr, 2013), including peer instruction (Mazur, 1997a; Mazur, 1997b; Crouch & Mazur, 2001), collaborative work in small breakouts (Macpherson, 2015), debates (Kennedy, 2007), Socratic method discussion (Faust & Paulson, 1998), task- or problem-based learning (Allen & Tanner, 2007), role-playing (Deneve & Heppner, 1997), and game-based activities (Lepper & Cordova, 1992).

Using the prototype activities as a base, we developed and characterized approximately twenty-five different types of activities and in-class work products, each of which has a distinct "tag." One set of tags is used to track the student work product or output for an activity. Examples include *writing, speaking, presenting, diagramming, math,* and (computer) *code.* A second, larger set of tags tracks the type of activity—or, in many cases, a pedagogically relevant facet of it. Some of these are self-explanatory: *discussion, debate,* and *brainstorming,* for example. Other activity types are less obvious but proved to be recurring and useful ways to ensure that every student be actively engaged at least 75 percent of every class session. Examples of these include *focus questions*, which are written at the time the lesson plan is crafted to address particular material in that lesson (these questions are sufficiently difficult and nuanced that after one student responds, others typically are called on to add to or modify the response); *synthesis,* in which students must bring several lines of inquiry into a single coherent view; and *evaluation,* in which students provide and defend a holistic appraisal of a target view or work. Each activity typically is tagged in more than one way. Below is an example from one of the sophomore courses in our College of Natural Sciences. The tags are flagged with an "@" sign, in italics, right after the name of each step in the activity.

ACTIVITY: HC Use in Gould and Lewontin (1979)

1. **Introduction** *@infotransfer* (**2 minutes**) (**SLIDE**). In your breakout group, discuss the central arguments that Gould and Lewontin (1979) make about the adaptationist program. In bullet point form, identify the three to five most important arguments and describe how the authors employ specific HCs to support the arguments you identify.

2. **Breakout groups** *@discussion @analysis @writing* (**10 minutes**). [Students follow the instructions provided in the slide above.]

3. **Debrief** *@discussion @synthesis @focusquestions @speaking @presenting* (**15 minutes**). The instructor should call on students at random, asking them to add an argument to the shared document. The

student who presented the argument should then call on another member of his or her group to discuss how a specific HC was used to support the argument. Gould and Lewontin may or may not have used the HC well, and once the member of the group has described how the authors used a specific HC to support an argument, the class should be asked to use the mastery rubric to grade the authors' use of the HC in the chat.

4. **Activity Summary** *@synthesis @speaking* (**3 minutes**). Ask a random or quiet student: "How did your use of HCs in this activity help you to understand the learning objective for this session?"

A few aspects of this example are worth calling out specifically. First, the *@infotransfer* tag in the activity introduction means "information transfer." In some situations the instructor must provide information to students so that they know what is being asked of them, but this is kept to an absolute minimum; a Minerva class is about learning to *use* information, not about memorization. The "(SLIDE)" notation in this step shows the content that will appear on-screen for students to preview.

A second point concerns what is *not* seen here, namely, the ALF configuration that accompanies each of the three steps within the activity. How the ALF facilitates active learning is discussed in the next section; for now it is sufficient to note that although the lesson plan author is relatively unconstrained in how he or she uses the technology to support instruction, there are some typical patterns. In step 2, for instance, the ALF breakout tool will segment students into groups of a specified size and give each group a "private room" and a blank document to capture their work.

In addition, step 3, the debrief, is important for fully active learning: Students know this is coming and that they can be called on, and this motivates them to pay attention. The ALF configuration for this step would probably display the group notes, two or three of the group members, and a few other students from other groups. Lesson plan designers wield these and other configurations with great precision to optimize the number of opportunities for each student to demonstrate active learning.

These tagging practices have an important application that complements pedagogical efficacy, and that is programmatic assessment. We are laying a foundation of structured data that will allow us to study systematically the types of techniques that work best in various circumstances. Those studies could include an inquiry into whether, for example, written synthesis activities work well (i.e., increase student mastery of the learning objectives) at the end of class (we suspect they do) or whether problem solving works better in groups of two, three, or four students (we do not have a hypothesis about this).

Explicit engagement prompts

A socially reserved student's learning experience can easily be neglected. Even a conscientious professor may end up involving just three or four extroverted students or relying on those perceived to be reliable contributors. This concentrated attention is undoubtedly educational for those few, but whatever it may be for the rest, it is not active learning. Certain features of the ALF help us avoid such problems, but we do not rely solely on them. As soon as an activity work product is defined, we immediately ask ourselves, "What is everyone else doing?" To help lesson plan authors create fully active learning exercises in which all students are engaged at least 75 percent of the time, we created more than two dozen engagement prompts that work for almost any discipline or subject and can be combined with each of our activity types.

We divide engagement prompts into two types: rolling and summative. Rolling prompts require students to pay attention because they will need to respond immediately to another student's contribution. These prompts can appear at any point in a discussion. A few examples are shown in table 12.1.

By priming the class at the beginning of an activity to be prepared to respond to these prompts, we increase the likelihood that a student will engage the cognitive processes that we know are associated with learning.

However, we have noticed a drawback to the use of these rolling engagement techniques. Even though we sample with replacement (i.e., the same

Table 12.1

Sample "Rolling" Engagement Prompts

Representing the view of a prominent figure	Explain what a specific prominent figure might contribute to the discussion. Sample prompt: "When I call on you, be ready to explain what Kahneman [2011] would say about the point made by the previous student."
Sharpest critic	Regardless of your personal view, articulate what the sharpest critic of the view just expressed would say.
Conjunction ("and/but") relay	Extend the previous student's idea by extending it (when prompted with "and") or disputing it (when prompted with "but").

Table 12.2
Sample "Summative" Engagement Prompts

Selecting the "best" response and explaining why it is the best	Which breakout group produced the best product? Which comment was most compelling? Which example was most useful? Explain why your selection was better than all of the others.
Summarizing key points	Summarize the key points made throughout the activity.
Characterizing underlying dimensions	Explain how the points raised varied along a specific dimension. What was that dimension? Illustrate the variation along it by providing several examples.

student can be called on repeatedly), students quickly learn that, on average, once they have been called on it is unlikely that they will be called on again soon. Thus they remain alert and engaged until they are called on, and then are less alert and engaged during the period afterward. Pairing rolling prompts with summative prompts, described next, mitigates this fall-off in attention.

Summative engagement prompts require students to attend throughout the activity in order to prepare for a response at the end. These responses require students to integrate the prior discussion and typically write down their analyses, and hence they must pay attention throughout. Table 12.2 presents some examples.

After students write their responses (which only the instructor can see), the instructor calls on several students to explain and expand upon what they wrote. The instructor often calls on a student who wrote a poor response and then one who wrote an excellent response. This verbal debrief is necessary because the social pressure inherent in the possibility of presenting their reply plays a role in ensuring that they pay attention, taking in what transpires so that they later can write a reasonable response. Furthermore, presenting and correcting a weak response is a means of clarifying potentially common confusions with the full class.

The main drawback we have found with such summative techniques is that they require a fair amount of time. Students often require three to five minutes to write reasonable responses, and then the verbal debrief requires another five minutes or so, which adds up to a noticeable fraction of a ninety-minute class. Nevertheless, the pedagogical value of such practices is clear, and so we view this time as well spent.

Technological Tools

All Minerva classes are computer-based virtual seminars held on the ALF. Some features of the ALF were designed specifically to facilitate fully active learning and complement the pedagogical techniques described in the previous section. Some of these features were designed to counteract computer-based distractions (e.g., the Internet, Twitter, Facebook, e-mail); others were designed to engage quiet students who might be overlooked in traditional classrooms. For example, the ALF includes a "talk-time" feature, a "feature quiet student" tool, and several types of polls, and it facilitates configuring and implementing flexible and highly reconfigurable breakout groups, as described below.

Equal access to participation for all students

Physical classrooms cannot provide equal access for all participants—access, that is, in the sense of seeing and hearing, and being seen and heard by, everyone else. Even in an intimate seminar, with ten students sitting around a table, no one person can see all of the others at the same time; no matter how you crane your head or twist your body, you will see some but not others. And in a lecture hall, students are oriented toward the front of the classroom, so for most of them to see others' faces, they have to turn to the side or completely around. Indeed, most of the time, most students in a lecture hall see the backs of their classmates' heads and only the professor's face, perhaps from some distance. The professor, meanwhile, may see only a few rows clearly.

Such lack of access is worth noting because interacting with others often is a prerequisite for full cognitive engagement and active learning. And to interact with someone, you need information about how he or she reacts to your comments and behavior, and vice versa. If you cannot see everyone all the time, by definition you are not receiving full information about such reactions. In contrast, the ALF provides equal access in ways that no traditional classroom could ever do. All faces are present in a row across the top of the screen, fully visible. Everyone, students and professor alike, is in the front row and equally visible and audible to everyone else.

Talk-time feature

The talk-time feature, triggered when the instructor presses the "t" key, superimposes a colored tint onto each student's video in the row across the top of the screen. Only the instructor sees this overlay. A green tint indicates that the student has spoken comparatively less than other students and should therefore, all else being equal, be called on soon to ensure that he or she has opportunities for active learning. A red tint signifies that the student has spoken comparatively more than others, and a yellow tint indicates approximately average levels of contribution. The feature is data-driven, updating in real time based on the total duration of the audio stream from each student. It does not force the professor's hand, but offers a fairer and more objective basis for calling on students than a professor's unaided memory could provide.

"Feature quiet students" tool

The talk time feature is triggered manually, but the ALF also features a more automatic way to engage students with lower than average participation. This tool is set up when the lesson plan is being written and is used in class. It is the "feature quiet student" tool. When a lesson plan author is designing an activity, he or she specifies when students should be asked questions or engaged in discussion. One option is to have the computer automatically select a quiet student (determined by the amount of recorded talk time) or a group of such students. Alternatively, the author can specify that the computer either selects students randomly or leaves it up to the instructor to select specific students on the spot. Typically the lesson plan author updates the ALF configuration at the beginning of each step within an activity, and hence can repeatedly feature quiet or randomly chosen students.

By automating this process and basing it on real-time data, the ALF allows the instructor to dedicate more attention to facilitating the activity—to listening carefully to the students, to thinking ahead, and to being strategic about asking questions and nudging the discussion in useful directions. Moreover, essentially for free, we help reduce the risk of favoring some students over others, which can arise from the understandable tendency to call repeatedly on reliable contributors.

Free response polls

The ALF also helps keep students engaged by requiring them to write responses. Most often, such responses take the form of "free response polls." The ALF interface presents a poll with a short prompt (such as a question they must answer, a comparison they should make, or a choice they must make and justify), and students write their responses in a text entry field. Typically these polls last three to five minutes, and the students write a few sentences.

We use two types of free response polls in virtually every class. First, at the outset of every class session, students respond to a *preparatory assessment* poll. Such polls are necessary because we use a type of flipped classroom, in which information acquisition (readings, watching videos, etc.) takes place primarily before class and class time is devoted to learning to use the information in various ways. Because the class activities rely on the students' having acquired the requisite background, we must provide incentives for students to do the work. These polls are one such incentive. In this case, the polls contain questions that can only be answered well if students have done the assigned reading and viewing and thought carefully about how the learning objectives apply to them. Before each class session students receive a study guide that suggests active learning exercises to complete as they read or watch a video; this guide also explains why we have assigned the reading or video and often tells the students how the material will be used in class. Thus the demands of the poll are not wholly unexpected, but neither are they easy.

The professor can see each answer as it is posted and can decide, once all students have finished writing, whether to spend a few minutes discussing the poll further. Whatever the decision, all responses are graded (using a rubric) after class and figure into each student's class grade. This grading serves as a spur to ensure that students arrive at class prepared and, equally important, that they know that active engagement with the assigned reading and videos is essential. The polls also lead to timely feedback for the students: professors often complete the grading within a day of the class session's conclusion, and the grades are posted immediately on each student's ALF assessment dashboard.

The second form of free response poll that appears in every class is a *reflection poll*, which is based on the "one-minute paper" technique (Angelo & Cross, 1993). These polls are administered at the end of class, typically in the last five minutes, and pose questions that can only be answered well if the students have been thinking actively throughout the session. Examples of poll prompts include "What was the most challenging concept focused on during this class session? Why? Make sure to reference one specific moment," and "Compare and contrast the way the new HC was used in the activities. What common threads did you see, and what was different?" Answering such questions well requires more than recall: students also must compare and contrast different moments in class and make a defensible evaluation, which in turn requires having paid attention. But more than that, such polls enhance learning by drawing on well-documented principles from the science of learning (discussed in chapter 11), such as the generation effect and the use of appropriate examples. Answers to these polls are also graded, using an appropriate rubric. In addition to grading both polls in each class session, professors have the option to attach comments to poll responses. This practice provides students with daily formative feedback.

Breakout groups

Breakout groups play a role in fully active learning in part because students cannot easily hide from their peers and there is social pressure not to be a "free rider." This is especially the case when the groups are small, with as few as two to three students per group. Such groups facilitate learning even when none of the group members has a solid grip on the material at the outset (Smith et al., 2009).

The ALF allows us to define breakout groups in three ways: (1) by assigning students randomly, as determined by the computer; (2) by assigning students as the professor sees fit; and (3) according to specific criteria (e.g., responses to a poll). In the future, we plan to include past performance (e.g., relevant HC scores) as an additional option, so that students with similar (or perhaps disparate) levels of mastery can be grouped together. Breakout groups can be defined in advance or on the spot. Moreover, students can be moved from one breakout group to another with the swipe of a mouse.

A huge advantage of the virtual classroom, and the ALF specifically, is that breakout groups can be created by the press of a button: students don't need to get up, drag chairs to corners of the room, and get resettled. Moreover, an enormous range of digital assets can be moved into breakout groups, ranging from notes and slides to computer simulation models. Furthermore, the professor can view and listen to each group—and the students may not be aware of when this is happening. And the professor can very rapidly cycle through the groups and only interrupt when necessary. Thus the ALF provides a level of accountability that is not possible in traditional classrooms.

Conclusion

Fully active learning takes good advantage of the principles of the science of learning: It ensures that students process material deeply, induces the generation effect, relies on spaced practice, and so on (see chapter 11). Moreover, fully active learning ensures that all students—not just the outgoing few who love to talk—have a chance to participate. In addition, fully active learning sets up structures (such as those provided by the ALF) and incentives (such as not wanting to look bad in front of one's peers) that keep students from drifting off or engaging in other activities (such as reading Twitter or the like).

Although our technology has been developed with fully active learning in mind from the start, one need not use our technology to benefit from many of these techniques. However, these techniques will not help lecturers encourage students to pay attention during their lectures—to benefit from fully active learning, one needs to use active learning!

References

Allen, D., & Tanner, K. (2007, Summer). Approaches to cell biology teaching: Learning content in context—Problem-based learning. *Cell Biology Education, 2*(1), 73–81.

Angelo, T., & Cross, K. (1993). *Classroom assessment techniques: A handbook for college teachers* (2nd ed.). San Francisco, CA: Jossey-Bass.

Barr, M. (2013). Encouraging college student active engagement in learning: The influence of response methods. *Innovative Higher Education, 39*(4), 307–319.

Bonwell, C., & Eison, J. A. (1991). ASHE-ERIC Higher Education Report (Vol. 1). *Active learning: Creating excitement in the classroom.* Washington, DC: School of Education and Human Development, George Washington University.

Crouch, C., & Mazur, E. (2001). Peer instruction: Ten years of experience and results. *American Journal of Physics, 69*(9), 970–977.

Deneve, K., & Heppner, M. (1997). Role-play simulations: The assessment of an active learning technique and comparisons with traditional lectures. *Innovative Higher Education, 21*(3), 231–246.

Deslauriers, L., Schelew, E., & Wieman, C. (2011). Improved learning in a large-enrollment physics class. *Science, 332*(6031), 862–864. doi:10.1126/science.1201783.

Faust, J., & Paulson, D. (1998). Active learning in the college classroom. *Journal on Excellence in College Teaching, 9*(2), 3–24.

Freeman, S., Eddy, S. L., McDonough, M., Smith, M. K., Okoroafor, N., Jordt, H., et al. (2014). Active learning increases student performance in science, engineering, and mathematics. *Proceedings of the National Academy of Sciences of the United States of America, 111*(23), 8410–8415.

Gould, S. J., & Lewontin, R. C. (1979). The spandrels of San Marco and the Panglossian paradigm: A critique of the adaptationist programme. *Proceedings of the Royal Society of London. Series B, Biological Sciences, 205*(1161), 581–598.

Jonassen, D. H. (1991). Objectivism versus constructivism: Do we need a new philosophical paradigm? *Educational Technology Research and Development, 39*(3), 5–14.

Kahneman, D. (2011). *Thinking fast and slow*. New York, NY: Farrar, Straus and Giroux.

Kennedy, R. (2007). In-class debates: Fertile ground for active learning and the cultivation of critical thinking and oral communication skills. *International Journal on Teaching and Learning in Higher Education, 19*(2), 183–190.

Kilgo, C. A., Ezell Sheets, J. K., & Pascarella, E. T. (2015). The link between high-impact practices and student learning: Some longitudinal evidence. *Higher Education, 69*(4), 509–525. doi:10.1007/s10734-014-9788-z.

Kuh, G. D. (2003). What we're learning about student engagement from NSSE: Benchmarks for effective educational practices. *Change: The Magazine of Higher Learning, 35*(2), 24–32. doi:10.1080/00091380309604090.

Lee, E., & Hannafin, M. J. (2016). A design framework for enhancing engagement in student-centered learning: Own it, learn it, and share it. *Educational Technology Research and Development, 64*(4), 707–734. doi:10.1007/s11423-015-9422-5.

Lepper, M., & Cordova, D. (1992). A desire to be taught: Instructional consequences of intrinsic motivation. *Motivation and Emotion, 16*(3), 187–208.

Macpherson, A. (2015). *Cooperative learning group activities for college courses*. Surrey, BC: Kwantlen Polytechnic University.

Mazur, E. (1997a). Peer instruction: Getting students to think in class. *AIP Conference Proceedings, 399*(1), 981–988.

Mazur, E. (1997b). *Peer instruction: A user's manual series in educational innovation*. Upper Saddle River, NJ: Prentice Hall.

Prince, M. (2004). Does active learning work? A review of the research. *Journal of Engineering Education, 93*(3), 223–231.

Smith, M. K., Wood, W. B., Adams, W. K., Wieman, C., Knight, J. K., Guild, N., et al. (2009). Why peer discussion improves student performance on in-class concept questions. *Science, 323*(5910), 122–124. doi:10.1126/science.1165919.

13   A New Team-Teaching Approach to Structured Learning

Joshua Fost, Vicki Chandler, Kara Gardner, and Allison Gale

Our commitment to the science of learning—and to class quality—requires a high degree of consistency across different sections of a course. At the same time, there are variables: instructors and students have varied expertise and interests, and no two conversations or class activities ever unfold in exactly the same way. To achieve consistency, leverage diversity, and maximize buy-in from faculty, we have adopted an unconventional but demonstrably effective set of practices. In this chapter we describe the work phases, team compositions, communication tools, and documentation practices used by our teaching teams. Because it has been in place longer, the emphasis here will be on our first-year general education curriculum, which we have taught for multiple years. Although as of this writing we are just now transferring these practices to our upper-division courses (sophomore year and above), it is clear that they can easily be applied widely throughout our curriculum.

The following discussion explains how our team-teaching model works in detail. As is evident, developing and teaching courses at Minerva are group activities, and the processes we have put in place are designed to ensure that the whole is much greater than the sum of its parts.

The Process of Course Development

To understand the role that teaching teams play at Minerva, it will be helpful first to understand the broader context of our course development process. Our team-based approach begins long before a class ever meets, though the workflow varies depending on the type of class. Syllabi, learning objectives, pedagogy, and assessment practices for the first-year cornerstone courses were developed and refined iteratively over a period of three years (indeed, refinement continues still) by a team that included the chief academic officer, deans of the four arts and sciences colleges, the associate dean of the faculty, the associate dean of institutional and educational research, the director of curriculum development, and a number of people who would later serve as development and instructional faculty. Because of the central role played by our general education curriculum and the breadth of the material covered, we dedicated and continue to dedicate a great deal of time and effort to this work.

A more recent and more common workflow, in terms of the number of courses developed, was crafted for our upper-division courses. The procedure is as follows:

1.   The college dean writes a one-paragraph overview for a course, ensuring that the course description fits well within the overall curriculum goals for the college.
2.   We engage a faculty member or consultant to write the syllabus. The dean and the syllabus author develop the course objectives, learning outcomes, and topics to be covered and select appropriate readings for each session; they iterate first to produce an outline, and then a full syllabus.
3.   The chair of the Council of Deans reviews the syllabus. More iteration ensues as needed.
4.   The syllabus is reviewed by two external subject matter experts, and more iteration follows as needed.
5.   A candidate final syllabus is reviewed by the chief academic officer. Iteration continues until final approval.

In our experience, this level of escalating inclusion and iterative development on a syllabus is unusual. One reason we go to such lengths is that the syllabus forms the foundation for a great deal more work, namely, the crafting of assessments and more than two dozen types of fully active learning exercises used in class, each of which may be used in many classes (each semester comprises twenty-eight sessions, and each session on average has two active learning exercises). If the foundations are weak, the later work that rests on them will be compromised.

Another reason we go to such lengths is that we seek strong integration and complementarity of courses within the curriculum for a particular major or subfield. As one of our faculty said, "At Minerva, it is important to think of a course one is developing and teaching as 'our' course, not 'my' course." At many other institutions, courses may be developed and taught by faculty members working in comparative isolation with little or no oversight. Classes developed in this way are likely to be highly variable—from year to year, section to section, and certainly instructor to instructor. In our view, this is problematic because, as concerned as we are with pedagogical efficacy, we are equally concerned with the reliability of that efficacy. Reproducibility is a foundational principle in science: to be true to the science of learning, we need blueprints for courses that can be followed by teachers here and at other institutions to achieve similar results, and for that it is not enough to identify reading materials—however worthy they may be in principle—and send instructors into classrooms with whatever tools they may (or may not) possess. This issue is particularly important at Minerva because our curriculum is highly structured: upper-division courses rely on the students having learned specific material in previous courses, and hence we must ensure that they in fact do so.

Communication Channels

The geographic freedom afforded by our virtual classroom model has had an interesting and beneficial side effect: we have become more intentional about ensuring easy and frequent communication within and among various constituencies. No doubt we benefit too from being a new institution: the prospects for innovation and creating a true "learning organization" have clearly energized our whole staff, and new colleagues come into Minerva expecting to do things differently. We direct that energy into at least four well-defined communication channels, which have been developed specifically to foster within- and between-team dialogue. Three of these spaces are, at least in their basic form, conventional meetings; they are synchronous conversations conducted on the Active Learning Forum (ALF) platform. There is nothing novel about a meeting, of course; what is novel is the level of consistency and the fruitfulness of these meetings. The fourth communication channel is harder to characterize. All are described below.

Weekly meetings
The canonical model for these meetings is as follows. We deliberately avoid scheduling classes on Fridays, largely so that students can exploit the rich cocurricular offerings available to them and explore the cities in their global rotation. A side effect of this scheduling decision is that faculty are freed of teaching in the classroom, creating space for each team (i.e., all the instructional faculty teaching a particular course, the course designer, and often the relevant college dean) to meet virtually on the ALF for one hour each week, usually on Fridays.

The primary purpose of these meetings is to conduct a "one week back, two weeks ahead" review. Typically the meetings open with a brief review of what worked or did not work in the week just concluded. The most important of these observations will have been captured in the lesson plan notes (for more on this, see the discussion under "Capitalizing on Individual Strengths," below). Then the lesson plan for the upcoming week is subjected to a detailed walkthrough, and the lesson plan for two weeks hence receives a lighter review. Faculty identify potential problems that in their view need to be addressed, or simply suggest ways to improve the plan. Examples of modifications that are considered include the clarification of assessment questions, the addition of fruitful topics for discussion, ideas for hooks (see below), and the addition of useful background readings for faculty. In some cases—rare, given the amount of collaboration and oversight that has already been incorporated into each lesson plan—there will be suggestions for substantial pedagogical changes, such as modifying an activity from a whole-class discussion to a problem-solving exercise in breakout groups. Cross pollination is common: instructional faculty have varied subdisciplinary backgrounds and can share distinct insights relevant to the lesson plan.

Some of us have taught at institutions where a model similar to this was in effect, at least nominally. In many of those cases, however, the schedule for the meetings slipped to perhaps once per month, then once per semester, or even not at all. The reasons for this slippage are neither complex nor important to delineate here; what is important to note is that because we place instructional efficacy rather than research efficacy at the center of our institution, team-based work like this is not compromised by unaligned incentive structures. Our weekly meetings really do happen, for every team, and they are productive and pleasant enough to be self-sustaining.

Slack channels

Slack is a multiplatform communication tool for teams. Its core feature is channel-based exchange: users create channels for whatever purpose; people join those channels, post to them, and are alerted when others post. Direct person-to-person messages are also supported, and small working groups can create private multiparty channels, usually short-lived, to address emergent issues. Conversation within a channel is chronological, cleanly formatted, and easier to parse than a typical e-mail thread. Auxiliary features such as synchronous telephone-call-style conversation (using a computer instead of a phone) and custom integrations with other software tools are also frequently useful.

We use Slack extensively and in a variety of ways. The feature most apropos for teaching teams is the course-specific channel, accessible by all the core stakeholders. For example, we have a channel for our Empirical Analyses cornerstone course. Participants in this channel include all the instructional faculty currently teaching the course, the development faculty who wrote the original syllabus and lesson plans, the dean of the College of Natural Sciences, the director of the first-year curriculum, and the director of curriculum development.

In a typical week, channel conversation might address coordination regarding assignment dates and details and cross-section calibration regarding model answers to questions posed to students in class. The Slack channel might also be used to share useful background or accessory readings, place requests for and post reports about substitute teaching, post morale-boosting (and, occasionally, commiserating) reports on teaching experiences, pose calibration questions on assessments, and provide technical status updates on the availability of resources for faculty and students.

Because all of this traffic is posted and read asynchronously but persists in a mode that makes it easy to scan quickly, significantly less time is needed than would be required for in-person meetings designed to achieve the same end. Because the time demand is much lower, people are more likely to read the material posted and to remain fully active participants on the team. Further, because our faculty are often not in the same time zone, asynchronous reading is a very important requirement.

One novel use of Slack's software integration tool is indirectly relevant to team teaching, and that is the "HC of the Day" ("HC" is short for habits of mind and foundational concepts; see chapter 2 and appendix A). This piece of software once a day automatically randomly selects one HC, including its full description and a sample real-world application, and posts it to the general channel on Slack. Everyone in the organization, not just those on the academic team, sees these posts. By making everyone aware of our general educational goals, we effectively increase the size of the teaching team. Members of the student experience team, for example, become better able to plan cocurricular activities that reinforce the HCs. Members of the student life team can encourage students to apply these skills to problems they may encounter in their nonacademic life. Gratifyingly, it was a request from these and other teams that motivated us to create the feature, which is widely read.

Full faculty meetings

Once per month, the entire faculty body meets as a group. We initially met on the ALF but have now have switched to a commercial large-capacity video conferencing system; the ALF is limited to about thirty people, and we've outgrown that. We do not have a "not invented here" syndrome; if another provider better serves our needs, we will use it (but we will also be thinking about how to grow our own technology to serve our needs, so that we don't have to depend on others).

In a recent and representative meeting, the agenda included a review of the expectations associated with academic advising and the tools available to help advisors; a "design sprint" to help support the collaboration between the student experience team (the team that organizes cocurricular events) and the faculty, a report on the status of special initiatives (in this case, workshops to help students struggling with mathematics, writing, or computer programming), and general announcements—all of which was followed by an open Q&A discussion.

Faculty advisory committee

The mechanisms described above help us tackle a range of issues, from the tactical (affecting a single lesson plan) to the strategic (affecting the institution as a whole). The fourth mechanism we designed to capture the more strategic issues. For this, we created a Faculty Advisory Committee (FAC), which consists of one member per college (Arts and Humanities, Business, Computational Sciences, Natural Sciences, and Social Sciences), with one of those representatives appointed chair. The chair of the FAC facilitates the regular meetings and serves as a point of contact between the committee and other academic groups, such as the development faculty, curriculum directors, and the deans. The members and the chair of the FAC volunteer to serve, and their participation is approved by the other instructional faculty in their colleges.

The FAC was designed to collect information about the instructional faculty experience and share that with the curriculum directors and the deans. The FAC also serves as a point of contact when directors and deans require faculty input. The committee has a monthly meeting, in advance of which the chair collects agenda items from its members. The meetings are attended by all committee members, the associate dean of the faculty, and one of the five college deans, who serves as a representative. After each monthly meeting the agenda and notes are shared with all members of Minerva's academic team and posted on our intranet.

To ensure representative sampling, we are considering limiting the term of each committee member to one semester. Although that could lead to continuity problems, we suspect this will not be a concern; most of the decisions made at this level are implemented within the semester in which they are made.

To highlight meeting outcomes, share general announcements, collate, and preserve all communications from these disparate communication channels, we produce a weekly newsletter. All newsletters are filed on an online portal where they can be referenced later by faculty and staff.

Capitalizing on Individual Strengths

Our first-year curriculum comprises the four yearlong cornerstone courses, which demand much from our faculty because their learning goals and applications are so diverse. For example, our Formal Analyses course includes learning goals (HCs) in formal and informal logic, computer science, probability and statistics, game theory, and decision theory—all of which are embedded in applications in advertising, biotechnology, climate change, artificial intelligence, epidemiology, psychology, and political science. We do not expect each of our instructors to have a strong background in all these areas. Instead, we help them learn how to "teach what they don't know" (e.g., by asking them to read; Huston, 2009) and we rely on the skills and backgrounds of a diverse team. In a variety of ways, we nurture rich interaction and rely on peer instruction among the faculty to help every instructor become an informed and effective facilitator of active learning exercises in all these areas.

Invited comments on lesson plans

Our ALF and Course Builder (described in chapters 15 and 16, respectively) tools include nudges that encourage instructional faculty to provide comments on lesson plans they have just taught. These comments do not have to be lengthy to be useful. The key is to capture them when the instructors' reactions are fresh—specifically, when class has just concluded.

Feedback captured in this way is consumed at least three times. First, it is reviewed by the course developer and discussed in Friday meetings or, if more time-sensitive matter is involved, in e-mail or on a Slack channel. Second, such feedback is used to help revise our courses. All of our courses are revised periodically and in a way that makes the changes visible to the entire teaching team, so that all instructors are using the same lesson plans and all students have equal access to our best effort. Heavy reviews are likely for the first two or three iterations of a course. This was especially true of the cornerstone courses, which were subjected to deep overhaul after the first year—only about 10 percent of the material from the original courses survived—and then major revision after the second year—about 60–70 percent was saved then. During these revisions, we use the comments from the teaching teams. We also include more broad-based feedback from faculty and students concerning what might be thought of as "structural" factors, which occur at levels of analysis greater than the individual lesson plan or even the course or the college. For example, through a series of ad hoc conversations and later full-faculty meetings, we realized during our second year of offering classes that we had not calibrated our grading expectations especially well. More to the point, we had asked instructional faculty to provide more scores than could feasibly be provided. We score students on the approximately 115 HCs, roughly 30 per course. If each student receives three scores on each HC, each professor would have to generate just over 1,700 grades per course section. Reducing that target to something more achievable, given the other demands on faculty time, while preserving the highly granular and frequent formative feedback we demand proved challenging. In the end, input from the faculty proved critical to creating a grounded, realistic plan that met the pedagogical requirements.

The third way in which we use lesson plan feedback is in performance reviews. The deans provide career guidance to faculty based in part on the instructor's involvement in ongoing curricular revision, and offering constructive criticism on lesson plans is an example of such contribution.

Field reports

Teaching Minerva students from the lesson plans is extremely rewarding and challenging. We ask very bright students to come to class fully prepared to discuss, critique, and debate the materials for the class session, extend ideas introduced earlier or in another class, and apply them to real-world situations and their own interests and projects. Sometimes students ask sophisticated and insightful questions that cannot be adequately addressed in the time available or to which faculty do not know the answer. On other occasions matters of classroom management call for a creative response—for example, if a student critiques the pedagogy of an activity rather than the material or learning outcome itself. In all these cases it is helpful for faculty to share experiences they encounter in the classroom and how they handled them. Very often the best practices that emerge from these conversations make their way into the faculty instructions provided for each activity in the relevant lesson plan, or into the feedback database that we use to refine the activities in the next iteration of the course.

Grading support

A challenge when navigating team-taught courses is not just to ensure comparable (not to say identical) experiences for students in the classroom but also to maintain consistency in the assessment of student performance. New Minerva faculty commonly wonder whether they are grading students fairly and accurately, and whether their colleagues would grade the same work the same way. This cross-professorial calibration is a novel demand that may cause some initial anxiety.

To address this uncertainty, faculty have found their own creative, effective approaches. During their monthlong orientation and training in how to teach at Minerva, faculty receive a primer on rubric-based grading. This primer is a start, especially because it includes sample exercises to improve inter-rater reliability. But for new faculty there is no substitute for the real thing. Faculty during the semester have thus continued to cross-calibrate in two main ways: (1) by real-time sharing of sample student responses via Slack or other messaging services and (2) by initiating group meetings over the ALF to establish general principles for grading a particular assignment or poll question. These two approaches are not either-or solutions; faculty make use of both, in real time, to ensure grading consistency.

An occasional issue with rubric-based grading is that many of the HCs have broad scope. For example, the HC #dataviz, introduced in Empirical Analyses, addresses effective visual representations of data—any visualization, any data. Clearly, there are many determinants of an effective (or ineffective) visualization, so faculty teaching that cornerstone course arranged on their own to meet before grading an assignment in which students graphed data using multiple visualization techniques. The meeting helped clarify what exactly constituted a "2" versus a "3" rubric score. For example, the teaching faculty discussed how to handle and discriminate incorrect axis labels versus incorrect legend labels. Of course, such meetings can lead to lively discussion and even disagreements. But finding common ground is possible with the team-minded faculty at Minerva. The rubrics provide blueprints but cannot anticipate every situation, so ultimately the faculty fine-tune and implement them, just as they do with the lesson plans themselves.

This situation is far different from that at most institutions of higher learning, where faculty have enormous independence in what and how they teach, typically answering only to themselves and, on some occasions, their students. Because of the granularity of our assessments, the strictures enforced by rubrics, and the need for inter-rater calibration, grading at Minerva is time-intensive. Still, this investment yields dividends: the faculty develop bonds with their colleagues and feel (and are) part of a larger mission. One faculty member, experienced but new to Minerva, reported: "Within the first couple of months at Minerva, I feel not only a deeper and more meaningful connection to my colleagues, but a clear sense of how I fit into the bigger pedagogical picture. The distinct feeling of not wanting to let my colleagues down motivates me to be better every day. It is energizing."

Although our HC rubrics and within-course faculty collaborations go a long way toward achieving tightly calibrated scores, the diversity of student work means there are times when external support is needed. This is particularly likely to occur when faculty find themselves grading HCs that were introduced in a course they do not teach. An example might be a professor with no background in music assessing a student on the #music HC. In such cases, what is needed is something like a medical consult, an ad hoc, brief review of the student's work and guidance about what level of mastery was demonstrated. Slack is a good tool for this because the requesting professor can post the sample to the channel for the multimodal communications course, in which the #music HC is introduced, and the entire teaching team for that course would see it. It would not be unusual for one or more answers to arrive within minutes.

Another more proactive approach to the same problem, and one we have used to particularly good effect, is for the subject matter experts to contribute to a short addendum, a "grading guide," to the HC rubric. This grading guide explains what competent application of that HC might look like in the context of a particular assignment. Such addenda are captured and included in the faculty-facing sections of the assignment for use in future years.

Although it is clear that the grading style at Minerva requires more time from the faculty, the results have been positive in perhaps more far-reaching ways than originally intended. Yes, the main goal is consistency of grading across courses, but an important side effect that should not be overlooked is the bonding it creates among colleagues and the genuine sense of being a valued member of a team that it fosters.

Lesson plan development

Every class session at Minerva is highly structured and detailed lesson plans are drafted in advance. These lesson plans not only specify the readings but also include a quiz on them (administered at the beginning of class), a description of preclass homework (if any), detailed instructions about the activities (typically two, but ranging from one to three), and a "reflection poll" at the end, along with a wrap-up summary activity.

In a typical upper-division (sophomore or later) class, the person who writes the syllabus will also write the lesson plans. In the case of the highly interdisciplinary cornerstone courses, however, no single course developer has all the expertise required. Each of these courses spans a wide range of topics, many of them outside the normal purview of the college that hosts the course. For this reason, course developers sometimes asked for and received assistance in writing lesson plans. This came in degrees: sometimes the consultation was limited in scope to providing readings, "teaching the teacher" before lesson plan development began, critiquing a set of focus questions to be used in class, or designing the entire plan. A few examples will make this more concrete.

To get a sense of the range of materials in the cornerstone courses, let's consider the fact that the multimodal communications course introduces HCs not only about written and verbal communication but also about artistic composition and interpretation, both in the fine arts and in multimedia. Even the process of "design thinking" is introduced in this course; we introduce it here to encourage students to consider the full array of expressive tools before deciding on what will work best for a particular communicative purpose. Design thinking is more common in engineering than in literature and the arts, and indeed, this lesson plan was developed by a faculty member with a background that included teaching engineering. In the Complex Systems course similar occasions arose: although the course is in the College of Social Sciences and most of the subject matter lies cleanly within those boundaries, some of the topics, such as dynamical systems theory and agent-based modeling, are not as commonly encountered, even by an interdisciplinarian. So in that course too, some of the lesson plans were developed through consultations between the course developer and a subject matter expert. Some of these needs arose in the moment, as the course developer realized that he or she was not the best equipped to deal with a topic, whereas others were anticipated well in advance, and consultation was scheduled accordingly.

Hooks

By "hook," we mean a vivid and often surprising anecdote or example that motivates the need for, or provides an application of, a particular learning objective. When a good hook is available, it can engage students and facilitate learning by tapping into the *evoking emotion* and *creating associative chaining* (a.k.a *using storytelling*) principles from the science of learning (see chapter 11). By their nature, however, hooks are not widely known, and sometimes only a single person is aware of material that can be used as a hook for a particular lesson. Teaching teams are an effective way to share the wealth that these stories can provide. For example, our Empirical Analyses cornerstone course introduces the HC #perceptualbias. The concept itself—that our expectations influence our perceptions—is not complicated, but neither is it especially resonant for students with little or no training in psychology. A great example of the phenomenon is the *checkershadow illusion,* which professors with a background in perceptual psychology are likely to know. Yet many of the professors teaching Empirical Analyses have a background in the natural sciences and don't know the illusion. A second example: our Formal Analyses course introduces the HC #correlation, which includes both the mathematical calculation of correlation and learning the essential distinction between correlation versus causation. To vividly illustrate the distinction, professors might mention that the divorce rate in Maine is strongly correlated ($r = 0.9926$) with the per capita consumption of margarine (Vigen, 2016), though one strains to imagine a plausible direct causal connection. A short discussion helps anchor the concept in students' minds. Clearly, this is not a standard example in mathematical instruction—which is part of what makes it a memorable and effective hook.

Setting the stage: Faculty orientation
Teaching from highly structured lesson plans helps us maintain consistency across multiple sections of a course, and our rubrics help ensure that all faculty apply consistent standards when evaluating student work. Nevertheless, faculty come to Minerva with backgrounds in different disciplines and varied experiences in the classroom. Academics typically receive little or no training in how to teach effectively as part of their doctoral and postdoctoral work. We have found that the orientation of faculty to Minerva plays a crucial role in the implementation of our pedagogical structure. All new faculty must participate in a monthlong training course to learn about the science behind our approach to teaching and to get hands-on experience in both the implementation of lesson plans and the assessment of student work.

During the first week of our training, faculty are introduced to Minerva's overall pedagogical approach. We facilitate the sessions on the ALF, and the classes are structured in a manner quite similar to our undergraduate classes. Faculty have readings and assignments to prepare ahead of time; they take polls to assess their preparation at the start of class; they participate in active learning exercises (e.g., they work together in breakout groups, approaching problems and questions using peer instruction); and throughout each session, facilitators call on faculty members at random to share answers. This format provides faculty with the opportunity to play the role of students, allowing them to build empathy and understand what it is like to be a student in a Minerva classroom. Most important, they engage deeply with key topics—the science of learning, types of active learning, Minerva's HCs, our curriculum, assessment, and rubrics—using fully active learning.

After one session of technical training on how to run the ALF seminar classroom, faculty take a few lesson plans from their fall semester courses and run practice classes for their colleagues, deans, and (when possible) Minerva students. Each practice teaching session is followed by a feedback session. Every observer must tell the facilitating faculty member what he or she did well and what might be improved. During these sessions, faculty learn how to navigate the ALF and bring lesson plans to life. Often, lesson plans are taught multiple times by different instructors. This allows faculty to see how every class session can be authentic, natural, and responsive to student contributions, while also following a set of structured activities with clearly defined learning goals.

After their practice teaching sessions are completed and recorded, faculty learn how to assess student learning outcomes and HCs by scoring their class videos. They also grade sample papers and meet with their teaching teams to do inter-rater reliability exercises. By the end of the monthlong training, faculty have initial hands-on experience with all of the instructional tasks they will perform during the semester.

Conclusion

Our training sessions are extensive, and faculty are well prepared when they enter the classroom on the first day of class. Still, new challenges are encountered every day when working with students. Deans and academic directors provide support throughout the academic year, answering questions daily by Slack channels and keeping faculty informed through a weekly academic newsletter. Monthly faculty meetings allow us to tackle as a community issues that arise, and we also hold periodic pedagogy sessions to share strategies and best practices. Our faculty strive each day to build a community united in a common goal: helping our students meet their full potential.

References

Huston, T. (2009). *Teaching what you don't know*. Cambridge, MA: Harvard University Press.

Vigen, T. (2016). Spurious correlations. http://tylervigen.com/spurious-correlations

14   Teaching from Lesson Plans

Vicki Chandler, Stephen M. Kosslyn, Richard Holman, and James Genone

Lesson plans (LPs) at Minerva are a crucial bridge between the syllabus and the classroom. Because Minerva's classes are all small seminars, multiple sections are the norm. Following a model that has been used successfully for decades at Harvard Business School and in the Columbia University core program, all faculty who teach the same course use the same lesson plan. This practice ensures that the pedagogy is implemented consistently in different sections of the same course, that the same materials are covered, and, crucially, that students have comparable opportunities for engagement and learning.

The LPs also allow substitute faculty to cover for a professor if an emergency arises, without compromising the students' progress. Another benefit of using well-designed and well-articulated LPs is that they provide a record of what was taught previously and therefore a basis from which to modify and update each class session for future semesters. This helps us both to improve the curriculum each year and to provide consistency across years.

However, our use of LPs does not minimize the role or the contributions of the professors. The professor is not a "sage on the stage" but is also not simply a "guide on the side." Our professors are experts in their fields, which is necessary because they must direct the discussion and adapt the flow of the class to ensure that students are in fact learning the requisite material.

We now review what is contained in each LP, the pedagogical purpose of each component, and the professor's role in achieving this purpose. We provide examples that illustrate how Minerva's LPs facilitate dynamic teaching, with ample opportunity for each professor to bring his or her expertise, skill set and personality into the classroom.

Preclass Work: Setting the Stage for Active Learning

Minerva employs a "fully active learning" model (described in chapter 12) in each class session, whether the class is part of the general education cornerstones or the major core and concentration courses. Fully active learning is defined as all students being engaged at least 75 percent of the time, digging deeper into and reinforcing their learning of the material. For this method to work well, students must absorb specific information before class.

Moreover, Minerva's "radically flipped classroom" approach puts both the homework and primary knowledge dissemination before class, so that the ninety minutes of class time are reserved for learning how to use the information productively—which is consistent with our emphasis on practical knowledge. Specifically, we design the in-class activities to lead students to *use* the information they acquired through doing their preclass work (watching videos, reading papers, doing homework), perhaps by applying the ideas to solve a problem, engage in a debate, or role play applying the concepts in different contexts.

Faculty do not lecture at Minerva. Our seminars are not designed primarily to transmit information. Instead, faculty help students learn to use information productively and in novel ways. Faculty devote their energies to facilitating active learning, not to reading aloud from lecture notes or working through PowerPoint slide decks.

This approach makes identifying appropriate readings and other preparatory work a crucial aspect of course development: students must prepare on their own before class, and there are no lectures during which faculty can fill in gaps in the materials.

To help students prepare for class, each LP has a "why/use" statement for each reading or video. This statement explains why the material was assigned and what key aspects the students should attend to in order to prepare for class activities. The LP also provides a study guide, which further explains what students should concentrate on—for example, it might ask students to define key terms, summarize the main components of a theory, or compare and contrast two readings—and often provides questions for students to answer as they prepare for class.

For some class sessions the LP also specifies work that students do before class, either individually or in small groups, and then bring to class to use in a specific way. Such preclass work may require students to prepare pro and con arguments that will be debated in class, to set up and solve mathematical problems that form the basis for applying the concepts and methods to a new (often more complex) problem in class, or to analyze a data set and generate hypotheses to be critiqued in class. Such homework is always used in one of the in-class activities, all of which were designed to build on that preparation. This allows in-class activities to achieve a greater level of depth than would otherwise be possible.

Learning Outcomes and Activity Learning Goals

At the core of every lesson plan are two or three activities that are designed to reinforce the learning outcomes introduced in that class session. The learning outcomes for the cornerstone courses are the habits of mind and the foundational concepts, or HCs (see chapter 2 and appendix A). The learning outcomes for upper-division courses depend on the specific topic of the course and typically are specialized aspects of practical knowledge, or skills and knowledge that will lead to practical knowledge (see chapter 9).

Every activity is introduced by an "activity learning goal," which emphasizes a specific aspect of one of the learning outcomes targeted in the lesson. This activity learning goal motivates the activity, which is designed to achieve this goal. The activity learning goal often takes a relatively abstract or general learning outcome and drills down to a specific concrete aspect of that outcome—which in turn allows us to design an activity.

The activities themselves are structured to include an introduction (which includes a slide with the activity learning goal), the activity itself, and then a "closure moment." During the closure moment after the students have completed an activity, the professor may ask specific "focus questions" that direct students to the aspects of the activity that bear directly on the activity learning goal. These questions do not have simple yes/no answers; rather, they are prompts for deep engagement and discussion, which the professor utilizes to maintain the appropriate level of attention. Because different students will answer these questions in different ways, the discussions in two sections of the same course will never be exactly the same—and in all cases the professor must be able to pose illuminating follow-up questions and respond to questions from the students. Thus faculty must study the lesson plan carefully and be prepared for both common pitfalls and ways to help students go beyond the prepared material to reach deeper levels of insight.

The two examples below illustrate the relationships between and among learning outcomes, activity learning goals, and activities. One example is from the cornerstone course Formal Analyses and one is from a major core course in natural sciences.

In the Formal Analyses cornerstone course, a learning outcome is the HC #assertions ("Identify and analyze premises and conclusions"), which is introduced when formal logic is discussed. The LP contains two activities that give students practice in parsing statements into premises and conclusions. In the first activity, the activity learning goal is "Identify and classify logical sentences and arguments." To achieve this goal, students see a set of sentences; they then take a poll to answer such questions as "Do these sentences form an argument?" or "How many of these sentences are contingent?" After going through the polls, the professor conducts a debrief session in which the answers are discussed and focus questions are asked, such as "Is each logical statement a tautology, a contradiction, or a contingent sentence?"

Once the professor determines that the students are secure in their ability to identify logical statements and their types, the class moves to the second activity. The activity learning goal for this activity is "Determine consistency or inconsistency in groups of statements." This goal strikes to the heart of logical reasoning, and is something the students clearly should master. First a list of very similar sentences is presented, and the students read the statements carefully. They are to decide whether the sentences form a logically consistent argument. Then students go into breakout groups to create their own sets of statements, which either are consistent or (subtly) inconsistent. During the debrief portion of the activity, the professor asks one of the groups to present its sets of sentences and the other students to classify each set. (The students enjoy the challenge of trying to design a set that is only subtly inconsistent, which may fool their classmates into thinking the set is consistent.) The professor then asks the students to suggest small edits of the sentences that could convert them from one type to another, and guides this discussion. Clearly, the professor needs a level of expertise above and beyond what is required simply to lecture; he or she must understand the material deeply in order to guide the discussion appropriately.

As another example, in the Evolution Across Multiple Scales major core course (taught in the sophomore year in natural sciences; see chapter 9), one learning outcome is "Distinguish modes of selection and analyze their impact on genetic variance within and between populations." The first activity of the class has the activity learning goal of "Distinguish different modes of selection and their consequences for change in traits." In this activity the professor shows the students a series of graphs (from primary research papers) that represent different modes of selection. The professor asks students to identify the type of selection represented by each graph and to answer deeper focus questions. The graphs are related to, but distinct from, what was in their readings—which requires students to apply the underlying ideas from their pre-class learning.

The second activity in this class session has the activity learning goal of "Design, critique and interpret selection experiments." Students go into breakout groups of three to four students. The professor reminds the students of an article they read prior to class that relied on an experimental design to test for frequency-dependent selection. The professor then asks the students to modify the design to test instead for density-dependent selection. In the debrief after the class reconvenes, students share their experimental designs and predictions. The professor calls on students who are not presenting to ask a question or share an improvement. Depending on what is said, the professor corrects, amplifies, or nudges the class in certain directions. The activity ends with the professor's revealing an actual study of density-dependent selection, which students compare to their own designs.

Teaching in the Active Learning Forum

Once they have been designed and reviewed, LPs are automatically loaded into the Active Learning Forum (ALF; discussed in chapter 15), which is where the seminars actually take place. The ALF facilitates many different types of activities. The professor executes the LP but has control over the sequence of events in class. The ALF has a timeline that displays each of the major steps in the lesson and enables faculty to monitor the time spent on each section and to adjust the pace. Professors typically proceed through the timeline in the preconfigured order, but they can easily change the order if they believe a different one will be more effective in class. For example, if based on the initial discussion in class the faculty member decides that it would be best to begin with activity 2 in the LP rather than with activity 1, he or she can readily do so with the click of a mouse. Steps within an activity can also be reordered or adjusted.

As an example, the LP may specify that a debrief following breakout sessions should occur sequentially by groups. However, after monitoring the breakout groups and seeing that most of them arrived at similar conclusions, the professor can decide instead to debrief across all groups simultaneously and change the ALF configuration with a key click. Similarly, if students are struggling with the material in a lesson, a professor may opt to forgo the scheduled breakout sessions and instead adapt the planned tasks to work with the entire group in the main classroom. This flexibility enables faculty to monitor each activity and modify it to facilitate learning in the class; in all cases, however, the professor continues to emphasize achieving the activity learning goals. Understanding when and why to modify the sequence of events in a LP is one of the most important skills Minerva faculty must cultivate.

Other examples of the ways that faculty can adjust LPs include adding more time to a breakout session, ending a breakout session early, sending messages simultaneously to all breakout groups to amplify or modify the instructions (e.g., if the professor notes confusions when listening in), creating a poll on the fly, adding a repoll and comparing pre- and post-poll results after a particularly rich debate, calling for a yes/no vote spontaneously, introducing a new whiteboard, screen-sharing to run simulations (or prompt students to do so), and launching resources from the web. The professor can also specify how many students, from one to eight, are to appear on the main stage of the classroom (see chapter 15; all students and the professor are visible across the top of the computer screen, and below this is the main stage, which can have one to eight windows loaded with the professor, students, or documents); the professor can change this number quickly, as appropriate.

Making best use of these affordances requires faculty to judge both the needs of individual students and the progress of the class as a whole. In some cases the professor can challenge students who have already grasped the main idea of a lesson to explain it further, which will both solidify these students' own understanding and help bring their peers along. To do this effectively, faculty must accurately gauge what students have understood, based on their contributions, and must have adequate facility with the content and classroom technology to respond to the needs of the moment.

Engaging Students

Active learning is successful only if the students become engaged with the material. The principles that have emerged from the science of learning require that students actually think through and organize material in specific ways—and they need to pay attention to do so. Thus an important part of the professor's job is to ensure that students are paying attention, that they are engaged. The LPs are designed to promote this in several ways, as summarized below.

Incentives to prepare

A successful Minerva class requires all or virtually all students to come to class fully prepared to engage with the materials that were assigned to be read or viewed before class. One incentive that we use to encourage students to prepare in advance is a poll given near the beginning of each class, which is specified in detail in the LP. For the cornerstone courses the polls cover the preclass materials (readings and videos) that explain the HCs introduced in that class. In the major core and concentration courses the polls assess deep understanding of the assigned preclass materials for that day's learning outcomes. The questions in these polls cannot readily be answered by a quick Google search; instead, to answer the questions, the students must have read or viewed, thought about, and synthesized the material prior to class.

Cold calling

Another incentive for students to prepare for class is that faculty typically "cold call" on students throughout a class session. Although the ALF allows students to raise their hands (symbolized by a hand icon that occurs over their thumbnail video at the top of the screen), professors typically start a discussion by calling on students, often those who have not been active participants. To facilitate this, the ALF includes a "talk time" feature that allows faculty to see the relative amount of time each student has already spoken during class. The students never know when they will be asked to answer questions or apply the class material in a new way. If they haven't done the work prior to class, it is obvious to all.

Engagement techniques

To ensure that students are fully engaged, we have developed "engagement techniques" that are designed to encourage students to pay attention. As LPs are designed, the designer must always be thinking, "What is everybody else doing?" As discussed in chapter 12, we spend a lot of time and effort trying to ensure that those not being called on are nevertheless paying attention. We have found that students are more likely to pay attention when discussions and debriefs move quickly among multiple students, which requires considerable skill to manage without appearing rude. This is something we explicitly address when training faculty how to teach at Minerva. We avoid long presentations by students, keeping their answers succinct and to the point. Students are aware that they may be called on at any time to respond to what a previous student said or to offer a counterargument. In addition, before a debrief or discussion the professor alerts students that at the end of the activity he or she will call on a few students to analyze, synthesize, or compare/contrast specific aspects of the discussion. For example, the students may be asked to compare and contrast different positions that were discussed or to summarize succinctly the multiple pro or con arguments. The professor may ask all students to type into a free-response poll their answers to such a question, and then select a few students to expand on their answers to the class.

Wrap-up session

The LP also specifies a final "wrap-up session," which requires students to look back over the class session and consider how the learning outcomes and activity learning goals were addressed. Part of this session is a "reflection poll," which is designed as another way to motivate students to stay engaged throughout class (see Angelo & Cross, 1993); this poll requires students to reflect either on threads that cut through the entire session (requiring both analysis and synthesis) or on specific moments in class during which some aspect of the learning outcome was discussed (and because students are not aware in advance of which particular moment will be relevant, they need to pay attention throughout class). The professor scores each answer and often provides written comments, giving students richer feedback to help them learn what they understood well and what needs improvement.

At the end of the wrap-up session the professor asks a few students to summarize the main take-home message of the lesson and asks additional students to supplement this summary until all of the important points have been mentioned.

Conclusion

The LPs structure the ninety minutes of each class session by specifying components in a standard order. However, this structure is by no means rigid and does not prevent the professor from shaping the discussion or reallocating time to adapt to changing circumstances. Specifically, these components include the following. (1) At the beginning of class, the professor briefly introduces the learning outcome and activity learning goals of the class, which also allows him or her to ask and answer questions dealing with the preclass material. (2) Following this, a poll assesses students' understanding of the material assigned for preclass preparation. The professor leads a follow-up discussion, ensuring that the class understands the key concepts that are needed to achieve the learning outcome. (3) The professor then introduces and conducts the activities (typically two or three); the professor engages with students throughout the activities. (4) Finally, the professor conducts the wrap-up session and administers the reflection poll. A key part of the wrap-up requires returning to the learning outcomes and activity learning goals and discussing how the activities addressed them.

The LP structure leads the professor to monitor the class at every step of the way and to shape the flow to fit the evolving discussion. There are many opportunities for faculty to modify the structure on the fly to best achieve the goals of the class.

We must note, however, that although faculty do enjoy substantial flexibility, they are required to stick to the materials and to attain the learning outcomes and activity learning goals for each class. Our curriculum is highly structured, and we need to ensure that students have learned the prerequisite material for later classes. Furthermore, our professors are expected to incorporate active learning throughout the class (no lecturing) and to make sure that there is time at the end of each class for the wrap-up session, including the reflection poll. Significantly more skill is required to run a Minerva classroom than is required to give a lecture; we require all new faculty to attend a monthlong training course on how to teach using fully active learning and the ALF.

Because we encourage our students to be active learners and to come to class prepared to engage with and often challenge the material, faculty cannot readily predict ahead of time how each component of the class will proceed. Therefore, our faculty need to be skilled listeners and ready to adjust the structured plan as it plays out. This requires both a deep understanding of the course material and the ability to make good decisions quickly and appropriately. An effective Minerva professor knows when calling on one more student can help cement a key concept, and can identify the right moment to shift to the next topic. Moreover, our faculty must come to know their students well, and understand how to leverage different levels of preparation and ability to maximize individual and group learning.

In sum, teaching from lesson plans requires both expertise in the subjects we teach as well as expert facilitation skills. This expertise and these skills—in conjunction with the lesson plan itself—provide the opportunity for an unparalleled teaching experience for our faculty and a unique learning experience for our students.

Reference

Angelo, T., & Cross, K. (1993). *Classroom assessment techniques: A handbook for college teachers* (2nd ed.). San Francisco, CA: Jossey-Bass.

15 The Active Learning Forum

Jonathan Katzman, Matt Regan, and Ari Bader-Natal

As we began work on the Active Learning Forum (ALF), we not only had to work with Minerva's academic team to determine how best to teach our students, we also had to design a learning experience that far exceeded what students imagine takes place in a traditional university. To do this, the Minerva product team collaborated with the academic team to consider the implications of research on teaching and learning. One seminal piece that inspired us was Bloom's "2 Sigma Problem" (Bloom, 1984), which found that one-to-one tutorials offered a two standard deviation improvement in learning over traditional classroom instruction, a conclusion that has subsequently been buttressed by many other studies (e.g., Freeman et al., 2014).

Recognizing the exorbitant cost of scaling an education system based purely on personal tutoring, Bloom posed a challenge: How might we approximate this impressive gain using an alternative form of instruction that would be economically viable at scale? He proposed and evaluated one such alternative, mastery learning, and his framing of the two sigma problem led many other researchers and practitioners to develop and evaluate other alternatives over the past thirty years and more. One class of approaches, generally characterized simply as "active learning," emerged from a growing body of positive results (largely in the physics education literature). Active learning techniques aim to directly engage each student in a series of structured activities, in stark contrast to the large lecture hall instruction typical of introductory physics courses. Specific approaches or components ranged from peer instruction (Mazur, 2013) to team assignments, group problem solving, and more (see chapter 12; see also Willingham, 2010).

In our effort to create a class that surpassed the learning outcomes associated with a traditional seminar classroom, we explored how technology could be used to facilitate intimate conversations between students and professors, exploit the wealth of material online, enhance collaboration between students in class, and record every class so that the information could be used as a source of feedback for both students and faculty.

As we developed prototypes of the ALF, we learned from our own experiences and a few outside trials of our technology. We quickly realized that we needed to satisfy three critical conditions in order to achieve the above goals. First, we needed every student to feel as though he or she were sitting right next to the professor in every class; this is the position that gets you the most attention in a traditional classroom, which in turn leads to intense and interactive experiences. Second, we needed the technology to fade so far into the background that it virtually disappeared. The focus of the class had to be on the discussions among the students and the professors and not on the technology at their disposal. And finally, we needed to ensure that the seminar experience didn't disappear into the ether after class ended but was recorded so that it could be replayed for individualized feedback and improvement.

The result of this work is the ALF. Below we describe both the methods we used to create the ALF and the results we are achieving with the ALF as we strive to help our students deeply learn to use the material, be able to transfer it to novel situations, and remember these skills long after they were taught.

Creating the Active Learning Forum

The birth of the ALF took many forms and directions. Very early classes were piloted by faculty and staff, teaching each other on a crude yet functional prototype. This exercise produced invaluable data about the sorts of techniques that most engaged participants and led to lively classrooms.

The prototype was then continuously refined based on the results of these early classes and on the results of internal design exercises that were structured as "design sprints" (see Google Ventures [n.d.] in the reference list). New and proposed features were tested on current college students to validate some of our thinking. After months of testing and sample classes we had the initial production version of the ALF, but it lacked a certain level of emotional power.

We decided to return to our founding product design principles to determine how to address this problem. These principles are (1) engage deeply, (2) enhance focus, (3) eliminate friction, (4) promote collaboration, (5) support interconnections, and (6) be meaningful.

Because prospective students were eager to know how ALF looked and performed, we designed and produced a short video that embodied an aspirational design which pushed the limits of both what our most recent version of the ALF was capable of doing and what it looked like. The team was inspired by this future-looking version and over the next three months worked tirelessly to get the initial version as close as possible to the one promised in the video.

We finished in March 2014, just days before our first preview weekend for prospective students. Silently observing that first class with actual students was our first real test; it felt as though we were watching an Olympic figure skater land a series of complicated jumps. We held our breath as one of our deans led students through polls, breakout groups, and other aspects of a typical Minerva class. The result was a very impressed classroom of prospective students—and a very excited product team!

That September, our founding class students started taking classes—two years and one month after we began pursuing the vision of what the ALF could be. We continue to observe classes and gather feedback from our faculty and students, resulting in a product that is always improving.

Fully Active Learning: Sitting Next to the Professor

Our founding dean taught the first full seminar on ALF to the Minerva product team in a series of classes focused on the science of learning (see chapter 11). For years, learning science research has produced amazing insights into how humans learn—but the classroom hadn't systematically changed to take advantage of those learnings. We set out to do just that.

One of the fundamental findings from this literature is that active, engaged minds learn much better than students who passively listen to lectures. We wanted every student to be actively engaged in the classroom activity as close to 100 percent of the time as possible. We were determined to use both product design and the science of learning to make this happen. This is an example of our product design principles to engage deeply and enhance focus.

Basic design of the ALF

The ALF has been designed from the ground-up to support active learning in small seminars. From a product design perspective, there is no back row, no way to hide or sit far from the professor. The professor and every student have a clear view of every other person in the class. Anyone speaking automatically occupies a spot on the large center stage (figure 15.1).

Figure 15.1
The ALF has no back row, no way for a student physically to hide or sit far away from the professor. The professor and the students all have a clear view of every other person in the class. The person who speaks automatically occupies a spot on the large center stage.

Sultanna Krispil, one of our founding class students, describes it this way (Minerva, 2015): "In a normal classroom there are people behind you, there are people beside you, but [on ALF] it's nice to be able to see everybody and their reactions to what's being talked about in class." We go so far as to randomize the order of videos of students in every class so that students are not always in the same place.

Many of our learning activities rapidly call on students to participate. While intense, these pedagogical techniques also create an immersive environment in which our students and our professors are fully absorbed. We frequently hear from both constituencies that Minerva classes are the most engaging classes they've ever been part of and that they have more emotional connection to their fellow participants.

We then combined the product design with a sharp focus on activities that would yield even better learning. The philosophy behind the design of the ALF continues to be to create relatively few features but make them great instead of merely good. We also strive to show fewer elements whenever possible to reduce cognitive load.

The ALF doesn't just incidentally support fully active learning: built into its core is a set of evidence-based activities that are rooted in the science of learning. Templates for activities that are based on the science of learning, such as peer instruction and Socratic sprints, exist in a shared institutional database that curriculum developers can draw from and then customize to design the lesson plan for any given course. By coupling the lesson plan creation with the teaching environment, we are also able systematically to gather data and subjective feedback—which allows us constantly to improve the courses. And through our constructing a long-term curriculum, lessons can build on past material and ensure spaced practice and opportunities for near and far transfer.

What results is a class packed from beginning to end with activities that have been designed to foster the greatest amount of learning (see chapters 12 and 13 for teaching on the ALF using the lesson plans), with technology playing a supporting background role.

Structuring the class

Students arrive in the classroom having already completed their readings and assignments on the subject matter for that particular class session and are fully prepared to prove what they have learned. They do this during a series of lively discussions and activities that not only improve their own grasp of the subject matter but also help their classmates understand it. Because all class sessions at Minerva are versions of a flipped classroom, we designed the ALF to excel for this type of pedagogy.

Because so much is packed into every ninety-minute class, efficient use of time is key. Many of the most common activities that the ALF supports would simply be too cumbersome and time-consuming to squeeze into a traditional class of that duration.

Breakout groups   The ALF is particularly useful when breakout groups are employed. In such cases, the class can easily be divided into a series of breakout groups, often with each group being assigned a different small assignment to work through or discuss (figure 15.2). Immediately after the breakout groups end, the groups present their findings one by one and are challenged by other students and the professor. In a real-world setting this would involve determining who would be in which group, physically moving chairs around, and then trying to get the discussion done in a noisy, incoherent space, then repeating the process for the next group.

Figure 15.2
Class can very quickly be subdivided into a series of smaller breakout groups, often with each group receiving a different assignment to analyze or solve collaboratively.

In the ALF, this breakout process is instead triggered by the press of a button, with students immediately placed in a private "room" where they can focus on the task at hand, ask questions of the professor, have access to anything on the desktop or on the Internet, and easily see how much time is remaining. Professors have the ability to see how students are interacting during their working sessions and what each group is working on. Furthermore, the professor can visit—join the breakout—or just listen in on the breakout group. Immediately after the breakout session ends the groups can be quickly rotated through, with their work displayed to the rest of the class and actively critiqued by their peers. The result is an activity that efficiently promotes collaboration.

Polling and voting   The ALF also makes it very easy to use various sorts of polling and voting. Polls are used in almost every class session to assess mastery of a topic or to take the pulse of a class's feeling on a particular subject (figure 15.3). This ability to provide rapid feedback (on the students' understanding of a problem) to both the students and the professor is part

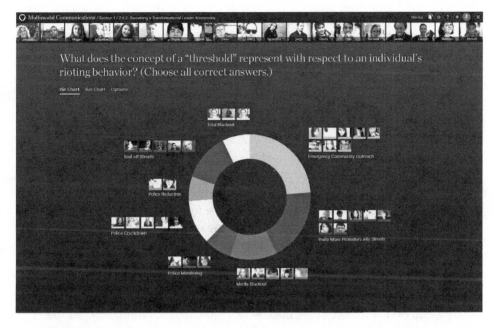

What does the concept of a "threshold" represent with respect to an individual's rioting behavior? (Choose all correct answers.)

Figure 15.3
Polls are used in almost every class session to assess mastery of a topic or to take the pulse of the class's feeling on a particular subject, and the results can be displayed to the rest of the class quickly, indicating how each student voted.

of engaging deeply. Polls can also be used as opportunities for graded feedback to students during class review.

Once a poll has been completed the results can be displayed in a variety of formats, but, more interesting, the same poll can immediately be rerun, allowing those students who changed their mind to be identified quickly and called on to explain their reasons for doing so. Most commonly, repeated polling will be interleaved with related activities: a poll, a classroom activity, and then a repoll. This is similar to what happens in collaborative learning or peer-to-peer instruction (Bonwell & Eison, 1991; Lee & Hannafin, 2016; Mazur, 2013; Prince, 2004).

The ALF also supports real-time continuous voting, that can be conducted over the course of time to gauge students' changing reactions. For example, students might flag when they agree or disagree with other students who are debating. Or they might use the flags to moderate a debate and determine when one of the debate participants is not following the rules. Real-time voting opens up interesting pedagogical techniques, such as reviewing a class to see where various students diverged in their assessment of a debate performance or how different presentations of the same concept affected student perceptions.

Collaborative whiteboards   Collaborative whiteboards allow actions not possible in a traditional classroom. With a scientific chart or an artwork displayed in class, students can be called on to plot a curve or highlight a point of interest.

For any type of activity that requires resources that are not built into the ALF, professors and students can screen-share any application on their desktop or Internet browser. This capability effectively allows our faculty and students to quickly and easily bring material from the world at large into class. Furthermore, students can show a wide range of work, whether it is a coding exercise, an essay, or a piece of art. This feature allows us to support interconnections that we cannot design ahead of time.

All of these activities were designed hand in hand with the academic team as it was designing our pedagogy and curriculum. In particular, we focused on the science of learning, which provided the foundations for the activities and shaped the overall arc of learning across each class session, each semester, each year, and the full college experience. The science of learning guided us when we designed tools that would induce students in particular classes, for example, to engage in deep processing or to experience the generation effect and spaced practice.

Discussion Is Critical, Technology Is the Stage

Although technically robust and intentionally packed with the ability to mount activities based on the science of learning, it was critical that the ALF facilitate learning while simultaneously being unobtrusive and allowing class discussions to occur uninterrupted. We aimed for engaging interactive classes that would promote discussion, dialogue, and active thinking, not passive receptivity while showcasing splashy technology for technology's sake.

Teaching a great seminar is hard work in and of itself. Professors find themselves with a powerful arsenal of tools, but we learned early on that if we weren't careful and deliberate, directing the class might interfere with teaching the class. We wanted the technology-rich classroom environment to enhance rather than overwhelm the learning and teaching experience in small, participatory learning environments. We needed not just to encourage discussion and active learning but also to figure out how to simultaneously reduce the professor's cognitive load while enhancing the focus on teaching.

We focused our thinking in these areas on how to eliminate friction and promoting collaboration. We eliminated friction by improving fluidity of the discussion and removing barriers. We also anticipated the needs of the classroom. We promoted collaboration by removing cognitive barriers for the professors and allowing them to attend to the discussion at hand. We also support multiple modes of communication, such as chat or discussion in breakouts, in which many students can participate at once.

Decision support tools

One mechanism for simultaneously enhancing the seminar experience and reducing the cognitive load on the professor is to provide professors with easy access to relevant data that can help inform their in-class decision making. We sought to understand what data or signals our professors would find useful if available to them so that we could automate the collection, processing, and visualization of those signals. We wanted to make such data or signals quickly accessible to professors in the classroom. This general approach—augmenting expert faculty with technologies that make available the relevant data to support and inform their decision making—guides faculty decision support at Minerva. Because decision support is a general approach and not a single specific technology, we begin the discussion by sharing a few findings from our early experiments that we have since applied to the design of our current and future decision support tools:

• *It should be up to the individual professor to take or leave any insight that our tools provide.* Decision support should inform and not limit decision making, so we leave it up to the professor to determine how best to combine automated insight with her own expert knowledge of the students and of the curriculum.

• *Decision support tools should be informative at a glance.* If a tool requires too much concentration to use effectively or otherwise distracts the professor from class discussion, it could make the class worse rather than better.

• *It is better to provide professors with relevant data as an overlay that enhances the primary view than to provide a separate dedicated display or dashboard.* Although a dedicated view sounded promising, this required professors to watch two displays rather than one, which significantly increased the cognitive load.

With these findings from past experiences as a foundation, we consider one specific use case for decision support at Minerva and describe in detail the tool that we designed and incorporated into ALF as a result.

A significant portion of the assessments that factor into a student's course grade at Minerva is based on verbal contributions in classroom discussions throughout the semester. Thus, if a small group of students dominates a discussion, those students inadvertently limit the opportunity for other students to contribute and be assessed. To avoid this situation, professors do their best to provide each student with ample opportunity to participate. Unfortunately, all of us are prone to various cognitive biases (including availability heuristics and gender stereotypes), and these biases affect whom a professor chooses to call on. Beyond the goal of being fair in calling on students, a professor would ideally also take into account which students could benefit the most from specific opportunities to participate. Depending on the question or topic being discussed, different students may benefit to varying degrees from the opportunity to participate and receive feedback. A student on the cusp of mastering the underlying concept or habit, for instance, could benefit more than a student who has already demonstrated mastery repeatedly. In this sense, there are more and less efficient allocations of the opportunities to answer questions in the classroom.

Although a professor in a traditional classroom could theoretically collect relevant data and bring it to bear in class discussions on the fly, the additional time and coordination required to do so are prohibitive. In the ALF, on the other hand, we can help professors make use of relevant participation and performance data in a way that doesn't require extra preparation before class or cognitive load during class. In this way we can offer professors a tool that helps them engage students in a more equitable and efficient manner.

The decision support tool that we incorporated in the ALF to support professors in this regard was dubbed "talk time." We designed this tool to maintain a running tally of the amount of time that each student had been talking in class and to provide the professor with an easy way to see which students had talked significantly more or less than the others. The talk-time tool works as follows: when the professor depresses the "t" key while in class, every student's thumbnail (along the top of the screen) is overlaid with a red, yellow, or green tint, indicating the amount of talk time relative to other students in the room during that session (figure 15.4). A red overlay indicates that a student has talked significantly more than others, a yellow overlay means that the student is near the classroom average, and a green overlay means that the student has spoken significantly less than others. Professors can use this information quickly and easily to identify which students have not yet participated and which students have already had ample opportunities to contribute.

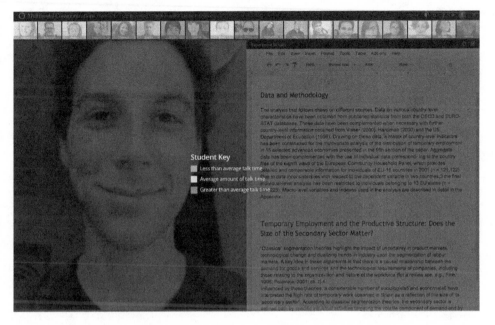

Figure 15.4
The professor can use the "talk time" feature to ensure that all students have comparable amounts of time to contribute to the discussion. When the professor depresses
the "t" key while in class, every student's thumbnail is overlaid with a red, yellow, or
green tint, indicating that student's average level of talk time for that session.

Preparing for a particular lesson

Another tool we developed to reduce the professor's cognitive load was the
timeline. Professors who taught the earliest Minerva classes had to change
the class layout manually, had to drag resources and students onto the
"stage" (i.e., the central area of the display), and had to find and choose
specific polls and breakouts. It became painfully obvious that this was a
large burden and unsustainable. To address this problem we designed what
we call the timeline. Essentially, every lesson plan is broken down into a
machine-readable format that subdivides the class into a series of activities,
each having a number of steps. Each step can be anything from reconfigur-
ing the classroom to a breakout discussion. (Chapter 16 provides a detailed
discussion of the technology used by course designers to design and prepare
a timeline.)

The timeline can be viewed only by the professor. The professor can pull
up the timeline simply by tapping a key, and then see an overview of the
class from beginning to end (figure 15.5). However, actually displaying the

Figure 15.5
The timeline allows professors to see an overview of class from beginning to end, to change the classroom from one state to another easily, and to remain on time.

timeline isn't necessary; professors can keep it out of view if they wish to keep their interface uncluttered and advance to the next step of class by way of a keyboard shortcut.

When the timeline is displayed, every step in it is clearly labeled with a title and a time indicator that indicates how many minutes should be spent on it. If professors start to spend too much time on a particular step, the timer begins to turn from green to orange and then to red to indicate that the pace should be increased.

The timeline is also able to draw on talk-time information. For example, the timeline can automatically pull up the six least talkative students and place them on the main stage of the classroom to discuss a topic. In addition, every timeline feature has a series of action buttons that the professor can use to move an activity forward: For example, the professor can press a button to display a given breakout group during a postbreakout review step.

Getting the interface out of the way

Equally important for improving the professor's ability to teach a great class was an interface that would get out of the way. We ruthlessly cut extraneous features and the user interface so that both faculty and students could focus on the current learning activity. We also enabled tools to appear at the right moment. For example, poll results can be brought in and then easily dismissed when no longer needed. Interesting questions or comments typed in advance by students can be quickly featured to the rest of the class to focus attention just when they are needed.

The main stage can be divided into one to eight divisions, or "panes," which can be filled by either faculty or student videos or by specific content. Collaborative documents, websites, videos, or anything available over screen sharing can be quickly and easily shown to the rest of the class.

Although deemphasizing the user interface and getting tools to disappear so as to enhance focus the teaching was important, it quickly became apparent that we needed to emphasize faces to create an interconnected, human-centric classroom. Whenever the classroom enters a discussion-heavy segment, large-view faces of contributing students quickly rotate through the stage; the larger views convey body language and expressions much more effectively.

We ensure that everyone in the seminar is focused on what's most important: either people talking or the content being discussed.

Allowing the professors to focus on teaching and simultaneously removing clutter from the product design led to classes full of intimate discussion. These intense seminars facilitate both great learning and deep connections between students and faculty. Many of our faculty report getting to know their students better while using the ALF than when teaching in traditional classrooms. Our students echo these sentiments. To quote Eugene Chan, a transfer student from a highly selective university into our class of 2020, twenty-three days into his first semester: "So far, I feel more engaged in these discussion-based sessions than any other classroom experience I have had. Even if I feel like a zombie when I wake up, by the time I log onto the platform and start class, my brain is fired up" (Chan, 2016). As Sherry Turkle (2015) discusses in her work on reclaiming conversation, we are actually creating a classroom environment that fosters the type of relationships between students and teachers that have often gone missing.

One of our professors, Randi Doyle, asked herself on taking the job: "How will I develop close relationships with the students?" She soon answered her own question: "It only took a few class sessions for this concern to fade. I feel I am closer with every student I teach at Minerva than any student I taught at traditional institutions. This is likely because I spend the entire class engaged with the students at Minerva, deep in discussion or debate " (R. Doyle, personal communication, October 25, 2016).

Technologies for Student Feedback

From the first days of the development of Minerva's technologies, we were tasked with enabling and supporting an unusual but principled form of assessment. In addition to assessing performance on course-specific learning outcomes, we needed to assess performance on a set of Minerva-wide learning outcomes, habits of mind and foundational concepts (HCs), associated with four core competencies: critical thinking, creative thinking, effective communication, and effective interaction. These HCs, introduced in the first-year curriculum, would be assessed across all courses and across all semesters for a student. We needed to assess students both on mastery and on their ability to transfer what they had learned to novel contexts. In subsequent years we would also need to assess students on the content-specific learning outcomes that would be introduced in the upper-division courses. In all cases, rather than relying extensively on written work and end-of-semester exams, we focused heavily on formative assessment, with a significant emphasis on assessing and providing feedback on what students demonstrated during classroom discussions.

As with other components of the ALF, a set of design principles informed how we designed the technology. These principles have served as a useful framework for several years of iterative design and development. Specifically, we aim to (1) grade consistently, (2) provide feedback in context, (3) aggregate meaningfully, and (4) show progress. (Chapter 17 provides a detailed discussion of how we assess student learning at Minerva and how each of these principles informed the design of the technologies that we developed.) Here we include a brief summary of the ALF-specific technologies that resulted.

Because many different professors would be assessing the students, in many courses over many years, we needed to be as consistent as possible in defining what a student was being graded on and what the criteria were for assessing each of the gradable comments or products. As a result, each of the Minerva-wide learning outcomes (HCs for all years, and then content-specific outcomes for upper-division courses) has a crisp definition and a detailed rubric for evaluation. All of our assessment tools—including tools for assessing written work, video-based multimedia, spoken contributions in class, and written reflections in class—use definitions and scoring rubrics for the learning outcomes. In each case, professors use rubrics both to provide specific scores and to elaborate on the scores by making written comments, with the emphasis placed on providing actionable feedback. All of a student's assessments, from all courses and from all semesters, flow back into the central assessment database. We do not ask our professors to provide overall letter grades on assignments that aggregate a set of observations across unrelated learning outcomes. Instead we record each underlying rubric assessment independently, which allows us meaningfully to aggregate performance on a single learning outcome across a variety of different contexts. Because these assessments of a given learning outcome were graded consistently across these contexts, they can be meaningfully aggregated.

Within the ALF, students can see their own high-level performance on each learning outcome, organized hierarchically under the course outcomes (e.g., Minerva's four core competencies for the four first-year cornerstone courses). For each learning outcome the student can view a wide variety of relevant information, including a detailed description of the learning outcome, model examples and applications, the complete grading rubric, links to the original course in which the learning outcome was introduced, visualizations of the student's scores (e.g., histograms), and a comprehensive data table of every assessment on this learning outcome, including hyperlinks to the archive of the student work being assessed.

When a professor provides feedback to a student, we want it to be a response to something specific that the student wrote or said, and we present each piece of formative feedback in context. "In context" means something different depending on the medium, so our grading tools anchor feedback differently depending on the medium of the work being assessed. For written homework, each assessment is anchored to a highlighted text selection within the student's written submission. For video-based homework, each assessment is anchored to a specific timestamp in the student's video submission. For software-based homework, each assessment is anchored to a specific piece of code or supporting comment, plot, or other type of rich media included in a Jupyter notebook (Kluyver et al., 2016) or other structured code submission. For in-class contributions to seminar discussions, each assessment is anchored to a specific contribution that the student made to the classroom discussion, whether it was a spoken comment in class, a typed comment in the chat, or a written response to a gradable poll question.

Our ability to anchor a rubric-based assessment to a moment in a classroom discussion is the most unusual aspect of this suite of assessment tools. To make this possible, we create a video recording of each class session and we align the video with an automatically generated event-based transcript of each individual student's contributions to the discussion. The professor reviews this transcript along with the video after class (akin to an athletic

Figure 15.6
Professors can easily review a class and provide students with written feedback and scores on the granularity of an individual spoken comment and a typed comment or a response to a gradable poll question.

coach's reviewing a game tape or a violinist's reviewing a concert recording), using a dedicated classroom discussion assessment tool, and the professor can attach rubric-based assessments to any student-produced event in the transcript. Each event is directly linked to a corresponding segment within the class video recording (figure 15.6), which provides a bidirectional connection between assessments and moments in the video recording. In this way the professor can easily review a class and provide students with comments and scores in response to very specific contributions they made to the classroom discussion. By making clear which of the student's contributions each assessment addresses, the professor can provide more meaningful and useful feedback to the student.

Conclusion

When our methods of achieving all three of our major goals work together synergistically, the results are engaging, unforgettable classes, amazing learning opportunities for our students, and deep relationships between our professors and students. As Dean Vicki Chandler says (Minerva, 2015):

"[The ALF is] interactive, very dynamic and very fast paced. I feel like I'm in a room with all of my students. I simply forget that I'm on a computer." For our students this elicits the sort of experience Haziq Azizi Ahmad Zakir expressed (Minerva, 2015): "It's the kind of learning where we're an active participant instead of a passive recipient. Both the student and teacher are engaged in not only dialogue but debate and role-play, and it's so much more fun than a traditional classroom." The computer melts away. Students and professors immerse themselves in the material at hand. And, last but not least, our students engage in deep learning that can only be achieved in an environment that facilitates and augments human coaching. The result is that we achieve our last design principle: be meaningful. We enable students to advance their self-discovery in collaboration with their fellow students while creating strong bonds both with their classmates and with their professors.

Acknowledgments

We thank the entire product team at Minerva that worked on the ALF. In addition to the authors of this chapter, past and present team members include Asher King Abramson, Avery Anderson, Jason Benn, Javier Cerviño, Ben Chun, Andrew Collins, Paul Craciunoiu, Casen Davis, Brian Fields, Cheng Gong, Laurence Favrot, Nick Fishman, Gene Hallman, David Jacobs, Jason Morrison, Jan Nelson, Eylem Ozaslan, Arthur Rio, Pedro Rodriguez, Jeff Root, Erin Spannan, Michelle Tilley, and Nick Zarczynski. We also thank the Minerva academic team for being amazing partners on this journey.

References

Bloom, B. (1984). The 2 sigma problem: The search for methods of group instruction as effective as one-to-one tutoring. *Educational Researcher, 13*(6), 4–16.

Bonwell, C., & Eison, J. A. (1991). ASHE-ERIC Higher Education Report (Vol. 1). *Active Learning: Creating Excitement in the Classroom.* Washington, DC: School of Education and Human Development, George Washington University.

Chan, E. (2016). "23 Days Later. ..." https://mystudentvoices.com/23-days-later-cc6fad6d9d27.

Freeman, S., Eddy, S. L., McDonough, M., Smith, M. K., Okoroafor, N., Jordt, H., et al. (2014). Active learning increases student performance in science, engineering, and mathematics. *Proceedings of the National Academy of Sciences of the United States of America, 111*, 8410–8415.

Google Ventures. (n.d.) Design Sprints. http://www.gv.com/sprint

Kluyver, T., Ragan-Kelley, B., Pérez, F., Granger, B., Bussonnier, M., Frederic, J., et al. (2016, May). Jupyter Notebooks: A publishing format for reproducible computational workflows. In *Positioning and Power in Academic Publishing: Players, Agents and Agendas: Proceedings of the 20th International Conference on Electronic Publishing* (p. 87). IOSPress.net.

Lee, E., & Hannafin, M. J. (2016). A design framework for enhancing engagement in student-centered learning: Own it, learn it, and share it. *Educational Technology Research and Development, 64*(4), 707–734. doi:10.1007/s11423-015-9422-5.

Mazur, E. (2013). *Peer instruction: A user's manual.* New York, NY: Pearson Education.

Minerva. (2015, September 17). *The Active Learning Forum: A New Way to Learn* [Video File]. https://www.youtube.com/watch?v=Gk5iiXqh7Tg

Prince, M. (2004). Does active learning work? A review of the research. *Journal of Engineering Education, 93*(3), 223–231.

Turkle, S. (2015). *Reclaiming conversation: The power of talk in a digital age* (pp. 211–248). New York, NY: Penguin Press.

Willingham, D. (2010). *Why don't students like school? A cognitive scientist answers questions about how the mind works and what it means for the classroom.* San Francisco, CA: Jossey-Bass.

16 Building Lesson Plans for Twenty-First-Century Active Learning

Ari Bader-Natal, Joshua Fost, and James Genone

During the first three years at Minerva, all courses rely on lesson plans, and all faculty teaching sections of the same course share the same lesson plan (the method for achieving congruence is described in chapter 14). We initially wrote these lesson plans with standard document-editing tools, but as the need to scale up the number of courses became more acute, certain questions became unavoidable: How might we collaboratively design, systematically coordinate, and iteratively improve on an entire curriculum of courses and lesson plans designed specifically for active learning? Moreover, how could we do this at scale, with dozens of authors and reviewers working on dozens of courses simultaneously?

As we created and refined our first four courses, we arrived at initial answers to such questions—or at least a clear vision of a need: we had to develop a set of shared processes, conventions, and templates. For the two years spent developing these initial four courses, we addressed that need with functional but labor-intensive solutions that consisted of document templates, tracking spreadsheets, email notifications and the like. In order to scale these solutions to support the much larger set of courses to be developed in subsequent years, we chose to develop custom software to integrate everything into one coherent course development workflow.

In this chapter we introduce Course Builder, our software-based system for designing, coordinating, and improving course syllabi and lesson plans created for Minerva's Active Learning Forum (ALF). We provide an overview of the design goals of the project and the key product features that resulted. We then share the lesson plan development process, as experienced by a course developer using the Course Builder system.

Design Goals

As with all software created at Minerva to support teaching and learning, the Course Builder project was the result of a close collaboration between the engineering team and academic team. Through a series of focused conversations between members of both teams, we identified and refined a set of goals for, and desirable properties of, the system we were going to build. To achieve our high-level objectives, we identified the following specific design goals:

1. *Course and lesson plan development should be treated as processes.* The technologies should facilitate our treatment of course design and lesson plan design as collaborative, multistage processes.
2. *Effective classroom activity designs should be reusable.* The technology for designing active learning lesson plans should support a shared library of effective activity designs and also support the reuse of these designs in courses across the entire curriculum.
3. *Lesson planning should automate the ALF configuration.* The technology for designing classroom activities should work hand in hand with the in-class technology for running these activities by preparing the ALF to automatically reconfigure dynamically as the lesson unfolded.
4. *Key processes and conventions should be built in.* The technology for course and lesson plan development should be "opinionated," biasing course designers toward developing lesson plans that would incorporate the shared conventions, goals, and best practices developed with the science of learning in mind.
5. *A course should be reviewed and improved each time it is offered.* The technology should facilitate program assessment and enable iterative improvements from one semester to the next.
6. *Deans should be supported in managing the development of multiple courses.* The technology should provide those team members who are overseeing the development of multiple courses or programs with a bird's-eye view of the state of development of each component of the relevant courses, maintaining all lesson plans and other materials in a common space.

In the following discussion, we take a close look at each of these six design goals in turn, detailing both the rationale behind each and the product decisions we made to achieve them. To anchor the discussions, we begin with a brief overview of some specific capabilities of the Course Builder system.

Capabilities of Course Builder

To make this concrete, we will trace the development of a brand-new course, from catalog summary through its second time being taught. The case we will examine concerns a new concentration course: one that a student would typically take in his or her third year in connection with a major.

The first step is to create the course in Course Builder by selecting from a list of course-level templates (e.g., cornerstone or upper-level course). Policies for assessment and grading vary for different course types but not for the same type of courses. By using a university-wide library of templates we ensure that the latest version of the correct set of policies will be included.

The second step is to set roles and permissions. Several people contribute to the development, review, and teaching of this course; each is added to the course, with a corresponding set of privileges. One faculty member with subject matter expertise is designated as the primary course author. Because we are considering a course in development for the first time, this subject matter expert will typically also be one of the professors teaching the course for its first iteration, so this person is given both the *author* and *instructor* roles in this course. The dean to whom this professor reports will be reviewing, revising, and ultimately approving the professor's work, so the dean is given a *reviewer* role in the course. The definition of roles and permissions is flexible and is used to customize the user interface that each person sees in Course Builder.

With the roles set, the next step is for the course author to construct the syllabus. A Minerva syllabus is unusually detailed, often running to more than twenty single-spaced printed pages for a fifteen-week semester. The author breaks the semester into a series of units (typically spanning three or four weeks each), summarizes the purpose of each unit, describes the specific topics that are addressed and the readings and assignments for each class session during that unit, and indicates the course objectives and learning outcomes addressed in each class session. As the author works through these details, he or she is able to discuss individual elements—everything from the overall summary of the course to the specific rubric descriptions used to evaluate student work on individual learning outcomes—with the course reviewer via discussion threads directly anchored to that element for context.

Once the reviewer is satisfied with the draft of the syllabus, Course Builder produces a shareable PDF, which the course reviewer sends to an external reviewer for feedback, which the course author and reviewer later incorporate into the draft. Once the syllabus is finalized by the author and approved by the reviewer, the course is published to the ALF with the click of a button within Course Builder. Among other things, this generates an updated PDF version of the course syllabus and adds it to the course page on the ALF, where it will be visible to enrolled students. If the syllabus is later revised and republished, the latest version is republished and prior revisions are archived.

The next step in developing a course is to write the lesson plans—a detailed walkthrough of this process is provided later in this chapter. Here we simply note that many characteristics of the syllabus authoring tool extend to the lesson plan authoring tool: the notion of role-specific interfaces, collaboration through anchored discussion threads, template customization based on available information, and document versioning and archiving. At the lesson plan level, however, Course Builder introduces a new style of interaction in the form of a drag-and-drop interface for defining and configuring a series of in-class activities (figure 16.1). When the

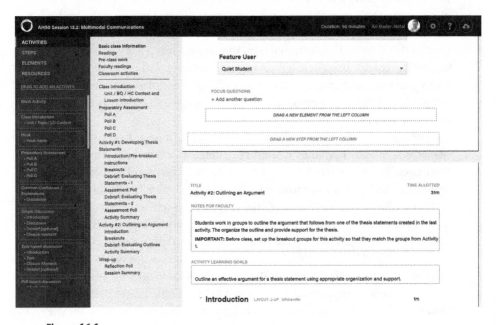

Figure 16.1
The lesson plan authoring tool is a three-column interface with the library of activity and step templates on the left, an autogenerated outline in the middle, and the detailed lesson plan editor on the right. The editor on the right notes each spot where an activity or step can be inserted through the drag-and-drop function from the library at left.

lesson plan is published to the ALF, this sequence of activities is made available to the professor teaching the seminar by means of an in-class interface sidebar that includes a sequence of buttons that reorganize the classroom to match that activity (see figure 15.5 in chapter 15).

Once the course author has finished drafting a lesson plan (see below for a more detailed walkthrough), it is ready for review. Because the dean responsible for reviewing this course is also likely to be involved in the development of several other courses, a dashboard view is helpful. When reviewers first log into the Course Builder system, such a dashboard is the default view, showing the state of development of all components of each of the courses in which they have a role (figure 16.2). This view serves as a project management dashboard, a navigation tool, and an interface for quickly answering certain questions about the curriculum.

With this picture of Course Builder established, we can now draw connections between each of our design goals and the components of Course Builder that resulted.

Design goal 1: Course and lesson plan development should be treated as processes

We start by recognizing that writing a lesson plan, when done well, is a process of drafting, revising, incorporating feedback, refining, and improving whenever possible. Whether or not we acknowledge it, the tools we use shape the processes that we adopt and the work that results. When we started, lesson plans were authored using Google Docs, a web-based collaborative document editor. This tool facilitated collaboration in the design process, and we made heavy use of it.

Tools for developing courses within a learning management system (LMS), on the other hand, are designed around the entry of content in form fields that are generally stored as structured data in a relational database—something that Google Docs does not do. But form entry interfaces aren't designed to facilitate the types of collaboration that we rely on when developing new courses, nor do they nudge users to integrate material in a way that will enhance student learning. In these systems, any collaboration among multiple authors or between author and reviewer needs to take place in a separate space using a different set of tools (e.g., an e-mail discussion thread, a Word document sent back and forth with "track changes" enabled, or a shared Google Doc annotated with suggestions and notes).

Based on the collaboration and review processes that we developed when using Google Docs, we sought to build a new kind of curriculum design and management system that vastly exceeds what is possible in a standard LMS.

Figure 16.2
The dashboard provides a bird's-eye view of the state of development for all lesson
plans, assignments, and syllabi for each course in which the viewer has a design role.
The left-hand sidebar includes tools for filtering and querying across the curriculum.
The icons and colors next to the titles indicate reviewer comments, postinstruction
feedback, video-graded sessions, and state of development.

Course Builder facilitates discussion and feedback directly in its authoring interfaces, and we wanted these discussions to be anchored directly to the specific element being discussed. As a result, every element of every syllabus, lesson plan, and assignment, from high-level elements, such as the overall purpose of the course, to low-level specifics, such as the wording of a preparatory assessment question, allows commenting, personal notes and reminders, collaborative discussion threads, and formal feedback from reviewers. Taken together, these features illustrate how Course Builder supports an iterative design and authorship process with collaborative discussions anchored to an interface for editing structured data.

The iterative design process that we refer to here is a well-structured, multistage review workflow. To begin, the course developer (typically a faculty member with appropriate expertise who will initially teach the course) and the course reviewer (the college dean or experienced faculty member appointed to this role) discuss the goals and aims of the course. The course developer then creates a draft syllabus, as described above. The draft syllabus undergoes both an internal review by the college dean and the chief academic officer and an external review by experts at various universities.

Course Builder includes specific features to facilitate this workflow. For example, prior to the development of Course Builder, Minerva's schoolwide academic policies were manually pasted into each syllabus. When those policies were updated, however, inevitably some course syllabi were overlooked, and so were not updated to reflect the change. Course Builder solves this problem by centralizing the contents of cross-course shared text, such as academic policies, and then providing a mechanism for republishing the set of automatically updated syllabi.

Lesson plan and assignment authoring involve a similar process. The course developer and course reviewer discuss initial ideas and then the course developer writes a draft of the assignment or lesson plan, which is reviewed and iterated until the reviewer approves it for publication to the ALF. The college dean reviews and approves lesson plans from the major core and concentration courses. Cross-college coordination of course development and training is provided by the associate dean of undergraduate studies and the chair of the Deans Council. The chief academic officer monitors the overall process and has final approval authority for all major core and concentration course syllabi.

The collaboration features described above greatly facilitate this design process by ensuring that all discussion of a lesson or assignment under development is contained in one place, rather than being scattered across multiple external communication channels.

Design goal 2: Effective activity designs should be reusable
In designing a single lesson plan for fully active learning (discussed in chapter 12), one must explicitly or implicitly answer a wide range of questions: Which core concepts should students grapple with during class? Which in-classroom activities and pedagogical approaches would best support those concepts? What questions should be raised during class? While two students are participating in a debate, how will the rest of the students be engaged? During the design of the 29 lesson plans in a full course, these same questions come up again and again, and a set of reusable patterns starts to emerge. During the assembly of those courses into a well-designed catalog of courses, these activity design patterns can serve as a useful tool in creating consistently principled and high-quality classroom learning experiences.

As noted in chapters 11 and 12, a significant body of literature indicates that active learning techniques are highly effective. Many approaches to student engagement have been described (Barr, 2014). They include peer instruction (Mazur, 1997), work in small breakout groups (Macpherson, 2015), debates (Kennedy, 2007), Socratic discussion (Faust & Paulson, 1998), task- or problem-based learning (Allen & Tanner, 2007), role-playing (DeNeve & Heppner, 1997), and game-based activities (Lepper & Cordova, 1992). Our initial approach to lesson plan design drew from these and other activities, which we then adapted and refined to be implemented on the ALF.

We quickly learned that lessons have a specific structure: course-level learning outcomes lead to lesson-specific learning goals, which in turn guide the design of activities—which are used to introduce and extend student mastery of the learning outcomes. We also recognized that many activities have interchangeable parts: a peer instruction activity and a debate may both involve breakout groups, and all activities require a brief introduction and a closure moment before transitioning to the next activity.

Identifying this structure allowed us to create a set of templates for frequently used sequential parts of activities, which we refer to as *steps*. Two examples of step templates are (1) those introducing the upcoming breakout discussion and (2) those featuring a group of students on-screen for a discussion or debrief. We identified particular sequences of steps comprising a complete *activity* that were particularly effective for reaching learning goals. Like steps, activities can be saved as templates that can be reused in other lesson plans. A poll-based discussion, for example, is an activity template that comprises this sequence of steps: a poll question, breakout discussions with students grouped by mix of poll responses, a post-breakout discussion, a repoll with the same question, a debrief, and finally a closure moment.

In our initial approach, when we authored lesson plans with Google Docs, this library took the form of a shared document, and lesson plan authors relied on copying and pasting text between documents to reuse steps. Among other drawbacks, we found that when curriculum developers subsequently customized these templates for use in their own lesson plans, the results were not always well suited to the ALF. For example, a lesson plan might specify that members of breakouts groups should be sent to new breakout groups in a specific combination that could not be implemented without significant manual input of data to individual course sections. With Course Builder, we addressed this problem by creating a structured data representation for each activity and step template, and provided the academic team with graphical tools for authoring and publishing new templates and modifying existing ones. We then included these templates in a shared library that is displayed within the lesson plan authoring interface in Course Builder. From here, lesson plan authors can simply drag and drop a template from the shared template library into the lesson plan they are creating (see figure. 16.1). This creates a copy of the activity, and lesson plan authors can then fully customize this copy as appropriate within the context of that lesson plan. These templates and the options for customizing them provide constraints by only incorporating features that are actually available on the ALF.

Design goal 3: Lesson planning should automate ALF configuration

Because each class convenes in a virtual room that can be reconfigured to suit a particular learning activity, we wanted our lesson plans to encode and automatically reconfigure the classroom as the professor taught the class. During the 2015–16 academic year, we accomplished this by manually creating a machine-readable file that represented the sequence of activities (which we call a "timeline") in every single lesson plan. That file instructed the ALF classroom how to reconfigure itself for each activity.

This approach worked, but was problematic in a few significant ways: (1) an enormous amount of work was required to construct and test these files for even a handful of courses; (2) the technology allowed course authors to describe activities that were not scriptable (e.g., "automatically assign students to breakout groups based on their intended major"), leading to an ad hoc system for coordinating and resolving post-design revisions; and (3) the approach didn't provide any way for a new course designer to discover and explore the enormous space of classroom activity designs that were possible in the ALF.

To address these three drawbacks, we decided that Course Builder should automatically generate the machine-parsable instructions for classroom reconfiguration. The tools for authoring a new lesson plan would give the author a way to peruse the full list of ALF-supported activity steps and a curated list of effective activity templates, and a way to see and experiment with how each activity and step could be customized. By authoring lesson plans using a structured activity construction toolkit (rather than the unstructured authoring environment of a general-purpose document editor), we were able to codify the ALF configuration instructions directly into each element of each step of each activity in the lesson plan authoring tool. When a lesson plan is ready to publish, Course Builder validates that no required element is in an incomplete or ill-defined state, and then *automatically* generates the configuration script—which had previously been constructed manually—and sends it to the ALF to create and configure the classroom for that lesson plan.

With the classroom fully configured, the professor has easy access to the list of steps in the planned activities, with each step accompanied by buttons that rearrange the classroom specifically for that step (see figure 16.2). Clicking on a button associated with a post-breakout share-out, for instance, might change the screen layout from the current document-based view to a five-pane display, with the shared notes from group A in a large pane on the left and the four students from group A in smaller panes on the right. Clicking again would replace these notes and video feeds with those for group B.

The benefit of preconfiguring the ALF for the lesson plans is significant: the professor can focus on teaching the class and guiding the discussion rather than needing to think about finding the right documents or figuring out which students were in which breakout groups in order to feature their videos.

Design goal 4: Key processes and conventions should be built in

The processes and conventions that the academic team developed during the years of our initial approach to course development, while time-consuming to communicate and manually implement, were enormously useful in that they consistently led to excellent in-class experiences. Much of this early experience was explicitly documented in development guides for courses, assignments, and lesson plans that the academic team shared with every course developer. Those processes and conventions that were deemed most effective we sought to design directly into Course Builder rather than maintain as external written documentation.

Built-in processes and conventions in Course Builder take a variety of different forms. The following are a few examples, selected to illustrate the range of techniques that we use to bake conventions, processes and best practices directly into the Course Builder system:

• The syllabus editor automatically tallies the total cost of all required resources, helping the course designer keep the total below the $50 per course target maximum set by the academic team.

• The lesson plan template includes an "engagement prompt" field next to each activity that prompts authors to indicate what everyone else is doing when only a few students are directly participating (e.g., answering a question from the professor).

• When an activity is added to a lesson plan, the text fields in the steps of the activity template may include examples of the types of questions that have worked well in the past.

• When a new reading is added to a syllabus, an inline tooltip accompanies the input field, clarifying that the reference should use the APA citation format and linking to an external website that generates an APA-formatted citation for a reference.

• The ability to modify or comment on a lesson plan depends on whether the viewer is a course author, reviewer, instructor, or a faculty member with no role in developing this course.

Design goal 5: A course should be reviewed and improved each time it is offered

We want to understand when and where each of our habits of mind and foundational concepts (HCs) are introduced (during the cornerstone courses) and revisited (during both the cornerstone courses and the upper-division courses). We want to do this in a way that allows us easily to identify and explore uses, patterns, and relationships using software-based tools. In addition, once a course has been taught, we wish to collect action-able fine-grained feedback on lesson plans from each faculty member who taught the course. We want that feedback to be stored and viewable in a contextually relevant way, making it easy to review and incorporate in the next revision of the course. By representing every component of every course, lesson plan, and assignment in Course Builder as linked data stored in a relational database, this becomes possible. Combining these data with additional data from the ALF allows us to pursue these and other analyses, in this manner creating a system that far exceeds what is possible in designing and managing curriculum in a standard LMS.

Although each lesson plan goes through many revisions before it is used in class, our process for iterative improvement does not end in the classroom. Course Builder allows faculty to attach notes to each activity in the lesson plan to document what worked and what did not. When a course is being prepared to be taught again, the faculty member working on revising the course is able to review, evaluate, and incorporate feedback and suggestions recorded by faculty members when each lesson plan—and the experience of having taught it—was fresh in their minds. The combination of soliciting feedback on a lesson plan from professors at the relevant moment and making this feedback available later to faculty members when they revise the course creates a powerful mechanism for iteratively refining and improving each course.

Design goal 6: Deans should be supported in managing the development of multiple courses

With detailed instructions written for every class session, we produced over three thousand pages of lesson plans—spread across hundreds of documents—when we developed our first four courses. Relying on the per-document permissions system of the web-based file storage system meant that these hundreds of documents were owned, stored, and shared in inconsistent ways.

After the experience of creating and refining the four cornerstone courses and painstakingly preparing the ALF to support the activities slated for each individual lesson, we realized that replicating this process on a much larger scale as our course offerings expanded would be prohibitively complex. Moreover, we wanted to minimize the burden of training faculty to use our templates and procedures appropriately.

The Course Builder dashboard, which displays the state of development of course components (i.e., the syllabus, lesson plans, and assignments), works not only for the deans but also for those in other roles (author, reviewer). Moreover, the dashboard doubles as a powerful query tool, allowing a dean or someone else with a curriculum-wide role to answer quickly a wide range of questions about courses and their contents, such as "Which courses have assignments that are due during Week 3?" "Are we designing more individual assignments or group assignments?" "Which lesson plans for next semester have been started but not yet approved and finalized?" "Which class sessions in courses this semester focus on linear regression?"

Questions like these can now be easily answered through simple searching and filtering capabilities in Course Builder's dashboard.

Lesson Plan Authoring in Course Builder

In this section, we present a step-by-step overview of how lesson plans are authored using Course Builder. We will write in the first person—here, this would be a professor or other lesson plan author—to provide the reader with as clear a sense as possible of what it is like to use the tool. We begin the process midstream, at a point in course development where the syllabus is complete and the materials and course calendar have been determined but the lesson plans themselves are still blank.

1. I log in to Course Builder and see a dashboard presentation of all the courses relevant to my work. I quickly find the particular course I want to work on today. I click on the icon for the course, and the dashboard view (figure 16.2) shows me the sequence of topics and their associated dates. I select one.

2. The "blank" lesson plan that appears is not in fact blank. It includes section headings for basic class information; moreover, the learning outcomes and required readings or materials have automatically been imported from the syllabus. It also includes headings for preclass work, a student study guide, background readings for faculty, and classroom activities. I cannot edit this initial template without returning to the workflow that established this material in the first place (e.g., consulting the dean about the learning outcomes).

3. My first step is to write a paragraph summarizing the overall purpose and structure of today's session. I have not yet designed the details of the activities that will achieve this.

4. Although the readings were prepopulated when the lesson plan authoring tool first opened (the full bibliographic entry for each reading was carried over from the syllabus), I now need to write a few sentences so that students can see why I am assigning this reading and what I would like them to focus on as they read.

5. Now I complete a section on preclass work: homework I want students to do. Course Builder allows me easily to make this either an individual or a group assignment. Whatever my choice, Course Builder will modify student dashboards appropriately so that each student receives the necessary instructions; no e-mails are required on my part.

6. Now I am ready to begin writing the lesson plan proper. I think about which aspects of the learning outcomes should be highlighted. This leads me to specify the activity learning goals, which will motivate the particular activities I will design. Most lesson plans have two activities (though some have three, and some have only one). For the first activity, I know that one of the readings deals with a particularly important concept that is subtle and many undergraduates will misunderstand. I would like to allow this concept to emerge naturally so that students are surprised by the complexity and feel motivated to unravel it. From the collection of preconfigured activity templates, I choose one called "Common confusions with breakouts." When I drag this template and drop it into my lesson plan, a sequence of new data fields and menus appears. Taken together, these specify the sequence of steps that the activity template calls for: events such as a brief introduction with a slide, prompts where I can enter questions I want to pose to the students, and more. Each step has a target duration to ensure that I am budgeting my overall ninety-minute class time appropriately, spending the most time on the things I believe are most important.

7. The potential confusion I want to address is easily stated, requiring just a textual slide. I use the built-in slide authoring functionality for this, with no need to switch to a separate tool such as PowerPoint. I simply choose a slide template inside Course Builder, enter my text, and I am done; when I use the ALF at class time, I know that a button will be waiting for me. Press the button, show the slide.

8. After the slide, I want students to go to breakout groups. I decide that I want random groups of three students each; I select this option and fill in a document for the notes that each group will see (I can choose whether the groups will see the same instructions and notes or whether each group will have its own version). Here I write a concise description of the task I want them to do. I choose an appropriate duration, in this case twelve minutes, and this is automatically deducted from my ninety-minute full-class-time allowance. (I take a moment to remember that ten minutes of "flex time" is automatically included in every class as well, to accommodate the inevitable variances.)

9. In a "debrief" step following the breakout groups, Course Builder nudges me to enter an engagement prompt that I can deliver at class time so that every student will have something to do in the ensuing discussion. This is a crucial part of our fully active learning approach (see chapter 12). I complete this prompt. I also take this opportunity to set the ALF configuration so that it will feature the members of each

breakout group (i.e., their video streams) alongside the notes they developed.

10. I also take this opportunity to tag the steps of this activity with the labels for the relevant pedagogical techniques: activities such as problem solving, writing, and diagramming. This will not affect class flow or the ALF presentation, but it does provide metadata that can be used for large-scale programmatic assessment.

11. I repeat this process, more or less, for other steps and activities in the lesson plan, making liberal use of activity templates to (1) save myself time, (2) follow the "opinionated" best practices captured there, and (3) ensure that I make good use of the ALF features—and don't write a lesson plan that can't actually be implemented.

12. Once my lesson plan has been approved by the reviewer for my course, he or she will click the "publish" button. This does three things. First, it provides a PDF of the lesson plan that formats each section for easy access during teaching—for example, each activity heading is highlighted so that I can see it at a glance. Second, it condenses all of my instructions, poll prompts, breakout configurations, timings, and so on and programs the ALF accordingly so that the classroom is ready and waiting for me on the day of class. Third, it updates student dashboards so that all of the students receive the preclass instructions relevant to them.

There are many more details, but this represents an overview of the basic steps that a lesson plan author would take to design a new lesson plan in Course Builder.

Curriculum-Driven Development

Many organizations build educational software; some of the more popular producers of course management systems have produced powerful tools with attractive features. Many of these organizations have employees with backgrounds in education and pedagogy and make good use of focus groups, test releases, and the like to provide a useful product. We do all that as well, but one of most unusual properties of our process is that our engineering team sits in close proximity and remains in constant dialog with the members of the academic community: administrators, professors, and students. A typical software company is simply an independent corporation, working alone. As a result of our unique situation, our development cycle is very short and the alignment of features and needs is extremely strong. Here we review a few of the ways that the close relationship between software development and curriculum development manifested during the design and implementation of Course Builder.

We rely on an iterative design process at Minerva; that is, our engineers produce functional tools early, release them to end-users, collect experiences, revise, and release updates based on this feedback every few days. We initially saw the scope of the Course Builder project as centering on the creation of a more user-friendly graphical interface (rather than the prior text-based interface) for preparing lesson plans to be taught on the ALF. It turned out, however, that the problem we really needed to solve was much broader, as the list of design goals above reflects. As a result, our product engineers soon had a long to-do list and needed an intelligent way to prioritize.

In the first few versions of Course Builder, we used a simple heuristic to determine which features to prioritize: we began with a course we had developed outside Course Builder and attempted to enter the syllabus, all assignments, and all lesson plans into Course Builder. Anytime we encountered something that couldn't be entered, we verified that the missing features were on the development list, and prioritized appropriately. Almost by definition, this procedure uncovered major functional blind spots quickly, with rarer cases emerging later. By the time we had made it through the first semester, approximately nineteen courses had been entered by several dozen users, and we had converged on a system that was considerably more powerful than the systems it replaced.

We pursued a somewhat different path when we developed the activity templates that facilitate setting up active learning exercises in a lesson plan. We had initially intended to launch Course Builder with support for only a subset of the activities used in lesson plans from the previous year (with the goal of continuing to add support for new activities in subsequent versions). When we realized how much work would be required to rewrite lesson plans that we were already happy with, we revisited this plan, and decided to support as many activity designs as we could in the initial launch. We prioritized implementation of activity types based on frequency of use and complexity of implementation.

Another way we prioritized development tasks was by paying close attention to pain points and time sinks for the users. Once Course Builder included a working version of all of the planned core features, we identified several features that were functional but too time consuming to use, and explored alternative solutions that would be more efficient and less frustrating. The process of creating slides for a lesson plan was one such example.

Static resources could be created using third-party tools (e.g., PowerPoint or Google Slides) and then uploaded to Course Builder. This process required switching among multiple tools, however, and authors would need to keep track of where they stored the editable slide document (future revisions to the slide would require reopening it to make changes and generate a new PDF). The alternative workflow that we designed led us to build a custom slide editor directly into the lesson plan authoring tool, so no external tool was necessary and subsequent changes could be made without first tracking down a source file.

Conclusion

As with many projects at Minerva, we took a two-phase approach to developing a solution that both was capable of addressing the immediate problem and could grow with us in future years. The product we developed in the first phase was, as expected, unsustainably time-consuming to use but also enlightening to develop and experience. From this, we learned a lot about the nature of the problem, and we used this process as an opportunity to test variations and modifications. This experience helped us clarify how we wished ultimately to solve the overarching problem. In the second phase, we applied what we learned to the design of our custom-built technologies, dedicated to making our ideal system sustainable and scalable. The end result, in this case, was a novel technology. This technology allows us collaboratively to design, systematically coordinate, and iteratively improve on an entire curriculum of courses and lesson plans at once. This technology serves as a new kind of curriculum design and management system, designed specifically to support active learning in Minerva's ALF.

References

Allen, D., & Tanner, K. (2007, Summer). Approaches to cell biology teaching: Learning content in context—Problem-based learning. *Cell Biology Education, 2,* 73–81.

Barr, M. (2014). Encouraging college student active engagement in learning: The influence of response methods. *Innovative Higher Education, 39*(4), 307–319.

DeNeve, K., & Heppner, M. (1997). Role-play simulations: The assessment of an active learning technique and comparisons with traditional lectures. *Innovative Higher Education, 21*(3), 231–246.

Faust, J., & Paulson, D. (1998). Active learning in the college classroom. *Journal on Excellence in College Teaching, 9*(2), 3–24.

Kennedy, R. (2007). In-class debates: Fertile ground for active learning and the cultivation of critical thinking and oral communication skills. *International Journal on Teaching and Learning in Higher Education, 19*(2), 183–190.

Lepper, M., & Cordova, D. (1992). A desire to be taught: Instructional consequences of intrinsic motivation. *Motivation and Emotion, 16*(3), 187–208.

Macpherson, A. (2015). *Cooperative learning group activities for college courses.* Surrey, BC: Kwantlen Polytechnic University.

Mazur, E. (1997). *Peer instruction: A user's manual.* Upper Saddle River, NJ: Prentice Hall.

17 Assessing Student Learning

Rena Levitt, Ari Bader-Natal, and Vicki Chandler

In his 2007 article "Counting and Recounting: Assessment and the Quest for Accountability," Lee Shulman makes the following observation: "The story told by an assessment is thus ultimately a function of the dimensions of measurement that determine the possible directions the narrative might take. So accountability requires that we take responsibility for the story we commit ourselves to telling" (Shulman, 2007, p. 2).

From the beginning it was clear that Minerva's innovative approach to education required a novel assessment story. We have a core set of habits of mind and foundational concepts (HCs) that we want students to master (and transfer to new contexts) by the time they graduate, and we want to be able to track progress toward mastery through every course that the students take during their four years at Minerva. We introduce the HCs in the four yearlong "cornerstone" courses during the first year; the courses also provide initial opportunities for students to apply these HCs. In upper-level courses, taken during the remaining three years, we expect students to continue exercising the HCs, both during active learning class sessions and on course assignments.

One particularly unusual component of our curricular design is that we determine the letter grade for the first-year cornerstone courses retroactively: we assign a provisional Pass/No Pass grade at the end of the first year, and then adjust these aggregated course scores—up or down—each subsequent semester, depending on how well students applied the HCs in their subsequent courses. We assign the final letter grade only at the time of graduation. Aside from the practical complexity of retroactively assigning course grades, we needed a way to record and aggregate individual assessments of HCs across many different courses completed over multiple semesters.

To support this unusual approach to assessing students on the material introduced in the cornerstone courses, we developed a set of design principles for assessment at Minerva. As our suite of assessment tools has evolved and expanded over the past several years, these shared principles have served as a useful framework for making decisions about the design of the assessment tools built into Minerva's technology platform (discussed in chapter 15). In this chapter, we introduce and delve into each of these six principles:

1. *Implement learning outcomes.* Student assessment should be based on well-defined learning outcomes.
2. *Grade consistently.* Students should be assessed accurately and with minimal bias.
3. *Provide feedback in context.* When faculty provide feedback to a student, it should be tied directly to what specifically is being evaluated and should provide formative feedback for improvement.
4. *Aggregate meaningfully.* Course grades should be aggregated in a way that accurately measures a student's proficiency.
5. *Show (and share) progress.* Students and faculty should be able to access and explore assessment data in order to make meaning of the student's outcome scores, track progress over time and facilitate student advising.
6. *Supplement with external measures.* Student learning should be measured with externally developed tools when assessing the effectiveness of our curriculum.

In the following sections, we unpack the implications of each of these design principles and summarize the innovations they led us to implement.

Implement Learning Outcomes

Each course has a predefined set of learning outcomes that form the basis of all assessment. We first developed this model for assessing the HCs that form the basis of Minerva's general education program. The HCs are organized into a hierarchical tree: at the top level are the four core competencies of thinking critically, thinking creatively, communicating effectively, and interacting effectively; at an intermediate level are specific aspects of each of these core competencies (e.g., for thinking critically, two such aspects are evaluating claims and weighing decisions); at the bottom level are the HCs that are subsumed by specific aspects of the core competencies (see chapter 2). We wanted to give students feedback at each level of granularity—and in fact, we designed an HC assessment dashboard that can provide the scores at each level. Major core and concentration courses follow a similar structure, with course objectives fulfilling the role of core competencies and learning outcomes mirroring the structure of HCs. Course objectives are the overarching learning objectives for each major core and concentration course at Minerva. The course objectives define the key knowledge students are expected to acquire by the end of the course. Each course objective is decomposed into a set of two to five learning outcomes, the specific skills or knowledge nested within each course objective (see chapter 9, table 9.2, for an example). As with the HCs, faculty directly evaluate learning outcomes when they assess student work.

Because HCs and learning outcomes play a similar role in student assessment and the techniques and technological tools developed for both HC and learning outcome assessment are similar, in this chapter we refer to them collectively as *outcomes.*

When assessing student work products, faculty grade the outcomes targeted in the assignment description and any of the previously introduced outcomes that are relevant. The "relevant" outcomes are either self-identified by students—who briefly describe the application of the outcome using a footnote—or are tagged by professors during grading. Numerous different professors assess the HCs in a variety of courses over multiple years. Typically fewer professors assess the content-specific learning outcomes, which often apply only to the material introduced in a particular course.

Grade Consistently

One way that we improve the consistency of grading is simply by explicitly defining outcomes. We also improve consistency in the evaluation of student work by explicitly defining the criteria for assessment using descriptive grading rubrics. By using such rubrics, we not only improve grading efficiency and the quality of feedback to both faculty and students, we also improve the accuracy of evaluations provided by different faculty members who are teaching the same course and reduce bias when evaluating different students (Suskie, 2009).

We faced a unique challenge when designing the rubrics to assess Minerva's outcomes. Typically a separate rubric is designed for each work product. Such a rubric would include multiple dimensions that are aligned with the assignment goals, and each dimension would specify a scale for scoring student performance—and the criteria for each score would be specific to that assignment (Stevens & Levi, 2005). This method did not translate to Minerva's assessment goals for three reasons: (1) The evaluation scale had to be consistent across all outcomes to provide a valid basis for aggregation (e.g., as we combine scores from HCs under a specific aspect of a core competency, such as those under the different aspects of "critical thinking"). (2) The criteria descriptions needed to be flexible enough to apply to all relevant student work products after that outcome was introduced. (3) Finally, the rubric would be applied to student work across a long time scale; thus the evaluation scale needed to be broad enough to capture improvement over time.

To address these requirements, we developed the mastery rubric template (table 17.1). This scale provides a consistent framework for all outcome assessment at Minerva. The scale describes benchmarks for achieving mastery of the outcome over time, from lack of demonstrated knowledge to profound knowledge. The rubric template is *holistic* when applied to a single outcome; that is, we use a one-dimensional rubric in which each level describes multiple aspects of the student's work associated with the

Table 17.1
Mastery Rubric Template

Rubric score	Description
1. Lacks knowledge	Does not recall or use the learning outcome when prompted or does so mostly or entirely inaccurately.
2. Superficial knowledge	Recalls or uses the learning outcome only somewhat accurately, by partially quoting, paraphrasing, summarizing, outlining, or applying it, or recalls or uses the skill or concept in ways that fail to address the relevant problems or goals.
3. Knowledge	Accurately recalls, uses, paraphrases, summarizes, outlines, or reproduces standard or straightforward examples of the learning outcome and does so in a way that addresses the relevant problems or goals.
4. Deep knowledge	Demonstrates a deeper grasp of the learning outcome by explaining it, using it to produce a sophisticated, nonstandard example, differentiating component parts, or applying critical distinctions, or by analyzing relationships between component parts.
5. Profound knowledge	Uses the learning outcome in a creative and effective way, relying on a novel perspective (i.e., not one that was in course materials or is easily located in the relevant literature) to: improve an existing problem-solving technique or create a more effective one; devise a more elegant or beautiful solution than the standard; or produce an unusually clever and effective application.

defined knowledge level, as opposed to analytical rubrics in which each aspect is mapped to a separate dimension (Allen & Tanner, 2006). Each HC or learning outcome has a detailed rubric for evaluation, which has been customized from the mastery rubric template. Course design faculty develop the descriptions in the customized rubrics, which then are refined based on feedback from teaching faculty and inter-rater reliability testing (Jonsson & Svingby, 2007).

The entire set of rubrics, when applied to a student work product, includes a dimension for each outcome that was explicitly targeted in the assignment, along with any additional outcomes tagged by students and faculty. This procedure produces a rich, comprehensive evaluation.

Provide Feedback in Context

When a professor provides feedback to a student, we want it to be a response to something specific that the student wrote or said. When evaluating a student on a comment that he or she made during a class discussion, the assessment should be directly linked to that specific comment. When assessing a paper submitted by a student, each assessment should be anchored to a specific passage in the paper. In this way, students can view each bit of feedback in context. However, "context" is a medium-specific concept, so we needed to provide different grading tools to professors based on the medium of the work being assessed. We consider the different tools in the following sections.

Assessing class discussions

One major advantage afforded by the Active Learning Forum (ALF) is the ability to review and directly assess students' in-class contributions. To make this possible, we create a video recording of each class session and we automatically generate a text-based transcript of the class session that attributes each contribution to an individual student. The professor can attach a rubric-based assessment (a score and comment) to any individual entry in the transcript, which attaches the assessment to the corresponding segment of the class video recording. Figure 15.6 in chapter 15 shows how this interface appears to the professor during postclass assessment. In this way the professor can review a class and provide students with written feedback and outcome scores at the granularity of an individual spoken comment or a typed comment in chat. Chapter 15 describes the classroom discussion assessment technology.

Daily formative feedback

Students receive daily faculty feedback from the two polls that are always included in each lesson plan. One poll is administered near the beginning of class and assesses how well students prepared for class. These preparation polls are assessed on a mastery rubric, and these scores give students feedback on their grasp of the preparatory material, helping them to identity concepts for further study. The other poll is administered near the end of class and assesses how well students understood and integrated the material discussed during the session. Along with the rubric scores, students receive written feedback from faculty. These comments clarify any confusion and reinforce especially strong points.

Assessing course assignments

Students complete various kinds of assignments that are designed to assess their mastery of sets of outcomes. These student work products are in multiple forms, and we have developed different tools to assess different types of submissions.

• For written assignments: Outcome assessments can be anchored to a selected passage of the student's submission (e.g., a sentence or paragraph).
• For assignments involving video production: When students create their own videos for assignments, outcome assessments can be anchored to a specific moment in the submitted video.
• For software-centric assignments: Assessments can be attached to any code or text passage within a read-only view of a notebook-based submission, which can include a mix of computer code, rich text, mathematics, plots, and rich media.

As we expand our curriculum into more specialized areas represented by the major core and concentration courses, we plan to continue to develop our suite of assessment tools. We will ensure that these tools will provide comments in a medium-appropriate context for those specialized areas.

Aggregate Meaningfully

If a student's assignment is annotated with widely varying scores, what overall score should the student receive on the assignment? As an example, let's suppose that half the outcome assessments were very high (e.g., for using the outcome in a creative and effective way, relying on a novel perspective) but the other half were very low (e.g., for applying the outcome partially or entirely inaccurately). Although this scenario may seem unlikely, it does point to an important problem: how should we combine anchored assessments into a meaningful measure of student mastery? If we average together extreme scores from different outcomes, creating a middle-of-the-road average score for the overall assignment, and then aggregate these averages at the end of the semester, the resulting number conveys little information. We are reminded of the old joke about the statistician who was found sleeping with his head in an oven and his feet in a refrigerator because he knew that the average temperature would be just right.

To address these issues, we have developed an assignment and assessment structure that aggregates across outcomes rather than within an assignment. In this section we describe the model for the cornerstone courses, then discuss how that model is adjusted for the major core and concentration courses.

Assessment categories

One aspect of our scaffolded curriculum is the design of common assessment categories for the four cornerstone courses, each of which introduces a different set of HCs. Each type of behavior or work product that we assess (e.g., comment in class, written assignment) has an associated weight that corresponds to the expected robustness of the evaluation and how much work was required:

• HC-scored class sessions: Faculty review and score class sessions. These sessions are designed to prompt students to synthesize and apply outcomes recently introduced in class. HC scores assigned to class sessions are defined as the baseline weight in a course.

• General assignments: These are relatively short assignments that allow students to practice recently introduced HCs. We designed some of the general assignments (e.g., an outline for a paper) to build toward a more substantial signature assignment (see below). HC scores from general assignments have the same weight as a class session score.

• Location-based assignment (LBA): Each location-based assignment involves engaging in an activity in the student's current city of residence and requires applying targeted HCs in a new, real-world context. Cornerstone course LBAs have twice the weight of a class session score.

• Signature assignments: These are original works (e.g., papers, videos, models) that give students an opportunity to integrate a set of associated HCs. The work is graded against a mandatory set of HCs that students must address. In addition, the student may address other HCs introduced earlier in this or any other cornerstone course. Signature assignments fulfill the role that midterm papers or midterm exams play in many college courses (Minerva does not use in-class exams). Assessments of signature assignments have twice the weight of a class session score.

• Cornerstone final projects: Each semester, students complete a single final project across all four cornerstone classes. Near the end of the semester, students submit a detailed proposal for their projects. The proposal outlines the scope of the project and identifies the set of HCs the student intends to employ, which must include HCs from all four cornerstone courses. After an initial round of review and feedback from professors, students devote the final week of the semester to completing their work. Assessments of the final project have a weight of four times the weight of a class session score.

As noted, in addition to assessing each assignment against a set of targeted HCs, a faculty member can assess students on any HC that has been previously introduced in any of the cornerstone courses. For example, a research design assignment in Empirical Analyses could target statistics HCs that were introduced in Formal Analyses. The scores assigned to the statistics HCs on the Empirical Analyses assignment would be included when determining a student's performance on those outcomes, eventually determining the grade in Formal Analyses. Although professors give holistic, formative feedback to students through comments, we do not assign a single holistic grade to individual assignments.

Computing scores

We take a multistep approach when we initially assess a student's level of mastery at the end of the cornerstone course year. First we take a weighted average of all scores assigned to a student on a single HC. An overall HC score is then computed for each cornerstone course by taking the grand mean across the weighted means for all HCs introduced in that course. We implemented this two-layer averaging process for two reasons. First, providing a summative score for each HC gives students more detailed feedback on areas of strength and where improvement is needed within each course. Second, the two-step process controls for frequency of scoring. For example, a student might be evaluated more often on the problem-solving HCs than on the research methods HCs, all introduced in Empirical Analyses. This does not mean that problem-solving HCs are inherently more important than the research methods HCs. Taking a grand mean results in each HC having the same weight in the final overall score.

The provisional Pass/No Pass grade that we assign at the end of the first year for each cornerstone course is based on a student's HC grand mean scores. However, this is just the beginning of our assessment of HC scores. Faculty continue to tag and evaluate HC applications in other courses taken in subsequent years. We update the cornerstone scores over the entire college experience to accomplish multiple goals: Continuing to evaluate HCs in later years reinforces these key skills and knowledge—and provides feedback that helps student to improve their mastery of them. Identifying the application of an HC outside the cornerstone course where it was introduced measures a student's ability to transfer his or her knowledge to new contexts. Moreover, the use of HCs in later courses and the capstone project provides evidence of whether the student has mastered these key outcomes by the time of graduation. Thus HC assessment data are more heavily weighted each semester before they are aggregated with the earlier HC scores. When students graduate, they are assigned a final letter grade for each cornerstone course based on all HC evaluation data.

Our assessment model for major core and concentration courses is based on the cornerstone model, with a few changes to account for differences in course structure and goals. First, we do not assess major core and concentration learning outcomes outside the course in which they were introduced. Major core and concentration courses are focused on a specific discipline and designed to teach knowledge and skills necessary for that field. This results in outcome data for these courses over a single semester rather than over four years; the numerical scores for outcome data are converted into a letter grade at the end of the course. The second major difference is the aggregation level. In major core and concentration courses we use the initial weighted mean at the course objective level rather than the outcome level (as we do in the cornerstone courses), giving course designers greater flexibility in the distribution of learning outcomes and helping to reduce an overemphasis of outcomes introduced early in the course (this is not a problem for the cornerstone courses because the HCs are assessed over all four years).

Show (and Share) Progress

All of our assessment tools build on the fact that we have hierarchical outcomes and descriptive scoring rubrics. In addition to tagging and scoring outcomes, professors provide written comments, with an emphasis on providing actionable feedback. This holds true across grading contexts, including assessment of submitted work products and spoken and written contributions to class discussions. We have developed tools to help students and faculty explore this wealth of assessment data.

Cornerstone outcome data are available to students through an HC assessment dashboard. All assessments associated with a specific HC flow back into the central assessment database. Because the same rubric is used for all assessments of a given outcome, these assessments can be meaningfully aggregated into a multiyear, cross-course view of performance on the HC. For each HC within this dashboard, the student sees all relevant information. Such information includes a detailed description of the HC, examples and applications of it, the grading rubric, links to the course where the HC was introduced, a visualization of the student's scores on the HC, and a record of every assessment on this HC. The data are continuously updated as faculty add additional assessments. One feature of the HC assessment dashboard is the ability to view aggregated scores at each level of the HC hierarchy. For example, a student could choose to view the data collected on HCs within the critical thinking competency for the full competency, the subcompetency of evaluating claims, or at the level of a specific HC. This gives students and their advisers the ability to identify strengths and areas for improvement at multiple levels.

In addition to the HC assessment dashboard, each upper-division course provides a course-specific view of student performance on the learning outcomes introduced in that course. This dashboard parallels much of the HC assessment dashboard. This view includes aggregated course data and links to the data sources. Both academic advisers and faculty members have access to this information about their students. This has proved useful both for academic counseling and for identifying students in academic distress.

Supplement with External Measures

Finally, we close by turning to a set of measures that we did not develop. We sought summative measures of how well our students were learning, which we could use to determine whether our curriculum was in fact accomplishing its goals. For this purpose, we sought measures developed by others and that had been used with other institutions, allowing us to compare the results of a Minerva education with scores elsewhere. In other words, we turned to externally validated tests to obtain measures of how effectively our students were learning. We used three such measures, as described below.

Collegiate Learning Assessment (CLA+)

In our first year, we administered the *Collegiate Learning Assessment* (CLA+) three times: during student orientation in the fall, at the beginning of the second semester, and at the end of the academic year in the spring. The *Collegiate Learning Assessment* is a performance-based measure of critical thinking, analytical reasoning, and writing ability; this test has been widely used to assess learning on college campuses, most famously by Arum and Roksa (2011, 2014), who, based on results from this test, concluded that there is very little learning going on at typical American colleges. This test primarily assesses critical thinking, problem solving, and writing. Given the nature of our cornerstone curriculum, we expected Minerva students to do better on this test at the end of the first year than they had at the beginning of the year.

The administration of the CLA+ at the beginning of the fall term provided strong evidence that the Minerva admissions process does in fact identify high-performing and talented students from all over the world. The Minerva founding class scored in the 99th percentile compared to freshmen at other institutions.

Because our students performed so well at the outset, in comparison to first-year students at other universities, we had to compare them to college seniors to assess possible progress over the year. At the outset, our students were in the 94th to 95th percentile compared to seniors at other institutions. Between the fall and spring administrations of the CLA+, our freshman students' rank increased to the 99th percentile when compared to senior outcomes.

Without question, this level of performance provides evidence that our cornerstone curriculum is effective. Moreover, this finding supports our contention that our courses and expectations for student learning are set at the upper-division level; we do not offer typical freshman-level courses.

California Critical Thinking Skills Test (CCTST) and Disposition Inventory (CCTDI)

After seeing the results from the CLA+ for the 2014–15 school year, we realized that this test would not give us enough range to measure improvement over the full four-year curriculum at Minerva. Thus, during the 2015–16 academic year, we administered two other assessments, the *California*

Critical Thinking Skills Test and the *California Critical Thinking Disposition Inventory.* The assessments were administered twice, at the beginning of the fall semester and after the last week of classes of the spring semester.

When compared to U.S. undergraduates at other four-year colleges, the Minerva inaugural class scored in the 85th percentile. In the spring administration Minerva's rank increased to the 92nd percentile on the CCTST. On average, individual student performance increased by 9.2 percentile points between administrations. Comparative data for other institutions by school year are not available.

Students also completed the *Critical Thinking Disposition Inventory.* This assessment measures an individual's tendency to apply critical thinking skills. The assessment decomposes critical thinking into seven underlying dimensions: truth-seeking, open-mindedness, inquisitiveness, analyticity, systematicity, confidence in reasoning, and maturity of judgment.

Percentile rankings are not available for this test. Scores in the 30 to 40 range indicate inconsistent application, those in the 40 to 50 range indicate a positive disposition, and those in the 50 to 60 range indicate a strongly positive disposition toward the attribute. During the fall administration members of Minerva's class showed a "positive" or "strongly positive" disposition toward applying critical thinking skills. The results are presented in table 17.2. As is evident, the scores improved on six of the seven scales. Again, these results provide good evidence that our curriculum is effective.

Table 17.2

Results of the Critical Thinking Disposition Inventory

| | CCTDI assessment results, AY 2015–16 | | |
Dimension	Fall 2015 mean score	Spring 2016 mean score	Difference
Truth-seeking	38.8	42.2	+3.4
Open-mindedness	46.7	47.2	+0.5
Inquisitiveness	50.0	49.8	−0.2
Analyticity	45.5	46.25	+0.75
Systematicity	39.5	40.3	+0.8
Confidence in reasoning	46.4	46.5	+0.1
Maturity of judgment	45.3	46.5	+1.2
Overall score	312.0	318.7	+6.7

Conclusion

Minerva's assessment techniques and technologies tell a unique story. We have created an innovative assessment model that aligns with our unique educational framework by using our basic principles: implement learning outcomes, grade consistently, provide feedback in context, aggregate meaningfully, show (and share) progress, and supplement with external measures. The result is a novel approach to assessment that enables us to document and track student growth across multiple years and contexts. Moreover, our own measures are nicely complemented by externally validated measures, which provide converging evidence that our cornerstone courses are having their intended effects.

References

Allen, D., & Tanner, K. (2006). Rubrics: Tools for making learning goals and evaluation criteria explicit for both teachers and learners. *Cell Biology Education, 5*(3), 197–203. doi:10.1187/cbe.06-06-0168.

Arum, R., & Roksa, J. (2011). *Academically adrift: Limited learning on college campuses.* Chicago, IL: University of Chicago Press.

Arum, R., & Roksa, J. (2014). *Aspiring adults adrift: Tentative transitions of college graduates.* Chicago, IL: University of Chicago Press.

Jonsson, A., & Svingby, G. (2007). The use of scoring rubrics: Reliability, validity and educational consequences. *Educational Research Review, 2*(2), 130–144. doi:10.1016/j. edurev.2007.05.002.

Shulman, L. S. (2007). Counting and recounting: Assessment and the quest for accountability. *Change: The Magazine of Higher Learning, 39*(1), 20–25. doi:10.3200/chng.39.1.20-25.

Stevens, D. D., & Levi, A. (2005). *Introduction to rubrics: An assessment tool to save grading time, convey effective feedback, and promote student learning.* Sterling, VA: Stylus Pub.

Suskie, L. A. (2009). *Assessing student learning: A common sense guide.* San Francisco, CA: Jossey-Bass.

III Creating a New Institution

A university education is more than what one learns in classes. Minerva aspires to be more than simply a source of great skills and knowledge; we also want to create the conditions that will nurture the students' social and emotional lives, that will help them to mature and develop into fine human beings. The chapters in part III of this book describe the aspects of the Minerva system that take place outside the classroom and that, like the in-class activities, we designed with the concept of a truly global institution in mind.

The following ten chapters flesh out the remaining pieces of how we designed and operationalized a fully reimagined university experience. The first three chapters lay out the processes we use to define the institution, from our guiding principles to the makeup of our student body. Chapter 18, "Building a New Brand," explores how we define the essence of the Minerva promise, in part by explicitly formulating a set of guiding principles, and explains how we ensure that we live up to that promise as an institution. Chapter 19, "Global Outreach: Communicating a New Vision," addresses the practicalities of bringing our guiding principles to life as we convey the ideas in this book to millions of people. Chapter 20, "An Admissions Process for the Twenty-First Century," details our unique, principled approach to selecting students to become Minervans.

The next five chapters explain in detail how we both challenge and support students to enhance their personal growth, both during their years at Minerva and how we plan to continue this process after they graduate. Chapter 21, "Multifaceted Acculturation: An Immersive, Community-Based Multicultural Education," details the ways that we help students adjust to life at Minerva. The adjustment to college is almost always difficult, and Minerva presents additional challenges with our international student body, city immersion, intense academic demands, and global rotation. How we structure the institution goes a long way toward ensuring that our students can thrive in this type of environment. Chapter 22, "Experiential Learning: The City as a Campus and Human Network," explores what is perhaps the most well-known aspect of Minerva, our global rotation. But rather than focus on the logistical elements of the rotation, this chapter details how we integrate students into the cities where they live. Chapter 23, "A Global Community by Design," explains how we purposefully manage our community with international diversity in mind, a challenge unique in American undergraduate education. Chapter 24, "Mental Health Services in a Diverse, Twenty-First-Century University," describes how we tackle one of the biggest challenges facing universities, with the added constraints discussed throughout this part of the book. Chapter 25, "The Minerva Professional Development Agency," addresses something special that we do for all our students: actively help them not just begin their chosen careers but also continue to progress on their professional trajectory after they graduate.

The final two chapters in part III explain the organizational steps needed to make the theory of Minerva a reality. Chapter 26, "Accreditation: Official Recognition of a New Vision of Higher Education," provides both an overview of the accrediting environment and Minerva's journey through it. Despite the hundreds of pages in this book that detail how Minerva is different, at its core, Minerva is very much a liberal arts university program, and the accreditation process helped us to articulate that and ensure that we delivered on our goals. Finally, chapter 27, "A Novel Business and Operating Model," details how Minerva has avoided some of the biggest financial traps that contribute to the high costs of higher education and has built a new operating approach to achieve the best in higher education.

Altogether, the chapters in this part of the book lend color to how we operationalized a reimagined university experience for some of the most deserving students in the world. Common to all of these chapters is a shared mission, purpose, and guiding principles that continue to clarify our day-to-day decisions.

18 Building a New Brand

Ayo Seligman and Robin B. Goldberg

As the lunch hour approached on January 21, 2013, the office was almost empty and uncharacteristically quiet. Although we were still a small team at that point, lunchtime was typically spent exuberantly discussing the grand vision we were working to realize. The near-emptiness could be attributed to the fact that it was a holiday—the day we celebrate the life and contributions of Dr. Martin Luther King, Jr.—but the hush was the result of deep thought.

Moments earlier, our founder had posed a question: How did we plan to notify our first group of prospective students that they had been admitted to Minerva? Although the question may seem trivial and perhaps to have an obvious answer—the big envelope for admits—it led to a deeply engaging discussion and a solution that reveals much about how we operate and what we value. At this fledgling institution, the concept of innovation was already deeply ingrained in its DNA.

After a quick trip to the food trucks that were assembled on San Francisco's UN Plaza and glasses of wine poured from the founder's reserve, we gathered on the balcony overlooking the Civic Center to ponder potential approaches.

"What if they receive a mysterious key in the mail?" one team member suggested.

That idea spurred a four-hour discussion, followed by an intensive prototyping and design refinement process that yielded an extraordinary final result.

Two months later, in mid-March, the entire organization assembled: "Put on these white gloves; there cannot be a single fingerprint! Remember to hide the tape in the seams of the gift paper. Every detail sends a message, and we want to make sure each package looks perfect."

The admissions committee had just finished reviewing more than 2,500 applications, selecting a mere 2.8 percent of prospective students to receive an invitation to join the founding class. The invitations themselves had to signal a number of important qualities. They had to demonstrate acute attention to detail and a commitment to each student as an individual, they had to suggest the layers of meaning and depth of understanding at the heart of the educational experience, and they had to feel magical, hinting at the challenging journey that lay ahead. Above all, we wanted the students receiving these packages to respond emotionally, appreciating both the unique opportunity and the tremendous responsibility that joining the founding class at a first-of-its-kind institution represented.

By creating "the box"—a hinged walnut case emblazoned with the word "curiosity" that was custom-built to house an Apple iPad Mini and its various components—and the sequence of interactive steps recipients were guided to follow, we sought to eliminate any doubt from the minds of these first pioneering students about attending Minerva. In the process, we exhibited the core principles that have come to define the organization.

When Minerva was still a conceptual vision, summarized in a deck of PowerPoint slides, potential investors often asked how we planned to impart the kind of meaning and prestige to the Minerva brand that other university brands had taken many years to acquire. Those who were experienced in building institutional value understood the importance of name recognition and reputation in a competitive (or saturated) marketplace. For many, however, use of the word "brand" in connection with an educational institution still seemed anathema. The immediate perception among many in academia is that any institution that concerns itself with its brand will inevitably put financial—or, worse, commercial—interests above those of its students or some idealized version of higher learning. But when one considers the power of such names as Harvard, Stanford, and Cambridge and the weight of those names in student and parent decision making, it becomes clear that these universities are indeed brands as well. In fact, even the appellation "Ivy League" can be considered a brand: graduating from one of these elite institutions endows a halo effect for life. Branding in academia is real.

Defining a Brand

The term brand is difficult to define. A common misperception is that a brand refers to a corporate name and logo (e.g., Mercedes-Benz and its classic three-pointed star trademark). More critically, a brand is the sum of a corporation's legally protected assets and the ideas they stand for, ideas reflected in such things as the name and trademark. In practice, a brand is the suite of impressions awakened in a subject's mind on hearing the name or seeing the logo.

For Mercedes, its name and marks summon a collection of perceptions about the company, its products, and its services. These perceptions include shared beliefs about quality, reputation, product personality, cultural significance, heritage, and other associations. The Mercedes name, badge, and "trade dress," together with these shared associations, make up its brand. Although intangible, a brand is immensely valuable: the Mercedes brand is valued at $43.5 billion by global brand consultancy Interbrand (2016).

Because of the brand's importance to any organization, defining a brand should not begin with a name and logo design. Instead it should be the result of carefully considering what the brand should represent in the world, what it would mean for people.

Brand Value in Higher Education

According to the multinational advertising agency Young & Rubicam (Rainey, 2001), a brand's strength is defined along four dimensions: its differentiation from others in the category, its relevance to its audiences, the knowledge those audiences have of the brand, and the esteem in which they collectively hold it. In the private sector, global companies spend billions of dollars annually on brand-related efforts. Through activities ranging from broadcast advertising to product portfolio management, firms focus enormous resources on building, reinforcing, or repairing their brand equity.

Universities, by contrast, rarely have more than a communications office dedicated to public relations and crisis management. In the event of a student protest, these institutions may be well prepared, but when it comes to addressing other threats to the brand, they are less so. Also, because universities have, generally speaking, grown their brand equity organically and over long periods of time, they have not given much thought to differentiation or relevance, relying instead on only the public's knowledge and accumulated esteem. Although the Harvard, Yale, and Princeton brands are all highly regarded, it is difficult to articulate their differences. Further, it seems apparent that the educational experiences they offer lag the pace of change under way in the world. Owing to this lack of a clearly differentiated offering, an increasingly questioned relevance to student success, and numerous entrenched institutional norms, there is room for other institutions to enter the market and provide a stronger brand proposition than the incumbents.

Building a Foundation for Prestige

Although it is not common for universities to focus on building their brands, this is crucial for a new entrant in the crowded higher education category. Because we at Minerva are appealing to exceptionally bright, curious, motivated, and globally minded students, we are competing with top-ranked schools all over the world. To quickly establish a reputation for excellence at this level, we needed to ensure we could break through and reinforce Minerva as deeply innovative and highly selective, yet globally accessible.

To define this strategy, we knew we would need to articulate the essence of our brand—what makes it different and meaningful—and convey this essence coherently to internal and external audiences. A cogent brand framework, including our central promise and value proposition, would give us a basis for communicating the core tenets and behavioral norms of the institution. By defining who we are, how we operate, and how we engage with the world, we would be able to align all parts of the organization and ensure that our interactions with students, parents, counselors, and partner organizations, as well as with investors and the media, would be of a consistently high quality. Although Minerva is not perfect for all students, it does need to be recognized as ideal for the *right* students.

Determining Minerva's Position in the Category

The process of defining the Minerva brand began with clarifying exactly what we were seeking to accomplish, why, and how, and with gaining a deep understanding of the higher education landscape—including how top universities present themselves—and our intended audiences, primarily top students around the world. In this way we related the brand strategy directly to the operational strategy. However, an effective brand framework includes further articulation of these considerations. Gaining that level of depth demanded extensive discussion, research, and analysis.

To develop a brand framework, we first conducted a series of work sessions, which included everyone in the organization. Participants gathered in a room whose walls were covered with oversized Post-It notes. We delved into numerous topics, both internally and externally focused, starting with high-level questions: What key challenges were we trying to solve? Why was Minerva best positioned to solve them? Why hadn't anyone else tried to do so? (Or, if others had tried, why did they not succeed?) Why should our audiences care about Minerva? As these sessions progressed, our questions became both more specific—What about students who need remedial support? Should we seek to reach masses of students or be more targeted?—and more conceptual: What if Minerva were a person? What would he or she be like? Because strategy demands sacrifice, we also sought to determine what we would *not* do and how we would *not* present ourselves. Our ultimate goal was to distill and crystallize our mission, our vision for the future, our institutional values, and the concepts that would influence how we expressed the brand to our audiences.

Understanding the Target Audience

We then set out to understand key characteristics of the types of students we sought to attract. During a series of in-depth interviews with university-age students in multiple regions, we investigated how they would evaluate various university options to arrive at a first choice. We wanted to understand what factors were important to them, what aspects of higher education were exciting, and what parts of the decision-making process they dreaded.

Following the interview phase, we considered other audiences and their perspectives. We were particularly interested in those who would have a high degree of influence during the decision-making process—parents and counselors. Additionally, we reviewed a broad collection of communications materials from top universities, analyzing the language and imagery they used to present themselves. This helped us determine how successful institutions attract students, and, more important, how we might distinguish ourselves from other institutions in search of smart, motivated students.

Articulating Our Mission and Promise

With pages of notes in hand, we got to work refining the various components of our brand's strategic framework. On a fundamental level, our mission statement would provide a rallying cry for the organization through a concise expression of our long-term objectives. The statement needed to convey the impact we aspired to have in the future, but also the vision we would act on every day. It had to be simple and bold, an encapsulation of everything we stood for, in a single line. After dozens of proposed phrases, we rallied around the shared commitment that Minerva existed to make the world better by making its students wiser. This idea was honed to a succinct, nine-word statement: "Nurturing critical wisdom for the sake of the world."

This single phrase expresses the warmth of our student-centric approach to education, our core belief that imparting knowledge alone is not sufficient, and our expectation that equipping the world's brightest minds with powerful cognitive skills will lead to an improved future for us all. Moreover—and this was particularly important—it also does not restrict our influence to only those students educated at Minerva. Our mission captures our hope and belief that other institutions and organizations will adopt our best practices and curricular innovations (possibly licensing our curriculum, pedagogy, and platform, or using it as a model when creating their own) to impart critical wisdom to a wider population.

Although our mission statement conveys the organization's long-term, overarching reason for being, we also needed to define our central promise, a description of whom we are serving and what our specific commitment is to them. We deliberately chose to focus on the brightest, most motivated students because we believe they are most likely to become the next generation of leaders and have the highest potential to develop the kind of meaningful innovations needed to bring about positive global change. We aim to provide them with educational experiences that will accelerate their growth, as well as the skills needed to devise effective solutions to difficult systemic problems. After many rounds of refinement, we arrived at a clear promise:

We will equip the most exceptional students in the world to fulfill their enormous potential to solve the most complex challenges of our time.

Distilling Our Essence

With these fundamental elements in place, we turned our attention to distilling the essence of the brand. It was clear from the start that what we were undertaking was incredibly bold and innovative, but it was becoming increasingly evident that the level of excellence we were working toward was equally remarkable. We were doing something so different and comprehensive, and our points of distinction from traditional top universities were so numerous, that our positioning could focus on one central truth: Minerva is working toward *Achieving Extraordinary*.

By intentionally including the gerund form of the verb and eliminating a definite article, we sought to convey the ongoing nature of our efforts to work toward an idealized destination. The organization eagerly embraced this continuous drive toward apotheosis, the elusive point at which a great work is transformed into something sublime. In fact, the phrase quickly became shorthand for our entire endeavor.

Establishing Our Guiding Principles

As "Achieving Extraordinary" was becoming a touchstone for the organization, we realized we needed a way to communicate the nuances embedded in this simple catchphrase. By explicitly stating what we stood for and how we would evaluate what was right for both the institution and the brand, we sought to provide clear guidance for our collective behavior and decision making. After further detailing our organizational beliefs and philosophy, with input and agreement from the full executive team, we arrived at a set of seven guiding principles that describe how we approach our work: *being unconventional, being human, being confident, being thoughtful, being selective, being authentic,* and *being driven* (see appendix B).

Collectively the principles invoke everything to which we hold ourselves accountable; there are no superfluous concepts, nor is anything missing from the set. We then defined each principle in depth, including a clear description and related attributes, and, because each principle can be considered as existing on a spectrum, we also outlined the extremes to be avoided. For example, being too unconventional becomes quirky or eccentric; being too confident makes one arrogant.

From Principles to Practices

Next, each principle was translated into associated practices—specific behaviors for the organization to adopt—including the actions we take, the language we use, and the way we design. When we discuss a direction we want to take or a major decision to be made, we rely on the guiding principles as the common organizational language used to weigh various options. We ask ourselves, which among these is most aligned with our principles? Similarly, we use the principles to steer specific initiatives. When developing the program for our admitted students weekend, we pushed to make it extraordinary by ensuring that it was *unconventional*—no mere campus tour here—and deeply *human,* with numerous *thoughtful* details. The name of the annual event itself, Ascent, reflects the *driven* principle and is part of a progressive metaphor used for the major milestone events in each city.

By using the guiding principles as a decision-making tool, we are able to move efficiently from idea to action. Whereas most universities, especially those with vested interests in the status quo, incorporate new ideas very slowly (if at all), Minerva is constantly looking for opportunities to improve. In another example, our pre-arrival guide for students is a purposeful departure from the typical printed leaflet with its basic information on the campus, a directory of services, and information on how to move into the dormitory. Instead we saw an opportunity to engage and inspire our incoming freshmen. In addition to the practical information, we incorporated philosophical content related to the process of departing and arriving; an interactive map of the city, indicating nearby services as well as exciting points of interest; and even helpful advice on cultural integration. The point is that something as simple as a student guidebook is held to the same standard as major institutional decisions.

Equally important, the guiding principles help us decide when we should say no. When considering opportunities for partnerships, for instance, we utilize the guiding principles as a checklist to assess whether the partner organization is suitably selective, unconventional, thoughtful, authentic, confident, and so on. The right partners help us identify the right students, but the wrong ones could damage our reputation among this key audience, negatively affecting our positioning or, worse, calling into question our judgment regarding student well-being.

Expressing the Brand

In tandem with defining our brand's strategic framework, we developed visual and verbal systems for communicating with our audiences. Our "Achieving Extraordinary" positioning demanded a suitably distinctive—and nuanced—visual and verbal identity for Minerva. These systems needed to convey a depth of meaning, be expansive enough to adapt to various media, and, crucially, reinforce our brand attributes.

After countless rounds of exploration and refinement we settled on a symbol, rich with meaning, as well as a custom wordmark. The symbol is an artistic representation of a Möbius strip, executed by a master Japanese calligrapher and incorporating three twists. By blending the precision of mathematical geometry with the organic quality of calligraphic brush strokes—Eastern artistic tradition married to Western scientific innovation—we realized an elegant balance of contrasting ideas. Additionally, the negative space is shaped like the shields in Ivy League schools' crests, suggesting our movement beyond existing models in elite higher education.

With our symbol and wordmark designed, we created a suite of logo configurations, a flexible color palette, custom iconography, and a robust approach to imagery and typographic design. We then applied the visual identity system to a variety of communication tools, from business cards to outreach presentations to the school's website. To illustrate how seriously we take the representation of the Minerva brand, it took nearly three years from the first day of work until the first business card was printed.

The visual identity is complemented by a distinctive "voice" for the brand. Once we decided to appeal to only the highest-caliber students, our verbal expressions had to be suitably sophisticated, yet approachable enough to engage millennial students. Our verbal identity includes word choices and sentence lengths typically found at the graduate school level but utilizes pacing and other structural techniques that keep writing consumable. Also, despite our core audience's global nature, we communicate almost exclusively in English because it is the language in which all classes are taught. This counterintuitive tactic acts as a minimal barrier to entry for prospective students, reducing the likelihood of unsuitable candidates in the applicant pool. Our language intentionally challenges readers, thereby signaling both the rigor of the academic curriculum and the demands of global cultural immersion.

Conclusion

Though we have accomplished a great deal in a very short time, having established Minerva as an attractive, highly sought-after alternative to traditional elite universities, we still have a tremendous amount of work ahead. After admitting four rounds of incoming freshmen, as well as two small master's classes, the organization is now more than ten times the size it was when we began and now has personnel in every major geographic location. This rapid growth, while necessary, brings additional challenges for managing our brand.

How can we ensure that new faculty and staff adopt the same level of meticulous attention to detail as the founding team? How can we continue to consistently implement our principles and the application of our visual and verbal identity across the organization? How should we handle new initiatives, or extensions of the brand into different categories of education?

In addition to these questions, we are also continually incorporating input from our students and staff, as well as responding to new information and opportunities, to increase awareness, relevance, and esteem for Minerva. We endeavor to strike and maintain the crucial balance between consistency and flexibility, speed and quality, and vision and reality; the organization continues to grow, learning to understand and integrate the lessons in the guiding principles. If we are to continue "Achieving Extraordinary," this movement will proceed for decades—even centuries—to come.

References

Interbrand. (2016). Best global brands 2016 rankings. http://interbrand.com/best-brands/best-global-brands/2016/ranking

Rainey, M. T. (2001). *Inside the minds: Leading advertisers.* New York, NY: Aspatore Books.

19   Global Outreach: Communicating a New Vision

Kenn Ross and Robin B. Goldberg

A concerted effort to align outreach and communication is necessary to build awareness and appreciation for something new and different. This is especially true for Minerva, as we try to balance building broad key stakeholder awareness with targeting and engaging those select students who might qualify for the Minerva program. The institution's outreach efforts are intentional, thoughtful, and, not surprisingly, in many ways different from those used by traditional top university programs.

To find and reach qualified prospective students, Minerva's approach must be different for several reasons. First, we are looking for the brightest and most motivated students in every corner of the globe. We need to be clever at building awareness of the program among exceptional students so that they will want to learn more about Minerva and eventually apply, if they decide that Minerva is the right school for them. Second, we believe that certain aspects of the traditional recruiting model fall short because they rely on ineffective and expensive outreach methods. Instead of elaborate brochures and direct-mail campaigns, Minerva leverages public relations, localized direct outreach, and partnerships with like-minded organizations. As an institution dedicated to providing a financially accessible college education, Minerva's approach to outreach is fiscally responsible, and hence the channels we use to reach students were designed to be more cost-effective than traditional models. We are committed to getting the word out with maximum effect while spending as little of our—and our students'—money as possible. Third, our messaging has to be different: it has to be smart, compelling, and comprehensive. The students we seek are bright, and we must respect their hunger to learn about every aspect of the program before they make the decision to apply or enroll. It is our responsibility to be sure the promises we make in our outreach efforts are then fulfilled as the students progress through their four years at Minerva. The results of our outreach efforts since we began accepting applications are compelling: for our first three classes, 50,000 young people from nearly 180 countries around the world have applied to be a part of Minerva's four-year undergraduate program, with more than three quarters of those coming from outside the United States.

Strategy: Outreach, Not Recruitment

Minerva's outreach effort has some unique challenges. On the one hand, Minerva has no quotas or targets for the number of students who will be accepted based on background, country of origin, athletic ability, or any other characteristic. Minerva can and will admit all qualified applicants from any country or region. However, the high bar for admissions means that although potential Minerva students exist everywhere, finding these students takes considerable thought and effort. The reason we are so selective is that we need to ensure that the students we admit will be successful and thrive at Minerva. As special as this program is, it is not right for everyone.

For every one hundred students who apply, only two on average will meet this rigorous bar. How do we find them? How do we share our differentiating factors? How do we engage in deep conversations—in multiple languages, no less—about the value of a Minerva education?

Outreach

We define outreach as (1) any and all efforts to build awareness about Minerva (our vision, our model) among key constituents (students, parents, teachers, educators, counselors, relevant thought leaders) and (2) finding those bright and motivated students who may be interested in attending Minerva. These two objectives are related. We know from experience that effectively spreading the word will go a long way toward finding appropriate candidate students.

Editorial coverage has proved to be a viable way for Minerva to build awareness and reinforce basic understanding of the Minerva offering. In-depth reporting on the organization and our programs in national and international media gives audiences more confidence in the messages being shared. As awareness and understanding of Minerva grow within a region, it is easier to gain access to other key stakeholders throughout that region. Rather than Minerva's radically different approach being seen as a threat, we are largely perceived as a force for positive change in the world. The more people know about Minerva, the easier it is for us to attract the strongest prospective students from around the globe.

We find that we do not need to impose ourselves on students. Rather, we simply need to present the facts about Minerva's educational model, and ideally engage them in a deeper discussion about the meaning of and rationale for a university education built for the twenty-first century. Those students who are interested in and suitable for a Minerva education will proactively seek to learn more about this opportunity. Since one of the key traits that Minerva seeks in students is motivation or drive, this is a good filter for us. Instead of aggressively recruiting applicants, we are much better off ensuring that prospective students are sincerely interested in our program and want to pursue it because of their deep interest. That said, students the world over still need to hear our message, and we need to find the most effective channels and tactics to spread that message.

Not recruitment

Many schools are focused on putting bodies in seats to fill a class, yet many fall short of enrollment expectations even with that limited goal in mind. As part of our own global work, we see firsthand how other institutions operate. Admissions officers, recruiters, and third-party agents working on behalf of other universities spend weeks at a time on the road, going from school to school, from college fair to college fair, talking to anyone who will talk to them. Often they are focused on quantity versus quality. We hear them speak of the number of students they will recruit that year, and the need to make sure they find enough students to fill an incoming class. Apparently there is real pressure to ensure that 100 percent of the beds available for first-year undergraduates at any given school are filled. Some schools admit they are in the business of "curating" their classes—finding the right applicant to be the next quarterback, the next representative from Brazil, and so forth.

We are frequently asked by students, parents, counselors, and teachers how many students Minerva intends to accept in the next matriculating class or the number of students Minerva plans to recruit from country X. We do not know the answers in advance. In the absence of social engineering based on country of origin, family background, ethnicity, financial status, or the like, and remembering that our high bar for admissions defines absolute, not relative, standards, we do not know how many students will matriculate each fall until the entire admissions process is complete for the year. This fact is reflected in how we conduct outreach. We are intentionally staffed and resourced to pay equal attention to communities of students and relevant stakeholders everywhere around the world. We do not seek out groups from certain geographic areas over others; we interact similarly with everyone, regardless of where they live or their family backgrounds.

Why does Minerva utilize outreach rather than recruitment? It helps us identify students who have genuine interest in our program. We spend considerable time building awareness among key constituencies, educating in depth with every interaction and engaging with those highly accomplished students who express sincere interest in Minerva. We ensure that we focus our time and attention on the most motivated prospects so that they can apply to Minerva with a deep understanding of and appreciation for the unique aspects of what we offer.

Tactics: Effective Methods for Spreading the Word

We have developed numerous ways to inform and educate the public about Minerva, including media and public relations campaigns, targeted communications, and person-to-person interactions. Following is a summary of the different communication channels we have used to build broad awareness of Minerva's program as well as to directly reach prospective students and those who shape their perspectives on college.

Media and public relations

Unlike most universities, which appear in the press only when there are controversies and scandals, Minerva has received a tremendous amount of editorial coverage since we announced our intention to build an improved university program five years ago. Because the Minerva model is so different and breaks with the status quo, journalists spanning the globe have shown an interest in covering stories about our curriculum, our faculty, our cloud-based educational software platform, and our students themselves. To date we have had more than ten billion media impressions and have been featured in many of the most prominent print, online, television, radio, and other media, including *The New York Times*, *The Atlantic Magazine*, Al Jazeera, *Veja* (Brazil), *Die Zeit* (Germany) and KBS Broadcasting (Korea), to name just a few. Often journalists, themselves graduates of traditional elite universities around the world, quickly grasp the fundamental value of the Minerva model, based on their own college experiences and their paths since graduation. They, like many others, quickly comprehend the need for a university curriculum that teaches students transferable skills that will allow them to succeed in many contexts and careers, and to keep learning and adapting along the way. A simple online search for information about Minerva yields an enormous amount of editorial content, the bulk of it overwhelmingly positive. We have been fortunate because much of it is accurate, if not always complete in its detail, because Minerva is a complex concept and challenging to articulate succinctly.

Periodically, as one might expect when introducing something new and potentially disruptive, we have faced the cynical journalist who has questioned our approach. For these outliers, we have done everything possible to answer candidly every question and given them access to key aspects of Minerva. It is remarkable that some of those initially among the most cynical have wound up publishing some of the most glowing reviews of Minerva. However, it should be noted that editorial content cannot be controlled: if journalists are invited to tell a story, a few may write pieces that don't accurately represent the institution. It is a trade-off, but we have found that the accurate coverage has far outweighed anything inaccurate, so much so that overall the editorial support has been very helpful in telling our story.

Since our first year, some of the most compelling stories have originated with our own students. Many of them, pleased with what and how they are learning at Minerva, have taken it upon themselves to share their experiences. Stories from students hailing from multiple continents and with various secondary education backgrounds and stories written in multiple languages have combined to indicate a clear consensus among these young learners: this is a university system not only worth experiencing but also worth sharing with others.

Another effective practice regarding media and public relations is to start the conversation early and be as open as possible in sharing information. Minerva has worked assiduously to do this from the beginning. We began sharing details of our vision and model even before it was fully articulated and well before we had any students. This generated a deeper discussion about what we are doing early on and created a valuable channel for feedback from various constituents. Additionally, we have continued to build out social media channels on a global basis to sustain an ongoing dialogue. Even this book is an example of the level of transparency that we believe is crucial, both for the fulfillment of our mission and to provide a model for other educational institutions to embrace.

The complexities of explaining Minerva

When journalists write about Minerva, they take what they learn through interviews and investigation and put together an editorial piece with their own context and commentary. They control the message. Our website, presentations, and marketing materials, on the other hand, all provide opportunities for us to craft our messages as we believe they should be conveyed. The complexities of our model and the breadth of innovation we have pursued make it particularly challenging to communicate all the distinctive aspects of Minerva to audiences, but given sufficient time and interest, we can explain both what is different about our program and why those differences matter.

Communications become much more difficult when we try to be succinct because there is so much depth and detail in every aspect of the program—and in the intention behind each. Because we recognize that the interest level of prospective students grows as they learn more about the program, we are very conscious about how we structure messages, moving toward greater specificity at each point of interaction. We also work to anticipate their questions, building the answers into our communications when and where it is most appropriate.

In light of the challenge of conveying a great deal of information about our program, it might be assumed that our written communications would rely on simple language and the extensive use of bullet points intended to make the content more consumable. Instead, our writing incorporates complex sentence structures, advanced vocabulary, and a consistently serious and intelligent tone. While we considered the possibility that we might alienate prospective students (and others) with this sophisticated approach to communications, we made the decision not to compromise and "talk down" to our most important audience: the *right* students. We realized that the brightest students in the world would not be put off by complex language. To the contrary, they would find the challenge a refreshing departure from typical university presentations.

Developing this sophisticated approach to communications has been an iterative process. Initially our messaging was much more focused on the features and characteristics of the program because it was first necessary to explain what we were doing. The early version of our website, for example, was full of descriptive language about the curriculum, the class technology, the faculty, and student life. We soon realized, however, that mere descriptions lacked the power needed to convey our key points of differentiation. Additionally, the descriptions resembled the claims that other top schools were using in their marketing communications. Therefore, adding more information was crucial to demonstrating the ways in which Minerva actually does teach students to be exceptional critical thinkers, innovators, leaders, collaborators, communicators, and global citizens. Through our face-to-face interactions, we also found that audiences reacted much better to each description of what we were doing when coupled with an explanation of why. This insight became the basis for our next wave of written communications: we included the rationale for each key difference while explaining its various aspects. By adding this second layer of information, we were able to proactively address many of the functional concerns most students would have.

The next step was articulating a compelling emotional narrative, one that would appeal to the right students and help them decide whether Minerva might be right for them. In speaking with our current students, one concept stood out as particularly relevant: the excitement derived from taking on new challenges. Not only are academics at Minerva challenging, including both a new way of learning and an entirely new class setting, so too are the global experiences Minerva offers and the diverse, often contrasting perspectives evident in the student community. Even the admissions process hinges on a unique set of challenges that are designed to assess how students think across a variety of dimensions. Weaving the concept of challenge into our communications provided another layer for our messaging, and we are now better able to set student expectations about the demanding nature of the experience.

We want students to understand the program, the intentionality behind it, and the significance of their decision to attend. We want students—specifically those with extraordinary intelligence, ambition, and perseverance—to learn about Minerva and quickly recognize that it would be the most transformative way they could spend the next four years. It would be both energizing and taxing, different from any other university in the world.

A personal approach
A key element of Minerva's outreach, one seldom employed by other institutions, is placing team members around the world whose primary objective is to share information about the program. For Minerva's current size and scale, the fact that a healthy proportion of the nonacademic team is engaged in outreach activities is perhaps unprecedented. Many traditional universities, older and larger than Minerva, may not have anyone based outside the city, town, or village where that university is located. One reason for this is that, by coincidence if not by design, those schools primarily serve students from their home countries. Minerva set out to educate talented students from around the world, without geographic limitations, so the makeup of our outreach team naturally looks different.

Minerva's focus on local engagement with relevant communities around the world may not seem special on the surface, but the fact that these team members are not based in one central location, as is the case with most American universities, is indeed special. By hiring local team members, persons knowledgeable about their own countries, regions, and cultures, Minerva ensures that we establish and maintain deeper ties in each area. In addition, this local expertise heightens our sensitivity to and respect for the myriad cultures and communities around the world. We do not simply "pop in" for a recruitment tour. Instead, we continue to engage in and with each community to foster long-term relationships. We get to know the people and the institutions, from the schools, counselors, partners, and governments to potential employers.

Another key component of our outreach model is the purposeful decoupling of outreach from admissions. That is, our global outreach team members are not admissions officers and have no formal input into admissions decisions. This has basic and immediately obvious benefits. Specifically, it eliminates potential bias from the admissions process. In the conventional model, admissions officers travel the world, visiting specific communities only every year or two. This is problematic: not only are they perceived as outsiders, they are also more likely to be influenced by their "gut feelings" about individual applicants, their need to fulfill quotas, or, worse, outright favoritism based on personal gain. This lack of objectivity is one reason why most so-called merit-based admissions are rife with bias.

At Minerva, admissions officers focus on the assessment of each candidate using verifiable and quantifiable information, while the outreach specialists focus on developing awareness of the institution. We believe that this level of specialization, not just a firewall that inhibits potentially problematic practices, is necessary to support the specific expertise needed for both outreach and admissions.

Leveraging Partnerships with Like-Minded Organizations

To identify students who will be successful at Minerva, we have developed a number of partnerships with organizations that have access to talented, engaged, accomplished students; these organizations also share our belief that top students should have the opportunity to succeed regardless of their ethnicity, nationality, or financial situation. When identifying potential partners, we look for alignment with our values and objectives, as well as clear benefits for each party. We then agree on the components of the partnership from the outset. In a typical relationship, we communicate with their student population through a variety of channels, including e-mail, social media, websites, events, and other joint activities. In return, Minerva may offer a scholarship in the name of the organization to students with demonstrated need. Examples of such partner organizations include the National Speech and Debate Association (U.S.), the World Youth Alliance (global), Estudar (Brazil), and the Uganda Mathematical Society.

More than just opening up new outreach channels and helping generate interest, collaborating with partners procures their implicit endorsement of Minerva as a preferred option for their students. When partners send communications on our behalf, students are reassured, knowing the message is coming from a trusted source. Students also often rely on these organizations as authorities when considering to which universities they will apply.

While it is easy to get excited about partnerships that offer access to a large pool of students, however, we must be judicious about the organizations we work with. The same credibility that a partner confers can have the opposite effect: partnering with a frivolous or unscrupulous organization would cast doubt on our own integrity and prestige. At Minerva, we are highly selective about the organizations we work with, ensuring each aligns with our mission, brand positioning, and guiding principles (see chapter 18).

One Global Approach Does Not Fit All

We recognize that it is beneficial, at times even essential, to modify our method of engagement from region to region. While the content of our messaging remains constant around the world, exactly which channels and modes we preferentially use in each location may vary.

Minerva's regional outreach teams determine the specific mix of activities that will generate the greatest awareness in that region or country. This mix of activities may include varying degrees of traditional press, social media, partnerships, e-mail campaigns, localized events, and more. These variations are the result of diverse audience expectations and behaviors, as well as the cultural and political climate. For example, the traditional press is an important, well-respected channel for trustworthy news in most of North America, but is viewed with deep suspicion in many parts of the Middle East. These distinctions mandate very different use of limited resources, such as a heavy focus on editorial coverage in the United States and a much greater reliance on other tactics in other countries.

To give a more specific example, Minerva's outreach efforts in China differ not only from those in other countries and regions but even differ from region to region within that country itself. Although both social media and traditional press are important channels for communicating with students there, a vastly different Internet ecosystem and the expectation that official communications will be primarily in Chinese require a specific strategy. Additionally, more than 98 percent of high schools in China do not allow university visits; they have neither the infrastructure nor the cultural practice of accommodating these events. In this relatively insular and conservative environment, we utilize specific social media platforms, direct e-mail, and press coverage, with translated messaging tailored to students—and their parents.

Minerva continues to receive positive feedback from local community members regarding the thoughtfulness of this approach. Several years ago Minerva learned that we appeared to be the only American university program that regularly communicated with interested parties in China through WeChat (China's most popular social media platform) in Chinese (rather than English). Although other schools ran WeChat platforms, seemingly through staff based in their foreign locations, none of them were writing and posting in Chinese. Some readers even inquired if this WeChat account was really Minerva's official one because they "didn't expect a US school to be so local." They were pleasantly surprised to learn that it was.

More Than Students

Beyond prospective students, Minerva's outreach efforts engage audiences with direct influence on the university selection process, including school officials, counselors, and parents, as well as those with broader relevance to student success. From local governments to potential employers and other educational innovators, our work to build relationships and garner support in each region is already yielding results. Not only have we helped secure internships for current students at top global organizations, we have also been able to establish each of our residential locations—including housing, technical infrastructure, support services, and event partners—rapidly and with few obstacles. We now know that top employers in multiple industries are delighted to learn of a university program like ours, one that is thoughtfully and purposefully bridging the skills gap. Individuals in these organizations are often excited enough to enthusiastically urge students—including their own children and relatives—to apply to Minerva. By engaging audiences beyond students, we are able to build productive relationships that help us expand awareness of and interest in this innovative approach to higher education.

Conclusion

Minerva offers an education like no other, so logically our approach to outreach and communications is different as well. Whether through focusing on high-touch relationship building within diverse communities, using distinctive messaging and channel strategies, or working toward broader audience engagement, in a remarkably short time Minerva has been able to achieve global recognition and interest with limited resources. These outreach efforts will progress. As we grow and innovate, we will continue to think deeply about how we can be more effective, global, and personal, to help more communities everywhere understand and support our efforts to educate exceptional students, for the sake of the world.

20   An Admissions Process for the Twenty-First Century

Neagheen Homaifar, Ben Nelson, and Stephen M. Kosslyn

It is a truism that with global markets, climate change, migration, and dozens of other interconnected systems, isolated communities no longer exist in the world. As part of its core mission, Minerva seeks to nurture "critical wisdom" to help our students effectively address global challenges. Thus, selecting students to matriculate at our institution is a great responsibility that is both humbling and clarifying. As with everything else that forms the bedrock of Minerva, we are guided by first principles in designing the student selection process. In this chapter we review those principles and then explain how we have used them to create a new kind of admissions process.

First Principles: Goals and Constraints

First and foremost, we needed to decide what we wanted our students to be able to do after they graduated. Our entire admissions process is grounded in a conception of the sort of student who can succeed according to our criteria of success. We defined our goals as follows: We want our students to be able to develop into leaders and know how to work with others, to understand and be capable of innovation, to be broad, adaptive thinkers, and to adopt a global perspective. We reviewed the relevant empirical literatures and identified characteristics that students should have in order to be likely to achieve these goals. The structure of the admissions processes was shaped in large part by these goals and the associated literatures.

We also realized that the problems facing society in the twenty-first century are so large and complex that it is unlikely that any person working alone can solve them. Rather, in most cases the mega-problems we now face will be solved by teams—and the members of those teams will bring different strengths to the task. We wanted students who were open to working closely with people who are very different, which would allow the whole to function as more than the sum of its parts. But more than that, we wanted to select students who were very good in at least one subject, and help them learn to collaborate effectively with other students who have different strengths.

Thus, diversity is at the heart of our admissions process—but not in the usual way. Because the causes of and solutions to major global issues are by definition global, an institution purporting to help solve those problems would do well not to limit its student body based on geographic origin. Not only is geographic diversity crucial, so is diversity of socioeconomic status, personal interests, and abilities. Moreover, many of the world's problems are best solved by bringing together people with various experiences and perspectives. Without exposure to diverse perspectives, life experiences, and cultures, our future leaders will be at a substantial disadvantage.

Luckily, talent is broadly distributed across geography, socioeconomic class, gender, ethnic groups, and personal belief systems. We believe that it is our responsibility as an institution to provide the best possible systematic framework to recognize that talent and provide access to an opportunity such as Minerva.

Most highly selective universities rely on quotas in their admissions process to achieve diversity, for example by selecting representatives from as many countries as possible. This kind of social engineering, however, leads to negative secondary effects, such as having different standards for different students, which has a negative impact on the overall quality of the education.

Some have argued that without different standards for different types of applicants, an admissions process will exclude rather than include more countries and high-potential students.

They are exactly right—if they rely on traditional methods of selecting and admitting students.

That is why Minerva had to completely redesign the traditional admissions process. We needed to identify students from around the world who met our criteria, without compromising our principle of focusing on merit and nothing else.

Designing an Admissions Process from Scratch

At Minerva, we do not change traditional processes and procedures for change's sake. Instead, we begin with an analysis of the present state of affairs, and only after we identify problems do we consider possible changes. After carefully examining the existing admissions processes, we found that we wanted to customize and eliminate more than we wanted to keep.

Problems with the traditional admissions process

We observed the following opportunities for improvement in the traditional admissions process:

Essays. Generic essays garnered unhelpful information, were not a guaranteed reflection of the applicant's work, and provided a substantial advantage to students who could afford test or college preparatory services. Family resources clearly play a role in helping students write these essays, which disadvantages students who do not have the means to hire consultants or even the network to garner advice. First-generation college students are at a particular disadvantage because their parents are usually unfamiliar with the US admissions process and cannot provide assistance.

Letters of recommendation. Similarly, letters of recommendation often were mostly indistinguishable from each other. And, more often than not, the best recommendations came from counselors at private schools, where the student-to-counselor ratio is dramatically lower than the nearly one to five hundred ratio present in most American public schools (U.S. Department of Education, 2015). In nonelite schools, most counselors do not have time to get to know each of their five hundred students well enough to write a compelling letter. Moreover, most international students do not even have a counselor, so the head of the school or a teacher ends up filling out the recommendation forms. Neither can be guaranteed to have an accurate overall picture of the student.

Outside activities. By the same token, we observed that questions about how students spent their time out of the classroom (e.g., in extracurricular endeavors) often were limited to an official position title and the hours spent, and typically said little about what the student actually accomplished. Moreover, we were concerned that not all students have equal access to all types of outside activities—and there was no systematic way to compare unusual activities with the more common types.

Application fees. College application fees charged by universities in the United States average $70. For international students, these fees can be even more expensive. Applicants to selective schools often hedge their bets by applying to multiple schools because the chances of getting in are low and the criteria are often nebulous. They may spend up to $1,500 to gain an opportunity at one school (Kaminer, 2014). Students unable to pay these fees will either jump through hoops to qualify for fee waivers (if they exist), or worse, not apply at all because the returns are not guaranteed—and international students realize they have lower chances of getting into an American university, and so often are reluctant even to try to be admitted. In addition, some students know that they cannot afford to attend, even if they are admitted.

Standardized tests. Standardized admissions tests (e.g., the SAT and ACT) are a mainstay of the system. However, we found that students could regularly improve their scores by hundreds of points if their parents could afford to send them to a $1,000 test prep class or hire a private tutor. Unsurprisingly, test scores are more highly correlated with a family's income than with an applicant's intelligence (Rampell, 2009).

Backdoors. Even with all the existing advantages for certain segments of the population, highly selective universities go even further to advantage certain students. The two largest groups benefiting from this practice are so-called legacy admits and college athletes. At elite universities, legacy students, those whose siblings, parents, grandparents, or other relatives attended the institution, constitute nearly a fifth of the student body. What is worse, admission rates for particularly well-off legacy students are astronomically high compared to those for the general population. For example, a person who worked in the development office at a highly selective university with a single-digit percentage acceptance rate told one of us that the acceptance rate of children whose family regularly donated to the university was more than ten times higher than the average!

Athletes provide another convenient backdoor for universities. When one thinks of college athletics one usually thinks of football and basketball, but elite universities have far more varsity teams than that. Harvard, for example, has forty-two recruited varsity intercollegiate sports teams that constitute 20 percent of the entire Harvard student body (Harvard University, 2016). These teams include sports such as crew, fencing, golf, sailing, skiing, and water polo, among other activities often taken up largely by very wealthy students.

Feeder schools. Universities appear to provide a substantial advantage to students from particular high schools. The phenomenon of feeder schools is well known, and it makes sense that highly selective high schools would prepare students disproportionately well for highly selective universities. But Ivy League schools often complain about how few spots they have available and the overwhelming number of qualified applicants they receive. With that dynamic, it would be very easy to distribute high school acceptances more broadly rather than concentrating them among wealthy demographics, as currently happens.

In short, we noted that wealth afforded too many advantages, too many talented students were overlooked, and traditional application questions typically shed too little light on the applicant's potential. For a university to have a truly diverse group of uniformly high-quality students it must explicitly and intentionally design an admissions process to achieve this goal.

It is crucial to note that some advantages of wealth cannot be filtered out and that those advantages should not be a negative stamp on those applicants. Students who come from stable homes, who have parents who have benefited from elite educational systems, and who believe in focused study and preparation will often grow up with a value system that is aligned with hard work and achievement. Those values will serve these children well, and will serve society at large well. But given the built-in advantages that wealth often brings, it is even more crucial to neutralize systemic advantages conferred by the institution itself.

The students who thrive at Minerva have a combination of curiosity and intellectual horsepower, as well as a demonstrable passion for something; they are humble, open-minded, culturally aware, and extraordinarily hardworking; and they believe deeply in contributing their talents for the betterment of their global community. It is our responsibility to identify such students during the admissions process.

A Different Kind of Selectivity

Because of our mission and institutional design, and the qualities our students must have (curiosity, intellectual horsepower, and all the rest), Minerva must be highly selective. That said, we remove as many barriers to entry as possible, especially the barrier of limited financial resources. In so doing we have also implemented major innovations to address the problems noted in the previous section.

No application fees

We recognize that talent is distributed worldwide, and that for people in many regions of the world, application fees of $70 or more are a major hurdle. Thus we have no application fees.

No quotas or tips

One of the most significant ways that Minerva reduces the barriers to entry for historically disadvantaged populations is by eliminating an enrollment cap and having no quotas of any kind. We have no maximum number of

Asian, female, nonathlete, same-school graduates, or low-income students, for example. As a result, we do not have to engage in the horse trading that goes into choosing between two qualified applicants. If both candidates meet our standards, both candidates are admitted. The competition to get into Minerva is between the student and his or her potential, not between two different students. If an applicant is bright and curious enough to handle our curriculum, determined and persistent enough to work through difficult subjects that are not in his or her area of interest, proactive enough to make real contributions to the community, and mature enough to handle our culturally diverse and travel-intensive environment, the applicant will earn a spot at Minerva. We do not select students based on specific nationality, gender, area of expertise, or socioeconomic status. In fact, it is not until we have made all admissions decisions that we learn the demographic makeup of our student body.

If we find that we have an uncharacteristically low representation of a particular type of student, we don't change our admissions standards to accept a token student. First, we invest more time and effort to ensure that we are interpreting our applicant data as accurately as possible (e.g., ensuring that we understand the significance of winning a certain award in Kenya or have a better representation of academic performance than the punishingly grade-deflated Singaporean transcript). Then we make sure that we provide the best guidance possible to our applicants. Last, and most strategically, we invest more in outreach efforts to those populations. For example, the founding class at Minerva included no students from Eastern Europe or India, and it did not make sense for us not to have representatives from those regions, especially because they send a significant number of students to the United States. Therefore we increased our outreach efforts in those regions, and we did in fact succeed in having better representation of these populations in our future classes.

Just as we have no quotas for nationality, socioeconomic status, or gender, we reject the preferential treatment traditionally given to legacies, athletes, or affiliates of the university. These sorts of applicants are not at any disadvantage in our system, but we also do not change our standards for them, just as we do not change our standards for traditionally underrepresented groups.

Because of our unique teaching methods and distributed residential model, we can accept *all* qualified applicants. We have no classrooms and thus no fixed numbers of seats, no gyms that have limited numbers of lockers, and so forth. Instead we accept all qualified students and then hire additional faculty and find additional housing as needed.

Admissions Process

What determines eligibility at Minerva if not one's performance on the SATs, counselor recommendations, or eloquence on essays? Minerva has a holistic admissions process: we consider multiple factors, both cognitive and noncognitive, and the overall pattern of measures determines whether an applicant is admitted.

As noted earlier, we designed our admissions process to assess specific characteristics that would make a student likely to succeed, both at Minerva and after graduation (where success is interpreted in the context of our four overarching goals, noted above). Specifically, we use three major sets of measures to determine an applicant's qualifications: that individual's accomplishments, academic performance, and performance on a range of different assessments.

Accomplishments and impact in communities

We require our students to have a high level of initiative. One of our fundamental goals is to graduate students who will take the initiative to improve the world around them. Without this quality, students will not succeed at Minerva. Our curriculum requires students to prepare outside of class to a much greater extent than at traditional universities, and students who tend not to take the initiative will find it very difficult to succeed under these circumstances. Furthermore, many student organizations are created from scratch every year (because upper-class students are not colocated with first-year students), and students are ultimately accountable to their peers for establishing their own extracurricular activities.

As they participate in our global rotation, our students also have a responsibility to the cities they live in. Making a positive change in these communities is part of the genuine residential experience (e.g., leading a movement for more public toilets in key areas of San Francisco, a city with a dense homeless population). Students who prefer a fully tried and tested experience in which activities are predetermined and ready to use would not happily survive in an environment like this one.

It is therefore our responsibility during the admissions process to identify the applicants who not only are likely to make an impact on the world after graduating but also would thrive, not drown, in this environment. To gauge this likelihood, applicants are asked to document their personal achievements beyond a structured academic setting. We ask them to tell us what they are proud to have accomplished not through mandatory tasks but out of their own volition. What choices did they make, and how did they make the most of the time they invested? This information allows us to identify individuals who have overcome significant obstacles, demonstrated perseverance, and shown a passion for activities, causes, and subjects that transcend their own personal benefit. We look for students who have already set out to tackle some of their community's problems.

Many applicants to Minerva have accomplished incredible things without having resources, just by having the will and motivation to confront a significant challenge. On the other hand, many applicants were not admitted even with impressive titles or seemingly notable accomplishments because when we examined their reports closely, we discovered that the applicants did not really contribute much to reaching the goal. These applicants took credit for other people's work or did not do much to make a change. That is not what we are looking for.

With more than 70 percent of our applicants coming from outside the American educational system, Minerva has an interesting challenge in this component of the admissions process. We ask students around the world to articulate their accomplishments. The first step is to define what an accomplishment is, for the concept of accomplishment is understood differently around the world. Accomplishments are not just winning the traditional leadership positions in school or medals in science Olympiad competitions—they are also community initiatives developed, significant employment commitments kept while excelling in school, and personal obstacles overcome. Cultural differences mean that students may have very different approaches to representing themselves or talking about themselves. In the United States, most students have an easier time talking about their impact or the importance of a role they played, whereas students in Latin America or Europe are less likely to share certain significant details because they are not trained to do so or do not want to appear boastful. We often have to reach out to teach applicants how to be their own best advocates.

This coaching starts with informing prospective students that we receive applications from more than 160 countries. Therefore, understanding the significance of their accomplishments or efforts in their community is paramount. Among the applicants in our first year, one prospective student wrote that she had started an LGBTQ club at her school. Had she not also described the significance of that act (which was especially notable because she started the club at a religious boarding school) or had we not already been aware of the taboo nature of LGBTQ issues in her country, we would have missed a critical component of what her accomplishment said about the applicant. She had guts and was willing to go up against the status quo for something she believed in that many did not. Over time, we have refined our instructions and expanded the media through which we coach our applicants (webinars, prerecorded video tutorials, applicant outreach, blog posts). We continue to experiment with different strategies so that all applicants, no matter their interests or country of origin, can present themselves as strongly as possible.

In addition to describing their accomplishments, we also ask applicants to provide evidence that they did what they claimed—and we take the time to verify this evidence. Applicants provide evidence in the form of web links, document attachments, or contact information for references. The verification process for our applicants is a conscious investment that helps us ensure that our student body is equipped for the challenging experience that is Minerva. Moreover, it is ultimately in the students' interest for us to admit them based on their merits, which increases the likelihood that they will flourish here and not have to drop out later. Several applicants who would have been selected to join Minerva were discovered to have exaggerated or outright fabricated their accomplishments.

Academic performance

Another part of our holistic admissions process focuses on the applicant's academic performance. Given the goals of a Minerva education, we want bright students who also have the motivation to persevere over extended periods of time—and grades are a good indication of this combination of characteristics. Our interest in academic performance dovetails with our principle of not having quotas, because selecting people based on anything other than their capacity can result in accepting some students who are not academically capable of dealing with a rigorous curriculum.

However, admissions must be based on multidimensional criteria, and we sometimes face the decision of whether to be more flexible on academic qualifications when an applicant has impressive accomplishments. There are two customary ways of dealing with this issue. We could accept students who do not have the necessary capability and simply allow them to fail out of school, but this would not occur until after we and they had made a significant investment. Or we could lower our standards so that applicants who were accepted for reasons other than academic merit are guaranteed to progress.

We are morally opposed to both of these options. We think it is our responsibility not to select students who we believe cannot handle the rigor of our curriculum. We believe this to such an extent that we have tuned our admission system so that some students who probably would have been successful at Minerva are not selected. We do our best to minimize our false positives as opposed to minimizing false negatives because we believe that this is the moral thing to do. Over time, we hope to do so less often. We also refuse to lower academic standards or allow grade inflation that makes failing almost impossible, as occurs in many elite universities.

Consequently, grades are important for admissions at Minerva. One reason why we look at academic standing is that it represents a student's commitment, mental fortitude, and desire to reach a long-term goal. In addition, grades reflect a student's willingness—and ability—to think broadly and to engage with multiple subjects. The ability to excel in different subjects is important for our interdisciplinary environment; a student might be number one in the world in physics, but if she has disregarded everything else for physics, she is not an appropriate student for Minerva.

This is also the answer we give to a commonly heard critique, namely, if traditional educational systems are failing, why are we holding students to account for success or failure in those systems? On the face of it, this seems to be a compelling point, and there are certainly many "Minervas" of the future that should be built for students who are not able to succeed in those environments but would thrive in others. However, for every such student, there are plenty of others who could be successful in those traditional environments but were not motivated to do so; in many cases, they apparently chose not to do well simply because they could not be bothered. That kind of attitude does not work in our system. We have not been able to distinguish between these two types of individuals with any level of certainty.

Nevertheless, we are not simply looking for straight-A students. Yes, Minerva students are bright and motivated, but they are also interesting, mature, curious, and passionate. Often we accept students who excel at certain subjects and, although they are generally very good across the board, nevertheless have "imperfections" on their transcript.

Assessments

The last major component of our admissions process is our assessments. Although grades are a way of measuring an applicant's intelligence, perseverance, fortitude, and ability to commit to more than just narrow interests, we needed a way to understand whether an applicant had a strong baseline from which to navigate fast-moving classes in advanced topics. Existing standardized tests such as the SAT and ACT do not reflect an unbiased or accurate view of intellectual skills and abilities, so instead we administer a battery of assessments that measure different aspects of such skills and abilities, which range from creativity and mathematics to analogical reasoning, comprehension, and written and spoken communication in English.

In addition, we administer an on-camera, automated interview, which allows us to assess some noncognitive characteristics that should predict success in such a strenuous environment; we also use these assessments to triangulate what we see in the rest of the applicant's materials (accomplishments and academic performance). If we see inconsistencies, we sometimes reach out to the applicant to get a better picture of him or her.

We administer the assessments in a timed, online, proctored format so that anyone with access to a computer and the Internet can apply to Minerva. There is no need to travel to a brick-and-mortar testing facility. In addition to this more flexible testing environment, there is no testing fee, nor can one study for the assessments. Thus there is no expensive test prep material to purchase or time spent memorizing strategy. Another barrier to entry removed!

Evaluating Applicants

To summarize, the Minerva application focuses on three broad areas: (1) the student's personal achievements outside a structured academic environment, (2) the student's past academic performance, and (3) the student's performance on assessments that reveal his or her capabilities and characteristics in greater depth than is evident in the other materials. The evaluation process relies on the following procedures.

Quantifying responses

Some of our measures are quantitative (e.g., scores on assessments), but many are not. We convert qualitative data (e.g., submitted accomplishments and the interview) to numbers by using rubrics. The admissions and academic teams work very closely together to develop rubrics that quantify our qualitative measures. We invest a significant amount of time developing these rubrics, with the goal of reducing as much subjectivity as possible. Keeping in mind that the majority of our applicants are not from the same culture, we consider the range of answers we could imagine receiving to design rubrics that address as many permutations of responses as possible.

We also anticipate possible answers when we design the questions used in the interview and the assessment instruments we use. For assessments that are more word-based, for example, we pretest all our questions on a test population from around the world to ensure that the questions are clear and easily understood by any English speaker, not just American English speakers.

Video interviewing

As noted above, some of our assessment measures, especially the noncognitive ones, are obtained through an interview. To standardize the experience for our international applicants, we chose to use an automated video interview, instead of a live Skype or in-person interview, so that we could reduce any disadvantages an applicant may have in a live interview. There are inherent biases in all interactions and some may be greater than others. For example, the experience of a Caucasian man speaking with a young Asian woman may be very different from the experience of a North African woman speaking with another African woman. It is true that interviewers can be trained to avoid certain behaviors, but the experience will never be perfect. In our video interview, we establish a consistent environment for all of our applicants such that the questions, time allotted to answer, and the feedback received for the answer (none) are the same. To make the experience as comfortable as possible, we provide practice questions so that applicants can see what it feels like to watch a video and record an answer in a timed environment. Once they feel that they have had enough practice, we get to see how well they think on their feet, just as we expect them to do in the classroom. An automated interview also has the virtue of being scalable; we could not personally interview tens of thousands of applicants.

Scoring accomplishments

With a large and diverse applicant pool, we had to develop numerous criteria to evaluate accomplishments. The significance or the scale of an activity comes in many forms, and we had to account for multiple dimensions that we believe are important indicators of the capabilities of the applicant while minimizing others that are less indicative. We also needed to consider the context of where the accomplishment took place; different countries, environments, and social and economic conditions amplify or dampen the significance of various accomplishments. We needed to design rubrics to take into account the vast differences in where our students have lived and gone to school.

Reliable scoring

We take objective evaluations so seriously that we create decision trees for each of our rubrics, such that an evaluator answers a series of questions that then automatically generates a rubric score for the evaluation at hand.

This method greatly enhances the reliability of rubric scoring. Rather than evaluate on a gut feeling or an internalized sense of what a certain score on the rubric is, we base scores on multiple specific questions with specific answers. We find this method a better way to ensure that our evaluators use the same criteria, and when evaluators disagree (at least two independent evaluators code each qualitative response), we can determine the point of divergence more systematically and refocus our training or improve an answer choice or question to reduce any subjectivity.

Distributed review

Each component of the application—accomplishments, grades, and assessments—is first evaluated independent of the other pieces and often excluding the applicant's name, so that we do not bias our interpretation of one area based on what we saw in another. This means that an applicant without perfect grades will not be penalized in our interpretation of his or her accomplishments or video interview.

Algorithmic Scoring

Most university admissions processes include a negotiation in which members of the committee sit around a table and compete to have "their" candidates accepted. We do not do this, both because we question the ethics of denying spaces to qualified candidates and also because we do not have to do so, given our teaching model (which does not limit us to a fixed number of spaces in any given year).

Eliminating the requirement to cull the pool of qualified applicants liberated us to be extremely principled in our selection process. All of the scores for each person are combined into a single composite score that determines whether the student is above or below a bar. Although the bar for entry is the same for each student, our holistic admissions process allows students who have very different patterns of strengths and interests to be admitted without being superb on each component of the admissions criteria.

The admissions process at Minerva is undertaken with care and deliberation. We want to be sure that every applicant has a fair chance of being admitted.

Financial Aid

Minerva is one of only seven institutions in the United States that is both need-blind and meets needs for all applicants regardless of country of origin (Wikipedia, 2016). Most of our students do not come from privileged backgrounds and therefore need financial aid. At Minerva we believe that investing in students' future is a shared responsibility. We play a significant supporting role, and request that students and families help finance their education to an extent that is both equitable and manageable. We help families to afford a Minerva education in several ways.

First, the responsibility rests with Minerva itself to keep costs down. We ensure that the four-year cost of our education is far lower than that of our peer institutions (see chapter 27). Minerva is careful to ensure that every dollar spent goes toward the things that only we can provide to our students, including small classes of fewer than twenty students, an innovative curriculum, a roster of world-class faculty, and a first-rate student life experience. We do not spend money on products or services that do not address our central mission. For example, instead of investing in building expensive campus facilities and the amenities found at other universities, Minerva uses the vast resources of major world cities as its educational, extracurricular, and cultural infrastructure. At Minerva, the city is the campus. All in all, a Minerva education costs well below half of what a traditional private, four-year nonprofit university costs, saving families in excess of $160,000 over four years.

Second, the student's family is responsible for contributing to the student's education, based on the amount it is capable of paying. We take a principled approach to evaluating family contribution regardless of the student's country of origin so that every family is treated equitably.

Third, the students themselves must supplement their family's contribution (for those families that cannot afford all of Minerva's costs) through Minerva-arranged work opportunities and student loans that are designed to be paid back without creating a burden on graduating students.

Last, where there is still a gap, philanthropists who believe in the mission of Minerva have pooled resources to offer need-based scholarships to enable our high-potential students access to a world-class undergraduate education.

Our shared goal is to enable students to attend Minerva but at the same time to ensure that they do not graduate with a heavy financial debt burden.

Conclusion

After four years of admissions cycles and three years of matriculating students, we have had the privilege of learning from some 50,000 people who applied to Minerva, from 179 countries. Those applicants yielded students from more than sixty countries with no majority country, a nearly even gender split, and a socioeconomically diverse student body, with more than 80 percent requiring some financial assistance from Minerva.

Students from a myriad of religions, races, ways of life, and socioeconomic statuses have earned their spot at Minerva without our needing to "fill spots" or check boxes. The freedom to admit students solely based on merit gives us the confidence that each year's class has a strong foundation and enough diversity of thought to make learning and living together both interesting and educational. It is impossible to achieve this level of community diversity and quality within the constraints of the traditional admissions process. If our peer institutions plan to evolve gracefully and remain relevant for future generations of bright minds, we invite them not only to reform what and how they teach but, for the sake of the world, whom they teach as well.

Acknowledgments

The admissions process at Minerva is the product of bold and interdisciplinary thinking fueled by members of nearly every team in the organization. To conceive, design, build, grow, and operate an admissions experience that challenges, inspires, and serves students around the world required the collaboration and input from the admissions, academic, product design, marketing and branding, outreach, and student services teams.

We would like to give a special thanks to the following people, whose contributions played a significant and lasting role in creating the quality of experience and achieving the scale that we have achieved in the last three years: Laurence Favrot, Kara Gardner, Junko Green, Jonathan Katzman, Rena Levitt, Samantha Maskey, Jason Morrison, Chris Swimmer, and the admissions processors.

We also thank the following past and present contributors for the work they have done to support and improve the admissions process: Alex Aberg Cobo, Avery Anderson, Fatou Badiane-Toure, Eoin Brown, Teri Cannon, Andrew Collins, Lucian Cosinschi, Paul Craciunoiu, Terry Cumes, Linh Dao, Nick Frezynski, Robin Goldberg, Teshika Hatch, Emily Hendershot, Will Houghteling, Lillian Kivel, Michael Lai, Olivia Luo, Marianna Mirchuk, Kriti Parashar, Jamie Randolph, Matt Regan, Lisa Richards, Arthur Rio, Jeff Root, Kenn Ross, Tiffany Schoolfield, Ayo Seligman, Sally Shearer, Jules Shell, Erin Spannan, Joyce Tagal, Kevin Tran, Marielle Van Der Meer, and Hideki Yamamoto.

References

Harvard University. (2016). Harvard Athletics website. http://www.gocrimson.com/information/recruiting/index

Kaminer, A. (2014, November 15). Applications by the dozen, as anxious seniors hedge college bets. *The New York Times*. https://www.nytimes.com/2014/11/16/nyregion/applications-by-the-dozen-as-anxious-students-hedge-college-bets.html?_r=0https://www.nytimes.com/2014/11/16/nyregion/applications-by-the-dozen-as-anxious-students-hedge-college-bets.html?_r=0

Wikipedia. (2016, December 1 [last update]). Need-blind admission. www.wikipedia.org/wiki/Need-blind_admission

Rampell, C. (2009, August 27). SAT scores and family income. *Economix* (blog). *The New York Times*. http://economix.blogs.nytimes.com/2009/08/27/sat-scores-and-family-income/http://economix.blogs.nytimes.com/2009/08/27/sat-scores-and-family-income

U.S. Department of Education. (2015). *Common Core of Data State Nonfiscal Survey Public Elementary/Secondary Education: School Year, 2013–14, Version 1a.* Washington, DC: National Center for Education Statistics. https://nces.ed.gov/pubs2015/2015151.pdf

21   Multifaceted Acculturation: An Immersive, Community-Based Multicultural Education

Norian Caporale-Berkowitz and James Lyda

In contrast to most student bodies at U.S. colleges, Minerva does not have a majority enrollment of white American students who benefit from the inclusion of people of color, international students, and other minority groups. Rather, all students are international students and no one group is a majority. This is very much by design. Minerva is an institution built on first principles and does not adopt the default patterns of any existing educational system. Similarly, the Minervan student culture is not anchored in any majority group, nor is it rigid or calcified. Instead it is malleable: it shifts between classes and across years, reflecting emergent properties that arise as each class of students comes together and then moves from one country to another over the four years of college.

What is the effect of having such a dynamic student culture? Students' cross-cultural experiences are not limited either to assimilation into the majority or to adopting cultural elements from the minority. Rather, in the absence of a dominant group or culture, students experience acculturation from many different angles, and cultural exchange becomes central to the identity development of most Minerva students. In many ways the acculturation process works toward the formation of a new, collective Minerva culture.

In the following pages, we use the term "multicultural" to encompass the full spectrum of human diversity, which extends well beyond geography, ethnicity, or country of origin. Minerva's internationalism is not the limit or focus of our multicultural education; it is only a starkly visible starting point to anchor a community-driven, participatory student culture that is dedicated to living with and learning from interpersonal differences.

Our approach to multicultural education has two main components: (1) bringing together a maximally diverse group of students and placing them in equally diverse and complex environments, and (2) creating community practices that allow students to cross-pollinate their values and backgrounds, and then proactively explore the resulting learnings.

Together, these strategies reflect the evolution of multicultural education over the past several decades. Historically, this field in the United States stemmed from movements to include in schools the histories and experiences of minority groups such as African Americans and Latinos, women, and those with disabilities. The first manifestation of this movement was the somewhat superficial addition of programs on famous women or people of color, but by the late 1980s schools had begun to address structural inequalities in education, and later they came to recognize the importance of instruction in critical thinking, global awareness, and social justice (Banks, 2013; Gorski, 1999).

Accordingly, Minerva's approach to multicultural education moves past the inclusion of marginalized groups and focuses on creating a learning ecosystem in which all students are in the minority, structural inequalities are reduced as far as possible, and students are equipped to actively examine their complex cross-cultural experience. The result is a university program in which theory and practice are more closely aligned than in most traditional educational models. This creates a new definition of multicultural education, one that may be described as "multifaceted acculturation": the evolution of an individual's or group's culture through active participation in an environment so diverse that the frequent exchange of cultural stimuli causes one's cultural values to be questioned as deeply as any others'.

Creating a Diverse Student Community

Minerva brings together a truly diverse student community and then equips students to get the most out of meaningful cross-cultural exposure, dialogue, and learning through a variety of approaches.

Admissions

Minerva aims to train future leaders, with the understanding that many of the world's problems can be solved only by including perspectives from across cultures, geographies, socioeconomic strata, and other dimensions of the human experience. Because of this orientation, much of our work to create a diverse learning environment occurs through our admissions procedures, well before any students arrive.

Our approach to fostering this diversity is not through affirmative action or the deliberate inclusion of minority groups. Rather, we seek to create an admissions system as free as possible from biases and structural inequalities so that all admitted students are equally deserving of their space in the student body. For example, Minerva administers its own battery of admissions tests and does not require standardized exams such as the SAT, ACT, or TOEFL, which favor those with access to costly test prep resources. Minerva also gives no preference to legacy applicants whose parents may be donors or alumni, nor does it have admission set-asides for sports teams or similar organizations, which may consume a significant proportion of the incoming class spots in a traditional university environment.

Through partnerships, media engagement, school visits, and online outreach on five continents, Minerva works to attract a maximally diverse pool of applicants, and by reducing structural bias in the admissions process it seeks to create a student body that reflects the global distribution of talent. This commitment to equality in the admissions process means that students know their classmates are all equally worthy of admission—and of learning from—and their presence is not the artificial product of gaming the admissions process. Multifaceted acculturation requires students to question their own cultural values and actively work to create a new collaborative culture that works for the whole community. This requires a high level of respect for those who may be very different, and this is possible only if students know that every classmate is equally qualified.

Additionally, because there are no quotas that keep class composition geographically or demographically static over time, equality in admissions helps a new Minerva student culture to emerge de novo each year. Ultimately, our approach to admissions allows students to be part of an environment that is always changing. This increases students' willingness to develop their own personal culture, creating a fertile environment for cross-cultural learning and reciprocal acculturation throughout the student body.

Student Legacies

On admission, students are randomly assigned to one of twenty-five Legacies, or social groups, that connect students across classes. Each Legacy descends from a member of Minerva's founding class. These Legacies act as student families within Minerva. They are the default groupings for students' first social activities and city explorations during orientation, and they later serve as the community units in which Minerva fosters social and emotional learning and teaches its seven character outcomes.

The Legacy groups provide students with a family that follows them throughout their four years (and after graduation) and that links them to each class above and future classes below. Just as in biological families, students do not choose their Legacy group or their peers within the group, yet they are bound together throughout their Minerva experience. The diversity of Minerva's community can be overwhelming, and the default affiliation of many students when they enroll is with students from their same country or region. We designed the Legacies to challenge this linkage by providing students with a "home base" community where they can quickly develop a new set of roots. Thus the Legacies are an important vehicle for tightly uniting students who otherwise would never have been friends.

Each Legacy also creates rituals and artifacts that are passed down to future classes of students. The process of collectively creating a Legacy culture is representative of Minerva's multifaceted acculturation model: bringing together diverse groups of students, and then positioning them to engage deeply with each other and create a collective culture that draws from and amplifies their varied backgrounds.

Cohorts

In the same manner that legacies create both large communities across generations and microcommunities within a given class, cohorts are used to fill the space in between. Within each class, students are divided into cohorts ranging in size from 90 to 150 students, depending on the year in which students are admitted. Much like the Legacies, cohorts are randomly assigned and represent a mix of students from various backgrounds. The size of the cohort fits comfortably in the range of Dunbar's number (Dunbar 1992), which is the group size in which deep social relationships can be maintained between all members without resorting to fracturing or the formation of cliques.

Students live and learn together with the same cohort across their four years. The cohort comprises the set of individuals with whom students take their first-year core curriculum classes, share a residence hall in San Francisco, and travel and share lodgings in all six subsequent cities. It is common to hear students in a few short months refer to their cohort as their "Minerva family," an idea that should only increase in strength over their four years together.

Dunbar's number communicates to students that they can and should eventually develop meaningful relationships with every member of their cohort. If not for this expectation, students would be less likely to engage proactively with those who are very different from them or to invest in building a larger community and a culture that binds the cohort and fosters meaningful cross-cultural interactions.

Creating Culture

Minerva is unique among university programs in that each student class lives in a different country. In most colleges, incoming students are assimilated into a majority culture formed by previous generations of students; at Minerva, when first-year students arrive each fall, previous classes have already departed for their global rotation, and matriculating students must create a student culture from scratch. Because all new students enter at the same time and there is no majority demographic, this results in a process of cultural development that is truly multifaceted, drawing on the backgrounds and interests of all students rather than on an inherited set of values and practices.

New student orientation

As successive classes of students live and work at Minerva, they develop some "best practices." We do want to preserve those aspects of institutional knowledge and to connect students across classes. One mechanism for doing so is our live, online predeparture orientation experience, which we call Basecamp. During Basecamp, older students share the projects and extracurricular organizations that existed in previous years, and incoming students can decide which of these programs (if any) they plan to continue and which new ones they wish to create. This model allows us to provide students with the experience of creating a new culture and extracurricular ecosystem each year while still retaining elements of tradition and university culture that ultimately prove important for a cohesive college experience.

In addition, shortly after they arrive at Minerva all students participate in a weeklong orientation called Foundation Week. This serves to introduce students to San Francisco, the residence hall, their peers and faculty, and the various policies and resources they will need during their first year of college. During Foundation Week and at various touchpoints throughout their time at Minerva, students are challenged to think about the values and practices that shape their roles as individuals, as members of a student body, and as citizens in the broader urban community in each city they inhabit. For example, Foundation Week for the class of 2020 included a Minerva-wide colloquium called "Hearth," which explored different aspects of what it means to be a Minervan. Students attended three separate roundtable discussions (chosen from among many options) with faculty and staff. Each discussion was tied to one of Minerva's seven character outcomes and addressed such themes as respect, tolerance, humility, resilience, community, and personal achievement.

By having students collectively engage questions of community identity, values, and practices in their first days at Minerva and repeatedly throughout the semester, we aim to show students that they are the architects of their Minerva experience. This is important because the process of actively creating a student culture forces students both to become curious about the experiences of their peers and to appreciate the trade-offs that must occur to make this culture work for a diverse group.

Accordingly, students often have very different ideas for how to create an ideal community. For example, some students think dirty public kitchens should be eliminated by installing cameras to find and punish offenders, whereas others prefer to create cleaning rotations and celebrate those who altruistically clean up the messes of others. These discussions and the testing of various solutions to such problems are important for the community's development, and we hope the solutions they choose will evolve over time as the community matures and students gain exposure to new attitudes, habits, and philosophies in each city where they live. Because of this, Minerva tries not to provide an official answer where possible and allows the student body to solve these problems independently.

Crossing groups

Much of the acculturation students experience at Minerva stems from living in close quarters with peers who often have very different backgrounds, beliefs, skills, and abilities. We randomly assign roommates for the first year and then make adjustments to remove problematic incompatibilities (as may occur when an early riser is paired with a night owl). However, to facilitate cross-cultural exchange, we do not allow students from the same country to be roommates in their first year and heavily discourage it in upper-class years. We made this decision to push students to adapt to living situations outside their cultural comfort zone. Students often request room changes to be able to live with someone from the same country, for reasons ranging from a roommate's strong-smelling food to the desire to speak their native language in the room. We rarely honor these requests.

In addition to roommate pairings, we foster student contact across existing groups by having residence assistants organize social activities. RAs organize mixers for students on different floors and work to create many touchpoints for different groups of students to interact.

We also deliberately use the residential experience as an opportunity for students to create their own policies and norms for resolving community issues. For example, issues with kitchen cleanliness resulted in students' creating weekly traditions on Wednesdays and Saturdays whereby groups of students take the lead in keeping their residence hall clean. Although staff in the residence hall do have the final authority to intervene, this rarely happens, and we prefer student self-governance and self-construction of their own community policies. This approach is similar to participatory action research, in which communities are engaged as coresearchers and collaborators to solve their own problems (Kemmis, McTaggart, & Nixon, 2013). Through this practice, we seek to position students as active agents of community change, a process that results in faster and deeper reciprocal acculturation than simply being a passive member of a culturally complex community.

Community Programs

Fostering social inclusion and stemming feelings of isolation are both vital to the multifaceted acculturation model; students are willing to evolve their own culture only if they feel they are gaining relationships and resources by doing so. Culture is integral to identity in part because it binds us to others. Why would students challenge their culture if they did not believe this process would improve their relationships and increase interpersonal connectivity?

Our approach to fostering social inclusion in such a diverse student body has been to create community programs and practices. These programs and practices empower each student to shape his or her unique background into a gift that can be shared with the community. For example, every Sunday night students take turns cooking food from their respective countries and sharing the music, dance, and popular culture they grew up with. Every Monday a different member of the community presents his or her life story and talks about how cultural and social contexts have shaped his or her experience. All students are also part of supper clubs, where students first form friendships through group activities; the clubs then become spaces to teach social and emotional learning. Collectively, these programs both highlight the community's multiculturalism and equip students to explore proactively how this diversity mediates their global experience across seven cities and four years of college.

Dissolving cliques and nudging the withdrawn

We have also created programs that we hope will dissolve cliques and provide spaces for more withdrawn students to contribute their perspectives and experiences to the community. For example, our student affairs team regularly organizes social mixers at which students who we know are not friends, and who often come from different parts of the world, are given the chance to spend time with each other. We find that many friendships come from default groupings, such as living close together in the residence hall, being part of the same Legacy, and, in some cases, even coming to Minerva on the same flight. Knowing this, we actively provide opportunities for students to break out of existing patterns and engage other students and cultures that may have otherwise grown along different paths in the normal social group development process.

Encouraging student-created programs

In addition to programs created by staff, Minerva's student experience team encourages students to design and run their own community programs. For example, we have worked with work-study students to incubate a new program called Pirouette Puzzle, after a type of cookie students eat as part of this activity. The Pirouette Puzzle happens at a surprise time and date, often late at night, and any students who are awake in the residence hall when it happens are invited to participate. Fifty or more students may participate, and each student is given a turn to speak for as much time as desired about his or her experience in the community. Sometimes this lasts for many hours and can create very deep connections, allowing students to gain empathy for peers who may come from very different backgrounds and have very different experiences as students at Minerva.

Programs created by staff may appeal to different cross sections of the student body than those created by students. By including both approaches, we hope to achieve as many opportunities as possible for students to have deeper interpersonal experiences.

Feasts and traditions

Classwide feasts and traditions are another important means for students to create a collective identity out of their diverse individual cultures and backgrounds. At most feasts, the whole student body comes together to share a meal, and students run the cooking and cleaning, manage the setup and decorations, and serve each other food at mealtime. Feasts often end in a talent show or performances of some kind. These events provide a space for students to place their individual talents in service to the community and to contribute something original.

Additionally, feasts are a space where student culture and local culture intersect. Minerva's two main feasts (and the only two holidays we officially celebrate) are Friendsgiving in the fall and Quinquatria, the festival of the Roman goddess Minerva, in the spring. Although Friendsgiving derives from the U.S. Thanksgiving holiday, it has become a Minerva tradition and is celebrated each year—including by students in Minerva cities outside the U.S.—because it celebrates values of community and gratitude that are important to Minerva. As Friendsgiving is celebrated in each city outside the U.S., it adapts to reflect the opportunities provided by and constraints of the local culture and setting. As an American tradition that became a Minerva tradition, which is then adapted by each class of students to their local setting, Friendsgiving provides an interesting example of how students experience the acculturation process as they travel during their four years.

Quinquatria, which thousands of years ago was marked by pupils offering gifts to their teachers (and everyone making offerings to the goddess Minerva), has evolved to be the only celebration that includes all Minerva students, faculty, and staff. For us, Quinquatria serves primarily as a celebration of what we are working to achieve together and an opportunity for a good amount of self-effacement and collegial ribbing. Infusing humility into our most important holiday helps students gain a sense that every part of their Minerva experience is a work in progress (and always will be), which parallels the constant cultural evolution that occurs within their student community.

In each city, we have also prepared for students to celebrate local traditions, such as Nikolaustag (St. Nicholas Day) in Berlin, Halloween in San Francisco, and Carnaval in Buenos Aires. Some of these traditions, such as Halloween, are in fact celebrated in multiple countries that our students travel to, but with different customs and practices. As each of these traditions is replicated (or not) in each city, mediated by both the context of the local city and each class's interpretation of the traditions, this provides an additional setting for multifaceted acculturation across the Minerva experience.

Cocurricular and Extracurricular Activities

Minerva offers a wide range of cocurricular activities, which are organized by staff and intended to connect with the curriculum, as well as frameworks for students to create their own organizations and activities.

Cocurricular activities
Each Friday, Minerva organizes cocurricular activities in which students apply their knowledge outside the classroom in joint events with local

people and organizations. In addition to being opportunities for experiential learning, these activities also afford students a better understanding of the local culture and how it affects the way people live in each city.

For example, students participated in a cocurricular event in the Castro district of San Francisco (which is the epicenter of the local gay community). The activity focused on the evolution of the LGBTQ (lesbian, gay, bisexual, trans, queer) movement in San Francisco. As part of the cocurricular event, students were asked to reflect on the status of LGBTQ rights in the areas where they grew up, and on the factors that make it easier or harder for civil rights movements to form. As students from places as diverse as Taiwan, Norway, Argentina, India, and the U.S. compared the effects of politics, religion, and culture on rights movements in their countries, several students shared that they had never seen an environment as accepting of LGBTQ individuals as San Francisco. This environment, coupled with the Minerva community's openness to discussing these issues, had given them a new understanding of what might eventually be possible in their own communities and countries.

Conversely, students from regions that were relatively more accepting of LGBTQ individuals had the chance to learn why other countries might be less tolerant, even with the people's (perceived) best interest in mind. This type of reciprocal exchange of experiences and insights broadens students' understanding of the merits and limitations of their own home cultures and provides a window into new models that could be created, incorporating insights from each system.

Student-driven extracurricular ecosystem

Extracurricular activities are initiated and driven by the students themselves through Minerva Communities (or MiCos) that organize activities for the student body. These activities often vary as students travel, providing a vehicle for students to see how their own organizations and projects adapt to new locations and cultural contexts. For example, students in San Francisco volunteered with the social service organization Concrn to help the city's homeless residents, which is important because homelessness is one of the city's most pressing issues. In Berlin, however, students volunteered with Kiron, a new university providing refugees with higher education, which is important there because the refugee crisis is a major local issue. These experiences allow students to see how various cities and organizations deal with issues differently and force students to tackle a wide range of types of problems and solutions in each city and country. Minerva's global rotation provides students with countless opportunities for small moments of acculturation, and with chances to observe how local culture and context mediate their experience.

Students are the drivers of these experiences throughout their daily lives. For example, in a student-led Berlin Exploration Day, a group visited various eateries throughout the city, observing cultural customs and discussing how different cultural norms manifest themselves. Activities like this are created by students for students as a way of exploring their environment and facilitating their interactions with it. Where else do we see students proactively engage in questions of acculturation and identity as part of their daily search for lunch? Discussion of these themes in the classroom, in Minerva-curated activities, and in activities organized by the student body all contribute to creating an ecosystem of constant cross-cultural inquiry, exchange, and acculturation.

Conclusion

Minerva creates a multicultural education that is community-based, highly participatory, and deeply immersive. We bring together an exceptionally diverse group of students in equally varied locations, empowering them to create a culture de novo that draws from and amplifies their individual perspectives. Additionally, we provide them with tools and programs that encourage them proactively to navigate their cross-cultural experience. Through this process, Minerva builds an ecosystem in which the theory of multicultural education becomes more closely aligned with practice, creating a new twenty-first-century framework that we call multifaceted acculturation.

References

Banks, J.A. (2013). The construction and historical development of multicultural education, 1962–2012. *Theory into Practice , 52*(suppl. 1), 73–82.

Dunbar, R. I. M. (1992). Neocortex size as a constraint on group size in primates. *Journal of Human Evolution, 22*(6), 469–493.

Gorski, P. (1999). A brief history of multicultural education. http://www.edchange.org/multicultural/papers/edchange_history.html

Kemmis, S., McTaggart, R., & Nixon, R. (2013). *The action research planner: Doing critical participatory action research.* New York, NY: Springer Science & Business Media.

22 Experiential Learning: The City as a Campus and Human Network

Z. Mike Wang and Robin B. Goldberg

If you had an opportunity to build a new university from scratch today, where would you situate it? In a city or a suburb? In one location or multiple locations? In Palo Alto? New Haven? Cambridge? Shanghai? Washington, D.C? Why? In a world becoming increasingly flat (Friedman, 2005) and in which employers clamor for global experiences (Malicki & Potts, 2013), practical knowledge, and cultural competency in new hires, there is increasing demand for a more global education. This is no secret: the word "global" features prominently in nearly every U.S. university's marketing material. But what exactly makes an education global? How can we facilitate global understanding? What structures and frameworks are needed to accomplish what so many other institutions merely pay lip service to?

This chapter explores Minerva's uniquely principled and integrated approach to designing a global learning and immersion experience. We review the vision that underlies our global rotations, our approach to global understanding and city immersion, and our framework for experiential learning design.

Why a Global Rotation?

With a commitment to prepare our students to be *global* leaders and innovators (with a true emphasis on global), Minerva's vision has never wavered from providing our students a global experience as an intrinsic part of their education. Although many colleges and universities claim to value a global perspective in their educational offerings, Minerva's approach is very different from that of other institutions. At Minerva, we want our students to learn about the world by experiencing it.

Rationale for the global rotation

Minerva students live in seven different world-class cities over the course of their four years, immersing themselves in different geographic locales, cultures, economies, and lifestyles. We believe that by living in different cities and experiencing different cultures, students will gain a deeper understanding of and appreciation for the different perspectives and approaches that a society may bring to bear on both complex challenges and everyday matters.

The global rotation model exposes Minerva students to a wide variety of experiences. We want to ensure that they visit cities on different continents, cities with different current and past roles on the world's stage, cities with different cultures, cities in different phases of economic development, cities where different native languages are spoken, and cities with different religious foundations. To try to cover all these bases, and to create structures that align with our academic calendar and semester model, we decided to include seven cities in the global rotation. The obvious alternative would have been to select four cities, one per year; the choice of seven cities rather than four meant greater exposure to a broader representation of the world's diversity.

Our choice of cities and their ordering in the rotation sequence were not accidental. We wove together several complementary locations to define the global rotation initially and then, with student input, on-the-ground experience, and reactions to current events, modified and iterated the selection process until we arrived at the current rotation.

Often we are asked what considerations go into determining the cities in the rotation. It might seem obvious, but safety and security remain the top criteria when we choose locations. We then look for historical, economic, political, and vibrant cultural hubs that provide a welcoming environment in which our students can immerse themselves and become engaged in the life and culture of the city. Affordability, quality housing, good local transportation, Internet connectivity, political stability, an appropriate visa policy, an open culture, and a host of other considerations are evaluated for each location option. Finally, in determining the mix of cities, we sought locales that would provide radically different perspectives from each another.

The seven cities

We made the decision to start the student rotation in San Francisco, with that city as the hub for the entire first year. The relatively small size and manageability of the city make it an ideal initial location in the rotation.

San Francisco, though one of the world's most prominent cities and known for its innovative energy, has a population of less than one million. Because the freshman year is the first time that many students live outside their home countries (and for many represents the first time away from home at all), a city that is compact and accessible with an excellent infrastructure makes the transition as smooth as possible. San Francisco not only has a dynamic business community, it is at the forefront of progressive social trends in the United States, it has a vibrant intellectual life, and it has a minority-majority population in the second most densely populated city in the United States. These factors provide a foundation for a wealth of cultural, commercial, and social impact activities. During the freshman year, students immerse themselves in activities and projects to reinforce the common intellectual language they learn in the first-year cornerstone courses; this is relatively easy in a city that is often considered the global capital of innovation.

During their second year, Minerva students experience two radically different Asian cities—Seoul, South Korea, and Hyderabad, India. South Korea and India are postcolonial societies (of the Japanese and British empires, respectively), and both underwent existential rifts, with the separation of North Korea from South Korea and India from Pakistan. In Seoul and Hyderabad, students are exposed to two cities that have seen and continue to undergo tremendous growth: Hyderabad, a city grounded in Muslim traditions, is the fifth largest contributor to India's GNP, while Seoul, a mix of tradition and contemporary culture, experiences economic growth largely through family-run conglomerates. Although a little more than fifty years ago South Korea's per capita GDP was lower than India's, today it is more than fifteen times as large. At the same time, India's overall GDP, which was smaller than South Korea's a decade ago, is now almost 50 percent larger. The paths these countries have taken and their likely future trajectories offer an important comparative lesson in developing economies.

The third-year rotation offers experiences on two different continents, Europe and South America. The cities selected—Berlin, Germany, and Buenos Aires, Argentina—are a study in contrasts. Berlin has emerged from a century marked by war, economic devastation, and partition to become one of the most important cities on the European continent. In contrast, Buenos Aires has had a century of relative external peace, but continued internal upheaval has curtailed change and kept it much the same as it was a century ago. That said, both cities offer uniquely inspiring locations rich with opportunities for our students.

For the fourth year, the Minerva rotation takes students to London, England and Taipei, Taiwan. London, one of the most exciting, diverse, complex and energizing cities in the world, makes for a fitting location for the senior year. Though this city is large and much trickier to navigate, by this point the students have the maturity to handle the complexity of this global capital. Not only is there a wealth of opportunities for engagement, the abundant resources serves the students well as they focus on their capstone projects. And finally, we felt that the rotation would not be complete without an experience in greater China. This region could not be ignored because China continues to grow in importance on the world economic stage.

In sum, the comprehensive rotation through a variety of geographic locations should serve our students well in understanding the broader world. As Minerva's student population grows, we may add new cities to the rotation. Removing cities from the rotation may also occur as world events force us to alter our plans. For some time we expected Istanbul, Turkey, to be in the rotation but the turn toward a totalitarian government prompted us to rethink that choice of city. Istanbul might someday provide an extraordinary opportunity for our students when the situation there settles. That said, any future decisions on cities and locations will be made in a principled way, and with one overarching objective: to provide a safe, secure immersive experience in which the students can put into practice the tools and skills they learn throughout their Minerva experience.

Even seven locations, however, are simply not enough to cover the true diversity the world has to offer. The constraints we mentioned above, including safety, academic freedom, and a reliable infrastructure, have made large parts of the world more difficult for us to operate in. We very much hope that with time, those situations will resolve.

How Minerva Approaches Global Understanding and City Immersion

Minerva took a principled approach to building out an experiential learning curriculum for the selected cities, in the belief that global understanding and city immersion do not necessarily happen by chance. In the same way that the courses in the curriculum should build one on another, we designed a scaffolded experiential learning journey across cities over four years. We took a methodical approach to experiential learning design and prioritized core experiences in each city. To understand the world, you first must experience it.

Global arcs and city tracks

We decided on three "global arcs" or contexts for understanding and approaching a city: (1) evolution, (2) institutions, and (3) ethos. These three contexts assist in creating a common vocabulary and a mental model for approaching each city and for making connections and comparisons across locations.

The evolution global arc introduces the historical significance of each city, including political, economic, environmental, social, and technological trends. The institutions global arc provides exposure to influential individuals and organizations working to address challenges, advance causes, promote growth, and shape the overall civic character of each city. And the ethos global arc explores the ethnography of each city, from its distinctive subcultures and social norms and customs to its collective identity.

With this framework in place, we used the categories to design what we call "city tracks," each of which explores a specific global arc in each city—a theme unique to the location. For example, in San Francisco the city track for institutions is "Boom or Bust." Because innovation and failure are among the twinned concepts we wanted students to be exposed to while living in Silicon Valley, the city track explores the positive and negative impact of the "innovation economy" in San Francisco. The scope of this city track then informs the structured prioritization, curation, and design of cocurriculars and other Minerva programming. The structure holds us accountable for taking a diversified and balanced approach in what we expose students to in each location.

Connections and juxtapositions

Global understanding and empathy develop as students come to juxtapose and make connections across countries, cities, and cultures. Our San Francisco city track for ethos was "Counterculture," which makes sense because San Francisco is the birthplace of multiple social developments, such as the Beat generation of the 1950s, the hippies of the 1960s, the American LGBT movement, the maker movement, the organic food movement, and the startup culture. What is it about the ethos of San Francisco that helped spawn and propagate those developments, and what role did the worldview of the city's residents play? By grappling with such questions, students are able to glean lessons from the city and deepen their perception and understanding of it. This understanding, both of the overarching questions and of the cities themselves, only grows as they consider similar questions about each of the other cities where they live.

The City as a Campus: How Minerva Approaches Experiential Learning

Learning is not something that is location-bound. Learning is not limited by the four walls of a classroom or by the iron gates of a campus. Students hunger for an integrated learning experience, one that has pathways for students to connect what they learn in the academic classroom to the real world. Leveraging the city as their campus, the students are presented with a wealth of opportunities for application and mastery through real world experiences, where students can put their learning into practice, establish mentorships, and pursue passions and interests.

Although we do not have the formal infrastructure of a traditional campus, with its libraries, centers, classrooms, and auditoriums, we believe in building capacity by forming meaningful partnerships with local organizations, companies, and institutions across all sectors—private, public, and government—what we now call civic partners. We don't have a library, yet we partner with and can tap into the resources of the San Francisco Public Library. We don't have a center for entrepreneurship or a center for social impact, yet we can collaborate and develop civic projects with the venture capital seed fund and accelerator 500 Startups, the San Francisco Mayor's Office of Civic Innovation, or the Argentinian National Ministry of Education. Instead of infrastructure, we provide access to a curated community of practitioners and experts, identify projects and challenges, and design location-based experiences that foster serendipity, discovery, and far transfer of what has been learned in class.

Each city track includes four stages of experiential learning: (1) exposure, (2) engagement, (3) immersion, and (4) insights and impact creation. These stages of our experiential learning program provide a structured approach to city immersion and human development for Minerva students.

Exposure experiences

Exposure experiences are curated programs and opportunities in the city that are mainly focused on knowledge accumulation, information gathering, and community access. The goal of exposure experiences is to introduce students to a concept, topic, person, or perspective. Exposure experiences range from Minerva-designed programs, such as the "What I've Learned" series, which are intimate discussions with prominent thought-leaders and practitioners, to partnerships with organizations that host conferences or summits, to city events and experiences. An example of an exposure experience was a conference in Silicon Valley called the GSV Pioneer Summit; this event was organized by Global Silicon Valley (GSV), one of our civic partners and a leading venture capital firm. The summit brought together technologists, practitioners, educators, investors, and government officials to discuss challenges connected to San Francisco's future. This experience unlocked access to a community of civic innovators, entrepreneurs and investors for the Minerva student body, and increased student awareness of the latest initiatives and challenges connected to San Francisco's future.

Although exposure experiences do not go deep, they are meant to inspire a change in worldview or perspective—exposing students to various industries or potential career tracks, problems to be solved, and people in the city. They often introduce students to recurring events and meetups, which allow them to pursue passions, interests, and hobbies.

Engagement experiences

Engagement experiences are focused, Minerva-designed experiential learning programs that often take the form of a half-day cocurricular experience during which students sharpen their understanding of a certain topic or perspective, through an interactive exercise, discussion, or challenge. The goal of cocurriculars is to help students synthesize what they've learned in the classroom and apply it to a focused challenge or question, often with a civic partner. Cocurriculars may introduce students to specific skills sets that are required in certain job sectors while offering students an opportunity to engage meaningfully with leading practitioners. Although the actual work accomplished at a co-curricular will not be substantive enough to populate a portfolio, we hope that it catalyzes sustained engagement with the civic partner and project.

An example of an engagement experience is the cocurricular with the world-renowned architectural firm Gensler. We taught our students Gensler's method of "empathetic research" as it informs user experience in design and architecture—Gensler's version of human-centered design for buildings and public spaces. This cocurricular enabled students to engage deeply on the topic of human-centered spaces; students met with designers, architects, and strategists from Gensler and discussed the firm's approach to designing public spaces. The cocurricular provided a bridge between the classroom and the practical skills needed for a job in the design field.

Immersion experiences

Immersion experiences deepen understanding through sustained and recurring engagement with a local institution, company, or organization or through engagement in a student-driven initiative or club. The immersion itself may take the form of a research project, a challenge, or a civic project curated and co-designed by the student experience team, or a student-driven project.

Immersion experiences often arise as a continuation of cocurriculars, as sustained engagement with a civic partner. An example of an immersion experience is the civic project with the San Francisco Mayor's Office of Civic Innovation (SF MOCI). The SF MOCI office was grappling with two large problems: how to improve livability in SF by decreasing waste and littering, and how to catalyze innovation in its workforce by creating an eight-week "innovation bootcamp" to lead its employees to work collaboratively across departments. Students had an opportunity to immerse themselves in the first eight-week innovation bootcamp prototype, tackling the problem of littering and waste in San Francisco. Students met weekly with government employees and conducted research. This immersion experience was enhanced by earlier exposure and engagement experiences, such as events at Code for America and GSV and the empathetic research lessons gained from a cocurricular with the architectural firm Gensler.

Insights and impact experiences

Insights and impact experiences result in a deliverable project in response to a civic partner's expressed need. The goal of insights and impact experiences is to deploy current skills and knowledge in novel contexts and apply them to specific challenges. An example of this is the Living Innovation Zones and Public Life Survey Project. Students were challenged by the San Francisco Planning Department—a civic partner—to design studies to investigate new ways that the government could evaluate the effective utilization of public spaces in the city.

Another example of an insight and impact experience was initiated by the Argentinian National Ministry of Education, who challenged students to research and propose interventions to address the fact that half of high school students in Argentina do not graduate. Minerva students researched and proposed various solutions, which ranged from professional development programs for teachers to a technology platform for curriculum development.

Such civic projects connect students directly with practitioners and thought leaders working on real-world, relevant challenges, providing students with an opportunity to learn by doing and apply their knowledge and skills in a meaningful way.

These four categories of experiences provide a range of learning journeys that students can take in each city. These learning journeys are not always linear, and not every experience leads to a project or deliverable, but this purpose-driven learning approach provides a structure to help students explore, learn from, and have an impact on the city as their campus.

Integrated Learning: Aligning Academic and Experiential Learning Goals and Outcomes

Our design for a high-impact experiential learning program required us to align and integrate this program with academic milestones and learning outcomes. Rather than treating experiential learning and character education as cocurricular garnish on top of the main course that is the academic curriculum, we believe in marrying formal classroom learning with real-world learning. Students want to pursue their passions and find purpose in their assignments, and working on relevant and impactful questions, challenges, and ideas can help them do this. The classroom and the real world, inform one another, and it is valuable for students to marry classroom learning to learning by doing.

Working closely with the Minerva academic team, we have been able to design a successful prototype for integrated learning in the first year, which we plan to apply to future years. Our goal was to bridge the end-of-semester, team-based finals project for classes to location-relevant industry challenges and inquiry-based learning opportunities in the city. We challenged students to identify a purpose for their learning across the entire semester, integrating their personal, location-based interests and academic coursework.

A critical step in this integration process is the alignment of vocabulary between academics and practitioners, which is necessary if students are to see how what they learn in the classroom connects with real-world opportunities and how they can channel their passion and purpose to pursue them. Academic milestones include research and problem definition, proposals of interest, team formation, finals proposals and feedback, finals project completion, and presentation. These milestones aligned well with experiential milestones, such as changes in perspective, exposure to real-world challenges, opportunities to tackle these challenges and build a portfolio, and meaningful engagement with future potential employers (through pitches, presentations, and feedback).We plan to continue to evolve this integrated learning model with the academic team during the coming years.

Conclusion

At many universities, learning is confined to the classroom, and all other activities are disjointed experiences that fill a student's available hours. The extracurriculars and other activities that center on a physical campus can provide enjoyment and sometimes additional learning opportunities, but we deliberately took a different approach. At Minerva, the carefully curated global rotation and experiential learning activities are intentionally designed to be a key part of the Minerva experience and to provide enhanced global learning experiences for our students. Making the most of each location by deeply immersing themselves in local organizations and communities, Minerva students first and foremost secure an opportunity to explore a wide range of opportunities, while at the same time learn what it takes to live and thrive in a variety of unique cities throughout the world. Equally important, students build on what they learn through the curriculum, which enables them to apply knowledge and skills in the real world. Through the path of exploration, engagement, immersion, and insights and impact creation, students find challenges they are passionate about, that focus their energies, and that build their competencies working with organizations whose mission resonates with their interests.

References

Friedman, T. L. (2005). *The world is flat.* New York, NY: Farrar, Straus and Giroux.

Malicki, R., & Potts, D. (2013). *The outcomes of outbound student mobility: A summary of academic literature.* AIM Overseas.com. http://aimoverseas.com.au/wp-content/uploads/2013/08/UAAsiaBoundOutcomesResearch-Final.pdf

23 A Global Community by Design

Z. Mike Wang and Sultanna Krispil

It is 10:01 p.m. on a crisp Sunday night, September 28, 2014. The kitchen in "851" (the nickname given to the founding year residence hall) smells of a classic American breakfast. Fresh buttermilk biscuits, creamy cheddar scrambled eggs, hothouse tomatoes and avocados from the Ferry Building farmer's market, and thick-cut bacon—lots of bacon. All homemade by our Minerva Student Experience staff. Thump. Thump. Thump. The sound of hungry footsteps descending stairs. The founding class, twenty-eight students from fourteen countries, dances into the kitchen and dining room for the last seconds of 10:01 p.m, just before it slipped into 10:02 p.m. "We're done with assignments!" they celebrate, before learning about the origins of bacon and eggs as an American breakfast and then heaping food onto their plates as if they had not eaten anything the entire weekend.

On this evening, one of Minerva's most beloved traditions was born— the "10:01." In the founding year, cornerstone course assignments were all due at 10:00 p.m., and students would spend a stressful weekend and often Sunday hard at work, usually resulting in a final sprint to finish by the weekly deadline. After a few weeks, we noticed the impact this deadline was having on the culture and spirit of our student body. Students were not engaging with the city. Bedroom doors were closed and human connections were suffering, with eyes glued to laptop screens. No student initiatives were being launched.

This climate created an organic opportunity to address the well-being of our community. The idea was to create a way to re-anchor the student body with a sense of belonging and connectedness at the convenient inflection point of 10:01 p.m. on Sundays. We challenged students to form teams each week to create something they were proud of from their culture or background that they wanted to contribute to community. The core design principle of this tradition was that it needed to be student-owned— otherwise it had little hope of surviving, going forward.

The tradition, originally designed around the theme of "breakfast for dinner," quickly evolved, with student and staff brainstorming, into a weekly student-led celebration of culture, rituals, and traditions—often through food and performances. These 10:01s created a space for students not only to share their "whole selves" with the community, but also to have what they have contributed be accepted and embraced; 10:01s became a platform for intercultural collaboration and understanding. They led students to look up from their laptops to foster serendipitous collisions around shared experiences and hidden passions that they would not ordinarily discover.

Class assignment deadlines have since moved. Residence halls have changed. Course schedules have evolved. But the 10:01s might as well have been around for the last 101 years—a given, the way it's always been. They continue to be called 10:01s and continue to be on Sundays—a tradition rooted in the values of respect and empathy within the community, shared across classes and celebrated across countries, in years past and for the years to come.

In any collection of university presidents' remarks and speeches, one word appears over and over again, from convocation speeches to homecoming remarks to commencement addresses. That word is "community." It is a word with many definitions, a word that means different things to different people. Why is the word community so important to a university? What do we mean by the word? What is the purpose of a community? How can one build community?

In this chapter we explore how Minerva adopted an approach to designing a global community that was driven by first principles. We review our strategy for defining a set of character, or learning, outcomes through community values, the process of translating those community values into a "character curriculum" of experiences, programs, and traditions, and finally how these community structures translate into a global context during students' four years at Minerva and beyond.

The Foundation: Community Values

At Minerva, we believe that community does not occur by hosting a plethora of events or through an annual flurry of celebrations of traditions, nor can success at building community be measured through attendance numbers and participation rates. Community at Minerva is built through intention and curation. Serendipity plays a role, but it is a feeble influence in the absence of intention and curation. We have built a global community by design.

When people participate in events and traditional practices without a clear understanding of intention or purpose, those events and practices lose their potential for sustained meaning. In the same way that the curriculum follows a certain pedagogical bent, we anchored our community with a set of learning outcomes, which we framed as character outcomes and community values. We then created a portfolio of community programs (our experiential "classes") that evolved over the span of each school year and across each city to illuminate and teach certain values. The evolution of these community programs was location-based by design, adapting to the core values of each country and culture our students experienced.

Defining our community values

Our first step toward building a global community was to establish a set of community values that were unique and meaningful to our global student body. Minerva itself is a complex system of stakeholders, from faculty to staff to civic partners to students, each with different perspectives and priorities. All had to be considered if we wanted to prescribe a set of values that could be adopted globally. This would require a process that was both top down (driven by our founding goals and ethos) and bottom up (based on observations from our various stakeholders).

As a student-centric university, we wanted our community values to be the anchor for the ultimate success of our student body. Through an annual questionnaire we give to all of our students—the Passion-Interest Questionnaire, known simply as the PI-Q—we asked one critical question: "Share one personal value that you believe the community should live by at Minerva. Why?" This was our bottom-up approach. Using the responses on the PI-Q (we had 84 percent engagement on the questionnaire), we identified themes of values and character traits that our students proposed. We took these themes as indicators for the type of community that the students wanted and for practices they hoped to embrace.

We ended up with a student-suggested list of about two dozen unique values, including "purposeful action," "courage," "kindness," "being one's authentic self," "respect," "listen to understand," and "curiosity before judgment."

We then evaluated the guiding principles that Minerva was founded on, the seven guiding principles for the organization—being unconventional, being human, being confident, being thoughtful, being selective, being authentic, and being driven (see appendix B). We also considered our student experience team's assessment of the critical "character outcomes" that our students would need as global citizens. This was our top-down approach.

Then we combined the major components of the student-produced outcomes and priorities to distill seven core community values—respect, empathy, curiosity, collaboration, initiative, focus, and resilience. These values provided the backbone for one of the most critical steps of this process, the crafting of a manifesto, a list of Minerva-specific practices that would illuminate how our community uniquely interpreted these values and strived to put these values into practice.

Living the Community Values

The community values serve as the foundation of our learning outcomes for character education, which is how we believe students should strive to engage with, contribute to, and build a strong community. The final design component here was not only to share a list of values, which could be left open for interpretation, but also to create a system that would help students live by these values. As a result, we translated the community values into a series of living practices, preserving much of the original language used by students in the responses to the PI-Q.

Finally, to close the loop on the top-down (principle- or outcome-driven) and bottom-up (survey-driven) approaches, we shared with our student body the final list of community values and also our interpretation of living practices for these values, to get their buy-in and approval; we emphasized that this was a living document, one we would revisit each year to make sure it still aligned with the students' vision for the community (which is why it is "v3," or version 3). Our Community Manifesto is in table 23.1; each part corresponds to one of the community values.

For the class of 2020, we asked the entire class to sign this document before convocation, when they officially "became Minervans," to symbolize their commitment to striving to live these values. This process produced buy-in—and, even more important, expectations setting—when students were just entering Minerva. Signing this manifesto was not the end but the beginning. The process provided a common language for students to work through their collective and individual understanding and mastery of these values, and helped them to begin practicing them.

Developing Individual and Community Understandings of Values

With the foundation of community values in place and a list of practices identified as a guide to how members of the community should understand and embrace these values, we then began to create organizational structures for students to deepen their understanding of, grapple with, and practice these values. We wanted our students to be challenged to explore and understand these community values in different contexts: as individuals, as a collective, through microcommunities (in smaller groups), and as the entire Minerva-wide macrocommunity.

Individuals

When trying to build a successful community, it is first necessary to embrace the individuality and uniqueness of the members of the community. It is not possible simply to assign values and expect community members to live them because they are mandatory or listed on a website. Requiring action without facilitating understanding of the reasoning behind a given set of values will result in, at best, short-term success—but not long-term commitment.

To build a thriving, values-driven community at Minerva, we challenged students first to come to their own personal understanding and perspective on the set of community values. When designing experiences that explored a certain value, we were always intentional about including spaces within the group experience for personal reflection and introspection before attempting a collective discussion of individual understandings of the value. Collaboration and empathy mean different things to people from different countries, especially those not used to sorting the nuances of English from birth.

This approach enriched our community programs because students would come in with questions about and different perspectives on a specific community value (or several), which created an anchor for them as individuals—but then allowed the collective to grapple with the complex discussion of what it wanted to stand for and how to live the values as a collective (i.e., a macrocommunity), realizing that individuals' personal perspectives affected the various structures they were embedded in every day at Minerva, which in turn would them as individuals in a feedback loop.

Microcommunities

Within a global student body, one in which fewer than 20 percent of students hail from the United States and the label "international student" does

Table 23.1

The Minerva Community Manifesto, v3

We are a community.

We foster mutual understanding.

    Expressing our authentic selves,
    finding strength in our differences,
    and cultivating unconditional belonging,
    we create unity within diversity.

We demonstrate humility.

    Seeking to understand new perspectives
    with empathy and openness,
    we develop a spirit of appreciation,
    accountability,
    and care for others.

We explore courageously.

    Embracing ambiguity,
    seeking adventure,
    and confronting our fears,
    we discover new ideas,
    and gain insight through experience.

We go deeper.

    By investing our time and energy
    in things that truly matter,
    we achieve the focus needed
    to reach our full potential.

We take action.

    Through concerted effort
    and personal responsibility,
    we advance our ideals,
    thoughtfully doing more with less.

We adapt and persevere.

    By viewing every challenge
    as an opportunity for growth,
    we seek out difficulty, practice deliberately,
    endure through complexity,
    and persist to completion.

We champion communal success.

    Through sustained collaboration,
    we support each other, enhance the collective,
    and improve the outlook for future generations
    because we know we will go farther together.

Table 23.1 (continued)

We value respect, empathy, curiosity, focus, initiative, resilience, and collaboration.

We are a community.

We are Minerva.

---

not exist because everyone *is* international, microcommunities are a critical component of building meaningful relationships and deepening understanding. This type of interaction at a traditional university is often left to chance, which in some ways is reasonable. Serendipity can be magical. Unexpected friendships can form as students come together in residence halls, in cafeterias, at chorus rehearsals, in the biology lab. Often, however, leaving community up to serendipity results in missed opportunity, division, and a siloed experience that quickly segues into exclusion, into the creation of the other and the sacrifice of the whole.

At Minerva, we wanted to encourage microcommunities to form, but we also wanted to challenge students to develop a broader sense of their "inner friend group." How could they expand their microcommunities into something unexpected, diverse, and more meaningful than what would otherwise occur through chance and casual choice?

We instituted several innovations to address these questions. First—at the very foundation—"Minerva Communities" (MiCos) replaced the general conception of the club. The MiCos are inclusive, globally spanning, community- and civic-minded, and aim to collaborate rather than compete with one another. MiCos exist for specific topics and interests. Each city has its own chapters of MiCos, and, eschewing the traditional hierarchical structure in which more senior students run things, each class of students from first year to fourth year has the opportunity to run her or his "global chapter" of a given MiCo in a certain city. This arrangement provides opportunities for students to learn how to lead (and follow) while collaborating globally across MiCo chapters around the world. For example, the MiCo Minerva Quest, which focuses on journalism and media, had managing editors in both San Francisco and Buenos Aires—a broader opportunity for both the class of 2020 (first-year students in San Francisco) and the class of 2019 (second-year students, who that year were in Buenos Aires) to take on leadership roles, with clear mentorship opportunities as well.

The second way we encouraged broader microcommunities is to consider how we might group students from different backgrounds, cultures, and interests. In addition to MiCos, we wanted to create a structure that would give students a way to connect globally across cohorts (classes) and cities, not to mention with alumni, once we have Minerva graduates.

As a result, we created the Legacy groups as an organizational mechanism to foster microcommunities of support, understanding, and exploration. The twenty-five Legacy groups each include one of the founding class members and some members from all subsequent classes, thus forming a vertical linkage through the classes and a horizontal linkage through time (see chapter 21). The goals of forming the Legacy groups were twofold: (1) to have a way to organize students in future classes into small communities in order to deliver programs and the character curriculum that would deepen understanding and practice of our community values, and (2) to create a structure for students to feel connected to each of their cities and to each other. Legacy groups are moored to a physical location in each city, and we challenged students to ritualize how the group affiliated itself to the city. The Legacy groups facilitate connectedness among students in a microcommunity structure that is linked to physical aspects of a particular locale.

Macrocommunities

We believe that the most magical and transformational experiences occur within the structure of macrocommunities (cohortwide or classwide) at Minerva. We wanted to assist students in an entire cohort or class to have shared, formative experiences that would shape who they are and how they perceive the world, and would also strengthen a lifelong attachment to their future alma mater.

The macrocommunity structure also has trickle-down effects to the microcommunity level and to the individual level. Thus experiences at the macrocommunity level would be expected to influence students' priorities and intentions to engage meaningfully with each other and live the values of the community.

Community Programs and Traditions

With the foundation (the character learning outcomes and values) and structures (individual, microcommunity, and macrocommunity practices) in place, we could focus on content. We tied the content of the character curriculum to a series of signature experiences and workshops, which were intended to deepen students' understanding and mastery of community values within different contexts as individuals and as members of small and larger groups, up to the size of the entire student body. This design, we thought, would lead to a flexible, recurring structure for experiences and allow serendipity to reinforce the desired character traits.

One of the signature events we designed for individual growth was the weekly Minerva Talk, which challenge students to explore the community values in their own life prior to Minerva: in essence, students reflect on and become the storytellers of their own lives. Over the course of an hour a student provides an encapsulation of his or her life story and then responds to questions from other students. We also launched a Minerva Talk mentor program, which trains student facilitators to support future Minerva Talk speakers. This program proved to be successful and empowering for students.

One microcommunity program we designed for the Legacy groups at Minerva was the supper clubs. Supper clubs meet biweekly to explore one of the community values in depth, sometimes through a facilitated conversation, sometimes through a location-based experience (which we call "Signature Experiences"). Supper clubs are currently formed by combining members of different Legacies into groups of roughly fifteen students. This purpose-driven microcommunity then explores Minerva's values and character curriculum through exercises, workshops, and discussions. A group experiences the nuances and highlights of what each city and year (i.e., freshman versus senior) represents in terms of the values.

For example, because of the entrepreneurial and innovation-driven nature of San Francisco, the character outcome of resilience might best be understood through a signature experience of a half-marathon hike across the northern coastline of San Francisco. Students met at Ocean Beach in their supper clubs and then were given a set of instructions with seven checkpoints (each with a reflection topic and challenge) for the 13.1-mile or 21.1-kilometer hike. We designed the experience to give students the option of stopping at each checkpoint, while reinforcing the definition of resilience and persistence. Eighty-three percent of the freshman class began this signature experience and fully seventy-five percent finished the half-marathon-hike. The students then gather in their supper clubs to discuss what this experience meant to them and their deepening perspective on the character outcome of resilience.

Another example of a signature experience is from Buenos Aires. We designed this event to teach empathy through blind tango at Teatro Ciego. We believed that one way to develop students' understanding of empathy was to challenge them to tango with their partner in the dark. The constant need to figure out what your partner needs and how you should communicate your next movements is brought to life even more in darkness and in a large group. We hoped that blind tango would provide an experiential vocabulary for students to grapple with the concept of empathy and would challenge them to put it into practice in future contexts.

At the outset of this chapter we described one of our more beloved traditions, the Sunday 10:01s, which is a macrocommunity program; however, the frequency with which it occurs—weekly, on Sunday evenings—creates a space for microcommunities to form and serendipitous conversations and relationships to develop. The 10:01s create a space for groups of students to explore the value of taking initiative and propose ways in which they could add value to the community. This activity often revolves around food—creating a meal from scratch with fellow students—but has grown to become an experience designed around cultures and rituals that facilitates deepened understanding and acceptance of others in our global student body. Students who take the initiative to lead the 10:01s are also challenged to think deeply about the needs and desires of the community and to take action to address them, not just think of themselves as individuals.

At the macrocommunity level, a series of programs from Foundation Week and Elevations (community-building and training sessions for students in each new city) to Civitas (our opening introduction to civic partners, mentors, and projects in each city) to feasts (coming together to give thanks and reflect on the semester or give it a ceremonial start) to Symposium (celebration of accomplishments at the end of the semester) are milestones that bring together the entire student body to live with different values. As described below, these events help students explore and practice specific community values:

Curiosity: Civitas is an intergenerational ideas and challenge summit that kicks off each Minerva city residency, allowing students to begin their engagement and immersion with community members and leaders in the city. Students learn about civic projects that companies, institutions, nonprofits, and governments are working on, which catalyzes their thinking about how they want to channel their energy and knowledge into creating insights and having an impact on the city.

Collaboration: Feasts are Minerva-wide dinners designed and cooked by students, staff, and faculty to learn how to create something from scratch among people with different skills, expertise, working styles, and attitudes toward food.

Focus and resilience: Symposium challenges students to work on and showcase one long-term project in each city. This project should deliver insights or impact for the city and the world beyond.

Some universities require their students to sign honor codes, but Minerva does not. Rather than asking students to sign an honor code, Minerva challenges its students to adhere to a set of living values and practices, while deepening understanding through community programs that are explicitly linked to character development. As a result, we address not what students should not do but how students should strive to behave as a community, establishing a precedent for culture and for expectations about what it means to belong, to be connected, and to contribute to a community.

Scaling a Global Community

The key to the success of Minerva's community and programs is the scaffolded program that spans years and cities. In each new city, the class strives to build on the lessons, core experience, and insights gained in the previous one. The key is not just to repeat traditions and community programs but to develop them across years, through which process students gain the requisite skills, knowledge, and expertise to take on leadership roles in this iteration and prototyping.

One of the most important aspects of a global community is knowledge preservation, institutional memory archiving, and storytelling to preserve insights and lessons learned. In the next few years, Minerva will be operating concurrently in seven cities around the world, with hundreds of students in each city. In each city we will continue to promote activities based on community-developed rituals and traditions, run community programs, and immerse students in core experiences.

We are acutely aware of a major challenge in growing and preserving the Minerva culture: no upper-class students will be present in person with the newly arriving cohort in any city. Thus, Minerva culture will not be self-perpetuating in the usual ways. As a result, we intend to document, reflect on, and process students' experiences, which will be collected in a central repository called "Spoke," a sister website to our wiki page, "The Hub." Spoke is designed to function as a central repository for lessons learned, knowledge accumulated, insights gained, and tips discovered and revealed by students. By accessing this material students can learn from the emotional journeys of other students and have opportunity to reflect on the rituals and intentional practices of those who preceded them. These rituals and practices institutionalize cultural preservation, which is vastly better than randomly hoping that "seniors pass it down to sophomores."

Finally, our goal is not only to build a community of students but also to connect this community with city stakeholders of like-minded values and interests. The global nature of Minerva is realized only when students begin to explore these values and character outcomes beyond their own communities and move into the city and into the world—which represents the true honing of a set of skills and competencies for global citizenship. Microcommunities such as MiCos and Legacies provide structures for this community engagement, be it interest-based or value-based.

Conclusion

Community at Minerva comes about not through accident but by design. In a rapidly changing world, there is no established set of competencies or values for global citizenship, no well-accepted sets of criteria for how humans should engage with and treat each other.

We have designed our community programs, tied to character learning outcomes (our community values), to provide a common vocabulary and experiential learning journey over four years. This journey should prepare our students for both the workplace and their personal and interpersonal lives. We aim to help students develop the ability to engage, support, and interact with others through a program of character education for global citizenship.

24 Mental Health Services in a Diverse, Twenty-First-Century University

James Lyda and Norian Caporale-Berkowitz

As an institution focused on reinventing higher education with an emphasis on the science of learning, Minerva views student mental health as integral to the educational process. Regardless of their intellectual ability, many university students can and will experience mental health challenges that may inhibit their ability to function effectively. The transition from late adolescence to early adulthood brings with it certain stresses that, when combined with an academically rigorous environment, and in the absence of familial and other known support systems, can be psychologically and emotionally taxing. Moreover, Minerva's global rotation practice means that our entire student body lives as international students, with the added stress of moving to a different culture with each new semester of college. The particularly high demands of Minerva's academic curriculum, combined with the plethora of cocurricular activities, participation in various student communities, and the distractions of some of the world's most interesting cities, provide additional challenges for Minerva students. We therefore consider psychological support to be an essential pillar of student success. Students must be mentally, emotionally, and socially healthy to fully engage with and benefit from the innovative learning process we offer.

At the most fundamental level, mental health and counseling services are central to the mission of universities because these services promote the academic success and positive personal development of students. Well-trained counselors and psychotherapists assist students in coping with psychosocial concerns, provide crisis counseling services, offer short-term psychotherapy, and do their best to prevent mental disorders, suicide, and violence (Holm-Hadulla & Koutsoukou-Argyraki, 2015). This is true at Minerva, but with one very important difference: we have the unique opportunity to combine known best practices with novel approaches to develop a new model for university-based mental health services. The solution, however, is not simply to hire a handful of counselors and instruct students how to access them. This would not be a very innovative approach, nor would it accommodate the changing landscape of university mental health services over the past decade and a half. Instead, we have taken a preventive, integrated, and community-driven approach, as summarized below.

University Mental Health Services in the Twenty-First Century

The twenty-first century has witnessed an elevated profile of mental health counseling services at colleges and universities in the United States (Prince, 2015). Much of this attention has been driven by high-profile tragedies, such as mass shootings, suicides and apparent suicide clusters, and, most recently, an awakening to the problem of sexual assault on U.S. college campuses. In addition to these tragic, newsworthy events, there has been an almost universal increase in the number of students seeking support for psychological problems. This is not just an increase in demand; gone are the days when the university counseling center's primary role was to assist students dealing with developmentally congruent challenges in adjusting to college life, the transition to early adulthood, and career development. In addition to serving these needs, many major university counseling centers resemble outpatient mental health clinics and community crisis centers, serving students with a full range and severity of preexisting or emerging psychiatric conditions, including major depression, severe anxiety, trauma, bipolar disorder, psychosis, eating disorders, substance abuse, and suicidal ideation.

This shift in mission has presented a major challenge to colleges and universities that seek to provide adequate access to counseling services. Counseling and psychological services on many campuses are inundated with demand, forcing major changes in the way they deliver services. Wait-lists several weeks long with dozens of students are common, and limits on the number of counseling sessions per student have become a necessary operating policy.

Despite differences from their U.S. counterparts in the scope of and approach to services, in parts of the world such as Europe (Rückert, 2015) and China (Yang et al., 2015), mental health services have also been elevated as essential to the educational mission of universities. Internationally, we have seen trends toward increased student stress and a subsequent increase in demand for services.

The "New Normal" in University Mental Health

How did we get here? Answering that question in any depth requires its own book and is not the aim of this chapter. Briefly, it is the result of a complex amalgam of factors, including but not limited to the greater attention now paid to mental health issues by society; various sociological factors of the "stressed-out" millennial generation, not the least of which is the influence of social media; socioeconomic pressures in the aftermath of the global financial crisis of 2008 pertaining to costs, gaining admission to selective universities, and high academic performance in the pursuit of jobs in an economy where a college education is increasingly the minimum requirement; improvements in pharmacological and psychotherapeutic treatments that have allowed students to attend college who would not have done so in the past, but who may require ongoing treatment to persist; successful public health efforts to increase awareness of mental health and reduce the stigma surrounding mental health and help seeking; efforts to make campuses less homogeneous, including diversifying the student body in terms of ethnic, racial, national, and socioeconomic backgrounds; the influx of international students, who experience added stress related to cultural adjustment and isolation while also paying the highest tuition; and, last but not least, the influence of modern parenting on and parental expectations of students, ranging from those of "tiger parents" to those of parents who themselves never attended college and therefore cannot provide guidance to their first-generation college student children.

What we do know is that the game has changed, and there are no signs of the situation's reversing. Based on the American College Health Association's annual assessments (which demonstrate robust findings year after year), during the course of an academic year a major U.S. residential university typically can expect the following to be true:

• About three quarters of students will feel overwhelmed at some point.
• About 30 percent of students will feel so depressed that at some point they will find it difficult to function.
• Approximately one-third of students will experience anxiety and one quarter will experience depression that interferes with their academic functioning.
• Some 6 to 7 percent of students will seriously consider suicide.
• One percent will attempt suicide (American College Health Association, 2015).

In 2014, the same year that Minerva matriculated its founding class, the American Council on Education, the Student Affairs Administrators in Higher Education, and the American Psychological Association collectively published a strategic primer on college student mental health (Douce & Keeling, 2014). The report, inspired by President Obama's call for attention to mental health issues, convincingly documented how mental health concerns disrupt students' ability to learn and retain information. The report presents a compelling argument that mental and behavioral problems are learning problems; they are critical impediments to students' academic success. This observation underscores the role of college and university counseling services as central to the mission of higher education.

Delivering Mental and Behavioral Health Services at Minerva

Minerva and its students stand to benefit greatly from a focus on mental and behavioral health. Whereas other universities have had to quickly adapt existing systems to students' rapidly changing mental health needs in a manner tantamount to turning a massive ship in a storm, Minerva had the advantage of starting with lessons learned and an evidence-based understanding of the challenges. Moreover, Minerva started from scratch: there were no stakeholders to convince, no legacy to overcome or institutional inertia to confront. Minerva's model and the nature of our students make the school fertile ground for innovation.

According to Douce and Keeling (2014), "Not all students who could benefit from mental or behavioral health services will come to the counseling center today, or any day. Students may not recognize the need for or recognize the availability of available services" (p. 6). This is especially true of our students, who come from a variety of cultures and hold a wide range of beliefs regarding mental health. Some are open to consulting a mental health professional; others come from places where stigmas or taboos exist regarding seeking help for mental health issues and mental illness. Still others may be considering for the first time what mental health and balance means for them.

Douce and Keeling's (2014) strategic primer outlines five key goals to establish a safety net of support, which we have modified to accommodate the realities of the Minerva model and our diverse, international student body. These goals form the groundwork of Minerva's approach to mental health services and are as follows:

1. *Eliminating fragmentation and improving access in supporting students' health, well-being, and learning.* One of the biggest challenges to creating a mental health safety net for students is fragmentation caused by departmental siloing and territorialism. Students who are engaging in concerning behavior or who appear to be struggling emotionally can fall through the cracks when faculty and staff do not collaborate or communicate with each other and counseling services providers.

At Minerva, much of the typical fragmentation is mitigated by the simple fact that we operate in an open administrative office space where the director of mental health services has a workspace next to the chief accreditation officer, across from the founder and CEO and ten paces from the academic deans. Although individual counseling services occur in a private office space, away from the main administrative offices, the director of mental health services has regular meetings and can provide curbside consultations with any staff or faculty member in the office, or working remotely. This arrangement allows student-facing staff to have direct access to consultation, and in some cases, crisis support when students demonstrate concerning behavior. It promotes a culture in which every faculty and staff member owns his or her responsibility to student health and well-being and understands that mental health is inextricably linked to student learning and success.

Access to individual counseling services is facilitated by a clinical services model with three key components: (1) ensuring that students—and the faculty and staff who support them—are aware of how to initiate counseling services and access support; (2) the continual acceptance of new students on a week-to-week basis throughout the year through a short-term counseling approach that includes informal consultation, initial assessment, and referral to local services if a student needs more intensive or specialized treatment; and (3) the active promotion of counseling services and the counselors themselves, ensuring they are highly visible through outreach and community involvement.

How does this work on a global scale across as many as seven cities? Doesn't this cause fragmentation? To address this challenge, each city has its own counselor on the ground who works with local student affairs and operations, student experience, and academic teams to create a local safety net. In turn, the various city safety nets are connected through regular meetings and communications. When students move from one city to the next, mental health services staff work with one another to ensure that students who are in need of services have continuity of support. Continuity is facilitated by having a cloud-based electronic health record, where counseling staff can access a student's treatment record as the student moves from city to city. Regular cross-functional and cross-campus working groups are integral to providing a cohesive mental health ecosystem as students travel the world throughout their four years of college.

2. *Recognizing patterns in campus life that suggest mental and behavioral health concerns.* Minerva is a data-driven, science-based institution that uses rapid iteration to improve our ability to educate and support students. This means we regularly evaluate (both formally and informally) how students are doing, and how the academic life, residential life, and institutional culture contribute to student mental and behavioral health. In addition to direct student surveys, weekly cross-functional meetings with members of our student experience, academic, and student affairs teams (including mental health services teams) provide an opportunity to surface potentially concerning patterns across our many touchpoints with students and to deploy equally cross-departmental solutions. Building a university from the ground up requires all of this. Because of the close collaboration across departments, it is difficult for students to go unnoticed, and insights and ideas are collected from across the organization.

We also understand that the global rotation model whereby students live in seven cities across eight semesters is intense and requires ongoing adjustment, acculturation, and transition. We therefore provide students with a predeparture orientation in advance of travel to each new location, as well as an in situ reorientation in each new city. As noted earlier, we have mental health counselors available in every city to support students through any stresses caused by their global journey.

3. *Providing outreach education and consultation to prepare the community to recognize and respond to students with mental or behavioral health concerns.* One of the most important aspects of mental health services at any university program is outreach education and consultation made available to students, faculty, and staff. This aspect of Minerva's mental health services' mission serves to promote a community perspective. We do so by extending the services of clinical providers beyond the confines of the private counseling office and into the community. Outreach and consultation provide deliberate, systematic, and creative educational programming and resources that emphasize a multicultural and developmental perspective on prevention, wellness, student development, and community building. Mental health services staff work collaboratively with other staff and programs to support the mental, emotional, and physical health needs of students.

According to the Campus Framework proposed by the JED Foundation, a leading U.S. nonprofit organization that exists to protect the emotional health of high school and college students and reduce the risks of substance abuse and suicide:

It is ... important to promote emotional health awareness among those who interact with students the most—"gatekeepers" such as residence hall staff, academic advisors, faculty and even fellow students – as it is vital for these people to be able to recognize and refer a student who might be in distress (The Jed Campus Framework, 2016).

At Minerva, we achieve this in several ways. We provide resident assistants (RAs) and a select number of student community leaders with an adapted Student Support Network mental health bystander training (Morse & Schulze, 2013) and Question Persuade Refer (QPR) suicide prevention gatekeeper training (Quinnett, 2007). Faculty and advisers are also trained to recognize signs of distress, talk to students effectively, and properly refer them to support services. Additionally, at orientation, we provide students with psychoeducation about common experiences such as adjustment, academic stress, imposter syndrome, acculturative stress, and burnout, and we discuss how these experiences negatively affect mental health and emotional wellness. Our mental health services are involved with planning for orientation, predeparture training for each new Minerva city, and other university-wide events, all with an eye toward preparing both faculty and staff, as well as the student community, to recognize and respond to students in need of assistance with mental or emotional wellness issues.

4. *Using surveys, presentations, self-assessments, activities, and special events to identify students whose lack of psychological well-being is interfering with their development, learning, and achievement.* Minerva is data-driven, feedback-oriented, and highly engaging, making it difficult for students to fall through the cracks. We take advantage of multiple channels to monitor students' psychological well-being. For example, we solicit regular student feedback through both formal classwide surveys and smaller, primarily qualitative feedback dinners with randomly selected groups of students. Other events are designed specifically to discover and support those students who may be withdrawn and less proactive in seeking support from staff. For example, in a program affectionately dubbed "Brownie Corners," select students are invited by staff to attend a dessert party and student mixer. RAs are asked to periodically update staff about students who are less engaged or who fail to attend RA group meetings and programming, and

these students are likely to get an invitation (where appropriate). When we have evidence through any of the above channels that students are struggling academically, socially, or emotionally, we guide them toward effective support services.

5. *Nurturing a supportive tone and attitude, challenging stereotypes, undermining prejudices and stigmas attached to counseling, and encouraging students to reflect on their own mental health and seek services when needed.* Minerva's model results in a close-knit community that is fully international, with students coming from fifty countries and exhibiting a full range of cultures and beliefs regarding mental health. Given the diversity of our student body in this respect, we actively work to create a "Minerva culture" that embraces help seeking, values mental health, and is affirming of the presence of mental health issues. Doing so in a manner that is respectful of different belief systems and worldviews is important. Our approach has been to create multiple avenues for students to discuss what mental and community health means for them and to normalize a discussion of mental health care as an integral part of the college and community experience at Minerva.

We are fortunate that by building an institution from the ground up, we are able to foster new levels of cross-departmental programming and collaboration. In addition to student affairs and mental health services, Minerva also has a student experience team dedicated to student community building, experiential learning, and character formation. Through a weekly meeting that includes members across these teams, we are able to both design collaborative programming and position our mental health support services as an integral and safe part of student life. For example, both our Student Support Network mental health bystander training and the "fishbowl" discussions (Kane, 1994) we use to engage students in considering community well-being have been developed and implemented collaboratively across these teams. In addition, we have grouped students into supper clubs, groups where students form organic friendships and which also become the learning units where we teach social and emotional learning and Minerva's seven character outcomes: curiosity, empathy, resilience, focus, collaboration, initiative, and respect. By running this programming through existing community units and across teams that regularly interact with all students, we strive both to remove any stigma around counseling and to create natural spaces for students to discuss emotional and interpersonal development, as well as to make support resources available in these areas.

Conclusion

Students' mental health is inextricably linked to their academic success. The job of counseling centers is to offer diagnostic assessment, individual counseling, crisis intervention, and group counseling, with a view toward enhancing social competence. Enhancing social competence enables students to cope with academic problems and overcome mental and emotional health problems. Achieving these goals has become increasingly challenging in a world where the "new normal" for universities entails high demand for and a high severity of student mental health needs. Minerva strives to establish an approach to student mental health that draws on evidence-based practices and lessons learned. Additionally, driven by our unique model of education and our diverse, international student body, we are fertile ground for innovation. Minerva holds promise for becoming a model of effective mental health services provision in higher education.

References

American College Health Association. (2015). *American College Health Association— National College Health Assessment II: Reference group executive summary spring, 2015.* Hanover, MD: American College Health Association.

Douce, L. A., & Keeling, R. P. (2014). *A strategic primer on college student mental health.* Washington, DC: American Council on Education, Student Affairs Administrators in Higher Education, & American Psychological Association.

Holm-Hadulla, R. M., & Koutsoukou-Argyraki, A. (2015). Mental health of students in a globalized world: Prevalence of complaints and disorders, methods and effectivity of counseling, structure of mental health services. *Mental Health & Prevention, 3,* 1–4.

The JED Campus Framework. (2016). The JED Foundation Campus Program. http:// www.thecampusprogram.org/framework-for-success

Kane, C. (1994). Fishbowl training in group process. *Journal for Specialists in Group Work, 20*(3), 183–188.

Morse, C., & Schulze, R. (2013). Enhancing the network of peer support on college campuses. *Journal of College Student Psychotherapy, 27*(3), 212–225.

Prince, J. P. (2015). University student counseling and mental health in the United States: Trends and challenges. *Mental Health and Prevention, 3*(1–2), 5–10. doi:10.1016/j.mhp.2015.03.001.

Quinnett, P. (2007). QPR gatekeeper training for suicide prevention: The model, rationale, and theory. Spokane, WA: The QPR Institute. http://citeseerx.ist.psu.edu/ viewdoc/download?doi=10.1.1.471.5942&rep=rep1&type=pdf

Rückert, H.-W. (2015). Mental health of students and psychological counseling in Europe. *Mental Health and Prevention, 3*(1–2), 34–40. http://dx.doi.org/10.1016/ j.mhp.2015.04.006

Yang, W., Lin, L., Zhu, W., & Liang, S. (2015). An introduction to mental health services at Universities in China. *Mental Health and Prevention, 3*(1–2), 11–16. http:// dx.doi.org/10.1016/j.mhp.2015.04.001

25 The Minerva Professional Development Agency

Robin B. Goldberg and Anne Kauth

One of the promises we make to our students is that we will prepare them to go out and make a difference in the world. We want them to be successful when they graduate, and we are committed to putting them on a trajectory better than if they had spent four years doing anything else. The students have to do their part—namely, to engage in everything Minerva requires of them, from academics to student experience to working on their career readiness. This is not merely a desire on our parts. Our mission obliges us to ensure that those possessing critical wisdom are able to deploy it for the sake of the world. Thus, we see it as our responsibility to give students guidance and support in planning their professional lives, starting from the time they arrive at Minerva and continuing for the rest of their lives.

Ensuring that our students do well also enables the acceleration of our institutional mission. As our students graduate and take on meaningful roles in society, they will carry the Minerva name with them. We anticipate this will be our best form of marketing in the long term, both for generating student interest in attending Minerva and for encouraging other institutions to adopt the philosophies, methods, and curricula outlined in this book. The value of a Minerva education will no longer be analytically self-evident, it will be evident from graduates' contributions to the organizations they join and those they start. Our students in their postgraduate careers will be our proof points that this education has the outsized impact the research on which it is based has demonstrated.

With the stakes so high, the combination of opportunity and obligation required us to reinvent the traditional university function of "career services" offered by most institutions. The typical career services office on most American college campuses offers résumé review, mock interviews, career fairs, and interview scheduling. For Minerva's goals, this was too simplistic. The challenge then became envisioning how best to support our students in a more compelling and holistic way.

We began by thinking through what models exist currently that support professionals to achieve and sustain success in their chosen field. A good example is the talent agency model that serves celebrities and artistic talent in film and television. Effective talent agencies that support artists offer a number of crucial services and personnel: agents and managers to protect their interests, casting teams to find and place talent, publicists to connect artists with the best possible audiences to promote their work.

Artistic talent benefits from such professional support; we believe that the impact from heightened attention to professional development and support could have an even more dramatic impact on intellectual talent. To that end, the Minerva Professional Development Agency is designed to support students and then as graduates, for the rest of their lives. Each individual has someone advising her or him on a personal level, a team that makes introductions to interesting and relevant opportunities, and a group of experts to help build professional skills and promote the graduate's career. This is the foundational aspiration of the Minerva Professional Development Agency.

Advising and Coaching

Imagine having someone looking out for your career, giving you guidance about the kinds of roles to take on, missteps to avoid, how to bridge from one role to another, how to find the best fit for what you want to achieve. Someone who contacts you when a brilliant opportunity surfaces or just as readily helps you find funding when you have a brilliant idea. Someone who remembers that you are building your personal brand throughout your career, ensuring that your work and accomplishments are recognized, acknowledged, and shared.

Working with coaches

As early as the freshman year, each Minerva student starts working with a coach on an individual basis. Using a combination of exercises, assessments, and workshops, the coach spends time understanding what makes each student tick, and, equally important, the student gets a better sense of himself or herself. What are the things the student values at the core? These are things that no student should compromise, regardless of what they want to do in their career going forward. Is the student a talented writer? A verbal communicator? An analytical thinker? As the coach devotes time to understanding the student's interests, passions, and strengths, the coach helps the student recognize existing abilities to be complemented by skills the student should grow over the four years. The coach spends time to understand what the student is excited about, be it industries, functions, or even the role models the student would like to emulate. Through one-on-one coaching sessions, exposure to professionals in fields of interest during co-curricular activities, and conversations with members of the broader Minerva network, each student has an opportunity to explore all the areas that she or he might find intriguing and can start identifying and evaluating the multitude of options available.

One of the keys to good one-on-one coaching is honest conversations. This sounds simple but takes significant time and maturity on the part of the coach. Let us look at a scenario. A student comes into a session very anxious. All of his friends are starting to lock down internships for the upcoming summer, and this particular student doesn't have anything lined up. He arrives at the coaching session determined to solve this problem by proclaiming his desire to work for Google. The job of the coach is to help the student assess what is really driving him to that conclusion. "Do the values of the organization match the ones you said were so important to you? Would you be a good fit? And, as important, let's look at what the organization needs, and see whether you have the right skills and strengths to add value to that organization today."

There are times when the feedback can be harsh. It can be very difficult for a student to hear she will likely not be a good fit in an organization she has set her heart on. Yet, just as a talent agent might tell an up-and-coming actor not to accept a certain role because it might hurt her career in the long run, Minerva coaches are candid and honest to ensure that the student they are working with views the world with open eyes. The role of the coach is often to encourage the student to be open to new ideas, to consider industries, functions, or locales that may not have been on her radar before.

The individualized attention provided by the coaches is invaluable, yet we also find that offering a variety of workshops, ranging from time management, to professional networking, to interview preparation, can be a strong complement to build students' professional development skills. The Minerva Professional Development Agency not only provides direct support in the present but also increases self-efficacy for the future. Thus it enables deeper and broader exploration of opportunities, confident outreach to key contacts, and continued progress on a desired professional path. One less often articulated goal of the agency is to equip students with the tools and techniques to take a more proactive and forward-thinking approach to career considerations for the rest of his or her lifetime.

Serving a wide range of goals

We established the Professional Development Agency to help students
determine how to transform their passions, interests, and skills into action,
but we recognize that students may not be interested in joining an established institution. The entrepreneurial spirit is palpable at Minerva, and
a good percentage of our students are interested in starting something of
their own. We designed the Professional Development Agency to help support these students as well. Although each student needs to have his or
her own idea about what to start, the agency team can help support that
student as an entrepreneur by helping him or her understand the skill areas
that need to be developed and focused on and by connecting the student to
complementary resources that might be useful. In addition, as the student
advances deeper into idea development, the agency can help to connect
the budding entrepreneur with others who might serve as team members.

We have already seen Minerva students who have strong business ideas
and are finding cofounders within the class. We envision facilitating this
process at a greater level as student and graduate populations grow over
time. Additionally, startup ventures typically require funding. Minerva
has a number of connections in the venture capital community and can
point students with the most compelling business ideas to those who might
potentially fund the venture. Of course, the students must make a compelling case to actually raise the funds, but Minerva helps these students get
their foot in the door.

The coaches of the Professional Development Agency are charged with
supporting students and graduates regardless of what they may choose to
do after concluding undergraduate studies. Some have no interest in entering the workforce or starting a business but want to further their education and obtain an advanced degree. Some students enrolled at Minerva are
interested in pursuing degrees in law, medicine, business, and other professional areas after graduation.

Paving the way for our students to apply to graduate programs, all of
the Minerva deans have reached out to peers and colleagues across other
institutions to ensure those individuals are aware of the strong educational
foundation that Minerva provides. Then the coaches work directly with the
students (and often with the relevant dean) to help the students best position themselves for these advanced educational programs and opportunities. In some cases the coaching involves suggesting certain experiences the
student should have over a summer to strengthen his or her résumé. For
example, a student interested in science should acquire some lab research
experience over the course of four years at Minerva. At other times the

coaching may help the student identify skills and interests and present them in a compelling way on applications for advanced study.

Regardless of the desire of a Minerva student or graduate, coaching supports the individual and his or her interests for a lifetime. Regardless of what path the students take after graduation, we anticipate they periodically will want to change the course of their career, look for new opportunities, or just talk with a coach about how to continue to excel in the roles they have adopted. Minerva promises to support its graduates for life, so that at any stage there is a coach waiting to support their efforts.

The Employer Network and Recruiting

The Minerva Professional Development Agency is committed to helping students take the guidance they receive from their coaching and use it to turn their passions, interests, and values into research, internships and job opportunities. Again, Minerva approaches this process in a completely different way from other institutions. Minerva balances the needs of students and employers in navigating the matching and placement of students into the most appropriate internship opportunities.

Engaging employers

To open up opportunities for Minerva students, the Minerva Professional Development Agency seeks to engage employers in an authentic conversation about how they are experiencing the skills gap—and helps them understand how Minerva's curriculum and student experience prepare Minerva students to be the most competitive, well-prepared candidates not only for current roles but for the jobs of the future. These conversations have led to the development of a robust employer network that includes global employers big and small in the fields of consulting, banking, technology, the creative industries, and more. Employers respond favorably upon seeing the value of the Minerva education in preparing effective future employees of their organizations. As employers quickly grasp, starting in their freshman year Minerva students learn the foundational skills to be adaptable, highly competent professionals—and they continue to grow throughout their academic journey. This foundation enables our students to join organizations and start making contributions with little to no on-the-job training.

This sounds straightforward, but it is not the experience most employers have when seeking to hire undergraduate students. In fact, there is a distinct disconnect in the understanding universities have of how well their students are prepared for the world of work and the realities as seen by recruiters and professionals across industry areas when working with millennials. According to a recent study by Gallup (Gallup-Lumina, 2013), a breathtaking 96 percent of chief academic officers at institutions of higher education say that their institution is "very or somewhat" effective at preparing students for the world of work. This is astonishing, if one considers how poorly U.S. business leaders and the American public increasingly judge higher education institutions on this same measure of "return on investment"—successful placement across industry areas and core functions. The same study found that a mere 14 percent of Americans strongly agree that college graduates are well prepared to achieve success in the workplace. And barely one in ten (11 percent) business leaders strongly agreed that college graduates have the skills and competencies their workplaces need (Gallup-Lumina, 2013). This college-to-career skills gap is a threat not only at individual and organizational levels; it is also a threat to economic and labor dynamics across the country and throughout the world. Nor can these statistics be thought of as a problem only for nonelite universities—quite the opposite. At many nonelite universities, job skills training is the primary focus of the institution, whereas at many elite universities preprofessional education is looked down on. Minerva's commitment to closing this gap by preparing our students with the four core competencies—thinking critically, thinking creatively, communicating effectively, and interacting effectively—as well as with deep expertise in their chosen field ensures that our students will have an outsized impact in a variety of organizations and institutions.

Matching students to employment opportunities

With students prepared and ready to contribute, and with a high level of support from their coaches, the next key is matching students with the right opportunities. Minerva's professional development team is dedicated to identifying exciting, productive, relevant opportunities for students and graduates. By building and maintaining connections with employers across disciplines, the professional development team provides an extensive global pipeline to a wide range of corporate, educational, nonprofit, and government organizations.

Building these relationships takes time and energy but has been rewarding. We have found that employers become excited once they learn about the curriculum that Minerva offers, so much so that a number have designed a unique process for Minerva students, allowing them to bypass the traditional paths for securing internships in their organizations.

For example, Dalberg Global Development Advisors is a strategic advisory and policy firm founded by two McKinsey and Company alumni. The firm has a unique approach to solving the most pressing problems in global development, in areas such as agriculture, information technology, education, and resource management. Their mission aligns well with Minerva's and requires a particularly talented, productive, mission-driven team to achieve the firm's goals on a global scale. Dalberg showed an early interest in Minerva and, once students were enrolled, was particularly enthusiastic about creating a targeted track for recruiting Minerva students to its offices in Dakar, Nairobi, and Dar es Salaam.

Dalberg previously recruited directly from top MBA programs and university students in their penultimate year. Dalberg's management team recognized that even in their earliest years, Minerva students have the unique ability to identify the right problems, think critically and creatively, and apply their raw intellectual horsepower to the most pressing live business issues. Dalberg solicited résumés and applications directly from Minerva and opened up opportunities for students immediately following their first year of studies. The Minerva Professional Development Agency worked to identify students with the appropriate skill sets and a clear topical interest in the work of Dalberg to ensure a strong match. The summer 2016 pilot program was a success and has been expanded for the summer of 2017 to include opportunities with teams across service lines and offices in the region.

This example illustrates well the alignment between an industry leader's talent needs and Minerva's approach to talent development—the kind of alignment that will eventually serve to close the college-to-career skills gap at the highest levels.

Another such example comes from the entertainment industry. A major well-recognized corporation shared with Minerva's professional development team that it receives some 13,000 applications for internships for each annual cycle. After seeing the academic curriculum, the professional development approach, and achievement proof points thus far, the corporation agreed to fast-track Minerva students through the process by expediting application review and consideration by hiring managers. Our students still must earn the internships through an interview and selection process and prove that they are competitive for the given role. Yet, as we've seen, their experiences at Minerva prepare them well for these situations. The goal of Minerva is to open doors. It is then up to the student to make the most of the opportunity.

Minerva's approach is different from that of most other colleges and universities because we deliberately focus on matching each student to appropriate opportunities. In contrast, at other colleges and universities, where a typical career services office has a service ratio of one staff member to 850 students (National Association of Colleges and Employers, 2012), most of the effort is focused on bringing companies to campus to interview and allow students to compete with each other for the coveted interview slots. This practice leads to an imbalanced dynamic in which students interview with companies just because of the brand and not because they have done the personal soul searching to determine what they really want to do with their lives. This isn't helpful for employers or students.

For employers, on-campus recruiting is far from the best approach to securing the right talent and establishing a positive, fruitful trajectory for both parties. On-campus recruiting is an expensive, time-consuming endeavor requiring companies to host interviews for large numbers of students without a clear view as to how well prepared they are or who would be the best fit for different functional roles. Minerva seeks to eliminate the wasted effort on the part of employers by ensuring that students who engage in interviews are prepared and sincerely interested in the organization or company. Through the guidance given to students and the deliberate matching to opportunities, the entire process is made much more efficient and effective for all parties involved.

We maintain authentic, ongoing communication with industry, keep our fingers on the pulse of what employers are thinking, and develop a deep understanding of what they look for and need in candidates. To that end, Minerva has developed an Employer Advisory Board to ensure that the practical skills students learn at Minerva are applicable to the current and future needs of employers. These skills are passed on to students through talent development training sessions, tailored for relevance in each global location and delivered in an appropriate developmental progression that tracks the academic curriculum. For example, when students are learning about identifying the #rightproblem (see appendix A) in the Empirical Analyses cornerstone course, they are simultaneously offered talent development training in effective problem solving and professional teamwork and communication skills that can be applied in their summer internships and term-time professional experiences. In this way we enable students to be immediate and effective contributors, with tangible applications and outcomes, ultimately preparing them for long-term success.

Ongoing Professional Development and Support

We expect Minerva students to make meaningful and compelling contributions over the course of their lifetime, and we want to provide platforms and channels for students and graduates to share their ideas, their successes, and their stories. It is not always the case that the most successful individuals know how to showcase their talents. For this, the Minerva Professional Development Agency also offers support.

Publicizing contributions

Minerva publicists act on behalf of the students (and eventually, graduates) to showcase the many successes of the community. With proven expertise in garnering editorial coverage from global media outlets, leveraging social media to amplify messaging, and securing keynote address and speaking opportunities through a wide variety of events, Minerva is committed to finding the right opportunities to publicize the success stories of our students. This type of service and support is highly unusual (perhaps unique) for any college or university to offer, yet we recognize that the success of our students will contribute to the ongoing success of Minerva. Therefore it is in our best interest to ensure that the accomplishments of Minerva students and graduates be publicized and celebrated.

Minerva's team works to secure editorial coverage, or support the effort if students secure opportunities themselves, that showcases both the students and others associated with Minerva. An article published in the *New York Times* (Miller, 2015), featuring an inaugural class student, and another in the U.K.'s *Sunday Times* (Cohen, 2015), featuring the writing of a founding class student, suggest what it means to "get editorial exposure." These students had the opportunity to share their insights and stories with a broad and interested audience. To date, Minerva students have been featured in a wide range of globally recognized outlets, including the *Atlantic* (Wood, 2014), *Newsweek* (Jones, 2014), the *New Yorker* (Guerriero, 2014), and *Die Zeit* (Drösser, 2014), to name just a few. However, Minerva does more than set up the interviews and hope the students will figure out how to handle the situation. Minerva prepares the students for a one-on-one interaction with journalists. Just as the most experienced politicians and executives have media training, Minerva provides this coaching to students as well. Learning how to handle the questions of a probing journalist, how to share compelling messages, and how to handle themselves with grace will benefit students for the rest of their lives.

Deep media training

Helping our students be featured in print is one aspect of gaining editorial experience and exposure, but at Minerva it doesn't stop there. Students have had opportunities to be interviewed for video productions with Al Jazeera, PBS Evening News, and the Korean Broadcasting Service, among others. Because they are prepared to feel at ease, the students articulately share their experiences with journalists representing global media outlets.

Students who participate in these media opportunities are not only learning a skill set that will be with them for the rest of their lives, they are also building their own personal brands and their portfolios. As they continue on in their lives and careers, they will have a documented piece that showcases them as individuals.

Other avenues of exposure

Not every student wants to be put in front of journalists or is hungry for camera exposure. For those students, we provide other options for getting exposure and building their personal portfolios. Students with strong writing abilities can share their ideas through bylines and blog submissions placed by the publicists at Minerva. Through these experiences, students learn the importance of key messaging, authentic storytelling, and understanding the audience—all skills they will use throughout their professional careers.

Our publicists aim to promote the accomplishments of students and graduates by highlighting their individual achievements, as well as those of the organizations they represent. We also want to ensure that students with the most compelling ideas have an opportunity to share them through speaking opportunities and keynote talks. To support this effort, the publicity team also oversees a speaker's bureau, which identifies and manages student and graduate appearances at relevant events such as SXSWedu. By providing a range of platforms for sharing ideas, expertise, and inspiration, this team helps develop students' public personas, positioning them as innovative thinkers and, eventually, experts in their chosen fields.

Conclusion

One of the first questions students and parents ask colleges and universities is how well the graduates of the institution do when seeking their first job. Published reports often measure a university's success by the starting salaries of their graduates. At Minerva we think much more long term than that. Of course, the first job should be meaningful and relevant. But we also have a responsibility to support our students and graduates for the rest of their lives, staying focused on serving the individuals in a scalable way. Our goal is to support our students and graduates in finding the ways they can best contribute to society and the opportunities to do so, and to ensure they have a platform to share ideas and contributions with the broader world. From first-year summer internships through leadership positions at top organizations, the Minerva Professional Development Agency provides lifelong guidance and support for successful careers on the world stage.

References

Cohen, K. (2015, January 25). Top of the class. *The Sunday Times*. https://www.thetimes.co.uk/article/top-of-the-class-nb0lftlrqj6

Drösser, C. (2014, September 18). Akademische Nomaden. *Die Zeit, 37*.

Gallup-Lumina. (2013). *What America needs to know about higher education redesign*. Gallup-Lumina Report on Higher Education. http://www.gallup.com/services/176759/america-needs-know-higher-education-redesign.aspx

Guerriero, M. (2014, April 22). Are college campuses obsolete? *The New Yorker*.

Jones, A. (2014, December 17). How to solve college debt: An online school may have the answer. *Newsweek*.

National Association of Colleges and Employers. (2012). *2011–12 Career Services Benchmark Survey for Four-Year Colleges and Universities*. http://thekeep.eiu.edu/cgi/viewcontent.cgi?article=1020&context=eiunca_resourcesplanning_docs

Miller, C. C. (2015, October 30). Extreme study abroad: The world is their campus. *The New York Times*. https://www.nytimes.com/2015/11/01/education/edlife/extreme-study-abroad-the-world-is-their-campus.html?_r=0

Wood, G. (2014, September). The future of college? *The Atlantic*. https://www.theatlantic.com/magazine/archive/2014/09/the-future-of-college/375071

26 Accreditation: Official Recognition of a New Vision of Higher Education

Teri Cannon

During the past twenty years, higher education has faced both dramatic changes and challenges to its value and efficacy. This context created the conditions under which Minerva was created and sought recognition by accreditors. In this chapter we first consider the challenges that must be addressed by any new program and then address the general constraints imposed by the accreditation agencies. Finally, we examine how Minerva navigated these turbulent seas.

The Environment for Higher Education and Accreditation

Accreditation of institutions of higher learning has evolved to be sensitive to a number of changes and problems that have emerged in the sector.

Poor quality of education

Among the most serious charges leveled against institutions of higher education, starting in the 1990s and continuing to the present, is that students do not learn what they are supposed to learn. A flurry of books and articles has addressed the failure of liberal arts education and the watering down of standards. The research of Richard Arum and Josipa Roka, published in 2011 in *Academically Adrift: Limited Learning on College Campuses,* validated many of these claims. In their study of 2,300 college students, the authors found that students experienced little in the way of learning gains between the first and the last year and devoted far more time to socializing than they did to studying and attending class. Some key findings of the study were that 45 percent of students showed no significant improvement in learning during the first two years of college and 36 percent showed no improvement in learning (as reflected in improved critical thinking, analytical thinking, problem solving, and writing skills) over four years (Arum & Roksa, 2011).

Other studies have revealed that a substantial proportion of employers believe that higher education is doing only a fair job or a poor job at producing graduates who have the skills needed to succeed in the workplace. The skills most commonly cited by employers align with those that most liberal arts educators seek to instill: critical thinking, problem solving, effective communication, the ability to apply knowledge and skills in the real world, skill in finding and evaluating information, and innovation and creativity (Arum & Roksa, 2014; Hart Research Associates, 2013, 2015).

In response to the challenges raised by such research findings, accreditors have promoted the assessment of student learning outcomes to encourage institutions to do a better job of measuring and demonstrating learning, even in the face of resistance from many faculty members and institutions.

Poor service, poor completion rates, and increased costs

Along with disappointing learning results, three other areas of growing concern have helped shape the accreditation process: higher education is not serving all groups in society equally well, students are not completing college in a timely way, and college costs too much.

Certain groups, especially African American, Latino, and Southeast Asian students and first-generation college students, are underrepresented in higher education generally and are enrolled at disproportionately low levels at comprehensive research universities and prestigious institutions. Further, students from those underrepresented groups who do attend college are less likely to graduate (and when they do graduate, need more time to do so) and are more likely to graduate with higher levels of student loan debt (Baylor, 2016; Huelsman, 2016; Kena, Musu-Gillette, & Robinson, 2015; Musu-Gillette, Robinson, & McFarland, 2016; Pell Institute for the Study of Opportunity in Higher Education, 2016; Scott-Clayton & Li, 2016).

Second, timely college completion itself became a compelling driver of policy change when research showed that the undergraduate four-year graduation rates in the United States were less than 40 percent and six-year rates were less than 60 percent (Bowen et al., 2009; Kelly & Schneider, 2012; Kena, Musu-Gillette, & Robinson, 2015). Failure to complete in a reasonable amount of time coupled with excessive student loan debt created a crisis not only for the students affected but also for the institutions these students attended. Policy makers thus turned their attention to student loan default rates as an indicator of institutional integrity and effectiveness. Most accrediting agencies have responded, at a minimum by asking for data, including disaggregated data, on retention and completion rates and pressing institutions to develop plans for improving completion.

Third, higher education has become increasingly expensive. The increase in the amount of individual student loans and in the proportion of borrowers has been driven in large part by the increasing cost of higher education. Annual double-digit tuition increases were common in the 1980s and 1990s at both public institutions, which increasingly came to rely on student fees and tuition, and private institutions faced with the rising costs of operations (Bok, 2013; Bowen, 2013; Carey, 2015; Craig, 2015; Kelly & Carey, 2013). More students are financing their education through Title IV student loans, and record high levels of student debt have featured prominently in news stories. The proportion of undergraduates with loans rose from 45 percent in 1992 to nearly 71 percent in 2014, and the average debt during that period rose from about $9,000 to more than $35,000 (MK Consulting, 2015). Rising loan default rates and the inhibiting effect of debt on graduates' economic and personal lives continue to be subjects of study and great public concern (Huelsman, 2016; Looney & Yannelis, 2015). Policy makers are beginning to ask accrediting agencies to monitor student indebtedness and default rates as part of the review process.

The Role of Accreditation in Addressing Higher Education Challenges

Accrediting agencies were first established in the United States in the 1880s as private, nonprofit entities. Colleges and universities joined as voluntary members with a shared interest in upholding quality and allowing transferability of credits. In the early 1900s, standards and processes were adopted. The basic attributes of accreditation, then as now, are institutional self-study in the context of a set of good-practice standards and peer review—by both a visiting team of colleagues from peer institutions and through decision-making bodies made up largely of institutional representatives.

Types and roles of accreditors

There are four kinds of accreditation: regional, national faith-based, national career-related, and programmatic. Most academic institutions seek regional accreditation by one of seven regional accrediting agencies in six regions of the country. Regional accreditors accredit about three thousand institutions, and there are in total about five thousand degree-granting accredited institutions in the United States (Eaton, 2012; Gaston, 2014; Council for Higher Education Accreditation, 2016).

The mission and character of regional accreditors were altered dramatically in the 1940s and 1950s when the federal government decided to use accreditation as the "gatekeeper" for institutional participation in federal financial aid programs, which were expanded with the Higher Education Act of 1964. This step meant that in a very practical sense, accreditation was no longer a purely voluntary, peer-based process; most institutions want or need federal aid. This status caused a sea change for the agencies, which were no longer accountable only to their members but became accountable also to legislators, the Department of Education, and the public, and became subject to many federal regulations that dictated their standards and processes.

Criticisms of accreditation

Over the past fifteen years, as the challenges in higher education described above came to the foreground, policy makers often focused their attention on accreditors. Policy makers have accused accreditors of failing to fulfill their public protection role by monitoring everything from recruiting and financial viability to student learning, completion, and loan default rates. The accrediting agency model of "quality improvement" has shifted to "quality assurance," carrying ever increasing demands for greater transparency and accountability.

Although there was opposition from educational institutions and accreditors, which called out excessive and burdensome government regulation (e.g., American Council on Education, 2015; Miller, 2015), voices within the legislature and executive branch advocated successfully for strengthening accreditation standards, especially as a means to exercise more control over for-profit institutions. A scathing report from a U.S. Senate committee (U.S. Senate Committee on Health, Education, Labor and Pensions, 2012) was prepared after Senate hearings at which accreditors were called to account for failing to identify and address recruitment abuses and low retention rates at for-profit colleges.

At the same time, other voices within academic and policymaking circles attacked accreditation as too time-consuming and expensive, claiming that it did not add value and advocating for reform or the decoupling of accreditation from financial aid eligibility. Among the reforms currently under discussion is adapting processes to the strength of the institution being reviewed (i.e., risk-based accreditation; Taylor et al., 2016). Other objections have been raised to the peer review process itself, one of the linchpins of accreditation, as inherently conflict-ridden, protective of incumbents, and posing a barrier to new entrants and to change. Finally, innovators and change-makers have found the gauntlet of accreditation long and unwieldy and stifling of innovation and new ideas that might improve and expand higher education (Gaston, 2014; U.S. Senate Committee on

Health, Education, Labor and Pensions, 2015; U.S. Department of Education, National Advisory Committee on Institutional Integrity and Quality, 2015). We at Minerva were particularly sensitive to this last criticism, which turned out not to be relevant for our circumstances.

Most recently, three senators have introduced the Accreditation Reform and Enhanced Accountability Act, which would require accreditors to enforce Department of Education–established metrics for student outcomes data, to evaluate college affordability, to take quick action on institutions being investigated or showing signs of instability, to increase transparency about their decisions, and to "clean up" conflicts of interest; accreditors would be subject to termination of their authority or fines for failure to meet these requirements (Senate Bill 3380, introduced September 2016).

The forces converging on accreditation are loud and clear, although the pressures from different sectors push accreditors in what seem like contradictory directions: how do accreditors do more, act faster, and be tougher while simultaneously easing up on selected institutions and being open to new models and innovations?

It was into this messy and contentious environment that the Keck Graduate Institute and Minerva stepped in 2013 with a new model of partnership and incubation, a global educational program, an unusual approach to the curriculum, and a science-based teaching-learning modality that had not been seen before.

The Pathway to Accreditation

One of the basic requirements of regional accreditation is that the institution has graduated students (WSCUC, 2015). This requirement means that new institutions must operate without regional accreditation for several years (a minimum of five, including the preparatory year for institutions offering only bachelor's degree programs) before they can be accredited. This requirement is in place for all institutions seeking accreditation, not just those also seeking federal financial aid eligibility.

This constraint was pivotal in Minerva's decision making about how it would get under way. Minerva's plan to be highly selective and academically rigorous would have made starting out alone very challenging. The most high-performing and qualified entering freshmen around the world are unlikely to attend a new unaccredited institution when they have offers of admission and financial aid from prestigious universities in the United States and elsewhere.

Alternative paths

Three options were available to those starting new institutions at the time we began (2013): (1) to start as a freestanding institution and wait until the first students were about to graduate to apply for accreditation; (2) to take over an accredited institution, ensuring that it retained its accreditation, and then start the new programs within that institution; (3) to find a like-minded accredited institution that could offer the new programs either permanently or for some period of time until the new programs had graduates and a separate entity could seek its own accreditation (this is known as the "incubation model").

Understanding that the first option was not desirable, we explored the second option and quickly rejected it. First, the institutions that might have been subject to takeover by another entity did not have a mission or culture that was compatible with Minerva's. None of them was global or selective in its orientation, and some were in dire financial condition and did not have a good reputation for quality. Most important, this kind of arrangement would be viewed as "buying accreditation." Some accreditors had rejected requests for takeovers that would result in a major change in mission or emphasis and that looked like the only asset of value was the accreditation itself.

The third option, finding an institution where Minerva could "incubate," was the natural choice. After meeting many college presidents and provosts in California, Minerva identified the Keck Graduate Institute (KGI), the most recent addition to the Claremont Colleges, as the best possible institution to house Minerva's programs. At KGI, Minerva found shared values and philosophy, strong and forward-thinking leadership, complementary degree offerings, and a culture that prized innovation, entrepreneurship, and active learning.

Fit with the host institution

KGI is dedicated to education and research that translates advances in the life sciences into applications that benefit humanity. The institute was founded in 1997 with a $50 million grant from the W. M. Keck Foundation; the first faculty member was hired in 1998 and the inaugural class was enrolled in 2000. KGI initially developed the nation's first two-year professional science degree, called the Master of Bioscience (MBS) degree. This degree program is designed to educate scientifically oriented individuals for leadership roles in the pharmaceutical, biotech, medical device, and diagnostics industries; the program has an interdisciplinary curriculum that integrates science, engineering, management, and bioethics. The curriculum emphasizes inquiry, project-based learning, and team building.

KGI also offers a postdoctoral professional master's degree in bioscience management, a PhD in applied life sciences, a master of science degree in applied life sciences, and two new programs: a master of science degree in bioengineering, started in 2016, and a professional doctorate in pharmacy, started at the same time as the Minerva Schools at KGI.

When Minerva and KGI first began to get acquainted, KGI was in the second year of a strategic plan that called for it to invigorate and expand its portfolio of programs. KGI was actively seeking to fulfill this goal. The PharmD program was in development at that time. In addition, the plan called for KGI to deploy active learning strategies across programs, which created a clear alignment with Minerva's educational philosophy.

A comparison of the values and operating principles of KGI and Minerva showed close alignment and established the foundation for a strong and durable relationship.

• KGI has a global orientation, preparing leaders for the life sciences. It has a substantial number of international students and offers coursework to biotechnology students outside the United States. Minerva seeks to enroll a global student body and to create global citizens and leaders.

• KGI has a highly rigorous, interdisciplinary approach emphasizing creativity and the application of multiple approaches to solve problems. Minerva's curriculum is interdisciplinary and emphasizes the application of approaches from all disciplines to solve important problems.

• KGI rejects traditional departmental and disciplinary silos, as does Minerva, which has no departments within any of its major areas of study.

• KGI has mainly full-time faculty members with multiyear contracts and with ranks and promotion, but no tenure. This is the faculty model that Minerva adopted.

• KGI has adopted effective learning strategies, utilizing team-based and active learning in all its programs. Minerva utilizes an active learning/ flipped classroom model based on the science of learning.

• KGI sought to make better use of technology in teaching and learning, and Minerva has developed its own active learning technology platform.

• KGI emphasizes the translation of knowledge and discovery for the collective good. Minerva emphasizes "practical knowledge," applying intellectual skills and knowledge to solve real-world problems.

• KGI was created just twenty years ago and has continued to be innovative to this day, developing new and cutting-edge offerings and realizing high levels of student and graduate success. Minerva values and lives a spirit of entrepreneurialism and reflection, encouraging experimentation and new ventures and tolerating risk.

Finally, it is worth noting that KGI's existing programs and Minerva's proposed programs had no degree overlap. KGI, as an example, had no undergraduate offering until the introduction of Minerva. This made a partnership much easier than it would have been with an institution that was already offering undergraduate or similar graduate-level programs as those proposed by Minerva.

Minerva and KGI worked closely together with counsel to form an alliance that would serve the goals of both entities and ensure that accrediting agency standards and policies were met. At that time, KGI had just opened its second school, and comprised the Schools of Applied Life Sciences and Pharmacy. With Minerva, KGI created a third academic unit—the Minerva Schools at KGI—to offer the programs developed by Minerva. The alliance agreement between KGI and Minerva calls for Minerva deans and faculty to report to KGI's board and president. Minerva's chief academic officer reports to the KGI president in the same manner as other KGI deans, with regular check-ins and reports. Systems are in place for approval of every new program, budget, and tuition; major changes to programs; major academic and faculty policies; and all faculty appointments. The Minerva Project provides the intellectual property and funding for curriculum, pedagogy, enrollment management, student services, and student life needed for Minerva Schools to operate.

Working with the accreditor

KGI's accreditor, the Western Association of Schools and Colleges Senior College and University Commission (WSCUC), had relevant policies and procedures in place in 2012–13 that continue to exist today, some of them in expanded form (see, e.g., the 2015 Policy for Review, Monitoring and Approval of Proposed "Incubation" Relationships with WSCUC-Accredited Institutions, and the older but recently revised Policy on Agreements with Unaccredited Entities, available on the WSCUC website at www.wascsenior.org). The key principle underlying these policies is that the accredited entity has control of the fiscal and academic elements of any program offered under its auspices, including programs offered through a contractual relationship with another entity.

In 2013, when KGI and the Minerva Project began discussions about forming a relationship, WSCUC was known as being both one of the most rigorous accrediting agencies and an agency that was open to innovation. Institutions that wanted to do something that had not been done before and that held promise to promote access, student success, and quality could consult WSCUC staff informally to understand the policies they would have to meet and the processes that they would have to follow to gain approval.

Specific steps toward accreditation

After consultation with WSCUC staff and discussions among counsel about the KGI-Minerva Alliance Agreement, KGI in fall 2013 applied for approval of a "structural change," defined as a change that reaches beyond a particular program or location and affects the institution as a whole. Offering the first degree at a level at which the institution does not already offer degrees is classified as a structural change. Because KGI had only been approved to offer graduate degrees, the proposed offering of undergraduate degrees triggered the structural change. In addition to the proposal supporting this application, KGI was required to submit the proposal for approval of the first undergraduate degree program, which was the BS in social sciences.

The preparation of these two proposals was exceptionally useful to KGI and to Minerva. WSCUC requires a level of detail in its proposals that exceeds that of other regional accreditors. Preparing these proposals ensured that both entities had looked deeply at the relationship and how it would work, the impact on KGI, the quality of the offerings, and the details of the faculty, curriculum and student services.

The structural change proposal required a description of the context for the change and the impact on mission, purposes, and strategic plans; updates on previous interactions with WSCUC, including the recent reaccreditation and other substantive changes; and the reason for the change and its effect on governance, leadership, relationships with external bodies, faculty, and staff, and KGI's capacity to deliver its existing programs. Detailed plans for the technology platform, global aspects of the undertaking, and new services to support the students were required. The alliance agreement was provided, along with detailed financial plans showing both the impact on KGI's finances (which were negligible) and the feasibility of the undertaking.

The substantive change proposal for the BS degree in social sciences, which was more than fifty pages and had more than forty exhibits, covered everything from KGI's expertise and capacity to offer programs at the undergraduate level to detailed explanations of the curriculum, global rotation/cultural immersion, faculty model, library, student learning outcomes, methods of assessment, student services, and financial plans. We also had to address the fit with KGI's mission, needs assessment, and plans for recruitment of students. An explanation of how the curriculum would meet WSCUC expectations for core competencies was included, along with a detailed description of the habits of mind and foundational concepts taught in the Minerva cornerstone courses. The philosophy of teaching and learning and the use of the Active Learning Forum for instruction and assessment were addressed in detail. Among the exhibits were sample student schedules and four-year plans; syllabi for courses, including the capstone; curriculum maps and assessment plans; the CVs of the founding deans and faculty; staffing models, and five-year budgets.

After an extensive review process, the WSCUC approved the structural change and the substantive change to offer the first undergraduate degree and classified the San Francisco location as a branch campus. In the months that followed, four additional undergraduate degrees and two master's degrees were also submitted and approved.

Reflections on the Accreditation Process

Many aspects of Minerva are new and innovative and have never before been seen together in one institution. Among these are the global student body and the global rotations; the high level of selectivity; the no longer common required first-year curriculum, made up of entirely new courses that no other institution offers, especially to freshmen; the synchronous instructional platform that has capabilities not found elsewhere; use of the science of learning to inform instructional methodology and assessment; and the highly structured lesson plans. Despite these innovations, some characteristics of Minerva are traditional and fit perfectly within the expectations for good practice in higher education:

• The undergraduate curriculum is four years, full time, and 120 semester credits, with seat time measured by traditional means. There are five undergraduate majors in common areas; the innovation in the majors is primarily within the courses and concentrations. No challenges to the conventions related to credit hour and online or compressed programs existed.
• Because Minerva is highly selective, fewer concerns would arise about whether students would be supported to completion and academic success.
• Minerva proposed to have primarily full-time faculty members, mitigating potential concerns that exist for many new programs that WSCUC sees, which are staffed by adjuncts or other contingent faculty members.
• The tuition for the program was set at the lower end of the range for all undergraduate institutions and no federal financial aid was being sought, decreasing any concerns about high student indebtedness.

• Class size was limited by the technology to nineteen students, so student interaction and engagement were bound to be high.

• Minerva's learning objectives aligned perfectly with the WSCUC core competencies for undergraduates and with the new expectation that student mastery of the core competencies be measured close in time to graduation.

• Student engagement outside the classroom and services for students to be supported into their careers and throughout their lives were more developed and robust than at most institutions.

• Finally, Minerva proposed to begin with a pilot that included a limited number of students for a full year and to grant those students full scholarships for tuition and housing. This plan demonstrated our sincere commitment to learning and refining all aspects of the plans before a large number of student enrolled.

The accreditation process served KGI and Minerva well. The staff, reviewers, and WSCUC commissioners were open-minded and fair, asked good questions, and challenged us to think deeply about our plans. At this point, four years after our first proposals were submitted, most of our fundamental assumptions and plans are the same and have served us well; however, we have refined and improved almost every aspect of our operations and academics, with an eye on the WSCUC recommendations made throughout the process.

Yet the same factors that made our process with accreditation so beneficial can illustrate some of the problems that other programs may face with this process. It isn't hard to imagine how a program that is based on decades of research, focused on the brightest students in the world, funded by tens of millions of dollars, and working within an existing, well-respected institution that is perfectly aligned with this radically new approach would be capable of navigating this kind of approval process. Other highly innovative programs that do not share all of these characteristics may have a much more difficult time.

Indeed, even with these great advantages, Minerva too encountered a couple of systemic barriers to innovation in higher education on this path. The first one, already noted above, is that institutions must have graduates before they are eligible to be accredited by a regional accrediting agency. As described above, this requirement results in new entrants to higher education having to operate without accreditation for several years before they can become accredited. This waiting period is quite costly, and in general only for-profit and public institutions have the wherewithal to start in this way. Although new policies for incubation, such as those adopted by

WSCUC in 2015, allow an alternative path to stand-alone operation and accreditation, it would be advantageous to allow new entities with sound plans and strong backing to start on their own with some kind of provisional approval. This option might even be offered only to new institutions that are not using Title IV funding until they are accredited, which would reduce the risk to taxpayers and encourage a viable business model.

Another challenge is the outdated definition and treatment of "distance education" that appears in the federal regulations and that accreditors are required to implement. Distance education is defined as delivery of instruction to students who are separated from the instructor. Distance education as defined includes both synchronous and asynchronous delivery using the Internet or one- or two-way transmission through open broadcast, cable, closed-circuit, microwave, broadband, fiber optic, satellite, or wireless, and audio conferencing. This catchall does not recognize the recent tremendous improvement in the quality of distance education offerings or the differentiation among kinds of instructional modalities. Minerva's courses, which are synchronous and face-to-face, meet conventional seat time measures and are limited to nineteen students, bear no resemblance to other forms of distance education in this definition. And Minerva's students live together in student housing and have a shared and deeply immersive experience in each city where they live and study.

The challenges to higher education and to accreditation will undoubtedly persist, as disagreements among academics, legislators, the Department of Education, policy makers, and influencers continue. For now, accreditation must be vigilant in meeting both its roles, as an agent for both quality improvement and quality assurance, and continue to serve as a constructive force in higher education.

References

American Council on Education. (2015). 2015 annual report. http://www.acenet.edu/news-room/Documents/ACE-Annual-Report-2015.pdf

Arum, R., & Roksa, J. (2011). *Academically adrift: Limited learning on college campuses.* Chicago, IL: University of Chicago Press.

Arum, R., & Roksa, J. (2014). *Aspiring adults adrift: Tentative transitions of college graduates.* Chicago, IL: University of Chicago Press.

Baylor, E. (2016, October). Closed doors: Black and Latino students are excluded from top public universities. Washington, DC: Center for American Progress. https://www.americanprogress.org/issues/education/reports/2016/10/13/145098/closed-doors-black-and-latino-students-are-excluded-from-top-public-universities

Bok, D. C. (2013). *Higher education in America*. Princeton, NJ: Princeton University Press.

Bowen, W. G. (2013). *Higher education in the digital age*. Princeton, NJ: Princeton University Press.

Bowen, W. G., Chingos, M. M., & McPherson, M. S. (2009). *Crossing the finish line: Completing college at America's public universities*. Princeton, NJ: Princeton University Press.

Carey, K. (2015). *The end of college: Creating the future of learning and the university of everywhere*. New York, NY: Riverhead Books.

Council for Higher Education Accreditation. (2016). Website. www.chea.org

Craig, R. (2015). *College disrupted: The great unbundling of higher education*. New York, NY: Palgrave Macmillan.

Eaton, J. S. (2012). The future of accreditation. *Journal of the Society for College and University Planning , 40*(3), 8–15.

Gaston, P. L. (2014). *Higher education accreditation: How it's changing, why it must*. Sterling, VA: Stylus Publishing.

Hart Research Associates (2013, April). *It takes more than a major: Employer priorities for college learning and student success*. Washington, DC: Hart Research Associates for the Association of American Colleges and Universities. https://www.aacu.org/sites/default/files/files/LEAP/2013_EmployerSurvey.pdf

Hart Research Associates (2015, January). *Falling short? College learning and career success*. Washington, DC: Hart Research Associates for the Association of American College and Universities. https://www.aacu.org/sites/default/files/files/LEAP/2015employerstudentsurvey.pdf

Huelsman, M. (2016). *The debt divide: The racial and class bias behind the "new normal" of student borrowing*. New York, NY: Demos.

MK Consulting (2015, December). Who graduates with excessive loan debt? www.studentaidpolicy.com/excessive-debt

Kelly, A. P., & Carey, K. (Eds.). (2013). *Stretching the higher education dollar: How innovation can improve access, equity, and affordability*. Cambridge, MA: Harvard Education Press.

Kelly, A. P., & Schneider, M. (Eds.). (2012). *Getting to graduation: The completion agenda in higher education*. Baltimore, MD: Johns Hopkins University Press.

Kena, G., Musu-Gillette, L. & Robinson, J. (May, 2015). *The condition of higher education 2015*. Report NCES 2015-144. U.S. Department of Education, National Center for Education Statistics. https://nces.ed.gov/pubs2015/2015144.pdf

Looney, A., & Yannelis, C. (2015, Fall). *A crisis in student loans? How changes in the characteristics of borrowers and the institutions they attend contributed to rising loan defaults.* Brookings Papers on Economic Activity. Washington, DC: Brookings Institution. https://www.brookings.edu/bpea-articles/a-crisis-in-student-loans-how -changes-in-the-characteristics-of-borrowers-and-in-the-institutions-they-attended -contributed-to-rising-loan-defaults

Miller, B. (2015). Up to the job? National accreditation and college outcomes. Washington, DC: Center for American Progress.

Musu-Gillette, L., Robinson, J., & McFarland, J. (2016). *Status and trends in the education of racial and ethnic groups 2016.* Report NCES 2016-007. U.S. Department of Education National Center for Education Statistics. https://nces.ed.gov/ pubs2016/2016007.pdf

Pell Institute for the Study of Opportunity in Higher Education. (2016). *Indicators of higher education equity in the United States: 2016 historical trend report.* Washington, DC: Pell Institute. http://www.pellinstitute.org/publications-Indicators_of_Higher _Education_Equity_in_the_United_States_2016_Historical_Trend_Report.shtml

Scott-Clayton, J. & Li, J. (2016, October 20). *Black-white disparity in student loan debt more than triples after graduation.* Economic Studies at Brookings. Washington, DC: Brookings Institution. https://www.brookings.edu/research/black-white -disparity-in-student-loan-debt-more-than-triples-after-graduation

Taylor, T., Saddler A., Little, B. & Coleman, C. (2016, October). *A framework for outcomes-focused, differentiated accreditation.* Council for Higher Education Accreditation Policy Brief 8. Washington, DC: Council for Higher Education. http:// www.chea.org/userfiles/Policy-Briefs/CIQG_Policy_Brief_Vol-8.pdf

U.S. Department of Education, National Advisory Committee on Institutional Quality and Integrity (2015, July). *Higher Education Act Reauthorization: 2015 accreditation policy recommendations.* https://www2.ed.gov/about/bdscomm/list/naciqi-dir/2015- spring/naciqi-finalpolrecom-jul222015.pdf

U.S. Senate Committee on Health, Education, Labor and Pensions. (2012, July). *For profit higher education: The failure to safeguard the federal investment and ensure student success.* https://www.help.senate.gov/imo/media/for_profit_report/PartI.pdf

U.S. Senate Committee on Health, Education, Labor and Pensions. (2015). *Higher education accreditation: Concepts and proposals.* https://www.help.senate.gov/imo/media/ Accreditation.pdf

WSCUC. (2015). *How to become accredited.* https://www.wscuc.org/content/How-to -Become

27 A Novel Business and Operating Model

Ben Nelson

Educating students is an expensive proposition. Minerva operates within numerous constraints that must be satisfied, and most of them require funding. Such funding is often structural, insofar as a Minerva education takes place over four years of study, two semesters per year, and requires 120 Carnegie Units to graduate. On the surface, one might think that Minerva's expenses would be much higher than those of traditional universities. For one, Minerva is the only highly selective university program in the United States in which 100 percent of classes are seminars taught by a professor, with fewer than twenty students in a class. The Minerva program is available to students residing in some of the world's most desirable cities, several of which are very expensive. In addition, the program allocates more money per student to mental health than 99 percent of other institutions of higher education; it employs a technology built from the ground up by a dedicated, top-notch Silicon Valley development team; and the program seeks the smartest, most motivated students in the world—and has a student outreach team in every major geographic area to identify such students. Despite the expenses involved in implementing Minerva, we turn away 98 percent of applicants. Finally, Minerva relies on a highly exacting process to create and develop new courses: approximately 100 person hours are invested for every 1.5 hours of class time before we consider a new class is up to our standards.

These factors do not sound like a recipe for an efficient, scalable model for higher education. Yet even with the many areas of overinvestment relative to other institutions of higher learning, Minerva is designed to be self-sustainable when we matriculate roughly fifteen hundred undergraduates across all four years, at a total cost of less than $30,000 per student per year for tuition, fees, room, and a budgeted living allowance. Furthermore, launching the most selective and arguably the most effective university in the history of the United States cost us less than $20 million in total.

The total cost of achieving a fully self-sustainable state will be less than the cost of constructing one building at a typical university, without furnishings. How can this be?

Once again, we appealed to first principles. When we designed Minerva's cost basis, we aimed to dramatically reduce or outright avoid five broad cost centers associated with traditional university systems. In this chapter we first identify the major reasons why traditional universities cost so much, and then turn to the principles that underlie the Minerva system.

Why Are Traditional Universities So Expensive?

In what follows we consider five major reasons why traditional universities cost so much and how we at Minerva have responded to each challenge. Then we take a step back and consider the overarching principles that have guided our business and operating model.

The amenities race

The most obvious and substantial way in which Minerva saves money is the lack of a traditional campus and the use of the cities in which the Minerva program is based as campuses. Various urban universities could easily take advantage of the same approach but choose not to. The main reason for that decision is known as the amenities race.

Even a few decades ago, university campuses were rather spartan. Dorms were sparse; student centers, if they existed, were often dingy; and classrooms were basic and functional. Today, much of a school's competition for students is based less on the quality of education that it delivers than on a combination of rankings and the offerings of the campus itself. This has led to the amenities race: tanning booths, lazy rivers, multimillion-dollar gyms, beautiful lecture halls, luxury dorm accommodations, impressive libraries, museums, cafeterias, and the modern upkeep of decaying but picturesque buildings constructed more than a century ago. All of this costs students dearly.

Let's consider two problems with racing to build a better theme park for students. First, universities are not adept at construction: substantial cost overruns are commonplace, and funding for buildings rarely takes into account long-term operations and maintenance. Second, once a university does construct and beautify its campus, the amenities it offers are rarely as effective as those available in the "real world," put up and managed by people who know how to build and operate those services. Few university museums are considered among the world's best. Few university cafeterias are run more efficiently than local restaurants or provide better food than what can be found in the world outside academia (nor should they; see Malcolm Gladwell's 2016 *Revisionist History* podcast). The examples mount up.

What's more, differentiating through construction as opposed to education invites a truly disruptive force into the sector. I was asked at a conference a few years ago to name a nonintuitive new entrant into the world of higher education. My pick, if universities were not to reform, was the Walt Disney Company. For an immersive living environment that feels like a real theme park, one need look no further than Disney's own Celebration Village—a working, living community in Florida that Disney has successfully run for more than twenty years. Why could Disney not do the same for students? Providing the education itself would not be a problem: Because the majority of current university credits even at elite institutions are delivered in lecture format (which, as has been noted throughout this book, is highly ineffective), new universities could offer the same or an even better education simply by offering a series of MOOCs—massive open online courses—and dispensing with the pretense that universities are actually about a quality education.

Minerva's model stands in direct opposition to this use of funds. The only physical investment we make is in residence halls—but we go out of our way to minimize the common space provided. We want students to take advantage of common spaces throughout the city and immerse themselves in the local culture.

The business of intercollegiate athletics

The second area of substantial savings is related to the first but deserves a category all to itself, namely, the business of intercollegiate athletics. Athletics programs at universities not only create tremendous costs, estimated to be as much as $10,000 per student per year for Division 1 athletic programs (such as Stanford's), but also have corrosive influences on the university itself. For instance, the University of North Carolina decided to offer classes that did not actually exist in order to give their athletes easy A's so that they would be able to maintain eligibility under NCAA rules. Although the university claims it knew nothing about the incident, this system existed for eighteen years, and recent testing of some football players showed that several of them were practically illiterate at the point of graduation (Beard, 2014; Wainstein, Jay, & Kukowski, 2014).

One could argue that this is a unique example, but the fact of the matter is that any university that recruits athletes in order to win at sports has to relax academic standards. Instead of creating fake classes, some universities offer courses such as Rocks for Jocks, or in other words courses that are meant for athletes and are much easier, have massive grade inflation, and enable students to meet specific requirements.

One of the most corrosive effects of lowering academic standards is that they often lead to out-of-control, overall grade inflation. An example is Yale University. In 1963, fewer than 15 percent of grades at Yale were A's (Adair et al., 2014; Yale University, 1979), but in 2013 more than 68 percent of Yale's grades were A's! Along with the overabundance of high grades has come the practical elimination of low grades. This means that effectively, a student cannot flunk out of elite institutions. Therefore the university can bring in recruited athletes and not worry about retention by simply lowering the standard of education for everyone.

This is not a small, niche population at elite universities. As an example, Harvard's athlete population is approximately 20 percent of the entire class (Harvard Athletics Recruiting Central, 2015). At small colleges such as Williams more than one-third of students are varsity athletes. Universities must pay substantial sums to staff these programs with coaches and administrators, build facilities for the programs, pay for travel, and so on—and universities rarely recoup those costs from merchandising or ticket sales (Burnsed, 2015). This is not to say that all college athletes are bad students—quite the opposite, many athletes are excellent students. But every football team needs its quota of wide receivers, linebackers, and quarterbacks; every water polo team needs a center, wings, and flats. A university may be able to find some exceptional students to fill certain of those positions, but the likelihood is very low that it can field a football team that can win the Rose Bowl rather consistently (as Stanford has done) and hold those same students to rigorous academic standards.

Minerva's approach to this problem is simple and straightforward: we decline to have athletic facilities of any kind and do not mount competitive teams. Instead, we encourage students to participate in intramural sports leagues in the city where they are living.

Tuition-subsidized research
The American university system is among the few in the world where government research funding is not used to subsidize education—in fact, the opposite is true. In many (if not most) instances, universities use high tuition fees to subsidize research, both directly and indirectly. Direct subsidies are

common at elite universities, where new professors are lured by new labs that may cost upward of $20 million—expenses that are rarely, if ever, grant supported. Furthermore, indirectly, professor salaries are rarely used just for the portion of their time spent on teaching: sabbaticals, low teaching loads (of one or at most two courses a semester), and semesters devoted entirely to research are examples of how tuition supports activities that have little to do with actual instruction.

In other countries, research activities are supported directly through government funding and grants, which provides a clearer accounting of the costs of education at universities. This is what allows elite British universities such as Cambridge to be clearheaded about the costs of undergraduate education, which they estimate to be about $25,000 per year. They acknowledge that 60 percent of this cost is covered by tuition and the balance comes from other university income sources, including overhead from research grants. This procedure stands in contrast to the $100,000 or more that elite American universities claim as the costs of undergraduate education, which clearly includes many costs not related to education per se.

The tenure system

A second faculty-related financial burden borne by students is the tenure system, and here again it is useful to compare the British and American systems. Tenure, much like mechanisms that alter free markets, creates distortions in what the market would otherwise bear in costs. However, unlike tariffs in trade relationships, tenure is a one-way cost generator. In less competitive, more stratified academic markets (e.g., in the UK, with Cambridge and Oxford, and in Israel, with Hebrew University, Technion, and Tel Aviv University), tenure is not as much of a cost issue. In those types of countries, universities can largely compete on luring faculty "up" the chain without needing to pay more—and increases in pay are rarely enough to keep promising faculty from going to the most well-regarded universities.

The situation is different in the United States, where many elite universities are highly attractive to academics: many American academics are enticed by a dozen or more elite universities, considering them exceptional places to work. Although colleagues, academic environment, and weather should not be underestimated as reasons for making a change, neither should higher salaries or institutional research support. In fact, salaries and research support serve as major bargaining points, especially when an academic's career is on the rise.

The reason tenure is relevant is that it forces universities to bet every time they appoint a new tenured faculty member. No matter how much they spend to recruit the scholar or scientist, if he or she has tenure he or she can stop performing, and there is almost nothing the university can do. Moreover, unlike in Britain and Israel, where there is mandatory retirement around age sixty-five, the United States has no legal forced retirement age, which can force a university to keep the inflated cost of a faculty member on the payroll for more than fifty years.

Much of American higher education has dealt with this problem by dramatically increasing the proportion of non-tenure-track professors at their institutions—growing from 30 percent of faculty in 1975 to more than 75 percent today (Edmonds, 2015). However, at elite institutions, the proportion of tenure-track to non-tenure-track faculty is much higher, and tenured professors are paid far more than at other universities (Chronicle Data, 2017).

This problem is widely acknowledged, but entrenched interests defend tenure as necessary for academic freedom. That notion is easily debunked. We need only consider the fact that non-tenure-track faculty are pervasive, and yet those faculty enjoy the same academic freedom protections as the tenured faculty. More to the point, academic freedom can be guaranteed in legally binding contracts that are easily enforced in today's courts, as opposed to through a lifetime employment agreement.

At Minerva, faculty members are initially hired with a one-year contract, which allows us and the individual faculty member to determine whether there is a good fit. Thereafter faculty have three-year, renewable contracts. We make it crystal clear exactly what criteria are considered for renewal, which emphasize teaching and student-oriented services (such as advising). We write the contracts to ensure that faculty do in fact have academic freedom, without guaranteeing a sinecure for life.

Managing administrative bloat

Administrative costs at universities have expanded at dramatically higher rates than the costs of the faculty (which were dampened by increasing the proportion of part-time versus full-time faculty) (National Center for Education Statistics, 2011). In fact, full-time nonfaculty professionals at universities increased by 369 percent from 1975–76 to 2011, while tenured and tenure-track faculty at universities increased by only 23 percent over the same period.

Minerva manages administrative overhead very differently than do traditional universities. University overhead costs suffer from three compounding components that enable unfettered growth.

Shifting responsibilities. First, the university itself decides to increase the number of administrators for jobs that were previously done by the faculty or not done at all. For example, having tenure enables professors at many institutions to shirk ancillary responsibilities, such as academic advising, without the threat of being fired. Therefore, additional people must be hired to fulfill those responsibilities, and total costs increase. Recent research has shown, as another example, that the presence of diversity officers at universities (Chronicle Data, 2017) is not related to the diversity of the university; their work apparently does not actually increase the diversity of the institution, even though that is their job. At first blush this appears to make little sense, but the outcome is in fact logical because diversity officers have no power to hire or fire in an academic setting; departments make those decisions. Perhaps a more effective use of the costs of the diversity office would be to allocate them directly to departments, to be used solely in appointing a more diverse professorate.

Although these may appear to be isolated incidents, according to an analysis of federal figures the number of nonacademic staff members has more than doubled in the past twenty-five years, while the number of students and faculty members has increased minimally (Marcus, 2014).

At Minerva, we have a "lean startup" culture. When faced with a problem, our first impulse is not to hire more people. Instead, we consider the actual nature of the problem (#rightproblem), and then devise ways to use existing resources to address it. Moreover, we have clear job descriptions (a rarity in academia), and all employees are evaluated according to how well they perform all aspects of their job.

Unfunded mandates. The university itself is not the only source of unnecessary administrative costs. Regulatory compliance costs have imposed a substantial economic burden on universities; ironically, these costs are largely intended to enable the use of federal funding to reduce the costs of higher education for a segment of the American population. A primary example of this is Title IX enforcement. Title IX was a law implemented in the 1970s to bring gender equity to sports programs at universities. Today it is broadly used to ensure a positive environment for women in university settings.

It is hard to argue with the goals of the expansion of the law—after all, campus environments, where drug and alcohol use is rampant, are inherently unsafe for women. However, the implementation of these regulatory rules has neither helped substantially to reduce crimes against women at universities nor helped reduce the high costs of education—quite the contrary on both counts. For instance, the rate of sexual assault at universities largely remained unchanged over the period of 2009–2013, when the bulk of these regulations were put in place (Sinozich & Langton, 2014). At the same time, it is unclear whether the incidence of sexual assault on campus is any lower than for similar demographics of women off campus (DePillis, 2014). What is clear is that the costs for universities to attempt to adjudicate certain criminal acts have skyrocketed.

In addition, universities are not equipped to act as judge, jury, and enforcer in such cases. Other than murder and manslaughter, forcible sexual assault is the most heinous crime in the FBI's UCR hierarchy of campus crimes (U.S. Department of Education, 2016), and in the criminal justice system forcible sexual assault is considered the worst possible felony other than taking a life. Because a university is not a government entity, the only punishment that it can mete out is based on the status of the student at the university. Imagine a university dealing with an alleged murderer. The worst punishment that a university could decide on would be to expel the student from school. In some cases, where the university could not determine whether the student was indeed guilty, it could move that student to a different residence hall or have him write an essay (all of which are remedies that have been used for similar cases of sexual assault). This is absurd. If one student were to stand accused of kidnapping another student or of setting fire to a building (both crimes considered the equivalent of aggravated sexual assault by most jurisdictions), the idea that a university would stand in judgment of the student as opposed to having the criminal justice system deal with the crime is almost inconceivable. Mere expulsion from schooling is not a societally acceptable punishment for a tier one felony.

Universities that are the beneficiaries of Title IV funding are now required to hire retired detectives and consultants to investigate crimes, rule on those crimes by assembling a group of faculty and administrators, and then, almost invariably, deal with the costs of one of the aggrieved parties who sue the university because the party is not satisfied with the verdict.

Title IX compliance costs are a small fraction of the overall costs universities face from regulation. Nonresearch compliance costs are estimated to cost four-year nonprofit colleges and universities $10 billion in the 2013–14 academic year (Vanderbilt University, 2015), which translates to approximately $1,000 per student per year in regulatory costs on average—with some institutions seeing as much as a $2,000 per student cost. At the high end, this figure is equivalent to more than 10 percent of tuition and fees at a public four-year institution or at Minerva.

Regulatory costs will and should exist, but when the goal is to lower overall costs of higher education, smart regulations are critical. Until such reforms are implemented, Minerva's approach has been to rely on the local justice system and to minimize taking funds from federal sources. Specifically, Minerva does not have its own police department, does not have committees that serve as courts of justice, and so on; if a crime has apparently been committed, we rely on local authorities. In addition, we do not take Title IV (Pell Grants) funding, which requires a substantial infrastructure. Because of our large percentage of international students, it simply makes no economic sense for us to have to cope with the accompanying regulations.

Parkinson's law. Perhaps the most insidious source of administrative bloat is commonly referred to as Parkinson's law, a tongue-in-cheek observation described in the *Economist* in 1955. Parkinson's law holds that bureaucracies naturally increase themselves. Although the article coining the name was a satirical exercise, it is hard to argue with the concept that the larger an administrative structure is the larger it tends to grow over time as administrators create work for one another—which in turn requires hiring more workers to do the work that those administrators now no longer have time to do. Universities, which are both highly regulated and less efficiently run than market-driven organizations, are fertile grounds for a large and growing bureaucracy. At Minerva we are mindful of Parkinson's law, and curb the impulse to hire more people whenever a new problem is encountered.

Minerva's Operating Principles

At Minerva, we utilize three core principles that help us avoid these five problematic cost centers. These principles rest on clear foundations, as summarized below.

Principle 1: Use available resources

The first principle is to use market-provided mechanisms wherever they are available and efficient. For instance, our students live in some of the world's great cities, and those cities come with an already well-designed and highly functional infrastructure. They offer world-class libraries, gyms, public parks, museums, grocery stores, and restaurants. All of these establishments are expert at what they do, as otherwise they would be out of business or would not obtain government or philanthropic support. Therefore, having our students utilize what the city already provides means we do not have to recreate all of those goods and services, which in turn keeps our overall costs contained. Yes, this means that the institutions that our students use are not limited to student access and that students do indeed have to mingle with the citizens of the cities where they live. We see this as a further benefit.

Principle 2: Directed tuition

The second principle stems from a deeply held belief that direct cost transparency and efficiency are critical for long-term services such as providing an undergraduate education. We do not believe that tuition dollars charged to students should be allocated away from services that directly benefit students. Minerva would never charge students tuition in order to pay the salary of a professor on sabbatical or to subsidize faculty research. Other sources of income such as grants or philanthropic support can easily be diverted to those goals. Similarly, we would not tax all students for services that benefit a small proportion of students. This is another reason why we don't build performing arts centers, football fields, or student labs.

Principle 3: Incentive structure

The third and possibly the most important element of Minerva's operating model is the natural incentives and disincentives built into our system. The incentive structure serves as a guard rail to keep the institution from losing focus on its mission. Minerva's stated mission is "To nurture critical wisdom for the sake of the world." We are conscious of the fact that the world needs wise decision making for humanity to thrive and we want to facilitate and increase such decision making. We realize that we cannot do this on our own. This book is a part of our efforts to fulfill our mission. So is allowing other universities to license the curriculum and technology developed by Minerva to enable systemic, scaffolded, and fully active education. The more successful the Minerva system is, the more other universities will want to follow in our footsteps and the more valuable Minerva becomes (from both a social and an economic perspective).

Therefore, every single one of our stakeholders—students, faculty, staff, supporters—has the same goals, and all benefit from achieving those goals. We are fond of saying that the only real metric of our success is the success of our students—and we have aligned the incentives so that this is true for all stakeholders. For example, faculty receive stock options, which become more valuable as the brand is strengthened, which will occur when our students learn material that helps them to succeed in the real world; hence, faculty are doubly motivated (both intrinsically and extrinsically) to help the students learn and succeed.

Moreover, we would not be able to attract any stakeholders of this caliber if our goals were different—it would be close to impossible to convince students or faculty to walk away from an Ivy League university if we were not providing a demonstrably better alternative. Similarly, it would be close to impossible to convince financial backers or employees to invest their time and treasure in a multidecade endeavor if it did not have the clear potential to deliver profound societal and economic benefit.

The result of this orientation is that we immediately push to the side temptations we may encounter to compromise on the quality of what we deliver. The temptation of short-term rewards is dwarfed by the value that we can generate in the long run by living up to Minerva's mission.

One example can be found in our admissions process. In almost any traditional university the admission rates that are published do not reflect the admission rates of the children of wealthy donors. Some of the most prestigious universities that have single-digit percentage acceptance rates accept the children of wealthy donors at up to ten times that rate. In many ways, those exceptions at "need blind" institutions make sense when examining their institutional design: they rely on large philanthropic gifts to support the infrastructure required by the five elements detailed above.

At Minerva, even though our students rely on scholarship money for access to the institution, the institution itself does not rely on donations to operate. The institution relies on having an attractive educational and experiential offering, and therefore relies on the tuition dollars that are associated with the cost of education. The incentives are no longer about pleasing the philanthropists but about pleasing a group of high-achieving students. If a donor were to offer $10 million to Minerva but expected special treatment for her child in the admissions process, we would simply turn that money down. The power of an unassailable institution of higher education is far more valuable than monetary value of any single financial payment. Even though we could do a great deal of good with that money, there is no calculating the harm that would befall our reputation with even one legacy or athlete admit.

Conclusion

We designed the business and operating model of Minerva by recognizing the problems faced by traditional universities and being clearheaded about why they have occurred and how they can be addressed. Our approach allows us to say that even though physical fitness and team competition are critical for a young person's social and personal development, we are not going to create our own sports program because every major city in the world has local intramural sports offerings and gyms. We will not allow administrative bloat to overtake our core mission; we will not use precious tuition dollars to support activities that we cannot justify. We have created a model where a lean cost structure and effective educational program go hand in hand.

References

Adair, R., Eyerman, R., Fair, R., Harms, R., Howe, R., Kalla, J., et al. (2014, February). Report to Dean Mary Miller from the Ad Hoc Committee on Grading. New Haven: Yale College. http://yalecollege.yale.edu/sites/default/files/files/gradingreport201402.pdf

Beard, A. (2014, October 23). Fake classes, inflated grades: Massive UNC scandal included athletes over 2 decades. *StarTribune.* http://www.startribune.com/fake-classes-inflated-grades-unc-scandal-included-athletes-over-2-decades/280072212

Burnsed, B. (2015, September 18). Athletics departments that make more than they spend still a minority. National Collegiate Athletic Association. http://www.ncaa.org/about/resources/media-center/news/athletics-departments-make-more-they-spend-still-minority

Chronicle Data. (2017, January 10). Full-time faculty salaries. https://data.chronicle.com

DePillis, L. (2014, December 19). Rape on campus: Not as prevalent as it is off campus. *The Washington Post.* https://www.washingtonpost.com/news/storyline/wp/2014/12/19/rape-on-campus-not-as-prevalent-as-it-is-off-campus/?utm_term=.120559854856

The Economist. (1955, November 19). Parkinson's law. *The Economist.* http://www.economist.com/node/14116121

Edmonds, D. (2015, May 28). More than half of college faculty are adjuncts: Should you care? *Forbes.*http://www.forbes.com/sites/noodleeducation/2015/05/28/more-than-half-of-college-faculty-are-adjuncts-should-you-care/#9dd3f9b1d9b9

Gladwell, M. (2016). Food fight. *Revisionist History.* http://revisionisthistory.com/episodes/05-food-fight

Harvard Athletics Recruiting Central. (2015, August). Website of Harvard Athletics Recruiting. http://gocrimson.com/information/recruiting/index

Marcus, J. (2014, February 6). New analysis shows problematic boom in higher ed administrators. *The Huffington Post.* http://www.huffingtonpost.com/2014/02/06/higher-ed-administrators-growth_n_4738584.html

National Center for Education Statistics. (2011). Fall staff in postsecondary institutions. *Digest of Education Statistics, & IPEDS Human Resources Survey 2011–12.* Washington, DC: U.S. Department of Education, Institute of Education Sciences. https://www.aaup.org/sites/default/files/files/2014%20salary%20report/Figure%201.pdf

Sinozich, S., & Langton, L. (2014, December). Rape and sexual Assault victimization among college-age females, 1995–2013. https://www.bjs.gov/content/pub/pdf/rsavcaf9513.pdf

U.S. Department of Education. (2016, June). The Hierarchy Rule. In *The handbook for campus safety and security reporting.* Washington, DC: U.S. Department of Education, Office of Postsecondary Education, Retrieved from https://www2.ed.gov/campus-crime/HTML/pdf/cs_hierarchy.pdf

Vanderbilt University. (2015, October). *The Cost of Federal Regulatory Compliance in Higher Education: A Multi-Institutional Study.* Retrieved from https://news.vanderbilt.edu/files/Regulatory-Compliance-Report-Final.pdf

Wainstein, K. L., Jay, A. J., & Kukowski, C. D. (2014, October 16). *Investigation of Irregular Classes in the Department of African and Afro-American Studies at the University of North Carolina at Chapel Hill.* Retrieved from http:/ /3qh929iorux3fdpl532k03kg.wpengine.netdna-cdn.com/wp-content/uploads/2014/10/UNC-FINAL-REPORT.pdf

Yale University. (1979, October). Women at Yale: A statistical profile 1969–1979. New Haven, CT: Office of Institutional Research, Yale University, http://wff.yale.edu/sites/default/files/files/1969-1979_Women_at_Yale.pdf

Afterword: For the Sake of the World

Ben Nelson, Stephen M. Kosslyn, Jonathan Katzman, Robin B. Goldberg, and Teri Cannon

We have a confession to make: this book is meant to recruit you.

Even if Minerva exists for a thousand years, graduates some of the most influential leaders, thinkers, innovators, and transformational figures of the future, and becomes the most desirable university program in the world, we can easily have failed in our mission. As we have mentioned repeatedly in this book, we exist to nurture critical wisdom for the sake of the world. This mission is simply impossible for us to accomplish alone.

When we talk about solving the world's problems, we may forget that we are talking about solving the challenges and problems that affect our own lives every day. Ineffective leadership—in government, business, journalism, health care, nonprofit organizations, and many other sectors of society—affects us all. At Minerva we believe that if we are to change course in this world, we must look to institutions of higher education as the primary solution.

Minerva was established to create more than just a good model of higher education. We aspire to create a qualitative improvement in higher education, and we find it alarming that so few others are trying to do so. This must change. Not only do we hope that other institutions will embrace Minerva's curricular, pedagogical, and operational philosophies but, far more important, we hope that other institutions will improve on them. We would never claim, and cannot accept the idea, that the current Minerva model is as good as education can get. Every week we are fixing problems, iterating solutions, and trying new methods to improve Minerva. And yet we are sure that there can be better models of higher education that have not yet been conceived.

This book serves as a meta-recipe book. It is meant to show the systemic logic, first-principles-driven institutional design, and uncompromising iterative process with which new models of education can be built. It is important to note that as daunting as this process may appear, there are fewer than one hundred faculty and staff at Minerva at the time of this writing. These few exceptional individuals built and now operate this entire system. Others can be much better than we are; we are sure of it.

And so we leave you with a challenge to embrace one of two paths: join us in implementing our mission or devise a superior plan and realize it. If you are seeking to further your education, join one of our undergraduate or graduate programs or demand that other institutions provide you with one that is as systematically and tightly designed to give you what you need and deserve. If you are an academic, join our growing faculty, come for a sabbatical to learn our teaching methods, or help your institution realize what can be accomplished with a fully active pedagogy applied to a scaffolded curriculum. Better yet, devise ways to improve on what we are doing and teach us how to evolve! If you are a reporter, hold us and every other university accountable. Our role in society is pivotal, and far too often institutions of higher education are criticized for symptoms (costs, completion, access) as opposed to the illness (not providing effective education). And perhaps most important, for those who influence institutions of higher education— employers, ministers and secretaries of education, legislators, donors—if you ever needed an excuse to demand higher standards, here it is.

The education sector is enormous and changes slowly. Even demonstrably better systems will take time to become the new normal. But positive movements have swept through higher education in the past, and they will do so again. As more and more students demand a better education (Minerva-style, perhaps?), other institutions will have to respond. As more professors innovate in the classroom and implement more effective pedagogical practices, others will follow. As reporters begin to highlight more effective institutions, the public at large will pay attention. And those who fund higher education could accelerate this transformation. Nearly two hundred gifts of $100 million or more have been made to institutions of higher education. What would be the result if half of those gifts were used to adopt effective new systems of higher education or create new systems that could exceed the bar we have set? How much better prepared would students be when they graduate? How much wiser would our society be? How much more optimistic would we be about the future of our world? For the betterment of society, let's nurture critical wisdom for the sake of the world.

Appendix A: Habits of Mind and Foundational Concepts

The Minerva curriculum is designed to help our students understand leadership and working with others, to become innovators, to develop into broad and adaptive thinkers, and to adopt a global perspective. Our learning objectives are informed by the literatures on leadership and creativity, as well as by interviews and surveys of large employers in a variety of disciplines. These data have led us to define four types of core competencies the students should develop in order to succeed in a wide variety of disciplines. Two of these competencies center on personal abilities: *thinking critically* (evaluating claims, analyzing inferences, weighing decisions, and analyzing problems) and *thinking creatively* (facilitating discovery, solving problems, and creating products, processes, and services). The other two competencies center on interpersonal abilities: *communicating effectively* (using language effectively, using nonverbal communication effectively) and *interacting effectively* (negotiating, mediating, and persuading; working effectively with others; resolving ethical dilemmas and having social consciousness).

The habits of mind and foundational concepts (HCs) are introduced during the first year, when all students take four yearlong cornerstone seminars: Formal Analyses (which focuses on core aspects of thinking critically), Empirical Analyses (which focuses on core aspects of thinking creatively), Multimodal Communications (which focuses on core aspects of communicating effectively) and Complex Systems (which focuses on core aspects of interacting effectively). This material is then used (and assessed) during the subsequent three years while students major and concentrate in specific subjects. As noted in the following, each HC has a hashtag name.

As noted in chapter 2, we are continually updating the set of HCs, based on feedback from students, faculty, employers, internship supervisors and others. Thus, this is a "living document," and will no doubt evolve in the coming years.

We indicate below the course in which the habit of mind or foundational concept is introduced:

CS = introduced in Complex Systems

EA = introduced in Empirical Analyses

FA = introduced in Formal Analyses

MC = introduced in Multimodal Communications

I. Thinking Critically

Thinking critically is essential in virtually any profession and is necessary in life more generally. However, critical thinking is not a single cognitive process. Its different aspects require different skills and may draw on different foundational concepts.

A. Evaluating claims

One aspect of thinking critically is evaluating claims, which requires identifying claims and their components. To do so, one must rely on one's ability to check whether conclusions are plausible and use principles of information literacy. In addition, one often must recognize whether claims are grounded in sound science and supported by probability and statistics. We introduce and assess the following skills and concepts that underlie this type of critical thinking.

1. Distill complex arguments, identifying and analyzing premises and conclusions:

    a. Identify and analyze premises and conclusions. (H) FA **#assertions**

    b. Actively and critically engage with texts and other forms of communication. (H) MC **#critique**

2. Use principles of information literacy:

    a. Define what information is needed to support an argument. (H) MC **#infoneeded**

    b. Distinguish between categories and types of information to determine source quality. (H) MC **#sourcequality**

3. Use estimation techniques to determine whether quantitative claims are plausible. (H) FA **#estimation**

4. Distinguish between scientific and nonscientific statements:

    a. Evaluate whether hypotheses are based on plausible premises or assumptions. (H) EA **#plausibility**

    b. Evaluate whether hypotheses lead to testable predictions. (H) EA **#testability**

    c. Identify and analyze pseudoscientific claims. (C) EA **#pseudoscience**

    d. Distinguish among scientific hypotheses, theories, facts and laws. (C) EA **#epistemology**

    e. Evaluate applications of the scientific method. (C) EA **#scibreakdown**

5. Evaluate probabilities and sampling appropriately:

    a. Apply and interpret fundamental concepts of probability. (C) FA **#probability**

    b. Apply and interpret conditional probabilities. (C) FA **#conditionalprob**

    c. Recognize and analyze sampling from different types of distributions. (C) FA **#sampling**

6. Evaluate and employ statistics appropriately:

    a. Use descriptive statistics appropriately. (H) FA **#descriptivestats**

    b. Apply and interpret effect size. (C) FA **#effectsize**

c. Apply and interpret confidence intervals. (C) FA **#confidenceintervals**

d. Apply and interpret measures of correlation; distinguish correlation and causation. (C) FA **#correlation**

e. Apply and interpret regression. (C) FA **#regression**

f. Recognize when regression to the mean is operating and adjust predictions to take this into account. (C) FA **#regresstomean**

g. Apply and interpret Bayesian statistics for inference and estimation. (C) FA **#bayes**

h. Apply and interpret statistical significance. (C) FA **#significance**

B. Analyzing inferences

Inference is the rational creation of new knowledge from old. The ability to draw appropriate inferences is broadly applicable. Even if a claim is correct, inferences drawn from it may not be. Formal logic provides a method for determining which inferences are valid and which are not. One type of logical thinking is inductive reasoning, which is about generalizations made from specific cases; another type is deductive reasoning, which is about what conclusions must follow from a set of premises. Because many inferences are based on human observation, one must be aware of specific biases in human attention, perception, and memory. And when drawing inferences about expressive works, such as works of art, one must appreciate the historical and cultural context of the work, its internal organization, and how individual experience shapes the recipient's interpretation of it. We introduce and assess the following skills and knowledge that underlie this type of critical thinking.

1. Apply and interpret formal deductive logic. (C) FA **#deduction**

2. Identify and correct logical fallacies. (C) FA **#fallacies**

3. Apply inductive reasoning appropriately; recognize that more than one generalization is always possible:

a. Formulate multiple plausible generalizations from available evidence. (C) FA **#induction**

b. Make predictions about short-term versus long-term behaviors. (H) FA **#prediction**

4. Identify biases (unreasoned tendencies) in attention, perception, and memory that may affect what inferences are drawn:

a. Identify attentional and perceptual biases that affect what we notice and how we recognize and estimate properties of patterns, and react accordingly. (C) EA **#attentionperceptionbiases**

b. Identify biases that affect the limits and fallibility of memory, and react accordingly. (C) EA **#memorybias**

c. Identify and minimize bias that results from searching for or interpreting information to confirm preconceptions. (C) EA **#confirmationbias**

5. Identify biases that affect inferences drawn from different forms of communication, and react accordingly. (C) MC **#interpretivebias**

6. Situate a work in its relevant context (e.g., historical, disciplinary, cultural). (C) MC **#context**

7. Identify, analyze, and organize characteristics of a work, and use these characteristics to interpret modes of communication:

    a. Identify, analyze, or organize characteristics to infer or craft possible meanings of a nonfiction work. (H) MC **#nonfiction**

    b. Identify, analyze, and organize characteristics to infer possible meanings of fiction or poetry. (C) MC **#fictionpoetry**

    c. Identify, analyze, and organize characteristics and use them to infer meanings of visual communications. (C) MC **#visualart**

    d. Identify, analyze, and organize characteristics and use them to infer meanings of auditory communications. (C) MC **#music**

    e. Identify, analyze, and organize characteristics to infer possible meanings in a multimedia work. (C) MC **#multimedia**

8. Describe interactions among events or characteristics at different levels of analysis to generate interpretations of phenomena. (H) CS **#levelsofanalysis**

9. Apply knowledge about the characteristics of a complex system to understand the whole, and vice versa:

    a. Apply and interpret decompositions of complex systems into constituent parts. (C) CS **#multipleagents**

    b. Recognize the role of attractors and sensitivity to varying conditions in the behavior of complex systems. (C) CS **#systemdynamics**

    c. Identify emergent properties of complex systems and react accordingly. (C) CS **#emergentproperties**

    d. Identify ways that multiple causes interact to produce complex effects. (C) CS **#multiplecauses**

    e. Identify primary, secondary, and further effects in networks, including social networks. (C) CS **#networks**

C. *Weighing decisions*

Evaluating claims and analyzing inferences are important in part because they help us decide how to act. To make decisions rationally, one must analyze the alternative choices and identify their respective trade-offs. Decision-support tools can help us with such analyses and with identifying and mitigating undesirable biases. We introduce and assess the following skills and knowledge that underlie this type of critical thinking.

1. Identify and evaluate underlying goals and the values on which they are based, as well as the guiding principles that determine how an individual or group will try to attain these goals. (H) CS **#purpose**

2. Recognize and evaluate foundational commitments. (H) CS **#firstprinciples**

3. Perform cost-benefit analyses for all stakeholders:

a. Consider different types of future costs and benefits for all stakeholders. (H) CS **#utility**

b. Identify ways that incentives affect decisions. (H) FA **#payoffs**

c. Identify and analyze the effects of sunk costs in decision making. (H) FA **#sunkcost**

d. Identify and analyze the effects of temporal discounting in decision making. (H) FA **#discounting**

4. Identify and analyze the effects of risk versus uncertainty. (C) FA **#risk**

5. Consider multiple choices simultaneously when making decisions. (H) FA **#broadframing**

6. Interpret and analyze decision-support tools to explore the consequences of decisions:

a. Apply and interpret decision trees to explore the consequences of alternative choices. (H) FA **#decisiontrees**

b. Apply heuristics to make and implement decisions efficiently. (H) FA **#efficientheuristics**

7. Identify decision biases that arise from emotional states. (C) EA **#emotionalbias**

D. Analyzing problems

Although actually solving problems requires thinking creatively, the analysis that precedes this process clearly is a form of thinking critically. This analysis focuses on identifying, understanding, and organizing the problem itself before trying different ways to solve it. We introduce and assess the following skills and knowledge that underlie this type of critical thinking.

1. Identify gaps (in knowledge, in market offerings, in a range of ideas, etc.) that reveal where a creative solution is required. (C) EA **#gapanalysis**

2. Characterize the nature of the problem. (H) EA **#rightproblem**

3. Organize problems into tractable components and design solutions. (H) EA **#breakitdown**

4. Identify and analyze variables and parameters of a problem. (H) FA **#variables**

5. Apply and evaluate game-theoretic models. (C) FA **#gametheory**

II. Thinking Creatively

Thinking critically focuses on analysis. In contrast, thinking creatively is about the production of something new, which often involves synthesis. Thinking creatively is at the heart of scientific discovery, the innovative solution of practical problems, and the creation of new products, processes, and services.

A. Facilitating discovery

There is no recipe or set of rules for how to make new discoveries. However, certain practices can set the stage, facilitating discovery. Among such practices is the ability to craft well-formed hypotheses, predictions, and interpretations of data. In addition, research methods can be used effectively to increase the likelihood of making a new discovery. Finally, one can facilitate discovery by considering systems at multiple levels of analysis and identifying the type of system being studied. We introduce and assess the following skills and knowledge that underlie this type of creative thinking.

1. Learn to generate hypotheses and informed conjectures:

   a. Evaluate the link between initial data collection and subsequent hypothesis-driven research. (C) EA **#hypothesisdriven**

   b. Evaluate the link between theories and the design of studies. (C) EA **#theorytesting**

   c. Recognize how models can be used to explain a set of data and generate new predictions. (C) EA **#modeltypes**

   d. Interpret, analyze, and create data visualizations. (C) EA **#dataviz**

2. Use research methods to conceive of ways to make discoveries:

   a. Apply and interpret principles of experimental design. (C) EA **#experimentaldesign**

   b. Design and interpret observational studies. (C) EA **#observation**

   c. Design and interpret primary research performed as interviews or surveys (individually or in groups). (C) EA **#interview**

   d. Design and interpret case studies. (C) EA **#casestudy**

   e. Evaluate and incorporate replicability in empirical study designs. (C) EA **#replication**

   f. Identify and evaluate appropriate controls for empirical study designs. (C) EA **#control**

B. Solving problems

A problem occurs when an obstacle arises en route to a goal. On first encountering a problem (for which no known solution is available), one must use creative thinking to solve it. Often such creative thinking relies on using specific heuristics (rules of thumb) and techniques. However, solving problems effectively requires one to be aware of biases and to mitigate their effects when they interfere with reaching a good solution. We introduce and assess the following skills and knowledge that underlie this type of creative thinking.

1. Use analogies in problem solving appropriately. (C) EA **#analogies**

2. Identify and apply constraint satisfaction as a way to solve problems. (C) EA **#constraints**

3. Evaluate and apply optimization techniques appropriately. (C) FA **#optimization**

4. Use problem-solving techniques:

   a. Apply heuristics to transition from one subproblem to the next. (H) EA **#problemheuristics**

   b. Apply "contrarian thinking" to devise new strategies. (H) EA **#contrarian**

5. Apply algorithmic strategies to solve real-world problems. (C) FA **#algorithms**

6. Apply and interpret simulation modeling to test a range of scenarios. (C) FA **#simulation**

7. Identify biases that result from availability, representativeness, and other problem-solving heuristics and learn to correct errors. (C) EA **#heuristicbias**

8. Apply effective strategies to teach yourself specific types of material. (H) EA **#selflearning**

C. *Creating products, processes, and services*
Various methods and techniques can help one to create new products, processes and services. Such methods and techniques include iterative design thinking, use of heuristics, and reverse engineering. We introduce and assess the following skills and knowledge that underlie this type of creative thinking.

1. Apply iterative design thinking to conceive and refine products or solutions. (H) MC **#designthinking**

2. Apply heuristics to find creative solutions to problems and to formulate new products and processes. (H) EA **#creativeheuristics**

3. Given a solution to a particular problem, use reverse engineering to abstract key elements that can be applied to solve other problems. (H) EA **#abstraction**

III. Communicating Effectively

The ability to communicate effectively is crucial for leaders and innovators who function as broadly educated members of a global community. This ability relies in large part on verbal expression, not only in terms of clarity of content but also in terms of appropriateness of form (i.e., pitching a message in the appropriate way for a given audience). In addition, communicating effectively relies on conveying appropriate information nonverbally, such as through facial expressions and body language.

A. *Using language effectively*
Most human communication occurs through language, both spoken and written; thus, it is crucial that one know how to use language effectively to communicate. We introduce and assess the following skills and knowledge that underlie this type of effective communication.

1. Write and speak clearly:

   a. Formulate a well-defined thesis. (H) MC **#thesis**

   b. Effectively organize communications. (H) MC **#organization**

   c. Communicate with a clear and precise style. (H) MC **#composition**

   d. Follow established guidelines to present communications professionally. (H) MC **#presentation**

   e. Understand and use connotations, tone, and style. (H) MC **#connotation**

2. Tailor oral and written work for the context and the audience. (H) MC **#audience**

B. Using nonverbal communication effectively

Communicating nonverbally often plays a crucial role in how well a verbal communication is received. These elements of communication not only convey connotations, they also color the entire message. We introduce and assess the following skills and knowledge that underlie this type of effective communication

1. Interpret facial expressions. (H) MC **#facialexpression**

2. Interpret and use body language. (H) MC **#bodylanguage**

3. Apply principles of perception and cognition in oral and multimedia presentations and in design. (H) MC **#communicationdesign**

IV. Interacting Effectively

We communicate not only to convey information but also as a key part of our interactions with others. However, such personal interactions involve much more than simply communicating. Interactions may be intended to have a specific effect on others (as when negotiating or trying to persuade) and may facilitate or impair team functioning. In addition, making ethical decisions plays a crucial role in how one interacts with others.

A. Negotiating, mediating, and persuading

Interacting effectively with people requires anticipating the effects of a particular message, registering the actual responses, and adjusting communications accordingly. Such dynamic interactions lie at the heart of negotiating, mediating, and persuading. We introduce and assess the following skills and knowledge that underlie this type of effective interaction.

1. Negotiate and mediate, including looking for mutual gains:

   a. Mediate disagreements. (H) CS **#mediate**

   b. Use a structured approach to negotiation to reach desired objectives. (H) CS **#negotiate**

   c. Prepare multidimensional best alternatives to a negotiated agreement (BAT-NAs). (H) CS **#batna**

2. Use principles of effective debating:

a. Evaluate the effectiveness of counterarguments by considering emotional, logical, personal, and other factors. (H) CS **#counterargument**

b. Recognize strengths and weaknesses in both your and your opponent's strategies. (H) CS **#debatestrategy**

c. Identify and analyze common ground to determine what you can concede, and react accordingly. (H) CS **#commonground**

3. Use persuasion techniques:

a. "Nudge" other people's decisions. (H) CS **#nudge**

b. Use cognitive tools to persuade. (H) MC **#cognitivepersuasion**

c. Understand and use emotional tools of persuasion. (H) MC **#emotionalpersuasion**

d. Consider the perspectives of others to design a compelling argument. (H) MC **#perspective**

e. Present views and work with an appropriate level of confidence. (H) MC **#confidence**

B. Working effectively with others

Each of us plays many roles when interacting with others, sometimes acting as a leader and sometimes acting as a follower or a team member. Specific behaviors and practices can facilitate such interactions. We introduce and assess the following skills and knowledge that underlie this type of effective interaction.

1. Use principles and styles of effective leadership:

a. Apply principles of effective leadership. (H) CS **#leadprinciples**

b. Learn to assign team roles appropriately, which requires being sensitive to the nature of the task and the nature of specific types of roles. (H) CS **#teamroles**

c. Influence group interactions by exerting different types of power. (H) CS **#powerdynamics**

d. Identify and analyze how reinforcement and punishment alter behavior. (C) CS **#carrotandstick**

2. Work effectively as a member of a team:

a. Mitigate the role of conformity in group settings. (H) CS **#conformity**

b. Recognize and leverage people's different skills, abilities, traits, attitudes and beliefs. (H) CS **#differences**

c. Understand the impact of organizational structure on individual performance and collaborative projects. (C) CS **#orgstructure**

d. Listen well and be open-minded. (H) MC **#openmind**

3. Discover and assess your own strengths and weaknesses:

    a. Monitor yourself to "know what you don't know." (C) CS **#metaknowledge**

    b. Identify your strengths and weaknesses, exercise humility, and mitigate behaviors and habits that result in overconfidence or impair effective performance. (C) CS **#selfawareness**

    c. Use emotional intelligence to interact effectively. (H) CS **#emotionaliq**

C. *Resolving ethical problems and having social consciousness*

The way one resolves ethical problems has a direct effect on how one interacts with others. One factor that should contribute to such thinking hinges on having social consciousness, which is a concern for others and the common good. We introduce and assess the following skills and knowledge that underlie this type of effective interaction.

1. Identify ethical problems, framing them in a way that will help resolve them. (C) CS **#ethicalframing**

2. Resolve conflicts between ethical principles by using the context to prioritize. (C) CS **#ethicalconflicts**

3. Recognize and work to mitigate unfair practices. (C) CS **#fairness**

4. Follow through on commitments, be proactive, and take responsibility. (H) CS **#responsibility**

Appendix B: Mission, Principles, and Practices

Minerva is guided by first principles. We are intensely focused on "Achieving Extraordinary"—on improving the future by enhancing students' potential and their ability to lead the development of innovative solutions to the most complex challenges of our time.

Our seven guiding principles inform all of our actions, ensuring that we continue to reinforce our strong reputation, support everything we stand for, and ultimately fulfill our mission: Nurturing critical wisdom for the sake of the world.

Upholding Our Principles

Our guiding principles and their implications are as follows:

Being Unconventional

We are unique, standing apart from traditional universities and other ways of learning. We believe there is a better way, and refuse to settle for the status quo. We challenge conventional thinking, anticipating needs and desires and championing novel approaches. By delivering the unexpected—that which brings a sense of mystery or a moment of delight—we encourage further discovery.

We never do things simply because others do them. Instead we develop different, more effective solutions.

Key Attributes: *Distinctive, Insightful, Inventive.* Never: *Obvious, Eccentric.*

Being Human

We are deeply curious and cosmopolitan. We embrace the energy and complexity of the world, seeking to understand the diverse cultures we live in. We build relationships through respectful, personal connections. By celebrating the power of different perspectives, we promote mutual understanding and shared ideas.

We eliminate barriers to human interaction, emphasizing meaningful contact.

Key Attributes: *Empathic, Inquisitive, Cultured.* Never: *Insensitive, Distant.*

Being Confident

We are bold and decisive, unwavering in our commitment and beliefs. We take informed risks and make prudent decisions, without fear of failure. We approach challenges directly, working through adversity and complexity. By acting with conviction, we are able to advance our progressive vision for the future.

We act with clear intent and strong judgment, yet understand that confidence does not mean hubris or arrogance.

Key Attributes: *Courageous, Assertive, Articulate.* Never: *Insecure, Arrogant.*

Being Thoughtful

We continually analyze, evaluate, and examine, incorporating depth and dimension. We look for things others do not see, including details and information that add nuance and levels of interest beyond what is immediately evident. We are considered in our own views, initiating discussion and debate and treating those who disagree with dignity and respect.

We never accept superficial thinking or lack of due diligence, and expect others to engage with the same level of depth and scrutiny.

Key Attributes: *Visionary, Considered, Rigorous.* Never: *Humiliating, Self-aggrandizing.*

Being Selective

We are prestigious, exacting, and rigorous, attracting the finest talent in the world. We focus our time and attention on the people, institutions, and initiatives that are most important for our collective success. We carefully consider what we present to the world, producing high quality with clear intention.

We are not suitable for everyone, but neither are we elitist.

Key Attributes: *Discerning, Intentional, Focused.* Never: *General, Pretentious.*

Being Authentic

We communicate openly and candidly, addressing people directly and conveying heartfelt emotion. We welcome honest dialogue, even about sensitive or controversial topics. We impart accurate information with genuine sincerity, building trust and establishing mutual respect.

We avoid anything artificial, false, or contrived; hyperbole breeds suspicion and erodes credibility.

Key Attributes: *Straightforward, Candid, Sincere.* Never: *Ironic, Unnatural.*

Being Driven

We are ambitious, always pushing to transcend the commonplace. We look for opportunities to improve, refining our approach, and enhancing the outcomes for our students and the world. We work to reach apotheosis, the highest point of achievement. Only by constantly striving to excel will we realize our full potential.

We never settle for "good enough." If we can't accomplish excellence, we pursue a different route.

Key Attributes: *Dynamic, Determined, Resilient.* Never: *Average, Overbearing.*

Editors and Contributors

Editors

Stephen M. Kosslyn, PhD, is the Founding Dean and Chief Academic Officer of the Minerva Schools at the Keck Graduate Institute. He served as Director of the Center for Advanced Study in the Behavioral Sciences at Stanford University and was previously Chair of the Department of Psychology, Dean of Social Science, and the John Lindsley Professor of Psychology at Harvard University. He received a BA degree from UCLA and a PhD from Stanford University, both in psychology. Kosslyn's research has focused on the nature of visual cognition, visual communication, and the science of learning; he has authored or co-authored fourteen books and more than three hundred papers on these topics. Kosslyn has received numerous honors, including the National Academy of Sciences Initiatives in Research Award, a Guggenheim Fellowship, three honorary doctorates (from the University of Caen, the University of Paris Descartes, and Bern University), and election to the American Academy of Arts and Sciences.

Ben Nelson is Founder, Chairman, and CEO of Minerva Project and a visionary with a passion to reinvent higher education. Prior to Minerva, Nelson spent more than ten years at Snapfish. With over 42 million transactions in twenty-two countries (nearly five times more than its closest competitor), Snapfish was among the top e-commerce services in the world in 2010. Serving as CEO from 2005 through 2010, Nelson began his tenure at Snapfish by leading the company's sale to Hewlett Packard for $300 million. Prior to joining Snapfish, Nelson was President and CEO of Community Ventures, a network of locally branded portals for American communities. Nelson's passion for reforming undergraduate education was first sparked at the University of Pennsylvania's Wharton School, where he received a BS degree in economics. After creating a blueprint for curricular reform in his first year of school, Nelson went on to become Chair of the Student Committee on Undergraduate Education, a pedagogical think tank that is the oldest and only nonelected student government body at the University of Pennsylvania.

Contributors

Ari Bader-Natal, PhD, is Chief Learning Scientist at Minerva, where he is responsible for anticipating and designing new technologies to support teaching and learning. These technologies have included the first version of Minerva's signature seminar classroom, tools for formative assessment of discussion participation and summative assessment of student performance, and technologies for curriculum design and management. Before joining Minerva, Bader-Natal was Chief Learning Architect at Grockit, where he developed the company's core social learning and assessment technologies and designed a central system for educational data analysis and learning analytics. Bader-Natal holds BA, MA, and PhD degrees in computer science from Brandeis University. As part of his doctoral research, he built peer-to-peer online learning networks to experiment with mechanisms for motivating appropriate challenges among peer learners. Bader-Natal also runs Studio Sketchpad, a website for creative coders to collaboratively create and share interactive visualizations. The site was initially intended to be a venue for informal learning but has since been used in introductory programming courses in more than one hundred universities, high schools, and coding workshops around the world.

Eric Bonabeau, PhD, is former Dean of Global Affairs at Minerva. In this role, he was responsible for developing institutional partnerships to extend the reach and impact of Minerva's proprietary curriculum and Active Learning Forum platform. He was previously the Founding Dean of Computational Sciences at Minerva, in which capacity he helped secure accreditation for the bachelor's degree in computational sciences and developed the first-year cornerstone course, Formal Analyses. In addition to being an inventor with fourteen patents and an angel investor in thirty-five companies, he is also the Executive Chairman of Icosystem Corporation, a strategy consulting firm he founded in 2000. Bonabeau is one of the world's leading experts on complex systems and distributed adaptive problem solving. His book *Swarm Intelligence* has been a bestseller for fifteen years and inspired Michael Crichton's novel *Prey*. Bonabeau received his PhD degree in theoretical physics from Paris-Sud University Orsay in France and is an alumnus of École Polytechnique and École Nationale Supérieure des Télécommunications.

Judith Brown, PhD, is Dean of the College of Arts and Humanities at Minerva and an accomplished scholar, educator, and administrator. A recipient of numerous awards, including a Guggenheim Fellowship and fellowships from Villa I Tatti, the Harvard Center for Italian Renaissance Studies, and the Center for Advanced Study in the Behavioral Sciences, she is a pioneer in the fields of Renaissance history and the history of gender and sexuality. Brown earned her PhD degree from Johns Hopkins University and her BA and MA degrees from the University of California, Berkeley. Having previously served as a faculty member at Stanford University, as Dean of the School of Humanities at Rice University and as both Vice-President for Academic Affairs and Provost at Wesleyan University, she brings a wealth of experience to Minerva. Brown believes that the solutions to the world's biggest problems require the application of interdisciplinary approaches in which the arts and humanities are essential. She strives to help students learn from the past, to be critical and ethical thinkers in the present, and to become persuasive communicators who are willing to take risks in the pursuit of knowledge and of having a positive impact on the world

Teri Cannon, JD, is Chief Student Affairs, Operations, and Accreditation Officer for the Minerva Schools. Before joining Minerva in 2012 she was a higher education consultant, working with universities and law schools on issues related to accreditation, student achievement, and organizational change and development. Cannon has more than thirty-five years in higher education, working in both law and undergraduate education and in both public and private institutions. She previously served as Executive Vice President of the Western Association of Schools and Colleges Senior College and University Commission (the regional accrediting agency for California, Hawaii, and the Pacific Islands) and was dean of two small California law schools and associate dean at a major public university. Active in accreditation work for multiple accrediting agencies as both a peer reviewer and leader since the 1970s, she is also a lawyer and author of two textbooks on legal ethics. She has served on several governing boards and accrediting commissions and has written and spoken widely on issues related to accreditation, the changing landscape of higher education, legal ethics, access to legal services, and diversity in the legal profession and the academy. She holds a JD degree from Loyola Law School (with honors) and a BA degree from UCLA in political science.

Norian Caporale-Berkowitz is Student Experience Manager at Minerva, where he leads programming to foster community building, social and emotional development, and experiential learning for all freshman students. Prior to joining Minerva, he was an early employee at Coursera, where he built the first community programs for MOOCs and developed partnerships with top U.S. and international universities. Caporale-Berkowitz earned his BA degree from Brown University, where he was a finalist for a Rhodes Scholarship and received the Biology Department's top senior award. He is also a graduate of the Interchange Counseling Institute and the recipient of the Harrington Fellowship, the most prestigious graduate fellowship given by the University of Texas at Austin, where he will begin his PhD in Counseling Psychology in Fall 2017.

Vicki Chandler, PhD, is Dean of the College of Natural Sciences. She has conducted critical research in the field of plant genetics for three decades and is recognized as one of the foremost geneticists in the world. In 2014 she was appointed to the National Science Board by President Barack Obama for a six-year term. She was also a Postdoctoral Fellow at Stanford University. She received a PhD degree from the University of California, San Francisco, and a BA degree from the University of California, Berkeley. Before joining Minerva, Chandler served as the Chief Program Officer for Science at the Gordon and Betty Moore Foundation while also teaching at the University of Oregon and the University of Arizona. She is passionate about helping students develop the skills they need to be successful in their future careers, part of which entails guiding them to be curious, lifelong learners.

Joshua Fost, PhD, is Associate Dean of Graduate Studies at Minerva, where he directs two master's degree programs, one in applied analyses and decision making and one in applied arts and sciences. Previously he was Director of Curriculum Development at Minerva, overseeing the development of Minerva's general education program. Before joining Minerva, he was Assistant Professor of Philosophy at Portland State University, teaching courses in neurophilosophy, cognitive science, human reasoning, and artificial life. In addition to his academic career, Fost has worked as a consultant with the Thomson Corporation and as Chief Technology Officer at Infosis (a web-publishing company) and Colliers International (a global commercial real estate firm). In 2004, *InfoWorld* magazine recognized him as one of the top twenty-five CTOs in the United States. His education includes a BA degree in neuroscience and philosophy from Bowdoin College, a PhD degree in computational neuroscience from Princeton University, and a Postdoctoral Fellowship at Brandeis University.

Megan Gahl, PhD, is Professor of Natural Sciences at Minerva. Professor Gahl joined Minerva after teaching biology and field ecology at Bates College, the University of Alaska-Southeast, and the University of Missouri. As an ecologist with unending curiosity, Gahl is motivated by puzzling scientific questions rather than discipline-specific projects. She served as Postdoctoral Fellow at the Canadian Rivers Institute at the University of New Brunswick-Saint John and earned a PhD in ecology from the University of Maine. Gahl's approach to teaching is to impart skills so that students can critically solve problems. She is excited to be part of the team at Minerva dedicated to designing creative active learning sessions focused on these skills to help students excel both within and outside the classroom.

Kara Gardner, PhD, is Associate Dean of Faculty at Minerva. Dean Gardner earned her PhD degree in music and humanities from Stanford University. As a Postdoctoral Fellow in the Humanities, she taught for four years in Stanford's Introduction to the Humanities program. In addition, she designed and led classes on popular music, music of the Americas, music appreciation, and music and gender at the University of San Francisco for more than ten years. In 2008 she received a teaching award for innovative pedagogy and commitment to student learning from USF. She also taught writing-intensive seminars for graduate students at the San Francisco Conservatory of Music. Her book, *Agnes de Mille: Telling Stories in Broadway Dance,* was published in 2016 by Oxford University Press.

James Genone, PhD, is Associate Professor of Social Sciences and Associate Dean of Undergraduate Studies at Minerva. Prior to joining Minerva, he was Assistant Professor of Philosophy at Rutgers University, Camden. His areas of expertise include the philosophy of mind and cognitive science, and he has both taught and engaged in research on topics such as the nature of sensory consciousness, semantic reference, personal identity, and perceptual knowledge. He has published articles in leading philosophy journals, and guest edited a special issue of *Philosophical Studies* on perceptual evidence. He is currently coediting a volume of essays for Oxford University Press titled *Singular Thought and Mental Files.* Genone earned his PhD in philosophy at the University of California, Berkeley, and was a Postdoctoral Teaching Fellow in the Introduction to the Humanities Program at Stanford University.

Robin B. Goldberg is Chief Experience Officer at Minerva, leading all aspects of the student experience. Goldberg is responsible for driving global student outreach, student life, city immersion, experiential learning, and the lifelong professional development and support of students. She is also responsible for marketing and creative, which includes managing the Minerva brand, building awareness, and driving engagement. Prior to joining Minerva, Goldberg worked at Blurb, where she held the positions of Senior Vice President of Marketing and Business Development, and Senior Vice President of Blurb International. During her tenure there, Blurb became widely recognized in the self-publishing industry. As head of Blurb International, Goldberg led the company's geographic expansion and was responsible for delivering more than half of Blurb's revenue. Prior to Blurb, Goldberg spent four years as Senior Vice President of Global Marketing for Lonely Planet, where she helped redefine how the organization approached marketing and successfully drove sales revenue up by 50 percent. Prior to Lonely Planet, Goldberg held several key marketing roles in technology and consumer brand companies, including Nestle, Clorox, and ClickAction. She earned an MBA degree at the Wharton School at the University of Pennsylvania and a BS degree in business administration at the University of California, Berkeley.

Richard Holman, PhD, is Dean of Computational Sciences at Minerva. He joins Minerva from Carnegie Mellon University, where he was Professor of Physics. His current research concerns the interface between particle physics and cosmology, with a particular emphasis on the inflationary universe paradigm. He also works on more speculative ideas such as models of dark energy and the possible observable effects of the multiverse. One of the brightest spots in Holman's career has been his interactions with students at all levels. His teaching awards testify to how firmly he believes in his role as a mentor to the next generation of physicists. He has long been an advocate for women in STEM, and has also worked with the Pittsburgh Public School System, as well as the Pennsylvania Governor's School for the Sciences, to encourage young students toward careers in the sciences. Holman was a Postdoctoral Fellow at the Fermi National Accelerator Laboratory and the University of Florida, and an NRC Postdoctoral Fellow at NASA Goddard Space Flight Center. He earned his PhD in theoretical particle physics and MA degree in physics from Johns Hopkins University and a BS degree in mathematics from Harvey Mudd College.

Neagheen Homaifar is Head of Admissions and Financial Aid at Minerva, where she is dedicated to ensuring that talented students who are passionate about having a positive influence on the world are able to attend Minerva. Her team is responsible for managing the operations of a selection process designed to be as objective as possible for all the students of the world. Before Minerva, Homaifar worked as a management consultant with the Parthenon Group. Her work there was anchored in solving public and private sector challenges in education. Prior to this, Homifar worked in the economic development sector in Latin America with both CIPPEC in Buenos Aires, a public-policy think tank, and with Compartamos Banco in Mexico City, the largest microfinance bank in Latin America. Homaifar graduated cum laude from Harvard College, where she earned a degree in Social Studies and a Certificate in Latin American studies. During university, Homaifar conducted ethnographic research in rural Latin America, focusing on microfinance communities, gender empowerment, and children's access to education.

Jonathan Katzman is Chief Product Officer at Minerva, where he leads development of the technology used to provide students an exceptional academic experience, including the hallmark Active Learning Forum platform. Previously, Katzman founded Xoopit, an email organizational tool created on the premise that personal data was moving off desktops and into the cloud. In 2009, Xoopit was acquired by Yahoo. Katzman went on to lead the Yahoo Social Bar product, which grew to become a top three Facebook application, as well as other social initiatives across Yahoo. From acquisition through 2010, Katzman also managed social and photo initiatives in Yahoo Mail. Prior to Xoopit, Katzman built and ran Tellme's directory assistance business, which accounted for nearly half of the company's revenue. Katzman has also served as an Entrepreneur-in-Residence at Ignition Corporation and worked at Microsoft on the Office and FrontPage teams as a development lead and program manager. Having contributed to three successful startups, Katzman gives back to the entrepreneurial community through both angel investing and advisory work. Katzman earned a BA degree in computer science from Harvard University, graduating with honors.

Anne Kauth is Manager of Employer Network and Partnerships at Minerva, driving the Professional Development Agency's approach to redesigning traditional career services. Kauth is developing a global network of employers, talent development professionals, and advisors across industry areas to advocate for Minerva students and solve the college-to-career skills gap. Previously she served as Director of Domestic Programs and Chief of Staff for Fullbridge, an education technology company creating blended learning programs for universities and government entities. Kauth has worked for the Women in Public Service Project, an initiative of the U.S. Department of State, and the John F. Kennedy School of Government at Harvard University. She studied at l'Institut d'Études Politiques de Paris (SciencesPo), was a Fulbright grantee, and a White House Intern with the National Economic Council. She holds an AB degree cum laude from Bryn Mawr College in political science.

Senator Bob Kerrey is Executive Chairman of the Minerva Institute for Research and Scholarship. He previously was Governor of Nebraska, Senator from Nebraska, President of the New School, and a candidate for President of the United States. He was born in Lincoln, Lancaster County, Nebraska, and attended the Lincoln public schools. He graduated from the University of Nebraska, Lincoln, and then served in the U.S. Navy SEAL special forces unit. He was seriously wounded in Vietnam and was awarded the Congressional Medal of Honor for "conspicuous gallantry and intrepidity at the risk of his life." He has also served on the National Commission on Terrorist Attacks upon the United States (the 9/11 Commission). Kerrey also is a cochair of the Advisory Board of Issue One, an organization that describes its mission as "fighting for real solutions to the problem of money in politics."

Sultanna Krispil is a passionate community builder, Founding Class student at Minerva, and bookworm, with a love for creating things and understanding the world. An Arts and Humanities and Natural Sciences double major, she enjoys creating bridges where they did not exist before and appreciating multiple perspectives on a problem. Her background includes such activities as building sets and directing productions at a theater school in Canada (her home), wrangling kids as a camp director with the YMCA, getting severe frostbite while cross-country skiing in Minnesota, and chopping bamboo to make pea structures in the mountains of northern Portugal.

Daniel J. Levitin, PhD, was the Founding Dean of Arts and Humanities at the Minerva Schools at the Keck Graduate Institute and is currently its Dean of Partnerships. He was previously James McGill Professor in the Departments of Psychology, Computer Science and Music at McGill University, from which he received the Principal's Teaching Award, McGill's highest teaching honor. He received a BA from Stanford University and a PhD from the University of Oregon, both in psychology.

Levitin's research has focused on the cognitive neurosciences of music. He has authored or co-authored more than one hundred papers on this topic, and has written three consecutive *New York Times* bestselling books on neuroscience for a popular audience. Levitin has been elected a Fellow of the Royal Society of Canada, the American Association for the Advancement of Science, and the Association for Psychological Science.

John Levitt, PhD, is Professor of Computational Sciences at Minerva. A former member of the mathematics departments at Occidental College and Pomona College, Professor John Levitt conducted research on the Minimal Model Program in algebraic geometry, derived categories, and enumerative geometry. He has also been involved in competitive machine learning. Levitt has a background in active learning strategies inside and outside the classroom and has been involved his entire career in transforming his students' views of mathematics as a body of facts to a problem-solving process. As a faculty member, he used these strategies in teaching a broad spectrum of mathematics courses, ranging from calculus and linear algebra to advanced seminars in geometry and set theory. Levitt has also been heavily involved in several community outreach programs.

Rena Levitt, PhD, is Associate Dean of Institutional and Educational Research at Minerva. Dean Levitt earned her PhD in pure mathematics from the University of California, Santa Barbara in 2008. Prior to joining Minerva, Levitt was a member of the Department of Mathematics at Pomona College, where she specialized in the design and implementation of inquiry-based and active learning techniques. During her time in Claremont, Levitt developed programs designed to improve diversity in higher education, focusing on recruitment and retention in STEM fields. She served as a faculty member for the Pomona Academy for Youth Success and developed Pomona's Learning Communities in Mathematics, a mentoring program for students traditionally underrepresented in math and the sciences. Levitt's current research is focused on active learning in higher education, learning outcome assessment, and the use of big data in education.

James Lyda, PhD, is a licensed psychologist and Director of Mental Health Services at Minerva Schools at KGI. Dr. Lyda's career has focused on mental health and wellness services for undergraduate, graduate, and professional students, with a particular focus on underserved/underrepresented populations, suicide prevention, stigma reduction, and crisis intervention. He has also worked with faculty and staff to enhance the university community response to students of concern. He earned his BA degree in psychology from Northwestern University, his PhD from the Counseling Psychology program at the University of Oregon, and was awarded the prestigious American Psychological Association Minority Fellowship. He had a Postdoctoral Fellowship and then a staff position at the University of California, Berkeley, where he developed a satellite mental health office within the UC Berkeley School of Law. Most recently, Dr. Lyda worked at the University of California, San Francisco, serving as campus coordinator of the University of California statewide Student Mental Health Initiative grant.

Matt Regan is the Director of Product Design at Minerva, where he heads product design on the Active Learning Forum. Previously an award-winning Director of Design at Yahoo, he led the design of the wildly successful Social Bar product and supported the company-wide socially focused redesign of all Yahoo properties. Prior to acquisition by Yahoo, Regan worked at Citizen Sports as lead designer on the Sportacular mobile app, one of the first applications chosen by Apple to be placed into the App Store "Hall of Fame." As an independent designer for many years, he led interactive online initiatives for clients including Oracle, Toyota, Adidas, and Microsoft. He is passionate about building elegant, human-centric products that facilitate efficient, effective teaching for the twenty-first century.

Kenn Ross, MBA, is Managing Director–Asia at Minerva, where he oversees the institution's activities in the Asia Pacific region. Prior to joining Minerva, Ross founded IFPASS, a nonprofit focused on promoting non-cognitive skills development in international education. He has held executive positions in Fortune 30 and midsized multinational companies in the clean energy, technology, and consulting industries. Ross is a regular figure in Asia media, and his book, *Academic Soft Skills* (2015), has been acclaimed in China as offering practical advice for students planning their global education experiences. Originally from the United States, Ross has lived in Asia for more than twenty-four years and is fluent in Mandarin Chinese. He is a graduate of Middlebury College, the Johns Hopkins-Nanjing University Center for Chinese and American Studies, and Harvard Business School.

Ayo Seligman is Creative Director at Minerva, a position to which he brings almost two decades of experience in branding and design. He is a proven team leader and creative manager, with more than five years previously as Creative Director at Landor San Francisco. Seligman has expertise in corporate and product brand strategy and brand identity systems, including all aspects of visual and verbal development. He is skilled in divergent and convergent thinking, in strategic and creative concept development, and in conducting presentations and work sessions with senior executive leadership. His specialties include visual and verbal identity systems, packaging, print and screen design, animation, video direction, brand strategy and architecture development, storytelling, user-interface design, advertising concepts and layout, brand name and tagline development, brand voice and messaging, creative team management, implementation, and process development.

Ian Van Buskirk is a member of Minerva's Founding Class. He has enjoyed doing research at the Santa Fe Institute and is interested in questions regarding individual agency in complex systems. He appreciates Minerva's innovative approach to education and is pursuing a major in the School of Computational Sciences.

Z. Mike Wang is Director of Student Experience at Minerva, where he leads experiential learning, community design, and global engagement across Minerva's world cities. Wang's team works to create a four-year experiential learning arc for student formation, from intellect to character to well-being. Prior to joining Minerva, Wang worked at Georgetown University, running special projects for the Chief Operating Officer, leading Innovation for the Chief Information Officer (resulting in the CIO 100 Award in 2014), and cofounding the Beeck Center for Social Impact and Innovation in the Office of the Provost, which led to the design of the first ever hackathon for the White House's My Brother's Keeper initiative. Formerly, Wang was an investment banker at Barclays Capital, focusing on global consumer and retail. He is on the Board of Directors of SxSWedu and Minds Matter San Francisco (a nonprofit that helps high-achieving, low-income high school students get into and graduate from college). Wang graduated magna cum laude from Georgetown University with concentrations in accounting, finance, and English. He loves his sous vide machine dearly.

Index